Mothering
Your Nursing Toddler
Revised Edition

Mothering
Your Nursing Toddler
Revised Edition

Norma Jane Bumgarner

La Leche League International
Schaumburg, Illinois USA

First edition, July 1980
Second edition, December 1982
Third edition, January 2000

©1980 Norma Jane Bumgarner
©1982, 2000 La Leche League International

Book and cover design Digital Concepts LLC
Cartoons by Kathy Grossman
Cover photos by David Arendt and Dawn Havener;
back cover photo by Dawn Havener

Photos on pages 1, 3, 23, 75, 95, 97, 167, 207, 209, 219, 2
249, and 267 by David Arendt; pages 7 and 279 by Norm
Bumgarner; pages 49, 175, 239, and 259 by Dawn Haver
page 121, used with permission of Allaiter aujourd' hui;
151, courtesy of Mimi de Maza; page 193 by Janice Try
page 233 by Judy Torgus.

ISBN 0-912500-52-2
Library of Congress Card Number 99-067379

La Leche League International
1400 N. Meacham Road
Schaumburg, Illinois, USA 60173
www.lalecheleague.org

For Myles, Maya, and Isaac, and for their
siblings and cousins yet to come.

The nursing days are long past for all of the children I wrote about in the 1980 edition. It was a great pleasure for me as I prepared the current revision to hear from a number of them, or from their mothers. Their satisfaction with the long-term results of what even today is considered a prolonged nurturing relationship warms me and encourages me to keep saying that a tot who can walk and talk can also nurse, and that the whole family can be better for it. My best wishes to every one of them, and to all families who are passing on civilized and supportive parenting to yet another generation.

Norma Jane Bumgarner, 1999

contents

Mothering Your Nursing Toddler is one of my favorite books on parenting.
I opened it frequently when I was nursing our daughter Hayden, our fourth child
but the first of our long-term breastfeeders. I read it again as Erin and Matthew
entered toddlerhood. (By the time Steven and Lauren came along, I have to say
that nursing toddlers no longer fazed me.) As the title suggests, the book is not
just about breastfeeding, but about being the mother of a child who is still
breastfeeding. It helped me cope not only with all the quirks of toddler nursing
but also with day-to-day toddler behavior.

Children in their second and third years of life are working on becoming
more independent, but at the same time, they need mother close by. This tug of
war between dependence and going their own way can frustrate mothers of
toddlers. Little ones insist on "I do it myself!" but also demand lots of mother's
attention. When the need to be close to mother takes the form of frequent
nursing, mothers wonder, "Will this child ever wean? Will I ever get a full
night's sleep?"

This is when parents need the reassurance that Norma Jane Bumgarner
offers. Yes, she says, every child weans eventually. The child who nurses eight or
ten times a day at one year of age will nurse less often at age two. And no, there's
nothing abnormal or worrisome about a little one who still loves to nurse at age
three. Even those of us who believe that nursing into toddlerhood is a perfectly
natural thing to do need to be reminded of this from time to time.

Mothering Your Nursing Toddler is the sort of book you read more than
once. Read it when your baby is about nine months old to get a look at what lies
ahead. Read it again when your toddler is eighteen months old and into
everything. Norma Jane Bumgarner will help you understand that as
independent as this little one seems, really he's just "a baby on wheels" who still
needs comfort at the breast. Pick up this book again when your child enters a
new stage or when you find yourself growing frustrated with night nursing or
when you're facing critical relatives.

Over the years, as a La Leche League Leader and a lactation consultant,
I have referred mothers to this book often, as often as I've referred them to THE
WOMANLY ART OF BREASTFEEDING. So I'm glad to see it updated and revised, newly
available for my daughters and daughters-in-law.

Mothering a nursing toddler is an intense and exciting experience.
Reading this special book can make you feel more relaxed and assured during
these years when both you and your child will grow and change. And may you
find lots of love—and fun—along the way.

> *Martha Sears, RN*
> Author with William Sears, MD, of
> *The Baby Book, The Discipline Book,* and
> *The Fussy Baby Book*

Reprinted from the 1980 Revised Edition

"Primum non nocere" (first, do no harm), is a well-known medical precept, eminently applicable to the question of how to mother or when to wean. It made a tremendous difference to your two-week-old baby whether you weaned or kept nursing. No question about it. The facts were there, the votes were in and counted. You wean, baby loses. So, despite sore nipples and sleepless nights, you decided to stay on the winning team and keep nursing.

At three months and at six months it was still pretty cut and dried. By a year, though, the pressures and the eyebrows began to go up. "Still nursing?" But you were hooked, (or unhooked, as the case may be) and actually glad your about-to-be toddler still needed you for that special something.

Now he's eighteen months, or maybe two, and you've settled in to being "just a mother." It's not a bad job after all. Your hours are flexible, and you can come and go as you please, provided you take the boss along. And who could ask for a nicer boss than that smiling, chubby little fellow who tags along with you wherever you go? He's such fun to be with. So you smile benignly on the doubters.

However, every silver lining has its cloud, and you're beginning to find out that mothering no longer includes giving in to your little one's every desire. You realize that the customer isn't always right anymore, and that you may have to work hard to convince him of that. What he wants and what he needs are no longer necessarily the same. He really doesn't need to run out into traffic, or take apart the morning paper, no matter how much he wants to. All you have to do is ask yourself, "Is it good for him? Bad for him? Does it matter at all?" Most of the time the answer is obvious. So, with infinite patience, cheerfulness, and lots of love and kisses, you set about showing him that, no kidding, there are limits to what he may do.

Nursing needs change, too. People may tell you that your two- or three-year-old doesn't need to nurse anymore. Maybe they're right. On the other hand, maybe they're wrong. It depends on your child. You know him better than they do. Also you know your circumstances better. Again, ask yourself, "Will it be bad for him?" (Will nursing spoil him, keep him a baby, dependent on mommy until he goes to college?) No, it won't hurt him to nurse. He enjoys it, maybe even really needs it, and with lots of "other-mothering" will shortly move on to the next stage of life better equipped to meet the challenges waiting to confront him.

On the other hand, must you nurse this busy little runabout every time he asks for it? Not necessarily. Perhaps your little fellow has just been trying to tell you that he wants more mothering, not just more breast. His real need is for you. Listen to him; look at him; have fun with him. Give him your time. That's quality mothering when your child is small. Turn down the job offers, turn off the soaps. Hang up the phone. Did you know that when you're on the phone you're gone from the neck up? Some kids draw on the walls, or flour the floors. Some just ask to nurse. Maybe the breast is their only reassurance that you still notice them at all. Don't give up nursing too soon. But take care that it is not your child's only link to a too-busy mother. Add more of yourself to your relationship with him and you'll probably find him wanting less of the breast. Talk to other mothers who have gone this route and read MOTHERING YOUR NURSING TODDLER.

You will come away with a better understanding of your own needs as well as those of your child. Your needs are important, but first you must sort them out. Mothers need to learn to sacrifice. They need to learn patience, kindness, and thoughtfulness. Mothers need, above all, a sense of humor to help them through these busy, crazy years. It is tempting to take the short view and make a decision on the basis of our immediate needs (comforts?) when we would be better advised to make a few more sacrifices and put our child's happiness ahead of our own for a little while longer. Later on we'll find out that in doing so we have taken care of some very real needs of our own as well.

Norma Jane has supplied us with excellent guidelines to help us sort out our questions. As one who has nursed her own children, she speaks from first-hand experience. Having talked with many other mothers as well, she reflects a variety of experiences and reactions.

The author explains why some children nurse past infancy, (and why their mothers let them). She tells us how some mothers have answered the curious, handled the pressures, and been good wives to their husbands during these sometimes frustrating, but always fascinating years. She tells us about love and limits at two, three, and four. (Have you ever heard of the "Spicy Burrito Method" of weaning?)

There are no absolutes when it comes to the question of when the post-toddler should wean, so don't look for them here. You have to supply your own answers. I believe Norma Jane has written the nursing mother's "cope" book, of inestimable value to all those who want to gain new insights into life with their little ones.

"There are joys as well as difficulties in every part of parenting," she says. "The nursing years are not the only, or even necessarily the best, of our lives with our children.... Good mothering is an investment, not a sacrifice."

I can guarantee that after reading this book you'll find life with your preschooler much easier and lots more fun.

Mary White
La Leche League International
Board of Directors
Founding Mother

acknowledgments

It seems a lifetime ago—and a lot does happen in seven years—when the idea for this book emerged in long conversations with Judy Greenwood and Elizabeth Hormann. These good friends gave me the confidence to undertake writing for parents of nursing toddlers—certainly the most ambitious project I have ever undertaken.

Pat Hudson deserves a special thank you here. How often, Pat, you will see your ideas reflected or amplified in these pages. For so much of my thinking about mothering grew out of conversations and correspondence with you.

I could never have succeeded without the patience of my husband and children. Nor would I have had much of interest to say without the lessons we learned in rearing our children through their preschool years.

I am grateful to Sue Forrester, my long-time friend and colleague in La Leche League, for sharing her experience with me, for fulfilling some of my commitments when I was too involved in writing to do other things I had promised, and especially for reading and commenting thoughtfully on the manuscript when it was still in unbearably rough form.

I owe special thanks to Dr. Gregory White of La Leche League's Professional Advisory Board, and to his wife, Mary White, one of the founding mothers of La Leche League, for their careful reading of the manuscript and their many helpful comments and suggestions.

I am grateful to Niles Newton, PhD, for information on nursing while pregnant, material from a study she did along with Marilyn Theotokatos. Karen Fitzgerald kindly shared some of her expertise as a nutritionist. Linda Kay Griffin did an excellent job proofreading the final typescript. Mary Ann Kerwin and the La Leche League International Book List Committee, including Alice Bicknell, were most helpful and encouraging. Judy Torgus provided invaluable assistance with many last-minute details.

My thanks go also to John Bowlby, The Tavistock Institute of Human Relations, London, and Basic Books, Inc., New York, for permission to quote excerpts from *Attachment*.

1980 Edition

acknowledgments

My thanks go to so many who have shared their thoughts and experience. Some are named in the text, but most are not. I lost count long ago of the people whose wisdom has come my way. Everyone who put pen to paper or fingers to keyboard has increased my resolve to pass on what all of us have learned together over recent decades. Everyone whose family is stronger and happier as a result of reading this book owes a "thank-you" to those who have gone before and who were generous enough to tell me what they learned from living with toddlers.

I received special and undocumented help from a long-time friend and colleague, Sue Forrester, RN, MSN, CPNP, and from new friend Barbara Mullings. Sue and Barbara have been ready with information and constructive advice on serious questions that most people would have thought bizarre, and this book is better for their contributions.

I also received invaluable assistance from the University of Oklahoma Libraries and from Carol Huotari at La Leche League International's Center for Breastfeeding Information.

Many thanks to the professional and creative editors and designers at La Leche League International for converting the drabness of a manuscript into the beauty of a book. Judy Torgus, Gwen Gotsch, and Katherine Solan did a wonderful and patient job of making me look good and of helping me say what needs to be said. Kathy Grossman added her touch of good humor with her cartoons throughout the book.

And, finally, thanks to Seth, Carmen, Myles, and Vincent. You taught me all I know about parenting. Now it is you, along with Madeline, Kevin, and Amy, who nurture me in the shelter of your love. The circle is complete.

2000 Edition

An Investment, Not a Sacrifice

When I first saw a walking child nurse back in the 1960s, I was horrified—horrified at the kind of sacrifices the mother must be making for her child, horrified at what I saw as the obscenity of it, and horrified at the lack of good parental management that had let this thing go on so long. However, as I got to know that mother and child better, my view changed. I did not see the mother making any unneeded sacrifices; she seemed to enjoy nursing. Nor was there lack of management when it was called for; both parents were dedicated to teaching their son how to care for himself and how to show respect for the rights and property of others. As time went on I saw that their nursing was not some weird perversion either; nursing was clearly a warm and tender part of their life together, one of many ways these two people loved and enjoyed each other.

I was so impressed with the kind of relationships this family had and what they told me about extended nursing that when my next child came along, I did not wean her. I let weaning come in its own time. Through example and happy experience I learned that weaning is not something you have to do to a child, but something shared, and that nursing can—and should—continue as long as mother and child want it to.

It turns out that I was not alone at the time. Throughout the industrialized world breastfeeding rates were beginning a slow rise, especially among mothers blessed with education and access to information. And among nursing mothers a sort of underground grew, women who not only nursed, but also nursed a long time. "Closet nursers" Jimmie Lynne Avery dubbed us in a pioneering article on the subject.[2] As we embarked on this "new" (in our own neighborhoods at least) venture, we ran into all sorts of unexpected joys and pitfalls. "Somebody ought to write a book," we all said. We needed information. Finally I decided that I would have to be that "somebody" and set out to collect our experiences in the first edition of this book, published in 1980.

Since that time a generation has grown up with the benefits of the encouragement and support their mothers got from that movement. Today many of these former nurslings have nursing toddlers of their own, such as the mother who wrote:

> *I raise quite a few eyebrows with my daughter's extended nursing, but for the most part it is a satisfying experience. I was nursed to age three and my husband to age two-and-*

a-half so we kind of figure we are just holding with tradition. We both feel lucky to have been nursed so long and partially attribute our happy, satisfying marriage to that fact. We share a trusting and respectful relationship, and I believe that an early childhood that includes a loving breastfeeding relationship can contribute to healthy adult relationships. I feel that a few years spent nursing a toddler can create a lifetime legacy of love and trust.

What a different experience it must be for young parents to be able to answer critics of their parenting style with, "Well, I was a nursing toddler, and look how great I turned out!"

Even if you weren't a nursing toddler yourself, somebody in the crowd around you probably was. Thanks to these new pioneers in what we'll see is a very old style of parenting, there is a good chance that the people you meet won't be as shocked at continued nursing as I was way back when.

Today you also have support within the circles of the health care community, support almost beyond my generation's dreams. In 1990 the World Health Organization and UNICEF arranged a meeting at Innocenti in Italy and there approved the "Innocenti Declaration." In this document they proclaimed it desirable that children be totally breastfed for four to six months and then partly breastfed up to two years of age or beyond.[9] The American Academy of Pediatrics in 1997 joined the world health community, recommending that breastfeeding should continue for *at least* one year and for as long thereafter as mother and baby want.[1] These policies are not necessarily promoted by all health care providers, but at the very least mothers of nursing toddlers can proceed with assurance that a majority of scientific minds in the fields of child health and nutrition have joined with loving parents in supporting the need children have for breastfeeding that is measured in months or years instead of days or weeks. (For examples of support for continued breastfeeding from popular books on childcare, see Diane Bengson's *How Weaning Happens* [3] pp. 58-59.)

Down with Martyrdom

Women have spent much of the twentieth century stirring, rising, and at last revolting against needless sacrifices that were long expected of us, especially in the name of children, including what many saw as the "sacrifice" of nursing at all, and especially nursing "forever." This was a necessary revolution, because in human relationships excessive sacrifice is a deadly trap. Mothers who thought their role was to do everything for everybody all the time, never asking anything for themselves, gave motherhood a terrible reputation. In Western culture, the tragic picture of the guilt-ridden son weeping over the grave of his mother, who spent her youth and beauty, if not her very life on him, is a romantic ideal that shows up repeatedly in our literature and art. Romantic or not, women have come to see this picture as one they want to stay out of. After all, everyone in it is—or was—unhappy.

Fleeing the notion that the only value women's lives had was in the "success" of other family members, mothers have withdrawn in great numbers from the care of children, often without even intending to do so, choosing to bottle-feed, forcing infants and young children to sleep all night and alone, and forcing toilet training as early as possible. Care for young children by someone besides mother has come to be seen as a parental right rather than as an option that benefits those children who enjoy having relationships with adults outside the immediate family. We have even allowed economies to develop in which many families need both parents to leave their children in order to earn enough to feed them.

As far back as we can see, there has been a tendency for the wealthy and powerful to delegate childcare to underlings. Wet nursing and childcare are industries with a very long history. Our movement away from care of children by their own parents may be just one feature of the common quest to enjoy the prerogatives of the upper classes. But turning the drudgery of small children over to others requires sacrifice, too. Perhaps royalty did not notice the drain on their treasuries, but others did. And in all classes such practices have often taken their toll in weakened family relationships and increased mortality for both mothers and babies.[5]

Thankfully there are women who can afford the best mother substitutes money can buy and yet choose to do the job themselves. Their example suggests that for them farming out the business of parenting is just too costly, and that their families are worth considerable investment of time and emotion.

Finding the Essentials

Industrial society has changed family economics so that it is often easier for affluent mothers to nurse as long as they want than it is for those of us who are more financially challenged. The problem for mothers—for parents—of limited means is figuring out what sacrifices are necessary to raise happy, healthy children. These are, therefore, not sacrifices at all but investments.

In devaluing sacrifice per se as the mark of a "good mother," we have to sort out the necessities, separate real parenting from the list of services that mothers in the past felt obliged to perform. We have become very confused about what we as mothers are committed to do for our families, what family members would be better off doing for themselves, and what we might want to do for them if we have time and energy left over.

Parents must see to the care of their children, provide and maintain shelter, obtain fuel and water, purchase and prepare food, and generate enough cash income to cover the services which most regard as indispensable (e.g., medical care). Breastfeeding requires a commitment of a mother's time, some of which might be devoted to other tasks. On the other hand, the reduction in lost sleep or in time spent tending to sick children that comes with breastfeeding gives a mother more time.[4] Nothing good in life is free, but the cost of intimate mothering may be considerably less than it first appears.

In our efforts to move away from duties of motherhood that have seemed uncomfortable and sometimes quite unfulfilling, we have left bare or even torn up the foundation of the family, a foundation which somehow got lost under a clutter of roles and obligations. That foundation is human need. As destructive to family life as some of humankind's flight from motherhood has seemed, we have at least been able to learn from it more about what is and what is not indispensable in family life—in our roles as mothers, fathers, sons, and daughters.

The family is a grouping of people that is ideally suited to meeting human needs. Families can provide for their own members better than any other social grouping. The family is not; we are learning at last, a gathering of people around a mother who takes care of them all, or around a father who takes care of them all. Families are groups of people who take care of each other.

Every member of the family, including mother, has certain biological and emotional needs. It is necessary for members of a family to see that the basic needs are met for every member of the family, for if someone is lacking the essentials, life will be difficult for the whole group.

It is only when the essential needs are tended to that we can begin to consider extras like a larger income and interior decoration. In the barrage of commercial promotion and even family pressure, we need to remind ourselves of the essentials listed above. The list does not include new or designer clothing. It does not include a separate bedroom for each child. It is in our ranking of needs and extras that we get ourselves into trouble—when we turn our backs on our families to get a new house or car (or to keep them clean and shiny), to keep ourselves shaped just so, to stay in this or that social circle, and so on and on. No doubt we can manage quite a number of these things while doing our part in seeing that everyone at home is faring well. It is the accumulation of too many "essential" things that does us in. When we turn away from a crying child to clean a carpet—or to buy a new one—we can be sure that our values are backwards. It should not be surprising how little pleasure there is in the spotless rug when someone in the house is unhappy. We have to help each other live with peace, satisfaction, and even joy. Everything else is extra—a pleasure to pursue and savor, but only if we have resources to spare above the human needs around us.

Tending to Basics Makes Life Easier—Not Harder

Making the commitment to help another adult meet his or her needs, as in marriage, may seem frightening, especially when we are very young. Yet such a commitment clearly makes life easier, because it is an agreement to help each other from the very beginning of the marriage relationship—or it should be.

With our children the commitment is one-sided at first. Babies and young children are totally dependent on us. The impulse to evade such total responsibility is easy to understand, especially the first time we are parents. It appears to be an impulse at least as old as human history. Yet experience shows that the more we can give ourselves to the needs of the young child—almost all of which can be satisfied by breastfeeding in the beginning—the easier life is.

Looking back on her first mothering experience, one mother said, "In retrospect, my attitude then seems so silly. My husband and I spent hours rocking her—at all hours of the day and night—when a few minutes at the breast would have been a great time and effort saver." Yet for many of us this struggle against giving ourselves fully to the baby seems to be a part of learning to be parents. I know it was for me.

A lot of ink is expended on the problems of weaning, toilet training, and bedtime—especially bedtime. Thankfully since the first writing of this book in the 1970s, pressure for early toilet training has diminished considerably. On the other hand, the "need" for children to sleep through the night seems to have increased. Advice intended to free adults for other "more important" tasks proliferates, not because the suggested techniques produce great and reliable success in imposing restrictions upon small children, but because in a lot of families non-nurturing child care practices fail, or even backfire.

It takes time for many of us to learn what one mother in Denmark discovered with her first child: "Laziness was probably the strongest urge that got me to nurse so well and to fulfill my child's needs in his earliest months, and it was also what kept me nursing. It is much easier to put a tired, bored, thirsty, hungry, and demanding eight-month, ten-month, fourteen-month-old child to the breast when you are visiting friends and want to talk. It is much easier to have enough milk so he will be satisfied in the early morning hours when I want to sleep."

I am always impressed by, even a bit envious of, parents who do not have to try avoiding their children's needs for a while before they learn how much simpler and happier life can be when needs are tended to promptly.

Giving freely to the young child is not a sacrifice, even though it may feel like a sacrifice at times. It is, as I have said, an investment. Before your child is grown there will doubtless be days when you in turn are totally dependent upon him (for example, when you come down with that twenty-four-hour "bug"). Your first-rate care for your child when he needs you will give him the resources to return the favor when he is old enough.

Meeting human needs in our children not only helps them grow into psychologically healthy adults, it also helps each of them to learn how to do their part in the family as a group formed to take care of each other.

Breastfeeding Is One of the Basics

Yes, breastfeeding does require commitment and dedication. It would be wrong to imply that it is effortless, because it isn't. It is often intense and demanding for about two years—maybe one, maybe three—although breastfeeding may continue at a more relaxed pace for much longer. During the times when the child's nursing is frequent and urgent, it is hard for a mother to see how what she is doing liberates her. Yet a desire to avoid drudgery is a very good reason to breastfeed and to breastfeed as long as the child expresses the need. To deny responsive mothering to a young child is to risk making family life much more difficult in the present and the future. An easy way to cope with tantrums and bedtimes is sufficient motivation for most parents. In the long run, breastfeeding makes the job of parenting easier, not harder.

Of course there are times when providing the care and attention required by small children can be maddening, but to abandon the task can have results that are even more maddening. It is far safer, and usually easier, to relax into human biological patterns of child rearing and turn away from some inanimate parts of the family's life for a while. It may seem like sacrifice at the time, but the sacrifice of things is only temporary. A movie that you miss will come out on video in a few months. An unmade bed will look just as nice once you get around to making it, no matter how long it stays unmade. A neglected career may be difficult to re-enter, but today's parents are fighting to make even that less true.

If parents turn away from their children instead of turning away from things, the children's unmet needs can grow in them and burden them and their families in one way or another for years to come. It is usually easier to do the job right in the first place—to do the hard work of parenting when it needs to be done.

One woman says on this subject, "As for my needs, nursing is the easiest, most pleasant of all the thousand things a mother must do for a child, so why begrudge him that?" A non-sacrificing mother, one who wants to be free "to do her own thing," will probably have the best opportunity possible if she helps and encourages other family members to do their own thing, too. Her little one's "thing" for a while will include nursing, using diapers, and needing lots of care day and night.

How We See the Nursing Couple

The way I saw that first nursling who was more than a tiny infant was probably a rather standard reaction at the time. I can only hope a generation of nursing toddlers now grown to adulthood is beginning to change that perception. There is a long way to go, considering the ways of thinking we have developed in the industrialized world.

Primate researcher Jane Goodall, with all the sensitivity and regard she has for the nursing relationship, still shows some effects on her thinking of Western culture's twentieth-century view of the older nursling—especially a demanding one. In her book *In the Shadow of Man*, she describes the behavior of Flint, a chimpanzee "toddler." A younger sibling had recently displaced Flint, and then the sibling died. Goodall interprets little Flint's renewed demands to nurse with concern for the wear and tear that he makes on his aging mother's energy and patience. She sees Flint as a youngster who was not weaned soon enough or firmly enough.[8] The description of Flint's regression to infantile behavior, however, makes me think of other little ones I've known. I see him as a youngster who has been through a rough time, possibly weaned too soon for his individual timetable. He is feeling his mother's distress and is desperate to have her back for a while.

More than this mild difference in viewpoint, a truly distorted picture of the nursing child has crept into out families and into our literature, like the grotesque account of Gussie's nursing and weaning in Betty Smith's classic novel, *A Tree Grows in Brooklyn* . In this story, the very young child is portrayed not as a small person who is unready to give up his babyhood, but as a little adult who is selfish, manipulative, and even a little obscene. No one in the story seems to be able to see how resourceful young Gussie is in showing his mother what his needs are.[7]

Nor did Betty Smith create such a harsh picture out of deliberate lack of warmth and kindness toward children; her writing is filled to overflowing with tenderness and concern for the very young. Rather her description of Gussie's nursing is a portrayal of society's image of a nursing child in the early twentieth century USA. It matches precisely the way one of my older relatives talked about a demanding nursling she remembered from Shawnee, Oklahoma, at about the same time.

More experience with older nurslings should provide modern cultures with appropriate, child-oriented frames of reference in which to see the behavior of the nursing child. We will be able to realize the special and wholesome kind of relationship there is between a mother and her suckling child, even if this child is big, even if this child is dressed in "big boy" clothes. Then a nursing child will not look to us like a horrid little man smoking a cigar. Instead we will see the baby still peeping out of those big-boy eyes. And we will see the joy in those eyes because mother is still there ready to care for that baby.

Managing Children's Lives

Somehow part of our distorted view of little children makes us distrust children and their ability to grow up. We jump in and try to take control. We overwhelm ourselves with things we must do for our children, and what is so ludicrous about much of this activity and interference with our children's lives is that all our work supposedly makes life easier for us adults. What nonsense!

We make up schedules for feeding babies, watch clocks, and carefully measure what they eat. We thrust spoons and cups into little hands that do not even patty cake very well yet. We may monitor their toilet habits. We insist on controlling their bedtimes and how they treat the statuary and potted plants. We decorate their rooms and fuss over how they are dressed and whether their toes point in the right direction. If they are not sleeping all night by six months we try hard to do something about the "problem." The day care center insists on toilet training. Despite the blessing of the American Academy of Pediatrics for extended nursing, in many families a year-old child who is not weaned, or certainly well on the way toward weaning, is still a sign that mother must do something and fast!

We clean our children's rooms, keep up with their clothing, and cook all their meals, sometimes for years. And then when they reach adolescence and need us again to be perceptive and thoughtful and loving, we wonder why we are too worn out to love them through the second major transition in their lives.

Our children do not need to have their lives managed or to have someone plan every aspect of their growth. Children do not cling to nursing or diapers, waking at night, or even fingering the household ornaments in order to trouble or control adults. One should not even describe these behaviors as bad habits. Children do these things because of needs and drives inside themselves. It is ever so much more wholesome for the growing child and easier for the whole family, especially for mother (believe it or not), just to forget managing infantile behaviors.

It is healthy, constructive, and ever so much more relaxing to go through life with your young child not dreading battles over night wakings, or worrying about when your child will eat next or need to use the bathroom.

Finding the Baby among the Teddy Bears

Of course many parents love some of the time-consuming tasks they can take on, such as providing elaborate nursery decorations. These niceties are the right of any parent who has the time and resources to spend on them. But they are for the parents, and no one should feel duty bound to provide a baby with such extras as traditional nursery surroundings. The infant does not care about them. Most young children prefer their parents' bed to the most beautiful nursery in the world. By the time a child is interested in how his room is decorated, he is old enough to do it himself, and will probably have his own opinions on how he wants it done.

The same is true for clothing. The young child enjoys comfort and variety, and hand-me-downs are often best in this regard. By the time he cares how they look, he will want to choose his own.

We parents do enjoy seeing our children nicely dressed, so we should feel free to put pretty clothes on them as long as doing so does not interfere with something important and as long as the children are happy with our choices. But again we must understand that we are dressing them for our own sakes. Clothing becomes an important issue with older children, as we can all remember from our own lives. But "failing" to dress babies and toddlers in handsome clothing during the time they are indifferent to what they wear deprives them of nothing.

The Real Goal of Parenting—Self-Sufficiency

In my parents' generation, mothers often kept the essential family business of preparing meals, cleaning house, and keeping clothes clean and sorted to themselves. Maybe this realm was preserved only for mother so that she was indispensable to the family, or perhaps, since this was "women's work," a mother would never dare ask for help with these duties. By keeping such tasks to themselves, however, especially as babies grew into children, mothers did their families no favor. Instead,

I believe they deprived family members of the security of knowing that, if necessary, they could survive.

Parenting is about teaching each child the necessary skills to take care of himself. Every daughter and every son should grow up knowing how to tend the house, prepare food, wash and mend clothing, do the shopping, pump gasoline, or change a tire. It is not our job as parents simply to take care of our children, but to make sure they learn how to take care of themselves.

So, rather than fretting over toilet training or weaning in the toddler years—these are developments that will come in their own time—it is more constructive to help children learn to do the things they want and need to do. This will likely include helping the child master the mysteries of slicing cheese or pouring milk, buttoning coats, and letting the dog out. By school age, most children should have learned to sort laundry and operate the washing machine. Soon they can prepare a hot meal from cans or simple recipes.

It should not be the parents' objective to manage children's lives, nor to be their caretakers. Nothing is more pitiful than to have a whole family in panic because a parent is down with the flu. All of us—mothers, fathers, and children—need to learn everything we can so that we can cope with circumstances and take care of each other. Second-graders make fine pancakes, and preschoolers can carry cheese and apples to a mommy who is under the weather. Daddies sew on buttons just fine. Mommies can put jumper cables on dead batteries. And big brothers can build a fire in the fireplace or wash and dry the family's clothing.

No member of the family can be sure of never being called on to do someone else's job. There is no guarantee that the person charged with an essential task will always be healthy or live forever. In love and kindness to ourselves and to our families we should spend less time, or better yet no time, on managing breastfeeding and sleeping and toileting. We should not try to monitor every bite our children eat, every item of clothing they wear, or exactly how they maintain their rooms. Rather we should have a long-range plan in rearing our children in which parents spend no more time than we need doing for other family members what they can do for themselves. (Note the phrase "than we need" in the previous sentence: family business does proceed more efficiently when there is a comfortable, and flexible, division of labor.)

The more people know how to do the more confidently they can live, and the easier life is for everyone, including mother. As a bonus, as if one were needed beyond the joy of self-confidence that we can give our families, when we mothers are not burdened by long lists of tasks we must do for our children for as long as they live with us, then the times of their lives when they need a lot from us will seem much less overwhelming. The breastfeeding years, for instance, are not an ongoing pattern of unending service from mother to child. Soon, perhaps even before breastfeeding is completely ended, mother and child will be doing for each other.

We waste precious time and energy, time and energy we could use for our many other and no doubt more pleasant ambitions, in trying to avoid the enormous investment of ourselves that a very young child needs. We hope we can avoid having to commit ourselves so fully, and we fear that the demands of the young child will go on forever. But that will not be our future unless we make it so. It is an economical move in terms of our own personal resources, even a laudably selfish move, to give ourselves fully to the infant and young child. As Dr. Lee Salk points out in *What Every Child Would Like His Parents to Know,* a child's needs for intensive parenting, like needs for food, go away once they are satisfied, and remain when they are not.[6]

There is no form of parental management that will teach a young child not to hunger for great helpings of attention. Rather than wasting effort, to say nothing of peaceful and potentially happy times, trying to teach a young child to get along with less of her parents' days and nights, it is far wiser to give that time freely, and to make good use of it for teaching really valuable and lasting lessons, like how to love, how to play, and where to find the peanut butter.

References

1   American Academy of Pediatrics. Working Group on Breastfeeding. Breastfeeding and the use of human milk. *Pediatrics* December 1997; 100(6):1035-39.

2   Avery, J. L. Closet nursing: a symptom of intolerance and a forerunner of social change? *Keeping Abreast Journal* 1977; 2:212-27.

3   Bengson, D. HOW WEANING HAPPENS. Schaumburg, Illinois: La Leche League, International. 1999; 58-59.

4   Berg A. and Brems, S. *A case for promoting breastfeeding in projects to limit fertility.* World Bank Technical Paper Number 102. Washington, D.C.: The World Bank, 1989; 11.

5   Fildes, V. A. *Breasts, Bottles and Babies: A History of Infant Feeding.* Edinburgh: Edinburgh University Press, 1986; 159-62, 85-89, 113-14, 199-203.

6   Salk, L. *What Every Child Would Like His Parents to Know.* New York: David McKay Company, Inc., 1972; 40.

7   Smith, B. *A Tree Grows in Brooklyn.* New York: HarperPerennial, 1998; 218-19.

8   van Lawick-Goodall, J. *In the Shadow of Man.* New York: Houghton Mifflin Co., 1971; 232-36.

9   WHO/UNICEF. *On the Protection, Promotion and Support of Breast-Feeding.* August 1990.

part one

Nursing Your Toddler — Why?

chapter one

Why Children Nurse into Toddlerhood

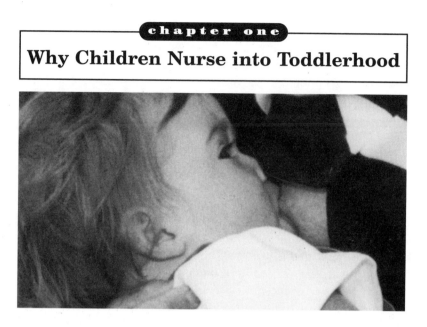

Sucking: A Tool for Growing

It may seem strange at first that a child who sits at the family table at mealtimes and is into the refrigerator many times in between would also ask his mother for nursing several times a day—and night.

Yet anyone who looks lovingly at a child at the breast can see that satisfying hunger or thirst is only a part of nursing. After a minute or two of nursing, the entire little body relaxes with contentment and pleasure. A child who is hurt begins to feel better. A child who has become overexcited calms down. One mother says of her nursing child, "She'll come up to me whining and refusing to talk. We'll sit and nurse; then she'll hop down and act like a big person again, having total control."

Nursing for the child is a kind of "fix," but a healthy one. It is not addictive, as suggested by Gussie's story in Betty Smith's *A Tree Grows in Brooklyn,* but just the opposite. The child's craving diminishes over time. It is no wonder that some families call mother's milk "joy juice." Nursing has all the restorative powers of a morning cup of coffee without the "caffeine jitters." It is as relaxing as an evening cocktail, with no bleary aftereffects.

Sucking is a necessary restorative for rapidly growing little people, so much so that most children who do not nurse seek an alternative—bottle, pacifier, thumb, fingers, hair, blanket-corner, etc.

3

They show us through the persistence of such behaviors that young children need the calming and reassuring effects of sucking as much or more than some adults need our "pacifiers." They are so young, so unfinished, so without experience in this world, while at the same time they are undergoing enormous growth and change.

Comfort from sucking is a blessing given to babies and little children which helps ease them through the physical and mental upheaval, greater than that of adolescence, that propels them from the womb into childhood in just a few short years. Children can be awakened and relaxed, soothed and pacified through sucking.

John Bowlby, a pioneering researcher in personality development, wrote that for primates sucking serves two separate purposes. One purpose of sucking, he writes, is nutritional. The other is what he calls "attachment," a term that describes the complex process in which a baby learns to trust and depend on other human beings, especially his mother. "Each of these functions is of importance in its own right," he writes, "and to suppose that nutrition is in some way of primary significance and that attachment is only secondary would be a mistake. In fact, far more time is spent in non-nutritional sucking than in nutritional."[1]

The best place for this sucking to happen is in mother's arms, at her breast, where it is entirely natural. The simple act of sucking, within the embrace of mother and child, is transformed into the complete act of suckling, where there is give and take and understanding between mother and child. And of course the child receives a bonus not possible with substitutes, the gift of his own mother's living milk, formulated specifically for this moment in the child's life.

"Nursing my son for comfort was a wonderful, peaceful time for us," a mother writes. "I didn't think about it, just held him close and let nature do the rest. About a year ago he weaned completely. However, the physical closeness we shared whenever he was upset or hurt or a thousand other emotions, continues to this day."

Mothers can distinguish between different kinds of nursing. "When he is hungry he nurses like he *means it;* he nurses strong through my let-down and then wants to switch sides. When he nurses for comfort his suck is different; he cuddles more and even pulls away during the strong flow of a let-down. This is as obvious to me as the times that he fiddles around and lounges as he nurses out of boredom." These different nursing behaviors are useful cues about the child's changing needs both within and beyond the nursing relationship.

Some people worry that comfort nursing encourages the bad habit of turning to food for comfort. Others don't see nursing that way at all, as the mother who points out that "the child is learning to go to a *person* for comfort ...." After all, the child is nursing for comfort, not food, that's the whole point. I personally think food should be comforting. And it is most comforting when part of a social ritual. Nursing is clearly better than handing a kid a cookie and telling him to go play. It's more like sitting down to a cup of tea with a sympathetic friend."

Suckling plays an enormous role in a child's growing up. Children weaned too soon often end up seeking ineffective substitutes, either behaviors or objects. Unlike suckling, which will cease all by itself once it has done its job, dependence upon less effective behaviors or upon objects may not go away until much later in life, if ever.

Nursing Children Speak for Themselves

As children grow older, some are able to put into words their reasons for nursing. And their reasons are neither manipulative nor evil as some people seem to think. At two-and-a-half, one of my children told me, "I 'nanny' when I feel like a baby."

Often we say that a child nurses only for closeness with mother after the first year or so, not for the milk. In a sense this statement is true, for a child who eats a wide variety of table foods may not require the nourishment of mother's milk. As one father put it, "She's no longer refilling her tanks; she's recharging her batteries!"

In another sense, however, children do nurse for the milk, because they like it. "I'm sure thirsty for your milk inside of you," one three-year-old told his mother. "Delicious!" announced a two-year-old when she had finished nursing. "It's my favorite!" said another, like a young gourmet offering compliments to the chef. According to one child, mother's milk is "the most delicious milk in the whole world."

What mother has to offer is so good that little ones often want their dolls and teddy bears to have a share—and sometimes even their playmates, although the playmates invariably decline. One little guy even asked his mother to refuel his new truck. He wanted only the best for his prized possession. A mother whose child is fond of dinosaur toys writes, "You aren't a real woman until you've nursed a triceratops!"

Children are quite aware, however, not only of nursing for milk, but also of nursing for comfort, and sometimes talk about this non-nutritive sucking, too. One two-year-old offered to nurse her mother who was not feeling well. "It will make you feel better fast, Mommy," she promised. A four-year-old, also thinking about nursing for comfort, modified "Jack and Jill" so that it made more sense to her: "Jack fell down, and broke his crown, and went home for num-num."

An articulate five-year-old had thought the matter of his continued nursing through quite thoroughly. He told his mother:

I think five-year-olds should be able to nurse if they want to. I think five-year-olds should enjoy nursing. Nursing is like drinking from a bottle except it's more comfortable. It feels very good, and I'm next to Mommy.

Although few children verbalize their thoughts about nursing so completely as this young man, we can be sure that children do think about it and that their thoughts and motivations run along similar lines. When children talk about nursing, they talk about something very warm and special to them. Nursing is their "soul food." They nurse because it tastes good and feels good and helps them feel happy.

References

1   Bowlby, J. Attachment. New York: Basic Books, 1982; 249.

chapter two

Why Mothers Nurse Their Children into Toddlerhood

Seeing a Need

When I ask mothers who have nursed longer than a year why they chose to do so, they usually say, "It just seemed natural," or "He seemed to need it still." Some mothers, taking their cues from the child rather than the calendar, say "I never even thought about it."

One mother describes the way she felt about her child's continued nursing: "I knew and felt her need for me and her desire to nurse. I love her, and it would break my own heart to disappoint her and refuse myself to her." If we look past the social rules at the children that these rules are supposed to benefit, it is not difficult to see the need children have for continued nursing, their joy in nursing, and their distress when it is denied. A simple but compelling reason for continuing to nurse is to please the child. More mothers these days are watching their children and responding to what they see.

A Health Plus

Research on infant health and mortality leaves no doubt about benefits of continued nursing, at least through the second year, in poor and transitional societies. Nursing toddlers grow better and have more resistance against infection.[18] For affluent families with good sanitation and access to safe alternatives to mother's milk, the health advantages of continued nursing are less dramatic. Still, the list of subtle, but statistically significant, benefits for nurslings continues to grow. For most children in the developed parts of the world, human milk may no longer be a life or death issue, but it still matters. Anthropologist Katherine Dettwyler says:

> At this point in scientific understanding, no research is available that looks at the differentials in disease and cognitive outcomes for children breastfed longer than two years, compared with those breastfed for shorter periods. All of the studies that have examined the relationship between duration of breastfeeding and health outcomes stop with an upper category of 24+ months. No studies have compared the health differential between children breastfed for three years compared with those breastfed for four years, compared with those breastfed for five years, and so on. Thus, stating unequivocally that there are significant or substantial health benefits to breastfeeding beyond two years of age is not possible. At the same time, stating unequivocally that there are no significant or substantial health benefits to breastfeeding beyond two years of age likewise is not possible. The additional health benefits, in a First World setting, of breastfeeding beyond two years may be very slight, or they may be significant; they may affect health in childhood, or they may not become apparent until middle age or later—the data are simply not available at this time. . . . All of the available research shows better health outcomes the longer the child breastfeeds, up to the current study limits of 24 months. If the mother and child want to continue breastfeeding, no reasons exist to suggest that they should not. In particular, no reasons exist to question the motivations of the mother who wants to give her child the best possible lifelong health, nor to accuse her of harboring ulterior motives for continuing to breastfeed well beyond two years.[1]

In classical times, even when weaning was encouraged at age two or three, physicians recommended later weaning for weak or special children. Various authors listed weaker children as twins, children who did not eat well, children born to older mothers, and males. They said that children of nobility—"treasured children"—should nurse longer, too.[2]

As you may have noticed in the movie *The Last Emperor,* the young heir to the Chinese throne, Pu Yi, nursed until he was eight. Continued nursing remains a way we can try to give extra protection to our own treasured children.

Although nurslings do experience illness, sometimes even severe illness, their time at the breast is an investment in their good health. Many mothers have commented on how much healthier their children were before weaning. "Old wives" have long warned against weaning in summer, knowing that nursing provided the child with protection against "summer complaint," gastroenteritis brought on by eating foods contaminated by bacteria in hot weather.

Your milk, of course, provides the optimal nutritional foundation for your child's good health. In addition, your milk carries antibodies to infectious diseases you have encountered. Babies are born with undeveloped immune systems, and colostrum and human milk provide important protection against disease from birth until the baby's own systems are able to function on their own. For example, breastfeeding has been shown to reduce children's susceptibility to *otitis media* (middle ear infection) for three years. The longer the exclusive breastfeeding period in the first year continues, the fewer the episodes of ear infection.[13]

Your milk is a living fluid, like blood, that carries your disease-fighting cells, the ones your body has produced in response to both past and current infective agents in your environment (and your child's). The list of substances produced by your experienced immune system and passed along to your child through your milk is long and exotic. Some agents act in your child's bloodstream, others in his respiratory or intestinal tract.[7,12] Some types of living cells in your milk may make their way into your child's gut or lymphoid tissue and persist there for months or years, influencing his developing immune system.[9]

Many different body systems and processes form these different substances.[11] Research so far has shown that the baby produces many of them on his own by three to seven months. However, production of the important immunoglobulin secretory IgA seems to remain low for eighteen months, and some aspects of the child's immune system may not operate at adult levels until age five or six.[3] Katherine Dettwyler spoke on this subject in 1999:

> *In humans, several physiological milestones occur around six to seven years of age, all of which can be linked logically to having breast milk as a component of the diet throughout this period. First, achievement of adult immune competence occurs at approximately six years of age. Until this time, the child's active immune response (both serum and secretory) can be enhanced by the*

lymphokines in maternal milk. Children need these lymphokines, even in small amounts, to augment and prime their own immune responses to stress until they achieve adult levels of immune competence (IgA, IgG, IgM) around the age of six years.[5]

As your child's immune system is developing, your milk can fill in the gaps. In humans, as in other mammals, there is a mirror-image pattern between immunologic development in the young and corresponding immune factors in the mother's milk.[4] In addition, the immune response in infants seems to be aided by factors in human milk which enhance immunoglobulin production.[3] The concentration of several substances involved in immune function increase through the weaning period so that it takes smaller amounts of milk for the child to receive the same levels of protection.[5]

Throughout the nursing period, your child exposes you to the bacteria she picks up in her expanding world. Your system responds with anti-infective agents that protect you and are transmitted to your child through your milk.[7] Or you may be exposed to an infective agent in your environment before your child is. Your milk will reflect your body's resistance against the infection and may give your child a head start in fighting it off once she is exposed.

In either case, your toddler's immune system will often produce adequate defenses on its own. Considering how subject even a mature immune system is to various stressors, however, logic suggests there may be occasions throughout the nursing years in which your milk might be able to provide protection your child is temporarily lacking, filling in for parts of your toddler's immune system that are weakened or not yet "on line." But we cannot say with certainty that this is true until research has been done on immunities in children nursing beyond the second year.

When a Nursing Child Becomes Ill

Mothers are most grateful for the ability to soothe children by nursing when a child is ill. Even breastfeeding will not prevent illness completely but besides the reduction in frequency and severity of illness, the nursling enjoys the advantage of being able to nurse through whatever illness she does experience.

Having an ill child can make an adult feel more helpless than any other problem in life. To be able to do nothing but sit beside a whimpering, miserable child, watching the clock for the next scheduled medication time is a wretched business. I don't know who receives the greatest relief from the misery of a child's illness through nursing, mother or child.

The first thing to do is get rid of the image of an ill child tucked neatly into bed with mother standing dutifully by. We should instead tune in to our own feelings and instincts. The best place for a small child who is ill is in a parent's arms if at all possible. Parents become even more anxious when he is anywhere else. Children come through illnesses, even serious ones, much less fretfully if they can be held, and if they can nurse, so much the better.

Even children who must be hospitalized can usually be held by their parents most of the time. And many a mother has never been more glad for her child's continued nursing than when she had to help him through an illness or injury so severe that it required hospitalization.

A long-recognized symptom of illness is an aversion to food. Lionel Chalmers, a seventeenth-century medical authority from South Carolina, wrote that weaning too soon risked death in the event of illness. "It is therefore safest," he wrote, "not to wean infants before they have all or most of their teeth, that they may have somewhat to trust in case of sickness; for they will take the nipple when all other nourishment is refused."[16]

Parents of a non-nursing child, in order to keep him from becoming dehydrated with fever, sometimes have to resort to feeding foods which one would hope they would rarely or never give to a healthy baby, sweet soft drinks or sugared gelatin. Pharmacies offer electrolyte solutions to be fed to sick babies and children. These are no doubt an improvement over highly sugared drinks, but a baby cannot depend on them for more than a few days at most.

The breastfed child who is too ill to take any other food will almost always nurse. Instead of running around fretting over what she can get a feverish child to eat and keep down, the nursing mother can rock her child and nurse, knowing that no fluid on earth is more suitable, and that nothing else will be more gently received by the child's struggling little body than her milk. One mother said, "When he was ill, nursing was his only comfort and his only nutrition. Nursing was my only comfort during his two bouts with pneumonia. It made me feel I was doing something during a time of waiting and feeling helpless."

Even following surgery or an intestinal upset so severe that the child cannot tolerate anything by mouth, the food he can handle first, well before any other, is mother's milk. Parents have often been surprised to find after a severe illness that their nursing children have lost little or no weight.

An ill toddler's return to nursing may be so complete for a few days that he even returns to the loose breast milk stool of infancy. It is important whenever you think your nursing child has diarrhea to think about what (or whether) he has been eating in the past few days and to remember the appearance and odor of the breast-milk stool. Many a child who has been well on the way to recovery from whatever made him return to "not much but mother" has been needlessly treated for diarrhea when his caretakers forgot that loose stools are normal for a little person of any age who is taking only mother's milk.

Even after little ones have cut back considerably on their nursing, in times of illness mothers have found that their bodies seemed to respond to their children's renewed need for milk. The ability to sustain her child completely when necessary is valuable to the mother of a young child. The ease of caring for a sick child through nursing and the rapidity with which these basically healthy little people usually bounce back when given their mothers' milk seem like reasons enough all by themselves not to abandon the nursing relationship before the child's maturation makes it necessary.

No doubt there are many still undiscovered chemical and biological properties of human milk that contribute to good health in our little ones. More beneficial factors in mother's milk are being found all the time. One of human milk's most significant health benefits, however, no doubt derives from how it is delivered. To the nursing child, milk is fed almost incidentally as part of a warm, loving embrace.

Nursing offers the child relief from the hurts, fears, and anxieties he encounters daily. The child who receives affection and a ready welcome into his mother's arms is likely to be a happy child, and happiness, including good self-esteem and freedom from anxiety, goes a long way toward creating and maintaining good health

Protection from Allergies

Avoiding or at least delaying allergy is a reason that some mothers nurse their children longer than a year. One long-term study showed that early non-human milk feeding was a stronger predictor of allergies later in life than was a family history of allergies.[14] In another study, strict dietary intervention, including breastfeeding with some limits on the mother's diet and "delayed and selective weaning" greatly reduced symptoms in at-risk babies and toddlers.[8]

> *[My 26-month-old daughter] had a late interest in solids (and was growing well without them), so I didn't discover that she had food allergies until she was 12 months old. I am glad we never tried formula, because now I know that she is allergic to not only the protein components, but the fats and sugars as well. . . . Her doctor says that for every year she avoids the problem foods, she has a 30 percent chance of outgrowing the allergies. By age five, she should be able to eat most foods. I'm sure we'll be nursing for a few more years.*

Some children are well past their first year before they are able to eat foods other than mother's milk without becoming ill. Children who cannot use cow's milk or other milk products especially benefit from extended nursing. Without their mother's milk they could be at risk of nutritional deficiencies because of their inability to use the nutrients in other milks.

Children who are prone to allergy may refuse solids until later than other babies. To force foods other than mother's milk on these children would subject them to allergic reactions that they may have been instinctively avoiding. For that rare child with severe allergies, the perfect food that mother can provide becomes his only food for as long as he needs it. And most mothers nursing on demand will produce plenty of milk to meet his needs.

Alignment of Teeth

There is also a tendency for children to take up thumb (or finger) sucking upon weaning, often as soon as weaning is initiated. Sucking a thumb or fingers can force the child's permanent teeth out of alignment if the habit persists into the school years. Nursing actually improves the dental arch. You can minimize the child's need for such self-comfort by nursing as long as the child wants to nurse. I do say "minimize" and not "prevent" thumb or finger sucking. Some children who can nurse whenever they want still seem to need thumbs or fingers in their mouths. But nursing on demand will keep the need for extra sucking and mouthing to a minimum and thereby reduce or eliminate some of those expensive orthodontist bills later on. Nursing more than a year in itself has been shown to reduce the incidence of malocclusion (teeth that don't meet properly). In one study as much as 44 percent of the malocclusion reported seemed to be related to breastfeeding less than a year.[6]

Better Skin

Your milk contains, among other things, fatty acids not available in other foods. These acids seem to help your child in forming the best possible tissues throughout his body. The one tissue in which the effect of these fatty acids is easy to observe is your child's smooth, silky skin. As your nursling becomes a toddler it does not seem to take more than a very small quantity of your milk to maintain that marvelous, touchable skin that we so enjoy in nursing babies and children. Even children nursing only once a day usually keep that special silkiness.

Not only does your milk make your child feel good to you; it also helps your little one feel good to himself by avoiding or minimizing skin disorders to which he may be susceptible. It is not at all uncommon for children who eventually develop some mild forms of eczema not to show any symptoms of the disorder until they are completely weaned. Whether prolonged nursing decreases the severity of eczema in these children we cannot say for certain. Many people believe it does. We can be sure, however, that nursing has postponed the problem until the child is more mature and can cope with it better.

Closeness

The good of the child, however, is not the only reason mothers keep nursing; they enjoy it, too. As one mother put it, "I think I would be crushed if a baby only wanted to nurse a year. This is because I probably enjoy nursing as much as the baby does." No matter how evil some people may want to make mother's enjoyment sound, being very close to a warm, cuddly child is what mothers like best about extended nursing.

A mother's pleasure in nursing is a good thing, one of the many wholesome pleasures available in life. "I used to believe," one mother says, "any mother who continued nursing after so many years had unmet needs of her own that nursing was satisfying." But this mother found as her own nursling grew older that those "unmet needs" she was worried about were actually normal, healthy needs that are easily met by nursing.

I have come to find nursing a toddler to be even more rewarding than nursing an infant. Even though he still nurses for most of his nutrition, he makes it quite evident that he also truly loves to nurse. Whenever he sees me without a shirt he gets a smile on his face, lays his head gently on my breasts and pats them. This gesture is so sweet and so full of love that I can't help but feel sorry for the mother who chooses to miss this experience.

Psychotherapist K. B. Walent regards distant and controlling approaches to parenting as today's version of "normative abuse," just as we have come to see the harsh punishments and restraints of nineteenth century child rearing as the "normative abuse" of that time. Once we realize how damaging detached, unempathetic child-rearing practices can be, and insist on "child-raising techniques that emphasize attachment, interpersonal involvement, and intimacy," then the number of detached, alienated personalities psychotherapists have to treat will decrease.[17]

No matter how much effort has gone into the selling of distance between mother and child, distance achieved by mother substitutes like playpens and pacifiers, and by child substitutes like hobbies and pets, mothers cannot be changed. We still are happiest when we can hold our children close. "I once heard," a mother told me, "that bottle-feeding is

like having a close friendship; breastfeeding is like having a love affair—
and I truly believe this just from my own experience."

So precious is the intimacy between mother and child, and unique
and irreplaceable in the lives of both, that it seems everyone who sees the
pair would make every effort to protect that bond. Artists strive to
capture the warmth between mother and child in poetry or paint, but,
sadly, over the years, people who have provided instructions and advice
on child care have developed systems that undermine every element that
we so admire in the relationship between mother and child.

It is little wonder that many of us are overjoyed to rediscover the
closeness we can have with our children. One mother said as she looked
back at her nursing time, "The memory of nursing my daughter as a
toddler is very pleasant for me. It is hard to pick out one best aspect.
I remember the closeness, how comfortable I felt having her always near
me. I remember how confident I felt in almost always being able to
comfort her and knowing instinctively how to meet her needs whether it
involved nursing or not, the beautiful loving feeling I had for her, and
which she returned, and the pride I felt at being the mother of this
beautiful, bright child."

Some of us may never have seen such an unaffected mother-child
relationship in all our growing up. Having discovered how good it feels to
be intimately attached to a baby and young child, we are unwilling to

ARE YOU THIRSTY?   NO, MOMMY, I'M *NURSTY!*

give up this closeness for anything besides the gradual progress of maturation.

Nursing helps establish intimacy between mother and child. In the beginning, the physical and chemical interactions involved in nursing help the bond to form properly. Continued nursing helps to maintain it by giving both mother and child an appropriate pattern for intimate behavior. Such loving behavior helps overcome other factors in the child's rapid development that can interfere with closeness.

Some children are very shy and tend to withdraw from close interaction with people, even mother. The shy child who is still nursing has a ready-made assertive behavior—asking to nurse—that can help him to learn how to get his other needs met, too. Other children are so active that nursing time is the only quiet, calm time in their busy waking hours. Nursing time is a refreshing time for the mother of a little runabout, and many mothers of active children especially treasure these moments. One mother says, "So many of my friends weaned early. They lost those special close moments as their children became more active. My son is just as active and independent, but we can both look forward to our special moments." It is much easier to feel close and loving toward a child in arms than toward one who is on top of the cabinets or dumping the flowerpots.

As surprising as it may seem, a small percentage of babies inexplicably form their primary attachment with someone in the family other than mother. In these families the mother's need for her child's attention (how seldom we think of what a mother needs from her child) could be at risk. One nursing mother wistfully told me, "My little boy has been a daddy's boy from the beginning. At least he comes to me to be nursed!" For her own sake a mother whose child chooses to spend most of his time with daddy or big sister or someone else in the household would be ill-advised to hasten weaning. Parents and family members need to be careful not to compete for such children's affections; nursing times can help soothe any hurt feelings and offer islands of closeness in which mothers can focus on accepting and supporting their children as they are.

There are children, too, who are challenging to manage, the ones William and Martha Sears call "high-need" children.[15] These little people are going all the time, active and headstrong. Responding warmly to the needs that these children show for nursing may be difficult at times because of the negative feelings their behavior can generate in parents. A mother described one of her children as "very demanding," "selfish," unfazed by his mother's feelings. "He turned me off," his mother said, and this worried her.

We can only wish these challenging little people were all fortunate enough to be born to mothers who resist their impulse to reject these children when they are at their worst, and who remain open so that they can delight in their children when they are at their best.

Many of us have the strongest reactions when our children are difficult or disruptive in front of other people. At home we can usually cope with our little "wild ones" much better. Also, at the same time that their behavior may ruffle mothers' feelings about nursing them, the calm of nursing usually helps to smooth over annoyances. Mothers who have nursed a demanding toddler until he became a reasonably civilized child look back on the experience and realize what an advantage nursing was for them. Without the regular intervals of loving that nursing provided, it would have been more difficult for them to keep the interactions between mother and child positive.

Mothers too can get into behaviors (usually referred to as "things I have to do") that can prematurely disrupt the mother-child bond. Just as nursing is the only time some especially active toddlers hold still for loving, so nursing is the only time some busy mothers sit still for that same loving, loving which these mothers need, too.

Comfort

Nursing is not only a pleasure, but also a convenience. A major task in mothering is helping your child several times daily to overcome fears or hurts or fatigue. There are various ways to comfort a crying child—walking, rocking, singing, but none is easier or more efficient than nursing. It has been described as a little bit of magic on your side: Presto! A fussy child is happy again.

How quickly a bruise or a scrape stops hurting when the first-aid includes nursing. If it is more than a bruise or a scrape, the fact that nursing does not seem to make the pain go away tells you quickly that you are dealing with a bigger hurt that may need extra attention. Other methods do quiet children, too, but the psychological network of the very young seems to be wired with nursing as the choice channel for feeling better. Though not all children will verbalize it, nursing toddlers no doubt appreciate nursing for comfort much as did the tot who said after a tumble, "Thanks, Mom, for nursing me. 'Bye now, I'll be okay."

Teething is a recurrent physiological cause for discomfort in little children, and when new teeth are making gums sore, little ones often ask for a great deal of time at the breast. Many a nursing mother has been pleased to help her child through the discomfort of teething with nursing alone, or perhaps with nursing for soothing and cold celery or a frozen bagel for biting. Of course medications or anesthetic ointments can bring relief when gums get really painful, but nursing acts as a natural analgesic and minimizes the need for chemical comforters.

Little people also manage to bump their mouths, especially while they still walk unsteadily, and even very small mouth injuries tend to bleed profusely. Toddlers usually hate having pressure and ice applied to their mouths to stop the bleeding. They do like to nurse, however, and nursing usually puts enough pressure on the injured tissue to do the job. For toddlers' ordinary small mouth injuries, nursing is the best first-aid, and usually all that is needed.

Comforting a sleepy child at bedtime and naptime is easier for families when the little one is nursing. Rarely do nursing families experience the fuss and tension others expect when a little one needs to go to sleep. Nursing is so effective a tranquilizer for tired children that fathers tease their mates about their "knock-out drops." Few families who have experienced a nursing child's bed or naptime will ever want to rear a child any other way.

Mothers also nurse their children to help them overcome emotional as well as physical upsets. Most mothers, even if they do plan to wean, refrain from doing so during an upheaval such as a family crisis or a move. Nursing is too beneficial to cut it off at a time when the child may especially need it. One mother whose family experienced half a year of illness and loss wrote about nursing her daughter during this difficult time: "Nursing has certainly helped her; it has been like an anchor in a storm. Whatever else has happened, Mummy's milk has always been there."

When There Are Older Siblings

Mothers who have nursed one or more children are almost always intent on repeating the experience with the next child. Nursing helps them take the time to build as special a relationship with the youngest as they did with the older ones when they were nursing.

Older siblings usually respect nursing time, especially if they have been allowed to outgrow their own needs in that department. In fact they frequently insist that mother nurse a fussy or pesky little brother or sister, usually out of sympathy, although occasionally they just want him out of their hair—or their Legos.

Some conflicts are inevitable, but with loving encouragement and firm persuasion older children can and do learn to restrain themselves from interrupting younger siblings' nursing times, even if they insist on being a part of almost anything else. Mothers come to appreciate nursing as a sometimes private haven in which they can give individual attention to the newest person making his place in the family.

Nursing from time to time triggers questions from older siblings, sometimes hard questions on very intimate subjects. By all means parents should take advantage of these moments to provide frank and simple answers. What you say, in the framework of the example of you at your parenting best, will serve your child well later when he is making parenting decisions of his own.

Other Advantages

One mother said she liked being able to take her little one with her everywhere using the excuse, "She won't take a bottle." Another said she found herself experiencing less anger toward her nursing child than toward her others. Reasons mothers occasionally give for continuing to nurse after the first year include maintaining a milk supply for a baby expected through adoption and keeping a nice bustline.

Proceeding with last things first, many of us who spend most of our lives in padded bras thoroughly enjoy the larger breasts we have while nursing. Though desire for a better figure is a wish that may be happily fulfilled through breastfeeding, it is hardly a sufficient motive to carry anyone over the inevitable rough spots. Fuller breasts are just a nice fringe benefit. They do tend to last to some degree almost as long as nursing continues.

For a mother planning to nurse an adopted baby, having an established milk supply can be quite an advantage. It is somewhat easier to increase your milk when you are already lactating than to start from nothing. Adding a family member this way can be a wonderful experience, as I know well from the warm relationship that still exists between my middle two children, now grown. My daughter was nineteen months old and still nursing avidly when her newborn brother joined the family through adoption.

Still, you must be very thoughtful about planning your care of one child to benefit another. Nursing needs to be done out of love and concern for the nursing child. Also, you need to give careful consideration to the personality of your child. Is he ready to adapt well to a new baby? Or does his nursing style or frequency tell you he needs you to himself a bit longer? Every child and every situation are different; the decision to adopt while your homemade child is still nursing is one that needs to be made with a careful eye to all the intricacies of your own family.

There seems to be no need to worry, however, about forcing nursing to go on too long in your efforts to maintain a milk supply. Although it would not be advisable to press your child to nurse when he clearly does not want to, the supposed dangers of nursing too long just have not been documented. Besides, the experiences of so many mothers who did not want to wean when their children did lead me to wonder whether it is possible to coerce a child to nurse even if you should want to. Children who do not want to nurse will not do so. If your child still nurses willingly, there is no harm in continuing.

Nursing is a complex relationship, and our reasons for entering into such a relationship need to be an equally complex mixture of warmly irrational and coldly logical hopes and objectives. Such a mixture of heart and mind enables us not only to overcome the obstacles we meet, but also to get the most out of a pleasurable interaction.

When Experience Speaks

Most parents who have had the experience of caring for a nursing toddler cannot imagine rearing subsequent children any other way. Only four or five of the nearly one thousand mothers who answered my original questionnaire about nursing past one year said that they would not do so again. And those few who did not want to repeat the experience were overwhelmed, not by nursing, but by the negative attitudes of people around them.

In my generation, in industrialized cultures, only a few fortunate mothers had more than their own experience to rely on to help them enjoy a long nursing relationship. Now many young parents, like my own children, have mothers who nursed them long and happily. One mother wrote, "My grandmother and great-grandmother both nursed their children as long as the children wanted to nurse, and I received encouragement and support from both of them."

People who have nursed well past infancy have learned in their own homes what a good thing extended nursing is and would rarely advocate any alternatives for themselves, or for their grandchildren. Such parents or grandparents will agree with the mother who wrote, "Of course I would nurse past infancy again—he turned out so cute and nice and smart." A Hindu woman in Pakistan expressed her approval of extended nursing in a traditional saying: "The more mother's milk a son gets, the more he'll take care of his mother when he grows up."[10] Satisfied American parents wrote, "We found that the longer we nursed our kids, the better they turned out."

References

1   Dettwyler, K. A. "Evolutionary Medicine and Breastfeeding: Implications for Research and Pediatric Advice." The 1998-99 David Skomp Distinguished Lecture in Anthropology, Department of Anthropology, Indiana University, Bloomington, Indiana, 1999.

2   Fildes, V. A. *Breasts, Bottles and Babies: A History of Infant Feeding.* Edinburgh, Edinburgh University Press, 1986; 367.

3   Fitzsimmons, S. P. et al. Immunoglobulin A subclasses in infants' saliva and in saliva and milk from their mothers. *Journal of Pediatrics* April 1994; 124(4):572, 570-72.

4   Goldman, A. S., Chheda, S., and Garofalo, R. Evolution of immunologic functions of the mammary gland and the postnatal development of immunity. *Pediatric Research* February 1998; 43(2):158.

5   Goldman, A. S., Goldblum, R. M., and Garza C. Immunologic components in human milk during the second year of lactation. *Acta Paediatrica Scandinavica* 1983; 72:461.

6   Labbok, M. H. and Hendershot, G. E. Does breast-feeding protect against malocclusion? An analysis of the 1981 child health supplement to the national health interview survey. *American Journal of Preventive Medicine* 1987; 3(4):227-31.

7   Lawrence, R. A. and Lawrence, R. M. *Breastfeeding: A Guide for the Medical Profession.* 5th edition. St. Louis: The C. V. Mosby Company, 1999; 159-95, 184-85.

8   Marini, A. et al. Effects of a dietary and environmental prevention programme on the incidence of allergic symptoms in high atopic risk infants: three years' follow-up. *Acta Paediatrica Supplement* May 1996; 414:10, 14-19.

9   Michie, C. A. and Tantscher, E. The long term effects of breastfeeding: A role for the cells in breast milk? *Journal of Tropical Pediatrics* February 1998; 44:2.

10 Mull, D. S. Mother's milk and pseudoscientific breast milk testing in Pakistan. *Social Science and Medicine* 1992; 34(11):1282.

11 Newman, J. How breastmilk protects newborns. *Scientific American* December 1995; 273(6):76-9.

12 Ogra, S. S. and Ogra, P. L. Immunologic aspects of human colostrum and milk. *Journal of Pediatrics* April 1978; 92(4):546.

13 Saarinen, U. M. Prolonged breast feeding as prophylaxis for recurrent otitis media. *Acta Paediatrica Scandinavica* July 1982; 71(4):569-70.

14 Saarinen, U. M. and Kajosaari M. Breastfeeding as prophylaxis against atopic disease: prospective follow-up study until 17 years old. *Lancet* October 21, 1995; 346(8982):1068.

15 Sears, W. and Sears, M. *Parenting the Fussy Baby and High-Need Child.* Boston: Little, Brown and Company, 1996.

16 Treckel, P. A. Breastfeeding and maternal sexuality in colonial America. *Journal of Interdisciplinary History* 1989; 20(1):36.

17 Walent, K. B. *Creating the Capacity for Attachment: Treating Addiction and the Alienated Self.* Northvale, NJ: Jason Aronson, Inc., 1995; 71.

18 Wray, J. D. Breastfeeding: An international and historical review. *Infant and child nutrition worldwide: issues and perspectives.* Ed. F. Falkner. Boca Raton, Florida: CRC Press, 1991; 61-116.

chapter three

Nursing: Still the Best for Your Child

Early Weaning—Not Recommended for Children

Most people unfamiliar with the concept of spontaneous weaning have the impression that prolonged nursing will harm the child. Yet, except for a few very specific serious medical conditions (See "Illnesses for which weaning is advisable," p.116), we have a hard time finding instances in which little ones are actually weaned for their own good.

It is true that many mothers have weaned because someone convinced them that it was best for their babies. But if we trace the origins of those reasons, we would find almost always that they really arose from an effort to make life easier for mom (or the physician or grandmother or husband or whomever mom complained to when life with her toddler became wearing and difficult). The modern mother did not invent busy-ness, nor laziness, nor impatience with demanding toddlers. Nor did our parents or grandparents. People have been making up rules about nursing and weaning for millennia and usually not to benefit the child, but to relieve the mother of one of her jobs. No matter what people tell each other, and no matter how long it has been said, there is no proof that a child's life is improved in any way by weaning before she indicates her readiness.

Making life easier for mom is a commendable goal, of course, and there is no need to make up other reasons for weaning in order to justify a mother's feelings about wanting to wean. When a mother gets tired of nursing and wants this part of her relationship with her toddler to be over, her feelings deserve respect, not judgment, from others. No mother should accept insult from anyone just because she wishes her child would wean. While it is constructive for us as parents to help each other evaluate the nursing relationship from the child's viewpoint as well as the mother's, it is not ever constructive to label someone as a "good" or "bad" mother, even in our own minds, on the basis of nursing or weaning decisions.

If a mother can face weariness with nursing with a good store of self-respect, she will be in the best state of mind to evaluate the nursing relationship in which she is involved. Many mothers, seeing that the only real obstacle ahead is the negative feelings they themselves may be experiencing, are able to relax and meet their little one's nursing needs in a casual way. They say to themselves, "Okay. All people do wean eventually; I'll get my way in the end." As one mother who kept nursing said, "I would rather nursing had ended sooner by my child's choice, but it's no big trouble." Others seem to need to try to change the nursing relationship in whatever ways are comfortable for their toddlers so that they can bring their own feelings to a manageable level.

What is not constructive is to hide or deny our feelings. To continue to nurse an older baby and hate it can become martyrdom—a poor basis for any family relationship.

Society's approach has not been honorable or constructive either. The "for the child's own good" propaganda spreads beyond individual families. Directives to wean "for the sake of the child" have been published by advice columnists and "experts," causing mothers who were enjoying nursing to feel compelled to wean lest they harm their beloved children. Today, fortunately, such critics face contradiction from people with impressive credentials in the areas of child health and nutrition. It would be better if each mother who really wants to nurse or really wants to wean would have the confidence to do what she and her toddler want to do without having to press others to follow the same course.

Prolonged Nursing and Dependency

Some people tell us that children who are not weaned (or not left with baby sitters or not taken to preschool, or . . .) will have difficulty becoming independent. Yet researchers experimenting with young animals have told us what observant grandmothers have always known: The fearful, clingy kids (by which I mean school-aged kids who should be pretty sure of themselves most of the time) are usually the ones who have been put into situations requiring too much independence too soon. A psychotherapist writes:

> *Our society's long-standing denial and devaluation of*
> *merger phenomenon throughout the life cycle have actually*
> *increased the likelihood of personality disorders and*
> *addiction, precisely because autonomy and independence*
> *have been encouraged* at the expense of *attachment needs.*
> *These disorders, which are so pervasive in our current*
> *world, illustrate that beneath the veneer of self-reliance*
> *lies the core of powerlessness, alienation, and detachment.*
> *The push for individuation and self-determination in*
> *young children has greatly affected the acting out and*
> *repressed behavior of adults we see later in our psycho-*
> *therapy practices.*[34]

The truly independent child will be secure in his independence, not shaky from being pushed away before he is ready to make the step himself. Most of us suffer in one way or another from the prevailing belief that separation is maturity and connection is immaturity.

John Bowlby in *Attachment* discusses research done by H. F. Harlow[17] that dramatically demonstrated the relationship between clinging, dependent behavior and the ability of infant monkeys to move away from mother, to explore, and to learn in new situations. Harlow's experiments also demonstrate that the reason clinging behavior occurs in these young animals is not, as Freudian psychology suggests, because it is rewarded by food. Clinging or "attachment" behavior is independent of the source of food and grows from the growing infant's essential need to cling in certain situations.

Experiments with young monkeys demonstrated this fact, both when they were alarmed and when they were in a strange setting. Some of these monkeys grew up with a "lactating" wire model as a surrogate mother, and others with a cloth model that was soft but did not feed them. When a monkey brought up with a non-feeding cloth model was frightened, it clung to the "mother" just as a wild monkey does under such circumstances. After a bit, it would become less afraid and sometimes even explore what alarmed it, using the surrogate mother as a base and returning from time to time. The infant brought up with a lactating wire model did not behave in the same way at all. When alarmed, it ignored the wire "mother" and remained frightened and unwilling to explore.

These experiments tend to support what many of us have observed in the real laboratory—our own homes with our own children. When our children are able to cling or be close to us as they need to (and for the preschool set this can include nursing), they usually behave better and pay more attention to growing and learning. They do not cling because this behavior is reinforced by mother's milk. They cling because this is a basic need in itself. When on the other hand mothers are preoccupied and are not as available to them as they need, children get cranky and waste much of their growing-up energy trying to get close and to get mother's attention.

Experience as well as experiment points toward the conclusion that the best way to help our children grow toward emotional maturity— and emotional maturity includes a reasonable amount of independence— is to meet their needs to be dependent and clingy while they are little. Normal toddlers are clingy in strange situations, when they're tired, frightened, or too far away from their anchor person.[7] Unlike handing your child a bottle or a pacifier (which might be likened to feeding with a wire dummy), nursing goes a long way toward fulfilling your child's dependency needs. Just as experimenters report that monkeys that have something soft and comforting to cling to overcome fear more easily than monkeys that do not, so hundreds of mothers have reported to me that they take pleasure and pride in the independence and self-confidence of their nursing children.

Nursing toddlers who are super-independent are common—the one who tries everything, accepts more people without fear than might be expected for any particular age. Nursing mothers take credit for this fine emotional development, and most of this credit is deserved. The freely nursing toddler is getting the bulk of his dependency needs met and shows the independence his personality and development allow.

The last phrase above is something all of us parents need to recognize. What you do with your child is very important in making independence possible. Your child, however, has a unique personality and timetable for development toward independence, and even in the best of emotional environments that timetable may be dizzyingly fast or painfully slow. One two-year-old is hysterical at the sight of a bug, but adores people—all people. Another plays with bugs, but is terrified of everyone, including grandma. Another is kind of in-between—bugs are okay; grandma and other "strangers" are okay at home, but not at grandma's house or the grocery store or anywhere else. I am very familiar with these particular variations, because these descriptions fit three of my own when they were nursing two- and three-year-olds.

Each child's special personality creates an individual pattern of fear and confidence at each age. The best way to develop a child's confidence and overcome fear is to provide opportunities for that child to enjoy his confidence. Make every effort to provide enough support—not excessive, of course, but generous—enough to make him feel protected when he is afraid. A readily available source of comfort and support for a frightened little one is at his mother's breast. For many children the more dangerous the things they may try to face (as they see danger, not necessarily as we see it), the more comforting and reassurance they will need, and this often includes more nursing.

As effective a source of comfort as nursing is for a frightened (or just tired and overextended) toddler, it is not really surprising how many parents of nursing toddlers are pleased with their children's independence. These children know that there is comfort for them if they meet fear or pain. "In a number of studies in the USA, children who were securely attached to mother as infants were later found to have relatively long attention spans, persistence, positive affect, empathy, compliance, ego resilience, and social competence."[20]

John Bowlby wrote that attachment in childhood is a falling-in-love process, something we can all understand. People of any age who are in love strive to preserve the relationship. When the relationship is threatened, people respond with some variation of clinging, then crying, then perhaps angry coercion.[5] We often see toddlers doing these things, and have probably indulged in at least some of these behaviors ourselves.

A few of us have had the incredible experience of watching an extremely clingy little one at three, at four, and still at five (this kid is never going to grow up!) blossom into a little drill sergeant, a child who at seven dances before an audience which includes the governor, and more importantly, fellow second-graders, without a sign of stage fright. Of course the possible need of the clingy toddler for several years of nursing is only a part of helping these little ones become self-sufficient. It is the experience of many families that these very, very easily distressed little people are able to learn confidence, not by being forced into situations in which they are expected to function independently before they are ready, but by having their mothers close for as long as it takes for them to develop confidence on their own. These children are clingy by nature; nursing does not make them this way. No doubt nursing helps both mother and child grow through this time of life into a secure future.

Nurturing Independence

Logic might give us the idea that children who are not weaned do not develop independence, based on the observable fact that people must experience success at functioning on their own in order to become independent. We need to make independence possible as soon as children can handle it. However, such experience is useful only when an individual is ready. Forcing independent behavior on a preschooler is just about as effective as forcing independent breathing on a very premature baby. It can be done sometimes, with lots of special know-how and equipment, but the risks are staggering. It is not something we would choose to do to a child.

Years ago an experimenter tried "teaching" independence to some puppies in a way that you have probably tried with your own child, although I would hope not as harshly. The experimenter studied following behavior, which is one way the young, including our own children, show their attachment.

One group of puppies not only received no sort of reward but were punished each time they attempted to follow "so that their only experience with human contact was painful." After several weeks the experimenter stopped the punishment. The puppies soon ceased to run away from him and, furthermore, actually spent more time with him than did control puppies whose approaches had been rewarded with uniform petting and kindness.[4]

The punishment did not serve to decrease dependency, but rather increased it in the long run.

Similar experiments "punished" infant monkeys for clinging to their dummy "mothers" by blowing jets of air at them from inside the dummy. To escape the hated blasts of air the infants needed only to move away from the "mother." Yet the more they were discouraged from clinging by the annoying blasts, the more tightly they clung to the dummies.[4]

These experiments have been repeated countless times with human youngsters and their mothers. Each of us has tried at some time or another to push away a child who wants to nurse or cuddle just when we sit down in front of the TV with a bowl of soup in one hand and a cup of coffee in the other, or just when we have picked up the hobby knife or crochet hook or paint brush. Oh Mom, you should have known! The harder we push them away, the more persistently they struggle to get near. Our experience confirms what the experimenters observed in their laboratories. Pushing away does not teach independence; it teaches fear and desperate clinging. The independent child is the one who has been held close when that was what he needed.

Many, many mothers tell me how chaotic their lives have become when they were either ill or too busy with other things to nurse and/or cuddle freely. Others describe similar situations when they were encouraging weaning at too fast a rate for their little ones. Their children were fretful, clingy, mistrustful, and very demanding. When the mothers made themselves more available, the children became happier and more independent again.

Abandonment—often suggested as a way of weaning—(see Chapter 17) is not a good tool for teaching independence either. The child who needs mother very much, especially the child who is not wholly at ease with other caretakers, is likely to be devastated by her absence. Rene Spitz's 1946 film *Grief: A Peril in Infancy,*[31] showing the shocking deterioration suffered by children left in hospitals without their mothers, should be required viewing for all who advise mothers to make their children independent all of a sudden by leaving them for a week.

A child is best equipped to develop the kind of independence that is based on faith that mother will always be there whenever he gets into a situation he cannot handle alone. The "escape clause" for the mother in this contract is the "situation he cannot handle" part. As each child grows older, there are fewer and fewer such situations. Provided your child is not prevented from exercising his developing capabilities, independence comes apace with his increasing competence.

I have no doubt that youngsters need plenty of opportunity to succeed as capable and responsible persons. Still, it is clear that there is nothing to be gained by racing with your neighbors to have the most independent child who assumes the most responsibilities at the youngest possible age. There is much to be gained, on the other hand, by being available to meet your child's needs to be dependent for as long as he expresses such needs. There is much to be gained also by continuing to be available for nursing, since nursing allows you to meet his needs in so

GOOD MILK, MOM*!*

many ways. It helps you convince your child that the world is an okay place, that he has a home base as he begins to experience more and explore more. It helps him feel better when he faces disappointment, frustration, and pain while he is still growing his own mechanisms for dealing with these hard things.

Being available to a toddler, however, does not mean that you jump in at every whimper the way you do with a tiny baby. Your child needs to learn how to solve problems herself, starting with very brief episodes and tiny problems, a toy being out of reach for example, and building up eventually to such challenges as haggling over prices or driving the freeway. Stay close enough to make sure your little one is safe and not too upset. It's good for her to work on getting herself out of the jams she gets herself into, but too great a challenge can topple her into despair that does nobody any good. You won't always get it perfectly right, but follow your heart and your tolerance for her frustration will grow at about the same pace that hers does.

If you put yourself in your child's place, you can see that it is very rough to grow toward independence if you have little relief from the bad feelings you face as a small person in a world built for big people. If you did not feel very much loved and protected, it would be ever so easy to lose that childish wonder and enthusiasm and just give in to fear and frustration. Things are so hard to do when you are little, and you get hurt so much. Nursing, rather than discouraging independence, can help it come more easily by providing the child a reliable way to soften her discouragement and fear in the difficult times.

Discipline without Weaning

Many people regard the decision not to wean or not to toilet train or whatever as the beginning of a whole pattern of parenting that does not include discipline. Yet I do not understand how weaning (or toilet training) got to be a part of discipline. As I remember all that Latin I studied back in ancient times when people studied such things, discipline has to do with teaching, not with the arbitrary alteration of normal, natural behaviors. Anxiety about discipline in the first few years of life is not part of every culture. When researchers asked mothers among the Turkana in Kenya whether a child was "bad" or "good," mothers laughed and said that they didn't know. They said it was a child, using a neutral, genderless word (*ikoku*) that indicated something little, not a person yet.[13] Similarly, in East Bhutan a nursing child is referred to as *mingbu*, a term also used for maize that is not yet ripe.[2]

Discipline has to do, not with conditioning these unformed little beings to respond to arbitrary commands like circus animals, but with helping children develop into adults who are both capable and kind. To be disciplined well, your children need to be able to trust you and your love. They need a relationship with you in which they can be sure, from their own repeated experience, that when you set limits on their behavior, the limits are truly for their benefit.

Limits are vital, but as William and Martha Sears point out, control is not.[29] The difference between limits and control is an important one, like the difference between a protective bubble and a straitjacket. We need to create an ever-expanding space for our children within which, in the years they are under our influence, we can safely and effectively encourage them toward kind and courteous behavior. On the one hand, we must not try to force them to become socially acceptable too quickly, while on the other we must not fail to challenge them to exercise and develop their growing consciences. Though we all stray one way or the other daily, to go too far either way consistently is to risk "spoiling" our children.

We have to teach our children many things. At first, in our arms, we teach them that love is available from people. We teach them whom to ask for love, and when, and how. Then as they move away from us we teach them how to behave so as not to hurt themselves or others.

As time goes on we teach them not to annoy other people needlessly. Many actions that irritate other people may be unimportant, but we want our children in time to become conscious of people's feelings and learn to evaluate behavior that may bother someone else. One of many ways we do this is by taking children who seem bent on obnoxious behavior away from the scene of the crime and explaining to them why we have had to leave.

Our efforts to teach safety for themselves and courtesy toward others will not succeed right away. As Dr. James L. Hymes, Jr., once described discipline, we are beginning the years-long process of "doing a selling job on decency."[21]

Closeness and loving, needed by all people, are critical to little people. It is without closeness and loving, and without sufficient attention to the business of teaching good behavior, that adults spoil children. One mother reminded me that things that are spoiled are things that have been left on the shelf to rot! Nursing does not contribute to such spoilage.

Without attention to their need to learn how to receive love through an intimate relationship and how to give love through slowly improving consideration for the feelings and property of other people, our children will be spoiled. You do not spoil a child by loving or by nursing, but by replacing his needs for both love and guidance with ignoring, scolding, and moralizing. Rather than setting the stage for undisciplined behavior, you can actually use continued nursing to help you create a secure environment in which to make your case for the decency Dr. Hymes talks about.

Nursing and Weight Gain

Sometimes mothers are advised to wean because their children seem to be growing too slowly. Every time I have been asked about this I have looked around for a thin, sickly child who obviously needed a change in diet. My experience has been among people with ready access to good food, so every time I've been asked, I have seen a firm, nicely proportioned, healthy little child.

Children in the second and third years are notorious for eating nothing, or so it seems to mother. (Actually they eat everything—you know, a dog biscuit, the last three drops out of your coffee cup, the little orange that was just beginning to ripen on your treasured miniature tree—everything except what is offered at mealtimes.) During this time in their lives, it should be more a comfort than a worry that a child has a regular source of nutritious food through nursing. And not all nursing toddlers who eat (or don't eat) this way are small. Many are average size or even big for their age.

Katherine Dettwyler observed finicky eating behavior among toddlers in Mali, children who were "not interested in food" or "refused to eat." Dettwyler writes, "Their mothers would offer them food at various ages, but they would not eat it, and were not forced to do so. When the family was eating they would play, or sit and watch the meal, but not partake themselves." Unless there was noticeable delay in motor development, nobody worried about the child's not eating.[9]

Elsewhere parents of slow-growing children may have to deal with anxious relatives or friends who fret over the child's lack of interest in food. One mother in this situation learned to tell people that he had just eaten a little while ago. "Most people accept that," she said. And in the case of a nursing toddler this statement is usually not a complete falsehood.

Many of us worry about little children, especially little boys—the ones who do not weigh as much as the charts say they "should" or who are not "tall enough." Why do we think that smallness at two determines smallness at twenty? What is wrong with being small at twenty anyway? Few of us are rearing professional athletes. I realize that voters seem to like our political leaders to be tall, but physical size doesn't seem to be of much concern among rocket scientists and brain surgeons. There are opportunities in the world for people of all sizes.

Even if it were bad to grow up small, and if being small at two meant that is the way the child would grow up, what makes us think there is very much we can do about it? It does not make sense to wean a normal, healthy child merely in hopes of making him heavier or taller. Weaning probably will not affect his size very much—he is going to get heavier and taller anyway, but at his own pace.

Look at your little child if you are worried about his weight and height. Think about the disturbing and ever-present pictures of starving children. Do his bones stick out like that? How well can you see his ribs? If your child's outstretched hand has dimples at the knuckles, or if he has dimples at the back of his elbows or front of his knees, your child is officially cherubic and plump and does not belong among the skinny ones. Back to the really thin ones—and I am not expecting to find true starvation in affluent societies, nor should there even be any real undernourishment if you nurse without limit and make nutritious food available every few hours throughout the day. We will be ever so much happier if we can learn to accept the fact that some children are short and some are thin and some are both, just as there are thin, short, and thin-short adults.

The nutritional problems that you read about resulting in stunted growth or impaired brain development do not occur in babies or young children who are free from disease and are being fed on demand by reasonably healthy mothers. Children develop normally while they are receiving good quantities of the superior nutrients in human milk.

Studies in some developing countries have found a tendency for nursing toddlers to be smaller than weaned ones, especially in the second year,[6] while elsewhere nursing toddlers seem to be larger.[32] The contradictory findings have stimulated a lot of discussion among people concerned with health care in nutritionally distressed populations. What none of the several studies have completely accounted for is the frequency with which the children are able to nurse along with the quality, quantity, and frequency with which other foods are available. he differences in results from study to study may tell more about feeding practices in varying cultures than about nursing itself.

A Brazilian physician who has puzzled over the phenomenon of slow growth in some nursing toddlers said:

> *The nutritional status studies we have carried out tend to show that at some stage around one year of age, children who are no longer breastfed tend to grow faster than those who are breastfed. . . . Again, there are many caveats because this varies from society to society. . . . I guess my reading of the literature on breastfeeding during the*

*second year is that most studies show this inverse
association, that is, breastfed babies grow less rapidly
than babies who are not breastfed. . . . On the other hand,
all the studies on mortality or infection in relation to
breastfeeding in the second year of life tend to show a
positive effect, although not all of them are significant. . . .
So we have this dilemma in the second year, whether this
poorer growth is enough to justify any policy change.
My feeling is that the positive effects of breastfeeding are
greater than the negative ones.*[33]

A researcher who has seen a few cases of actual malnutrition among nursing toddlers in Britain found the problem to result from inappropriate use of adult healthy-eating concepts with young children. "A few mothers mistakenly give a diet which is low in fat and high in fiber (and, therefore, bulky with low energy density) so that there is inadequate energy for growth."[39] This is the exact sort of diet that leads to malnourished toddlers in families plagued with food shortages. Low-fat, high-fiber diets are not appropriate for small children. If you are blessed with the resources to avoid a deficient diet (compared to people in some parts of the world who have to rely on little besides millet or polished rice), your child should not be at risk of stunted growth, physical or mental, no matter what anybody tells you.

When you have a child who is smaller than "normal," however, you need as much support as possible to help you feel secure when someone, maybe even a health care provider, gives you that psychologically devastating stab: "You are not giving your child enough to eat." A child must be severely deprived of nutritious foods over a period of time before any permanent harm is done. Since your child is receiving almost every one of the nutrients he needs from your milk, the odds are low indeed that he is malnourished. If you nurse freely and if tasty food is where he can get it himself whenever he is hungry, it is quite unlikely that he is even undernourished. There are probably genetic reasons that have to do with growth patterns in your family and with how big your child will be as an adult which dictate that your child should be the size he is right now.

However, deficiencies in certain nutrients, vitamin A, iron, zinc, or folic acid, can affect appetite and growth,[8] so you would be wise to make sources of these nutrients appealing to your child. You should pay attention to what nutritious foods your child seems to like, even in small quantities, and prepare those for him as often as you can.

If your child is thin enough to worry you, you do need to get a thorough check of his health. But low weight for age or weight for height does not by itself prove that there is a problem, especially if the growth charts being used are based on pre-1995 measurements of artificially fed babies and children. Weight for age in healthy nursing children is often significantly lower. Height for age, however, is usually comparable.

Other indicators of problems are a lack of normal fat in cheeks, buttocks, and extremities, hair in poor condition, and lethargy or an appearance of depression. A slowly gaining child needs to be checked for anemia, infection, intestinal parasites, and a host of other problems, any of which can result in reduced growth.[23] These include genetic, congenital, and chromosomal abnormalities, malabsorption, diseases of the heart or other organ systems, endocrine disorders, and so on. You will probably find none of these things, but it is important to your child's well-being that you make sure you are dealing with the run-of-the mill slow growth we sometimes see in the second year and not something that needs medical intervention.

Once possible health problems have been ruled out, you can just enjoy how much easier it is to pick up your little lightweight, how much less damage he does when he jumps on your couch, etc. I'm sure you can think of many more advantages.

Chances are, your child has his reasons for his food, or no-food, preferences, and time will likely resolve the situation:

> *I wrote you previously about my (then) thirteen-month-old son who refused solid foods. Well, he is now sixteen months old and eating food (not a lot, but he is eating). The week before he turned fifteen months old, he decided it was time to walk and time to eat. And when it was time, it was time—there was no mistaking his desire to join our family mealtimes. He loves to try new foods and takes great pleasure in new flavors and textures. He has finally confirmed for me my suspicion of food allergy—he has exhibited sensitivities to all of the foods that I ate in mass quantities during pregnancy (on a daily, or almost daily basis), including that food which most "experts" consider hypoallergenic—rice. He continues to nurse frequently, getting most of his nutrition from the breast, but I have finally been able to let go of those lingering doubts and have come to trust implicitly his body and his own unique timetable.*

If you have a small, slowly growing child who has had a thorough medical examination, make sure you have good answers to these questions: Are you nursing freely so your child gets plenty of milk and the loving that comes with it? Are other foods readily available to your little child? A healthy child who has access to food he likes will take in all the calories he needs. Make sure he can get a wide variety of foods in forms that are appealing to little people, and this can include your milk.

Don't let his taste get confused by sweets. Among the sweets that interfere with nutrition in some children is fruit juice. Excess juice can displace other more nutrient-dense foods, including your milk. In some children too much apple juice compounds nutritional difficulties by causing fructose and sorbitol malabsorption and diarrhea.[39]

Toddler foods need to be easy to pick up with still awkward fingers. Many little ones hate being spoon-fed and will begin to eat only when you put the food right on the clean table or high chair tray and let them do it themselves—almost always without the niceties of silverware. Follow the advice given to parents in 1540 by one unusually practical German physician: "Make for it lyttel pylles of breade and sugre to eate, accustome it so tyll it be able to eate all manner of meate."[28] (Well, not the "sugre" part, of course.)

In Mali, West Africa, children are fed (or not fed) this way. A mother there told Katherine Dettwyler that a child "cannot (or will not) wash himself properly until he is ten years old, but even a baby can be responsible for feeding itself because it 'will eat until it is full and then it will stop eating.'" This is an excellent philosophy as long as the child has frequent opportunities, several times a day, to try a variety of tempting foods. Researchers have observed that such a *laissez-faire* attitude toward feeding of solids is not advisable in times of famine, where food is severely limited and poorly suited to the likes and dislikes of toddlers.[10] On the other hand, it is definitely the best approach where there is plenty to eat and especially where we may be inclined to over-feed.

Self-feeding involves some sneaky, behind-the-scenes planning with attention to your child's likes and dislikes as well as her nutritional needs.

She's a peripatetic eater. She starts in her high chair and quickly wants to get down. I used to assume she wasn't hungry any more, but it turns out she'll keep eating for quite a while if I call her over and offer her a morsel from time to time. When her brother leaves the table she makes a beeline for his chair, climbs up, and cleans his plate. Trying to impose rules on her eating behavior (apart from keeping it in the kitchen) only creates fusses and lessens her intake.

A recent study in rural Peru found young children being fed in a way that produced "relative calmness" and "none of the struggles associated with young children and parents in middle-class US mealtimes."

> *Between-meal snacking is condoned and considered normal for children of this age. Recognition of a child's vulnerability is evident in women's behavior when food is distributed. By providing food between meals, women continue to adhere to the "demand" schedule until children are able to eat like adults and older children. Thus the transition from infancy to childhood is eased for young Ura Ayllu children who maintain a kind of free access eating pattern well after breastfeeding has ceased. Although weaned children are wholly reliant on the same food that adults eat, they are not expected to conform immediately to an adult meal schedule.[12]*

Frequent, unscheduled feeding (snacking) usually needs to continue for some time. Leaving food out the way you do for a cat is the only way to feed some active toddlers. William and Martha Sears recommend muffin tins with a variety of finger foods and dipping sauces like seasoned yogurt. One of my children would eat absolutely anything, as long as it had red spaghetti sauce on it, while my grandson prefers ranch dressing made from yogurt. You can use such sauces to interest your picky eater in nutrient-dense foods like avocado, brown rice, cheese, egg, fish, kidney beans, nut butter, whole-grain pasta, tofu, and turkey. I was surprised to learn how many children love steamed carrots and broccoli, because I disliked both these vegetables when I was a child. But then nobody ever served me child-sized portions topped with spaghetti sauce or a tasty dressing!

When you leave foods out for toddler grazing, make sure the amounts are tiny. That way you won't hesitate to throw out leftovers that have reached the end of their safe time at room temperature.

Too Fat? Too Thin?

How often you will find in the same room people who feel pressured to wean a toddler who is "too small" and people who feel equally pressured to wean one who is "too fat." I don't know how breastfeeding can be the cause of both problems; it seems we could settle on one or the other. But either way, breastfeeding—and breastfeeding well into childhood—is a normal, time-honored thing to do. Any influence breastfeeding has on your child's size is likely to be an influence toward being the size he is supposed to be.

Overweight in a toddler or older child can result from overzealous feeding or inadequate physical activity. Is your child still spending a lot of time in a sling or carrier? A chubby toddler may need encouragement to run and climb instead of sitting around with quiet toys or television. Being either overweight or underweight is sometimes part of a child's natural growth pattern, but either one can also indicate a need to better the child's emotional environment through an improvement in the mother-child relationship.

If you are worried about whether you are creating an optimal situation for your child's rate of growth, think about some basic patterns. Are you nursing freely so that your child does not insist on nursing more often out of anxiety that you will say "No"? Are you over-using nursing, many times each day, to "plug up" your little one while you attend to your own thoughts and conversations? (We all do some of this, and within reason it is fine; this is one of the happy conveniences of nursing past the first year. Just don't overdo it.)

You need to evaluate the kinds of foods that are left around or offered to your child. The sugar and white flour products should be under lock and key. A heavy child also should definitely not be spoon-fed; let her feed herself.

If baking makes you feel like a great partner or parent, perhaps it is time to forget cookies and desserts and concentrate on whole-grain breads and main course souffles. It is time to discover the joys of lean meats, raw vegetables, and grapefruit sections for snacks. A plump child has no need for whole cow's milk or for any milk but yours. Skim milk is a poor food for young children as it lacks milk's fat soluble nutrients. You should see that your child does not get an excess of sweet fruits, especially dried fruits. Try instead a good mixture of less-sweet colorful treats like tomato wedges, carrot sticks (cooked for younger toddlers), and strips of sweet red peppers.

Satisfy yourself that your child has a good nutritional environment—easy access to food, the right kinds of food, plenty of opportunity to nurse, and a reasonable level of "convenience nursing." If then your child still seems "too big" or "too small," I would urge you to change only one more thing—that is how you describe your child's size. Say that he is "his size" or "her size" and enjoy the advantages. Soak up the compliments that older people give you for your plump, healthy-looking child. In another time it was mostly the fat youngsters who survived, and you can enjoy the heritage of that time in the way so many people admire well-rounded preschoolers. Besides, most fat toddlers who are well-mothered and offered proper nutrition will thin out in time. Or, parents of tiny people, think of the new clothes you can have if your child can wear many of last winter's coats and overalls again with nothing more than a few altered hems and buttons. Relax and enjoy your child either way. Size is only one of the many things about him that are going to be decided by factors you do not control.

Nutrition and the Nursing Toddler

You will notice that in speaking of older nurslings (older than nine to twelve months) I do not say that your milk contains all the nutrients your child needs. Breast milk does not contain sufficient amounts of some minerals for toddlers. This is the case with iron, although the iron in human milk is in a highly bioavailable form that leaves nurslings less vulnerable to deficiencies than was once believed. The concern in years past about iron-deficiency anemia in infants and young children resulted from problems in formula-fed babies and toddlers who drank a large amount of cow's milk, not in nursing babies and children.

If you are selective about the foods that you offer to your nursing child, it is most unlikely that you will ever need to concern yourself about iron deficiency. The healthy, full-term baby has a store of iron in his liver that is sufficient for at least nine months, often even more. And he gets some iron from breast milk. Therefore most well-born nursing babies (70 to 90 percent) have no need for sources of iron in the diet for nine months to a year.[3]

Most babies, however, indicate a desire to taste other foods some time in their second six months and are able to enjoy a variety of foods without problems. Thus, provided the foods they eat contain bioavailable iron and vitamin C, they get adequate iron from their diet by the time their stored supply runs out. (Vitamin C helps the body absorb iron.)

Both my children have gone through a period in their second year when they were officially "eating solids" yet really ate very little, nursed a lot, acted clingy and hungry, refused many foods. In both cases I had the impression there might have been a tendency to anemia. It was mild and short-lived with the boy, but really went on too long with my daughter. I had to make a big effort to prepare foods she liked, market them seductively, and so forth— often with no results. Now that she's eating a good deal three to four times a day (and still nursing at night and a few times each day) she is much more sparkly and cheery and has ceased to be a "Velcro child." Some of the things that helped her make the transition: I made sure she (and I) got more vitamin C and iron in our diets. I'd heard that anemia could affect the appetite and I have the impression it worked that way for her.

If your child eats very little besides your milk and is anywhere past his first birthday, you should make a point of offering foods that are rich in minerals. The little bit he eats should not be cheese or other dairy products that contribute nothing beyond what he is already getting from your milk. His food should be mineral-rich and easy for people his age to eat, foods like tender meat, eggs, raisins, dried apricots, and foods made with wheat germ, including whole-grain breads. Some cereals are fortified with minerals, too. If you are worried about anemia, your doctor can check with a simple blood test.

Except for making some iron-rich food attractive to your child in his second or third year, it is usually best to trust your child's preference for nursing or for eating. Some children who refuse foods other than mother's milk are allergy-prone and seem to have food preferences that protect them from allergic symptoms, often delaying them for years.

> *My daughter is nineteen now. She was diagnosed with celiac disease at eighteen years. The doctor noted that she'd had few symptoms because she figured out what foods bothered her and simply avoided eating them. She's still small, but she's an inch taller than I am! She's also extremely confident, bright and independent. I attribute all that to her long-term, happy breastfeeding relationship. [Celiac disease is a chronic nutritional disturbance, caused by the inability to metabolize gluten. It usually shows up early in life.]*

Allergic children can sometimes nurse exclusively even longer than a year without any sign of deficiencies, but they need careful monitoring by a health care professional who is knowledgeable about pediatric allergies and breastfeeding. These children often thrive on mother's milk until they either outgrow their sensitivities or their caretakers develop a suitable weaning diet.

Vitamin D is present in your milk if your own vitamin D status is good. But breast milk alone does not always supply sufficient quantities for a toddler. Having a light-skinned child out in the sun for about 30 minutes a week in diaper only or two hours a week fully clothed[30] should keep his vitamin D levels adequate. The darker his skin, the more sun exposure he will need (or perhaps he will need another source of vitamin D).[22] Don't bathe your child for an hour or two after this exposure so the vitamin has time to be absorbed from the skin oils where it forms. Discuss vitamin D supplementation with your health care provider if your child's exposure to sun is limited by living where sunlight is reduced by latitude or pollution, by staying indoors most of the time, or by being covered with clothing for cultural or religious reasons.[39]

Vegetarian Toddlers

Many families adequately nourish small children on a vegetarian diet, but doing so requires attention to providing enough calories, protein, riboflavin, vitamin B_{12}, and various minerals, including iron. Milk products and eggs, of course, are good protein sources for families that use them and for children who are not sensitive to them. Egg yolk is also rich in iron. Other protein foods for these children include combinations of vegetable foods with complementary amino acids, such as rice and beans, or corn and beans. It is not considered necessary that these foods be eaten at the same meal. Additional possibilities are fermented soybean foods, soy-based milk or meat substitutes fortified with vitamin B_{12}, and a variety of legumes such as chickpeas and lentils, also nuts, almonds, bread, cereals, leafy vegetables, fresh and dried fruits, seeds, and peanut butter. Again, iron absorption can be helped by increased vitamin C intake.

Interesting some children in high-fiber protein foods like beans can prove challenging. Try different recipes. A toddler who turns her nose up at beans and cornbread may be enthusiastic about vegetarian chili or tortilla soup. Tofu and other soy-based foods have a smooth texture and can be prepared in numerous recipes that appeal to toddlers. Continued nursing can be especially helpful to vegetarian families by giving the toddler a good nutritional foundation for a gradual transition into the family eating patterns.

Night Nursing—A Factor in Tooth Decay?

Dentists have been troubled in recent years by what seems to be too many children developing cavities in their upper front teeth and upper molars at an early age. There is reason to believe that there is a greater tendency for children to develop this particular pattern of tooth decay if they lie in bed at night with a bottle of milk or (the dentist shudders) juice or a sugary soft drink; for this reason such a pattern of decay has been named "bottle-mouth syndrome" or "nursing caries."

Some nursing children also have serious problems with tooth decay, and children who nurse frequently may be more at risk than those who nurse less often.[36] Some studies show that in general the prevalence is lower among breastfed children than among those who were bottle-fed.[27] Frequent feedings of breast milk, however, like feedings of any carbohydrate-containing food, can contribute to tooth decay if we don't practice good dietary habits and dental hygiene.[16]

Because reduced flow of saliva during sleep makes teeth more vulnerable to the effects of milk in the mouth, some of the first advice parents get is that they should stop all night nursings. Nursing, however, even nursing at night, is not by itself the cause of tooth decay. And we know that night nursings contribute to quiet in the household, and that continued nursing contributes to the child's health in other ways. Besides, weaning from night nursings can be the most difficult weaning of all if the child is not ready.

More Than Teeth

It seems obvious that in the matter of tooth decay, as in others, we need to look at the whole child. The child is more than teeth. Too often dentists or pedodontists recommend weaning at night without any understanding of what such weaning might mean in the emotional development of the young child, especially in the child under two or so.

If it is easy to cut out night feedings, then it may be worth a try. Doing so would reduce the time that milk is available to acid-producing organisms in the child's mouth. But many children are so attached to nursing at night that there may be no perfect alternative available to you. You will have to weigh what you may hope to gain in dental health against lost sleep and possible damage to good feelings between yourself and your child from trying to wean at night. As one mother put it, "I've gained some relief and inner peace by refusing to look at the dental situation as an all-or-nothing package. The ideal of perfect baby teeth is not attainable for us, but we do what we feel is right for our child." [26]

The first thing to remember when thinking about night nursing and tooth decay is that the vast majority of nursing babies and children do nurse at night, and most of them are not troubled with much tooth decay. Researchers in Europe have found the syndrome in anywhere from one percent to 12 percent of toddlers, depending on the group studied and the definition of nursing caries. [25] Among one study group of nursing toddlers in La Leche League in the Netherlands, 14.5 percent had caries, 9.3 percent of them meeting the criteria of nursing caries. [36] These numbers suggest that, at the very least, 85.5 percent of us don't have to deal with the problem, and there is certainly no reason to worry about nursing and teeth unless your child shows signs she may develop decay. One indication to watch for is chalky white, gray-yellow, brown, or black lines or bands on the teeth, especially the front teeth, parallel to the gums. Such markings have been shown to be precursors to nursing caries in at least some children. [24] Something else to watch for is a history of extensive decay between and on the smooth surfaces of the mother's teeth, or those of someone else close to the child. Nursing caries may result from a contagious kind of decay, transmitted through saliva in kisses, shared utensils, etc. [15] A 1994 study suggests, however, that children of mothers with high levels of the suspect organism,

Streptococcus mutans, may be immunized and actually receive some protection against decay in the primary teeth by "frequent mother-infant salivary close contacts" in the early months, before the teeth erupt.[1]

If you find you have reason to worry about decay, you may want to consider some reasonable efforts toward reducing the time your child sleeps at the breast. As hard as it may be, during night nursings you may want to keep yourself awake until he falls into deep sleep so you can remove the nipple from his mouth. Some suggest rolling him on his side after nursing to keep him from lying on his back with a mouth full of milk. If you can manage to wipe the milk off his teeth with a soft cloth, so much the better.

Changes in Diet

There is research indicating that other foods have more to do with tooth decay than does breast milk. A 1996 study concludes:

> *The present study confirmed earlier findings that it is not the breast-feeding per se that causes dental caries but rather that other caries-promoting habits, like poor oral hygiene or intake of sugar-containing liquid when thirsty, co-exist in these children.*[37]

Another study, published in 1999, backs up previous researchers' observations with laboratory tests in which healthy teeth were immersed in various solutions. In cow's milk they decayed in about 14 weeks; in a sugar solution, in about four weeks. Breast milk, however, caused no enamel decalcification to teeth—the same result as for teeth immersed in water. In another experiment, minerals from breast milk even seemed to be added to the tooth material. On the other hand, when teeth were exposed to breast milk with a small amount of sugar added, tooth decay developed even faster than when the teeth were exposed to the sugar solution.[11] These findings are consistent with what some parents have observed:

> *My daughter is 2 years, 11 months old and has always been a "constant nurser" and until just recently has always been attached all night as well. She has decay in her top two molars (one on each side). I don't believe they are from nursing—she had a time of lollipops (blush) and of liking raisins and I saw the decay starting soon after that.*

Dental health practitioners don't recommend lollipops, of course. Neither do they have much good to say about fruit juice. They insist that items high in "non-milk extrinsic sugars" such as soft drinks and fruit juices or drinks, don't need to be given every day. Juices are a problem for teeth not only because of their sweetness, but also because their acidity can erode tooth enamel.

Juices do, however, serve some children as a major source of vitamin C. One of this vitamin's important functions is in facilitating iron absorption, and to do this juices need to be served at meals, together with the source of iron. Taking juice *only* at mealtimes serves this function while reducing the risk to teeth.[20]

These observations about use and abuse of fruit juices ring true for families like one in which five children were breastfed and nursed at night. Four of the children have good teeth, their mother writes, but "one of them has caps; he would take a bottle of apple juice on long walks."

I was surprised to see how happily my little grandson accepts water in his no-spill cup. He asks for water and walks around drinking it the way I remember my little ones doing with milk or juice. I noticed that his parents put a cube or two of ice into the cup, and maybe that increases the water's appeal. But whatever the reason, I'm sure this habit is good for his teeth.

Medicines containing sugar can also contribute to cavities. People interested in children's dental health now recommend that all pediatric medicines should be sugar free.[19]

One way to fight the decay problem is to do every sneaky thing you can to make whole, fresh, as-close-to-nature-as-possible foods become your children's favorites. Even people who have always been impatient with food fanatics find that this is the time to ban white flour and sugar from the family table, at least until the tooth problem is under control. They even say a sad farewell for now to nutritious but stick-to-the teeth favorites like dried fruit, raisins, dates, and honey. Sugar is sugar, whether natural to the food or added. They encourage instead frequent snacks of crunchy raw vegetables and crisp fresh fruit like apples, knowing that these foods actually help clean the teeth.

Such changes in diet may be difficult, but at least they come in the daytime when everybody is awake. And unlike weaning at night, this is a positive step that will not hurt anybody. Some parents may go into withdrawal symptoms for a while if there is no chocolate cake after supper, but big guys can surely make a temporary sacrifice for a little guy. Besides, adults too will be better off on this kind of diet.

Tooth-Brushing

There is evidence that daily brushing with parents' help starting by one year of age and use of fluoride toothpaste by two years reduce the risk of decay.[36] A dentist and his wife, parents of night-nursing toddlers, tell how they go about brushing little teeth:

Since decay is caused not by sugar directly, but by acids produced from food sugars by bacteria present in plaque (the white, sticky material that collects on teeth), the regular and thorough removal of plaque by brushing is one solution that may help susceptible children. Brushing should be done twice daily, with one session before nursing down for the night. The child may accomplish the morning brushing unaided, but parents must do the bedtime job. In our experience, this is easier said than done. Toddlers may resist having their teeth brushed and will probably require gentle, but firm restraint.

When we brush our toddler's teeth, the parent with the toothbrush holds the child's head in his/her lap while the other parent gently restrains the arms and legs. Whenever possible, we distract the child by talking about how beautiful the teeth are, any emerging teeth, what food items are being cleaned off, and of course, the "tooth germs." If the child is not made to feel that oral hygiene is a form of punishment, but rather an expression of loving parental concern, the nightly ritual may well be accepted in time.

Although this restraint may seem extreme, we believe it is far less traumatic than having to take the child for restorative dentistry. Dental treatment of caries is especially upsetting if pre-existing toothache is involved because much more aggressive physical restraint than explained above and/or sedation may be required. Negative feelings about early dental experiences involving pain and restraint may set the stage for long-term anxiety about dental care.

Other factors that can help prevent tooth problems are regular checkups by a supportive dentist (look hard), low dietary sugar (including candy and excessive fruit juice), and good parental modeling.[35]

If there is a problem with decay, the teeth need additional cleaning by being wiped with a washcloth after each feeding. Brushing with a small-head, soft bristle brush is even better. In these cases the dentist may also recommend daily treatment with a fluoride gel.

Fluoride

Fluoride at sufficient levels is important for proper mineralization of permanent teeth, which form during the toddler years. However, excess fluoride intake at this time can cause "opacities" or discolorations in the enamel of the permanent teeth. These changes seem to be of cosmetic concern only, but most of us would prefer to avoid them. Drinking optimally fluoridated water, and eating food cooked in fluoridated water are the best ways to get the right amount of this important but tricky mineral.[19] Bottled water may vary in fluoride content; some "natural" mineral waters may contain excessive levels.

Toothpaste is not usually necessary for babies and toddlers. Where the water does not contain fluoride, however, fluoridated toothpaste seems to offer some benefit. But a child who is too young to spit effectively might swallow too much fluoride, especially if you use relatively large amounts of toothpaste. If you use toothpaste with a toddler, put only an amount the size of a small pea on the brush and supervise the brushing closely,[38] instructing the child in how to brush and in the importance of spitting out all the toothpaste. You should discuss the best sources of fluoride in your community with your child's health and dental care providers, whether it is water, fluoride treatments, or toothpaste—perhaps a reduced-fluoride brand.

Choosing Your Dental Care Strategy

Above all, it is hard to accept that something as time-tested and as linked with the survival of humanity as is breastfeeding could be harmful to any significant number of normal children. Researchers who are convinced that breast milk can contribute to tooth decay still believe that in "virtually all cases, it does not." Nonetheless, they recommend that toddlers nursing on demand avoid regular consumption of other sugars, receive adequate fluoride, get good tooth brushing, and start visiting the dentist at an early age.[14]

Finding a dentist who is supportive and willing to work with you can make all the difference if you and your toddler have to deal with dental problems. It may take several interviews before you find the right one for your child. You need a dentist with whom you can be honest about your child's nursing pattern, someone who will respect your judgment about nursing or weaning decisions and help you work toward the best outcome for your whole child.

References

1   Aaltonen, A. S. and Tenovuo, J. Associations between mother-infant salivary contacts and caries resistance in children: A cohort study. *Pediatric Dentistry* March/April 1994; 16(2):110-16.

2   Bøhler, E. and Ingstad, B. The struggle of weaning: factors determining breastfeedign duration in East Bhutan. *Social Science and Medicine* 1996, 43(12):1807.

3   Bøorresen, H. C. Rethinking current recommendations to introduce solid food between four and six months to exclusively breast-feeding infants. Journal of Human Lactation 1995; 11(3):203.

4   Bowlby, J. *Attachment.* New York: Basic Books, 1982; 213, 215-16.

5   Bowlby, J. *Loss.* New York: Basic Books, 1980; 42.

6   Brakohiapa, L. A. et al., Does prolonged breastfeeding adversely affect a child's nutritional status? *Lancet* August 20, 1988; 2(8608):416-18. Michaelsen, K.F. Value of prolonged breastfeeding. (letter) *Lancet* October 1988; 8614(2):788-89. Briend, A. et al. Breastfeeding, nutritional state and child survival in rural Bangladesh. *British Medical Journal* 1988; 296:879-82. Nubé, M. and Asenso-Okyere, W. K. Large differences in nutritional status between fully weaned and partially breast fed children beyond the age of 12 months. *European Journal of Clinical Nutrition* 1996; 50:171-77.

7   Bretherton, I. The roots and growing points of attachment theory. *Attachment Across the Life Cycle.* Ed. C. M. Parkes, J. Stevenson-Hinde, and P. Morris. London: Tavistock/Routledge, 1991; 19-20.

8   Brown, K. H. and Bégin, F. Malnutrition among weanlings of developing countries: Still a problem begging for solutions. *Journal of Pediatric Gastroenterology and Nutrition* 1993; 17(2):133.

9   Dettwyler, K. A. *Breastfeeding, weaning, and other infant feeding practices in Mali and their effects on growth and development.* Ph.D. Diss. Indiana University, 1985; 139.

10 Dettwyler, K. A. Infant feeding in Mali, West Africa: Variations in belief and practice. *Social Science and Medicine* 1986; 23:658.

11 Erikson, P. R. and Mazhari, E. Investigation of the role of human breast milk in caries development. *Pediatric Dentistry* March/April 1999; 21(2):86-90.

12 Graham, M. A. Food allocation in rural Peruvian households: concepts and behavior regarding children. *Social Science and Medicine* 1997; 44(11):1705.

13 Gray, S.J. Infant care and feeding. *Nomadic Turkana: Biobehavior and Ecology of a Pastoralist Society.* Ed. M.A. Little and P.W. Leslie. Oxford: Oxford University Press, 1996; 247.

14 Hackett, A. F. et al. Can breast feeding cause dental caries? *Human Nutrition: Applied Nutrition* 1984; 38A:27.

15 Hale, K. J. Coping with dental caries: a pediatric dentist's perspective. NEW BEGINNINGS January-February 1997; 14(1):11-12.

16 Hallonsten, A. L. et al. Dental caries and prolonged breast-feeding in 18-month-old Swedish children. *International Journal of Paediatric Dentistry* 1995; 5:153.

17 Harlow, H. F. The development of affectional patterns in infant monkeys. *Determinants of Infant Behaviour.* Vol. 1. Ed. B.M. Foss. NY: Wiley, 1961, cited in: Bowlby, J. *Attachment.* New York: Basic Books, 1982; 214-15.

18 Hinde, R. A. Perspectives on attachment. *Attachment Across the Life Cycle.* Ed. C. M. Parkes, J. Stevenson-Hinde, and P. Morris. London: Tavistock/Routledge, 1991; 60.

19 Holt, R. D. Weaning and dental health. *Proceedings of the Nutrition Society* 1997; 56:136-37.

20 Holt, R. D. and Moynihan, P. J. The weaning diet and dental health. *British Dental Journal* October 5, 1996; 181(7):256-57.

21 Hymes, J. L. Jr. "Behavior and Discipline." La Leche League International Conference. San Francisco. 1976.

22 Lawrence, R. A. and Lawrence, R. M. *Breastfeeding: A Guide for the Medical Profession.* 5th edition. St. Louis: The C. V. Mosby Company, 1999; 896.

23 Lopez, R. F. and Schumann, L. Failure to thrive. *Journal of the American Academy of Nurse Practitioners* October 1997; 9(10):491, 489. Schwartz, R. Failure to thrive, ambulatory approach. *Nurse Practitioner* May 1996; 21(5):19, 20, 26, 27.

24 Matee, M. et al. Nursing caries, linear hypoplasia, and nursing and weaning habits in Tanzanian infants. *Community Dentistry and Oral Epidemiology* 1994; 22:290-92.

25 Milnes, A. R. Description and epidemiology of nursing caries. *Journal of Public Health Dentistry* 1996; 56(1):41-42.

26 Noonan, M. Toddler Tips. NEW BEGINNINGS March-April 1994; 11(2):59. http://www.lalecheleague.org/NB/NBMarApr94.tod.html

27 Roberts, G. J. et al. Patterns of breast and bottle feeding and their association with dental caries in 1- to 4-year-old South African children. 1. Dental caries prevalence and experience. *Community Dental Health* March 1993; 10:410-11.

28 Roeslin, Eucharias the Elder. *The Byrth of mankynde.* trans. R. Jonas London, 1540, quoted in V. A. Fildes, *Breasts, Bottles and Babies: A History of Infant Feeding* Edinburgh: Edinburgh University Press, 1986; 385.

29 Sears,W. and Sears, M. *The Baby Book.* Boston: Little Brown and Company, 1993; 520-33, 39.

30 Specker, B. L. et al. Sunshine exposure and serum 25 hydroxyvitamin D concentrations in exclusively breastfed infants. *Journal of Pediatrics* 1985; 107:372-76.

31 Spitz, R. *Grief: A Peril in Infancy.* Film, 1947 (16 mm), 1988 (1/2 in.).

32 D. Taren, and Chen, J. A positive association between extended breast-feeding and nutritional status in rural Hubei Province, People's Republic of China. *American Journal of Clinical Nutrition* 1993; 58:862-67. Castillo, C. et al. Breast-feeding and the nutritional status of nursing children in Chile. *Bulletin of PAHO* 1996; 30(2):129-33. Boediman, D. et al. Composition of breastmilk beyond one year. *Tropical Pediatrics and Environmental Child Health* 1979; 25:109.

33 Victora, C. G. Discussion of papers by Hanson et al. and by Victora, *Food and Nutrition Bulletin* The United Nations University, 1996; 17(4):398-99. Mølbak, K. et al. Is malnutrition associated with prolonged breastfeeding? *International Journal of Epidemiology* 1997; 26(2):458-59. Greiner, T. Sustained breastfeeding, complementation, and care. *Food and Nutrition Bulletin* 1995; 16(4):314-15. Victoria, C. G. et al. Prolonged breastfeeding and malnutrition: Confounding and effect modification in a Brazilian cohort study. *Epidemiology* May 1991; 2(3):175-81.

34 Walant, K. B. *Creating the Capacity for Attachment.* Northvale, NJ: Jason Aronson, Inc., 1995.

35 Weeks, S. and Weeks, M. Toddler Tips. NEW BEGINNINGS March-April 1994; 11(2):56-59. http://www.lalecheleague.org/NB/NBMarApr94.tod.html

36 Weerheijm, K. L. et al. Prolonged demand breast-feeding and nursing caries. *Caries Research* 1998; 32(1):50, 49, 137.

37 Wendt, L. K. et al. Oral hygiene in relation to caries development and immigrant status in infants and toddlers. *Scandinavian Journal of Dental Research* October 1994; 102(5):269-73.

38 Wendt, L. K., Hallonsten, A. L., and Birkhed, D. Analysis of caries-related factors in infants and toddlers living in Sweden. *Acta Odontologica Scandinavica* 1996; 54(2):136.

39 Wharton, B. A. Weaning in Britain: practice, policy and problems. *Proceedings of the Nutrition Society* 1997; 56:109, 110.

40 Zenel, J. A. Failure to thrive: A general pediatrician's perspective. *Pediatrics in Review* November 1997; 18(11):375.

chapter four

Nursing: Still the Best for Yourself

Most mothers at one time or another wonder whether continued nursing will drain their physical resources, weaken them, or make them prone to illness. At least from the time of the second century physician Galen, and no doubt before, overprotective people, even medically trained people, suggest that this is so. But women's bodies are designed for childbearing and breastfeeding so that with reasonable care neither pregnancy nor breastfeeding need produce physical stress. Although breastfeeding and short birth intervals may exacerbate health problems in severely malnourished women, the basic problem is underfeeding and not pregnancy and lactation.[27]

In well-nourished women, rebuilding of maternal reserves begins before breastfeeding ends.[14] In fact, breastfeeding can enhance a mother's health. Increased duration of breastfeeding seems to have a beneficial influence on fertility, bone mass, and the development of reproductive cancers. One study even suggests that the longer a mother nurses, the lower her risk may be of developing rheumatoid arthritis.[2]

Mother's Nutritional Needs

Women's bodies are very efficient at making milk, and studies on mothers' needs for food energy during lactation show that you don't have to eat as much as you might think (or wish). It is such a pleasure when baby is little and nursing a lot to be able to eat heartily without gaining weight. If you are determined to stay slim, however, it will probably be necessary for you to reduce your food intake and increase your exercise (not hard to do with an active toddler around) as your child nurses less and less frequently, especially after she becomes really interested in table foods.

In the early months of nursing a single baby, mothers seem to need approximately 2700 calories per day, that is an additional 500 calories per day.[12] Although maternal food energy needs grow as the child grows, we're still not talking about a huge increase. You can make up a 500-calorie deficit by adding the equivalent of a large sandwich, or 8 ounces of beef, or two 9.5-ounce cartons of regular yogurt to your daily diet. In the early weeks, adding just one quarter-pound fast-food burger to your usual diet would probably cause you to exceed your energy requirements without providing all of the extra nutrients your body needs. Many nursing mothers thrive on 2200 calories daily.[17]

The food you add to your diet needs to provide enough calories to maintain your weight or let you lose slowly, plus 12 to 15 additional grams of protein and increased quantities of other nutrients—different nutritionists emphasizing different specifics. One lists ascorbic acid, vitamin E, and folic acid.[28] Another lists calcium (from dairy products, fish with edible bones, some tofu, bok choy, cabbage family vegetables), zinc (from meats, legumes, seeds, whole grains), magnesium (nuts, seeds, legumes, whole grains, green vegetables, oysters), vitamin B_6 (bananas, meats, potatoes, spinach, prunes, nuts), thiamine (pork, fish, legumes, whole grains, seeds, nuts), and folate (leafy vegetables, fruit, legumes, whole grains).[12] Once your toddler is taking significant amounts of other foods, your caloric needs decrease until at weaning you are back to pre-pregnant levels.

Mothers have long been thought to be in danger of losing bone minerals to the baby during pregnancy and lactation, and you might think nursing a long time would increase this risk. Your body does in fact take minerals from your bones during pregnancy and early in the nursing period, and increasing calcium intake during those months may not have much effect on the process.[3] But over the months that follow the resumption of menstruation, your body remineralizes your bones.[13] In fact, some studies suggest that if you breastfeed and wean gradually, you are likely to end up with bones that are just as strong[11] or even stronger than if you had not breastfed.[6] And the longer your average duration of breastfeeding per child, the greater the positive effect seems to be.[4] It seems reasonable to assume that adequate child spacing is important so that circulating estrogen can return to menstrual levels and thus allow your bones to rebuild.[14]

Your diet needs to include sufficient calcium for this rebuilding to occur; the US National Academy of Sciences Food and Nutrition Board recommends that your diet provide you with 1200 mg/day.[12] Getting enough calcium is even more important if you are under 25, because your bones are still growing.

For most mothers in the industrialized world, if you are eating a varied diet with enough calories to maintain your weight, you are probably getting sufficient nutrients with the possible exception of calcium and zinc. The easiest source of calcium is dairy products. But if you don't use them, or if your child reacts to dairy proteins that pass into your milk, you can get calcium in generous servings of cooked bok choy, ground sesame seeds, blackstrap molasses, calcium-enriched tofu, collards, spinach, broccoli, turnip greens, kale, almonds, and Brazil nuts. Dietary sources of zinc are listed above.

Frequent nursing in the early months can reduce the drain on your iron reserves by delaying the return of menstruation. This is especially helpful for a mother who has to make up for a larger than normal blood loss at delivery. Once menstruation resumes, your need for dietary sources of iron increases.[12]

If you are restricting your diet for any reason, you need to pay careful attention to nutrition to protect your health. A low-calorie diet for a nursing mother needs to include a minimum of 1800 calories per day[9] and be made up of nutrient-dense foods, possibly including a vitamin-mineral supplement. Weight loss of one to two pounds a month does not seem to affect nursing, but four-and-a-half pounds a month is too much and would indicate that you need to eat more or exercise less.[24]

Mothers on diets that exclude some foods often need to replace certain nutrients. For example, a mother on a dairy-free diet needs other sources of calcium and vitamin D. A diet without animal foods would mean the mother needs another source of vitamin B_{12}. A mother whose diet is low in fruits and vegetables needs additional folate and vitamin C.[12]

A few thin mothers, although this is quite uncommon, do tend to lose weight or have difficulty maintaining their weight while nursing. If you are one who experiences more weight loss than you like, you are probably not in danger provided you are taking care of yourself and eating well. If you have trouble eating well, you might find a dietician's advice helpful. The Subcommittee on Nutrition in Lactation of the US National Academy of Sciences recommends that during the first six months of lactation a mother with low fat reserves consume 650 calories per day over what it took to maintain weight before pregnancy.[12] Your level of physical activity also affects energy needs from your diet. If you are exercising a great deal and having trouble maintaining your weight, you may need to cut back on exercise, but not stop, while nursing.

The milk-production system is so well designed that a mother has to be severely undernourished over a considerable period of time before we see evidence of a drain on her physical resources caused by lactation. Fortunately you are not required (as is a dairy cow) to produce milk at maximum levels for as long as possible. You can safely devote your energies to the well-being of your baby or toddler. When in time your little one becomes more interested in other foods, she will need less of your milk, and your body will again be able to use the food you eat to rebuild whatever stores are normal for you.

Prolonging Lactational Amenorrhea

For many women, continued nursing brings a longer period of natural infertility following childbirth. That breastfeeding can increase child spacing has long been recognized. In fact, in colonial America, while the European settlements were still small, families needed many children, and any attempt to limit family size could get a mother into trouble. The staunch Puritan, Cotton Mather, worried that mothers were nursing their babies to delay conception. An eighteenth century grandfather criticized his daughter-in-law for nursing so she would "not breed too fast." The birth-spacing effect of breastfeeding has been known for a very long time and may partially explain the widespread employment of wet nurses in medieval Europe among noble families who wanted many children. Intentional or not, the fact is that the birth rate among the upper classes did increase when mothers did not breastfeed.[7]

On the other hand, a colonial grandmother wrote of advising her 39-year-old daughter to keep nursing "that this might possibly be the last trial of this sort, if she could suckle her baby for two years to come, as she had several times done heretofore." Such advice was not often exchanged in public or in writing, but women probably shared it among themselves more than they wanted people like Reverend Mather to know. Few colonial mothers seemed to want to limit family size, but the desire for more children conflicted with what they may have seen as a need to space births in order to protect their own health and that of their children.[23]

In much of the developing world, breastfeeding has a greater impact on fertility than contraception. In Bangladesh extended breastfeeding reduces a mother's risk of dying by as much as 50 percent by reducing her exposure to the risks of pregnancy and childbirth in a dangerous environment.[29]

Of course breastfeeding directly reduces infant mortality. In addition, unrestricted, prolonged breastfeeding protects infants even further by increasing birth intervals. Some researchers predict that there would be a 20 percent drop in infant mortality from 1980s levels if worldwide birth intervals could be extended to at least two years, which could theoretically be accomplished by an increase in unrestricted breastfeeding.[29]

For families in the industrialized world, breastfeeding's birth-spacing effects are less profound, but they still matter, if only in reducing the bother and expense, to say nothing of any possible risk, of contraception in the first months after childbirth. Mothers also enjoy freedom from the mood cycles associated with ovulation.

The length of the infertile period varies from mother to mother, and is influenced by individual children's nursing patterns as well. By the toddler years, however, the time in which you can rely on breastfeeding alone to prevent pregnancy is past. What makes natural infertility a part of the discussion of older nurslings is the style of breastfeeding that best prolongs the infertile period following childbirth. The frequent, unrestricted nursing that leads to a long period of infertility tends to lead also to nursing toddlers. Even if your fertility should return before your child's first birthday, you would hardly want to suddenly abandon the free and healthy relationship you have developed with your child. "Natural" mothering is a fine and rewarding objective in itself, and natural infertility is just a bonus that many families enjoy. Prolonged nursing is usually part of that kind of mothering.

Even after the time during which nursing alone is a reliable contraceptive has passed, many mothers continue to enjoy freedom from menstruation and from the physical and emotional effects of ovulation and menstruation (PMS). You reap nutritional benefits as well. Although you pass the equivalent of 14 percent of your body's store of iron into your milk in six months of exclusive breastfeeding, this is about half the amount you would lose in menstruation. So a long period of amenorrhea increases your opportunity to rebuild iron stores after pregnancy.[12]

In addition, there is speculation among researchers that some of the long-term benefits mothers derive from breastfeeding, such as a lowered risk of breast and other cancers, are related to the period of amenorrhea or the hormonal state that produces it. There is no proof at the moment that this is so, but it might be worth thinking about the next time your child interrupts a project—or a nap—for the third time. Maybe your frequent nurser is doing you a favor by reducing your lifetime exposure to estrogen, in this case the estrogen produced by your own body after ovulation resumes.

The process of suppression and resumption of fertility is complex and not completely understood. In response to nipple stimulation your body produces prolactin, which in turn suppresses ovulation and other processes necessary for conception.[8] Since prolactin levels peak right after nursing and then fall off quickly, frequent nursing is necessary to maintain the effects of elevated prolactin. One researcher writes that nursing at least six times during the day for a total duration of at least 80 daytime minutes, plus sleeping with the baby and nursing frequently at night, was "highly predictive" of an 18-month amenorrhea.[22] Nursing fewer than three times a day results in prolactin dropping to pre-pregnancy levels.

To maximize the period of amenorrhea, nurse long and often from the beginning. Your chances for a long period of amenorrhea are best if you avoid pacifiers, nurse at night (especially if your baby sleeps with you), and delay introduction of other foods until the second half of the first year.

Thanks to recent public health research, the Lactational Amenorrhea Method (LAM) is now recognized as an effective family planning approach up to six months postpartum, and has been shown to be effective up to nine months in at least one population.[5] LAM is based on a woman's answering the following three questions:

1. Have your menses returned?

2. Are you supplementing regularly or allowing long periods without breastfeeding, either during the day (more than four hours) or at night (more than six hours)?

3. Is your baby more than six months old?

When a mother can answer "no" to all three of these questions, LAM will be an effective family planning method for her at that time. Research has shown LAM to be 98 percent effective, a statistic that compares very favorably to artificial methods of family planning. And while it does not provide guidelines for mothers nursing their babies into toddlerhood, it does call attention to factors that influence the return of fertility.

Often the first menstrual period a mother experiences is anovulatory, that is, it is not preceded by ovulation—and thus there was not the chance of the mother becoming pregnant. After the baby's first six to nine months, however, and certainly by the toddler stage, even if you continue to enjoy amenorrhea, you cannot count on the first menstrual cycle being anovulatory. You are less likely to conceive while still nursing frequently; but with every month that passes without a menstrual period, the possibility that you can become pregnant increases. Therefore, if it is important for you to avoid or delay pregnancy, you need to be using a reliable family planning method, either natural family planning or another approach compatible with breastfeeding, such as a barrier method with or without spermicides, an intrauterine device, contraceptive hormones (preferably progestin-only), or sterilization.

The American Academy of Pediatrics regards the newer hormonal methods as compatible with breastfeeding. Some practitioners, however, are uneasy about possible effects on babies of the hormones, which may pass into your milk. These hormones are probably less risky for a nursing toddler, especially if he is receiving a significant amount of his nourishment from other foods; but the truth is that nobody knows for certain. If you choose a chemical or hormonal contraceptive, do make sure your health care provider knows that you are nursing so the child's well-being can be part of your choice of method.

For a nursing mother choosing natural family planning (NFP), the method requires some modifications because of subtle changes caused by breastfeeding.[17] If you want to avoid pregnancy using NFP, it would be wise to consult books like Toni Weschler's, *Taking Charge of Your Fertility* or to consult an instructor in the method for further information. As the months go by, you should regard any bleeding or spotting as a sign of possibly returning fertility. After menstruation has resumed, increased nursing frequency, such as when your child is ill, can increase intervals between your periods. This is a delay rather than suppression of ovulation, and you should not regard it as a return to infertility.[25]

There is, however, considerable variation from mother to mother, either in production of prolactin, or in its suppressive effects on the menstrual cycle. A significant number of mothers who nurse frequently, day and night, still have an early resumption of menstruation and fertility. Any numbers for nursing frequency and the resulting length of amenorrhea are estimates—averages. Every mother is different, and individual experience varies widely, including some who become pregnant again with no intervening menstruation.

For some women, fertility does not return until weaning is complete. One La Leche League Leader wrote me about parents, unable to get pregnant while nursing, experiencing mixed feelings of longing for another baby while wanting to continue nurturing the one in their arms. The longed-for baby is just a wish, she writes. What if they weaned this child and still did not get pregnant? She says her own children are six years apart for this reason.

If you want to conceive again and your periods have not resumed, the first thing to consider is whether your child and your body are together telling you that he is not yet ready to be joined by a younger sibling. You know your child better than anyone, however. If you feel it is time to expand the family, it may be sufficient to cut back on the frequency of nursing for six to eight weeks. A long stretch without nursing every day may do the trick, provided you can keep your toddler content during that time. A long stretch at night could be even better, because the hormonal mix that prolongs infertility seems to be more dependent on nighttime nursing.

If you end up weaning completely, your periods should return in six weeks. If they don't, play it safe and consult a health care professional.[12] There are rare but potentially serious disorders (e.g., pituitary tumors) that first present themselves as unexplained amenorrhea, that is amenorrhea in a woman who is neither pregnant nor breastfeeding.

Variation in how long it takes for fertility to return is a reminder that there are limits to our control over a lot of things in life, including the size and spacing of our families. Some of us are surprised by babies much closer in age than we planned. Some of us are surprised by very long intervals between babies. There are advantages to having children close in age, and there are advantages to having them widely spaced. If we can turn loose of our yearning to control what is out of our control, we'll have a chance to enjoy the blessings of the family we have.

Other Physical Effects of Nursing

Another concern about extended nursing that people expressed in the past was about mothers' low estrogen levels while breastfeeding. One mother was even told by her physician that her uterus would atrophy if she kept nursing.

Natural estrogen is at a lower level during lactation amenorrhea (see above). Now and then a mother who does not menstruate because of nursing may notice changes related to low estrogen levels, such as vaginal dryness, tenderness, or itching. This condition can be relieved a bit with some of the vaginal creams available in pharmacies, K-Y Jelly for example. A few physicians prescribe estrogen ointments for mothers who complain of vaginal symptoms, and these products do eliminate the symptoms dramatically. Whether there are any long term risks to mother, father, or nursling from this small exposure to estrogen, no one knows for certain. Any possible discomfort from vaginal dryness disappears with the resumption of ovulation and menstruation.

The low levels of estrogen while nursing are natural. There is no reason to expect damage to the uterus or anything else from a normal hormone state. Quite the contrary, indications are that periods of low estrogen exposure may actually be protective against various cancers of the reproductive system.

There is evidence that breastfeeding provides a modest protection against breast cancer, and that nursing longer may increase the protective effect.[19] Having your first baby at an early age makes the greatest difference in breast cancer risk, but the reduction of risk in mothers who breastfeed a total of twenty-five months or more is also statistically significant.[15] Nursing more than just the first few weeks also provides some protection against endometrial cancer.[21]

For a mother with an adequate diet and a reasonable amount of rest, there is no more physical drain from lactation than from any other normal body function, such as, for instance, sweating or digesting food. On the other hand, mothering preschool children is quite a drain! If you frequently find yourself feeling tired, chasing an active toddler is explanation enough. Producing milk adds little or nothing to your level of fatigue, while nursing is a way to make caring for your toddler easier. At the very least, nursing is a part of the mothering job you can do sitting or lying down.

Dealing with Your Own Doubts

Nursing past your child's first birthday, or second, or fourth—or wherever you have put your own dividing line between confidence and doubt—is likely to require an intellectual decision on your part. And like most things we parents decide in our heads, it is hard for us to act without some ambivalence. Things we have seen done as we were growing up, especially patterns of parenting in our own childhood families, are the easiest for us to follow. When mothers nurse longer than anyone they knew as they were growing up, they are bound to feel unsure at times. Are we going to harm this precious child by making a bizarre, selfish, wrong choice about weaning?

When such doubts arise it helps to visit with mothers who are nursing or have nursed a child older than yours, and maybe even better, someone whose child nursed such a long time and is now growing up obviously okay. I could introduce you to my grown children and small herd of nieces and nephews who have obviously escaped whatever horrors were supposed to be visited on them because they nursed so long. La Leche League is made up of mothers with many kinds and degrees of nursing experience and can be a good source of empathy and encouragement.

Another person to look to for feedback about continued nursing— the first person really—is your child. How does he feel about nursing? How would he react if you tried to stop nursing now? Your child's feelings about nursing were not learned out of the latest child care book nor through conversations about nursing with the neighbors or with breastfeeding fanatics. Your child's feelings about nursing are an expression of what is going on inside him. Although your decisions about life with your child will not be totally decided by his feelings, nonetheless they do deserve consideration. If your child expresses a continuing need to nurse, you should weigh those expressions of need as you evaluate whether or not it is best for nursing to go on.

Doubts are greatest with the first child who nurses past a mother's self-imposed limit. It is hard to believe, no matter how many people tell us, that little people do quit nursing more or less on their own. Once you have experienced an uncoerced weaning, that doubt usually becomes much less urgent.

If you are nursing now and feeling uncertain whether it is best to continue, I really do not expect what I have to say to make you feel completely better. Almost all of us have to grow, as did the mother who wrote:

> *Now that I'm older and more experienced . . . I am much more inclined to ignore remarks from friends, relatives, and doctors. But the first baby seemed such a terrible responsibility, and I wanted so much to do right by him.*

Some part of the equipment built into good parents keeps us questioning and evaluating what we are doing, especially during that first "experimental" time we try a new (to us, anyway) approach in parenting. Your doubts are completely normal. In fact they are characteristic of a good parent on the way to becoming even better. You are watching and evaluating, striving to make life for your child the best it can be. How fortunate your children are to have parents with doubts!

But do not let the doubts get bigger than you are. Talk with people who support your viewpoint—again let me recommend La Leche League. There you will probably find the people who can help you most— parents whose little ones have nursed longer than yours, no matter how long that may be. When you are feeling uncomfortable about a parenting decision like continuing to nurse or not, expose yourself to people facing similar decisions. Bask in the warm support of those who are proceeding in a similar way. Give those who are making different choices a chance to "convert" you to what they are doing. You will feel better, enjoying closeness with those who agree with you, and a conviction that your decision is right for you since you have made it with full knowledge of differing viewpoints.

Most of all, you can overcome your doubts by looking at your child. Your happy, learning, growing child is evidence that you are doing fine. You are a good parent. Pat yourself on the back and feel proud.

Coping with Family Pressure

You have the tools to deal with your own doubts when you have them—
confronting doubt immediately by reaffirming your decision, or giving
doubt a fair chance by re-thinking everything, or just deciding to live
with doubt for a while to see what happens. You respond differently at
different times. Sometimes you look to other people to help you feel
better; sometimes you do it alone.

It is harder to handle doubts if others around us express similar
questions. Uneasy feelings we have been handling well can trip us up
when someone dear to us, especially a husband, talks about similar
misgivings.

> *My husband and I vehemently disagree about nursing
> our son. My husband is of the "old school," that nursing
> a four-year-old is gross, overindulgent, and out of line.
> I sense an intense need from my son to nurse. Several
> times a day, long nursings, and morning and bedtime are
> non-negotiable. There are other issues in our marriage,
> of course, so I think breastfeeding gets the brunt of it
> sometimes. I feel torn between my primary relationship
> with my husband, and the primary, timely, intense
> requirements toward my young children, who will not
> always be so young. Can I sacrifice what they need, in
> order to compromise with my husband? I have decided
> not to.*

What a tough situation to be in! Unfortunately, it is not at all
rare, and understandably so considering our culture's standard doctrines
about little children. Ideally, of course, parents would have their entire
nursing and weaning decisions worked out before the child is even
conceived. But often it doesn't work that way. Many of us have been
surprised to find ourselves led into extended nursing by our children.
And so our partners are likely to be surprised as well. So when the
subject of weaning is discussed, a mother may interpret her mate's
doubts as an attack on her and her choices and feel as though the person
closest to her is undermining the foundations of her still shaky decisions.
No wonder she reacts with emotionally charged defenses.

Keep in mind that the people you love usually have the same
kinds of concerns for your children that you do. They go through the
same worrying and questioning—maybe not as much or as soon in some
instances, but the same kind. Keep in mind when your husband says, "If
he's two (or 'three' or 'five') and still nursing, he probably won't ever quit

if you don't make him quit," how recently you believed the same thing yourself.

My husband was supportive of breastfeeding, felt "I knew best" and saw how healthy, strong, big, and happy it was making our son (our first child). Then he started to hear grumbling from his mother and others as our baby got older (so old —like eight months): "So, when are they going to stop?" He and I had agreed on a year of nursing, but as the deadline approached I could not imagine losing the one sure-fire, cure-all, good-eats, ever-ready that nursing is. My brilliant pediatrician said, "Your husband needs more attention." It was hard, but I cooed and cuddled more, and the weaning conversations stopped.

If someone very close to you, especially your husband, seems to feel that you should stop nursing, and if cuddling isn't enough to change his mind, be sure to acknowledge that he is concerned, as you are, about what is best for your child. Know in your own mind, and let him know you know, that his suggestions are made out of love for your child, not as an attack on you. Talk about your own doubts—ones you had in the past and ones you still have. Do this slowly; let him see how much you have thought about it. Listen to what he has to say carefully and thoughtfully.

Talk about how you arrived at the decisions you have made. Maybe he'll be willing to read what William and Martha Sears write about nursing toddlers in *The Baby Book* or *Becoming a Father*. Maybe he'll read "Fathering Your Nursing Toddler" in this book. Take your time, and give him time. Try to explain your reasons step by step. Give him a chance to think without threat, listening to what he has to say. He does not have a chance to come around to your way of thinking if you just get mad and shriek out the whole thing in under two minutes.

La Leche League's long-time friend and mentor Dr. Gregory White suggests, however, that it is not always bad to react emotionally. "There are times when one good 'explosion' goes further than hours of reasoning in showing how you feel," he says. The objective is to achieve communication, and it sometimes takes experimentation to find the channels that work for you.

It can also be helpful, both for you and for your mate, when you are with members of the family who might not be at ease in the presence of a nursing couple not to nurse too openly right at first, especially with the amount of breast exposure you are comfortable with at home. In the beginning you may need to nurse inconspicuously around certain people, sometimes even with husband or parents. Too much nudity too soon may be part of what causes some new grandfathers to find their daughters' nursing so distasteful. Of course you want to be able to relax and nurse in any way that is comfortable at home, but it is a good investment in the future of your nursing and family relationships to exercise discretion while the people who love you are coming to terms in their own minds with the way you have chosen to mother your baby.

Few family members understand extended nursing the way you do, especially if you are fortunate enough to be in contact with other mothers nursing into and past toddlerhood. People near us need us to understand their feelings—sometimes before we can ask them to understand ours.

In some instances it may be possible to improve the situation through the kind of empathy shown by the woman who wrote:

> *I helped my mother-in-law overcome her feelings of failure about not being able to nurse my husband as a baby. We talked about how few could succeed at nursing with the conditions she had in the hospital (ten days there, no nursing for the first two, rigid schedule, no night feedings). When she realized that she had tried and had not been at fault she could more easily accept my success at nursing.*

This grandmother had probably never before had her mothering efforts so accepted and affirmed by another mother, and it is no wonder that afterwards she had much greater faith in her daughter-in-law's ability to make mature and loving mothering choices of her own.

In general, however, we should not expect people whose peer groups are oriented toward eliminating baby "habits" as soon as possible to feel good about extended nursing, especially not when they first encounter it. How did you feel the first time you saw a nursing toddler? How long was it before you could think of nursing so long yourself? Do not be surprised that, like you, the other people who love your child need a while to ask questions and to satisfy themselves that you have made the best possible plans in your child's best interests. Husbands deserve special patience and attention, because without their support, enjoying the nursing relationship is almost impossible. Besides, fathers are parents, too! They have a right to help determine how their children are reared.

Coping with Pressure from Outsiders

Of course you can patiently discuss extended nursing only with people with whom you can spend a great deal of time. The time we have with many of the people whose opinions are important to us is just too limited. All too often we find ourselves blurting out a condensed version of our reasoning with these people and come out sounding like zealots on soapboxes. Or the end of a visit will come and close our discussion at an uneasy point, before we can even understand each other, much less come to some kind of consensus.

How many toddlers are weaned solely because of other people's opinions? Parents end up forcing weaning on toddlers because of embarrassment over incidents that involved other people—a three-year-old insisting upon his bedtime nursing when there was company, or a two-year-old demanding to nurse at church, and the like. What a shame it is when young parents say they are glad to have moved across country or spent time overseas just because it enables them to live many miles away from critical relatives.

Almost the only reason given by those few mothers who told me they would not plan to nurse future children past infancy was something along this line: "What other people think bothers me too much." "Nursing is not the problem, but what other people think of it." "If we lived on an island," one mother said, "where nobody else cared what we did, I would let her nurse as long as she wanted. . . . I know one thing for sure: My baby is a lot more independent than I am."

Although it can be difficult, mothers need to trust their own mothering urges as fully as their children do. Many mothers have indeed learned to tune out criticism of their continued nursing, change the subject, and enjoy the company of dear people in other ways. As one perceptive father pointed out, what most people express is not disapproval of extended nursing anyway; it is just surprise. One mother wrote:

> *I find that because it is so unusual to tandem nurse, that most just need to be informed that it is possible to do— and is safe. I usually empathize and remark that I did not plan to do this. If someone had told me ten years ago that I would be breastfeeding a fifteen-month-old and a three-year-old, I would have told them they were out of their minds!*

Facetious answers are sometimes enough too, when they are offered in good humor and love. When one mother with a toddler at her breast was asked, "How long do you expect him to keep that up?" she replied, "Oh, another five minutes or so." Another responded to "Are you still nursing?" with, "No, I stopped quite a while ago, but my son still is."

> *What do I say when the "are you still nursing" question arises? I smile and say, "I know, I'm a bad (or lazy) mother." It usually disarms the questioner, as that's the point they were trying to make. I say it gently, though, just in case they're even a little bit open to what comes next, which is the joy and benefits of extended nursing. This little speech gets a big boost from my visual aid, my happy, healthy, well-adjusted, and beautiful son.*

A few people are satisfied once you remind them how long many children use bottles, pacifiers, or thumbs. Another way to circumvent critical or surprised comments is to say, "Yes, we're giving more thought to weaning these days," and then talk about something else.

A mother writes about how hard it is to have differences in mothering style with her best friend:

> *She weaned her firstborn at two weeks, and refused to even start nursing her second. Although she is like a sister, and I love her dearly, we have chosen different parenting paths. I may not agree with hers, but I respect her. I just wish she would grant me the same courtesy, instead of suppressing a groan when I mention my toddlers' crawling into bed with me and the one still breastfeeding happily latching on as all of us get a little extra sleep after mom had a rough night. Some days, I want to tell her she wouldn't have these overly clingy children if she would just put their needs first while they are foremost. Nor would she spend half the time with one or the other in doctor's offices if she had breastfed. Not to mention the money she would save or the health benefits to her of extended nursing. But, that would add fuel to the fire, so I refrain.*

Would you believe that such differences with friends continue for some of us as grandparents? Of course by my time of life it is easier to change the subject from how our grandchildren are being reared, but I have been surprised to find it still necessary to do so.

Ducking the issue is not always the best approach, though, and you can tell right away when it's wrong. Some people really want to talk about weaning and will not let you change the subject. Other times you feel in yourself a strong need for that person's approval, so you really want to talk about it.

When discussion time is limited—when, unlike time with your mate, you do not have the evenings after supper, long chats over coffee, or the 2 A.M. "redeye specials"—there is probably no reason for getting into a debate. There is no chance for both of you to present all the facts and feelings each of you have so that you can examine them all and approach some kind of understanding. Besides, you don't need to "convert" everyone to your viewpoint. Instead you need to solicit their support and love for you as a person and their patience with the decisions you make as a parent.

Tell your mother-in-law or your sister who lives so far away—or whomever—how much you rely on her support for you as a parent. Tell her you know how much she cares for you and your child and wants things to be the best they can be for both of you. (Don't omit talking about either of the above two things; they are proof that you are listening and that you care about her, too.) Remind her that you are also acting out of concern for your child's well-being. You have learned from the experiences of other mothers you know and from reading, and what you have learned makes you sure that no harm comes from continuing to nurse. You can point out that the American Academy of Pediatrics[1] and the World Health Organization[26] share this opinion.

Without going into endless detail, point out that you know some good comes from extended nursing. Emphasize the enjoyable parts of your continued nursing relationship. Save your complaints for someone who can support you. Most people will respect your informed decision; they want to be helpful and feel a need to be sure this is not just a "bad habit" you have slipped into without thinking.

The Persistent Critic

Some people, it is sad to say, even after a kindly worded, direct plea for love and support, or at least for tolerance, feel an urgent need to talk you into weaning and continue to do so at every opportunity. These people are often genuinely alarmed at what you are doing, although some older people are not so much alarmed by what you are doing *per se* as they are by the very fact that you, still a baby in their eyes, are a parent at all. Other people nearer your own age may need to put down your decisions as defense for their own parenting choices on the assumption that one of you has to be wrong. (How much better it would be if we could, every one of us, think through what seems right and feels right for our own families and then be neither threatened nor threatening when the neighbors do not make the identical decisions!)

If a person keeps offering unsolicited advice to the point that it is annoying you or your family, it becomes necessary to be very firm. One mother dealt with such a situation within her family by leaving the room for ten minutes when the subject came up. If it came up again, she left for twenty minutes, and so on until the criticism stopped altogether. Usually it is best, though, to talk about the problem. "I know many people who feel as you do about weaning. But I've thought about it a lot and decided to wean my own way. I really don't want to talk about it anymore, please." By all means, stop the conversation about weaning there and go on to something else.

Now and then a friendship will seem to flounder because of how the friends feel about your nursing your toddler. If you are able to be easygoing about nursing, not defensive, then it is unlikely that a friendship would wane for that reason alone. There may be other wedges between you, and your decision not to wean your child may be the final excuse for drifting apart. When you have a stable friendship, you will be able to help your friends understand or at least to respect your decision. It is usually possible to say, as one mother does, "Friends accept his nursing. Some are a little amazed that I am such a good 'cow,' but my friends, my son, and I have grown together." True friends are like that; less flexible friendships are usually no great loss.

When Your Child Receives Criticism or Teasing

Now and then a person will criticize your continued nursing by teasing your child. When people criticize you directly, you can just ignore what they say if it is not making you too uncomfortable, or you can choose to respond. If your child is being used as a middleman, however, you must intervene for your child's sake.

Questions in your child's presence may be best met with, "That's private, and I'd rather not discuss it now." Help the critic see how unsettling it can be for a little person to face teasing for something that just comes naturally to him. It could also be enlightening to the critic if you point out to him or her that such comments are likely to put up barriers between that person and the child which could interfere with their future relationship. You can be kind and warm, but you must also be as firm as you have to be. Do not allow the teasing to continue or to be repeated.

Children will be aware of some of the negative opinions others have about their continued nursing. "You know, Mommy," one four-year-old observed, "I think Daddy's afraid I won't grow up." But as long as your child does not have to face a direct attack from those who disapprove, you can reassure him that he is fine and that not everyone has to agree on everything. With your help, the opinions of others should not trouble him too much.

Keeping Nursing Private

I have left until last the most satisfactory tool for dealing with people who might pressure you toward weaning before you want to—a closed mouth (and blouse). The older your child gets, the fewer the people who need to know you are still nursing. Too often we suffer for volunteering personal, private information to people who had no need to know it! Sometimes you can even avoid answering a direct question from somebody you would prefer not to know that your child still nurses by giving a silly or ambiguous response. For the most part, though, people who think your child should be weaned will assume he is weaned unless you tell them otherwise.

It is not even necessary to tell health care advisors that your child nurses if you think they would be inclined to criticize you, provided the nursing is not significant in evaluating a health problem. There is no need to set yourself up for comments when you want none. On the other hand, when you are feeling self-assured, it is good to let these people know that your child is not yet weaned. Such revelations are helping professionals in health care to realize what fine healthy children our little nurslings are and are moving us toward a time in which mothers can count on professionals, as Sharon Hills-Bonczyk writes, to "understand why women choose long-term breastfeeding, and provide support to maintain the breastfeeding relationships or to facilitate coping with the loss of the breastfeeding experience."[10]

Seeking Support and Approval

Mothers all need support and approval from other people in their parenting roles. After all, most are novices at the job, especially those with small families. When you need encouragement and a pat on the back for nursing, you should seek these goodies from people who share your enthusiasm. We make trouble for ourselves by seeking approval from people for things they are not likely to understand or to applaud. When you need a pat on the back from a beloved friend or relative, it is far wiser to seek their praise for things they feel good about, even if it is only your choice of laundry detergent or your little one's new haircut. It is foolish to ask them to support or praise you in matters that make them uncomfortable.

Mothers may be especially disappointed when they misinterpret the help and advice they get from people in health care. So often we expect our children's checkups to provide us not only with assurance that our children are healthy, but also with an "official" certificate of our good performance as parents. These expectations put additional pressure on health professionals. "In our society," Niles Newton wrote, "there is something embarrassing about a breastfeeding couple who thoroughly enjoy themselves. As the months go by the physician in charge, like almost any representative of our society, begins to feel uncomfortable."[20]

Doctors and nurses are trained in identifying and treating illness. It is not fair to them to expect them also to be experts in all aspects of child care and family living. Putting pressure on doctors and nurses to be everything and know everything by asking them for advice on matters beyond their training can lead to disappointment. Their advice on child care tends to be no better and no worse than that of other reasonably well-informed adults. This is as it should be, and it is a mistake to expect more.

I must add that, being as human as the rest of us, doctors and nurses are also just as likely as anyone else to offer unsolicited advice on child care. Years of studying pathology do not give them any better basis for such counseling than do years of studying computer science. What will qualify medical people to give good advice about child care is good family experience of their own. With such experience at home, many medical people give excellent advice on life with little people. So do many computer scientists. It is up to you to evaluate the advice you get very

SHE MUST HAVE HIT HIM OVER THE HEAD
TO MAKE HIM STOP CRYING SO FAST!

carefully according to what makes sense to you. As much as we might wish it to be otherwise, there are few, if any, physicians of the old Marcus Welby type—a fictitious character who seemed to know everything about every patient and to be totally helpful and right all the time.

Nursing When Other People Are Around

Maintaining that "closed blouse" I mentioned is not always possible around people, especially with younger toddlers. They can choose some of the most awkward company in which to be overcome with the need to nurse. Many of these little people are so active, picking up your blouse to see if the other breast is still there, running their hands down the front of your shirt, etc., that nursing inconspicuously is much more difficult than when they were tiny.

A vivid memory I have is of being in the back of a Jeep on one of those Rocky Mountain tours. I was sitting knee to knee with a family who talked and dressed as if they had just stepped off the set of the TV series "Dallas." Throughout the tour I coped well with nursing our tiny new baby off and on. Before it was over, however, our toddler decided she needed to nurse, too. Now, that scene fits my personal definition of an awkward place and company for nursing a toddler! We did survive, and without red faces, because of following several guidelines in living with a nursing toddler.

Clothing. First of all it is essential to plan ahead. Think about your clothing. As your child grows older you need to pay attention to what kinds of fasteners the bright little tot is learning to operate. Many a mother has not thought of this until after the first time she has looked down wherever she might be to discover her zippered front being unzipped by the innocent angel in her arms. This is a situation that calls for some immediate tickling and other distraction until you can get away and nurse, followed by the temporary retirement of such clothing for excursions away from home.

Code talking. For the first two or three years little people can be expected to ask to nurse anywhere the spirit moves them, and often their articulation far exceeds their sense of what is and is not socially acceptable.

In our industrialized society the breast is still a glorified object and its nurturing functions are of secondary importance in the minds of many. Despite the widespread flaunting of women's breasts that is so apparent in the media, women who breastfeed are encouraged to maintain a virgin-like modesty. These inconsistencies guarantee difficulties for breastfeeding mothers unless they manage a studied indifference to their social milieux.[16]

Not all of us achieve such indifference, not all the time anyway, and it is very difficult to keep nursing a private matter when your child announces, "I want to nurse."

"How cute!" remarked an aunt when a child made such a request, "He still remembers." "How could he forget," his mother thought to herself. "It's only been four hours."

It can be cute when little Lucy asks for "titty" or "boobie juice" at home. Think, however, whether you are comfortable having her make the same request with perfect pronunciation at the supermarket. What word will be best for you if your child should do what one New Zealand youngster did, patting his mother's jersey and announcing to all around "Mummy has drinkies"? Will it be comfortable for you if your three-year-old says "Mamma, get those nursers out"? How will his request sound to you shrilled above the strains of "Lohengrin" at a cousin's wedding?

This is not to say that your nursing relationship must be secret or that there is anything wrong with any term whatsoever that you may want to use for nursing. I just want to alert you to the fact that the word you use in the first or second year will usually be the word your child continues to use, and the pronunciation will become increasingly distinct. Though it may be possible to re-teach your child a new word later, it is bound to be difficult. So plan early, based on what will be comfortable to you.

Many families prefer to choose a code word for nursing. Since the "n" sounds come very early for most babies, the "n" words are very common code words ("ninny," "nanny," "nappies," "num-num," etc.). When the child starts saying something repeatedly in babbling, you can pick up the "word" and begin to use it to mean nursing. Some families choose real words connected with breasts and nursing, words like "all-gone," "jug," or "side."

I wanted something that I wouldn't mind hearing and wouldn't have to explain to others, so we picked "snuggles." When he first started talking, he couldn't make the "sn" sound, so it came out "cuggles" and now it is either snuggles or cuggles, but it just warms my heart to hear my two-and-a-half-year-old request his favorite form of comforting.

Others turn baby sounds into a code word like "dee-dee," "yum-yum," "ne-wee," "mim," "nummies," "nur-nur," "nurney," or "brr-brr." Nursing in one Kansas household became "oh," a baby-shortened form of "some mo'." In another family nursing became "mona" (Spanish for monkey) after the toddler saw a monkey nursing on television. Yet another family called nursing "night-night" and enjoyed the reaction of people when their "good" little child asked for "night-night" all by herself.

A hand sign or facial expression instead of a word has done the job for some families.

The advantage of the code word is that it is not a word in anyone else's language—just yours. In a crowded Jeep, or during a wedding processional, it becomes just child noise to the uninitiated and gives you a chance to handle the situation in the way that is most comfortable for you. In our case, the Jeep driver asked whether "nanny" was my daughter's doll, to which I replied, "No." Though she said frequently, "I want my nanny," she did not become frantic, and we made it through the remainder of the tour and into the privacy of our own car.

Delay. Often, as your child gets older, your wonderful private word for nursing will make it possible to use the next tool you can try for avoiding embarrassment, a tool I used in the Jeep: side-stepping nursing in situations that make you uncomfortable. Distraction often helps a toddler wait—walking around, jiggling, tickling, looking at new objects or toys. A verbal toddler can learn to go along with "Wait until we get home," or "After I'm through eating," or some such. A young child can learn where nursing is or is not appropriate and sometimes will accept a signal—such as your wearing something that fastens in the back on occasions when you don't want to nurse.

Do keep in mind, however, that avoidance, used too often, will add up to an initiation of weaning by you. You need to realize that if you find yourself delaying nursing, say for an hour or more once a day, you are in one pattern often recommended for weaning. If your child is far from being ready for weaning, the whole procedure could give you a result just the opposite of what you want—an increase in your child's requests for nursing at times you find embarrassing.

Avoidance of nursing in certain situations is fine, of course. To keep from setting up a weaning atmosphere, it is helpful to remember when you have distracted a little one from nursing and try to be quick to respond to the next request. If you've promised to nurse when you get home or after supper, by all means do so. Your credibility is at stake. So offer to nurse at the agreed-upon time, even if the child has forgotten about it.

Grin and "bare" it. Times arise, of course, especially with young toddlers, when their need to nurse is urgent, no matter how embarrassing you may find the circumstances. Many a mother in this type of situation has excused herself to "change a diaper" or "read a bedtime story" or "just to calm her down a little bit." There is no need to explain what you really do once the door is closed behind you.

You can sometimes avoid the need to nurse over a relatively short period of time, such as a trip to the grocery store or a brief visit at a neighbor's, by planning ahead. Your child may find it easier to go without nursing on these occasions if he is able to nurse just before you go.

If you cannot head off a request to nurse or cannot excuse yourself and your child for a few minutes, or if you would prefer not to, then use all the sneaky, unobtrusive nursing techniques you have been using all along—pull-up tops, or dresses with secret openings, your hair (if it is very long) helping to cover up. A wide-armed jumper outfit or dress with hidden slits can be especially helpful with a child who likes to pull your shirt up high while nursing, because the jumper front or the small openings make it harder for him to "overexpose" you. A poncho serves as a good cover-up at outdoor events. If you can lift your bra rather than having to unfasten the cup, it is easier to hide what you are doing. (Whether you can do this depends of course on how your bra is made and also on the size of your breasts.) If you do open the cup of your bra, you can usually put off fumbling to reconnect the closure—the hard part with most bras—until you are in private.

You may be able to persuade your toddler to be satisfied with one breast at times like these. Switching sides is just one more bit of commotion to call attention to what you are doing.

There will still be times when you have to cope with questions or stares you would rather not have come your way. But you can keep these uncomfortable times to a minimum while doing your best to meet the needs of your growing child. Besides, it is fortifying to think that every time you answer a question or comment about nursing with warmth (unsullied by evangelistic zeal), you bring just a little bit closer the day when what you are doing will no longer attract stares or comments.

Fun and Games

Nursing is not always a time for serious application of developmental psychology. It can be full of play and humor. "I remember the little fun games of peek," one mother says, "and the adoring eyes looking back at me. I wouldn't trade those times for anything." There are memories of nursing a little cowboy with his hat and guns, a little movie star in sunglasses, or a mechanic clutching hammer and screwdriver.

> *I'm an actress, so work is sporadic. The other day, I had to rush out to a shoot, but we had no more frozen breast milk. I grabbed the manual pump and got a four-ounce bottle in no time, then raced around the house looking for keys, purse, etc. As I said a hurried good-bye to the sitter, I looked over to find my son with his shirt lifted up, operating the manual pump like his little life depended on it. All I can say is, he's gonna be a great husband!*

There's the tot who parks her gum on mom's bra while she is nursing, while another forgot to take his gum out and got it stuck to mother.

A mother writes about playing with play dough with her two-and-a-half-year-old:

> We made a big ball and a little ball. My son called the big ball "Mama Ball," and the little one "Baby Ball." He then stuck the baby to the Mama, and exclaimed, "Drink milk!" We are planning to conceive another child later this year, so being curious, I made a tiny ball and put it on the table. (What would he do?) My son stuck the tiny ball to Mama ball, and said, "Drink milk, too." I guess he doesn't mind the idea of tandem nursing!

Toddlers start out with none of our inhibitions about their bodies, and no inhibitions about ours. It is up to each of us to teach them what is acceptable. Your family may get a kick out of watching a little one learn to express mother's milk and react with surprise when she gets a stream of milk in her face, the same mix of surprise and pleasure that the farm cat shows when the dairy farmer aims a stream of milk her way. Or you may find just the thought of such a game disgusting. However you feel about these things, you're in charge, so you can enjoy them—or never let them happen.

One word of caution: Young toddlers have trouble honoring the difference between public and private behaviors. So it is risky to permit or encourage any behavior in private that you can't be comfortable with in front of other people. The younger the toddler, the less likely that she can make the distinction.

Some nursing children make a great joke of trying daddy's nipples or trying to express milk from their own. One little guy pointed at the nipples of a large Buddha and gleefully squealed "Nur-nur!" A small copy of the "Venus de Milo" was much admired by the nurslings in my house. More than one child has had a much more wholesome response than was ever intended when he accidentally glimpses a topless centerfold. One of my favorite true stories came from a vacationing family who discovered they had stumbled by accident into a topless restaurant when their nursing toddler tried to help himself to what he innocently assumed to be the main course!

References

1   American Academy of Pediatrics, Working Group on Breastfeeding. Breastfeeding and the use of human milk. *Pediatrics* December 1997; 100(6):1037.

2   Brun, J. G., Nilssen, S., and Kvåle, G. Breast feeding, other reproductive factors and rheumatoid arthritis: A prospective study. *British Journal of Rheumatology* 1995; 34:543-45.

3   Cross, N. A. et al. Changes in bone mineral density and markers of bone remodeling during lactation and postweaning in women consuming high amounts of calcium. *Journal of Bone and Mineral Research* 1995; 10(9):1318.

4   Cummings, R. G. and Klineberg, R. J. Breastfeeding and other reproductive factors and the risk of hip fractures in elderly women. *International Journal of Epidemiology* 1993; 22(4):687-89.

5   Ellison, P. T. Breastfeeding, fertility, and maternal condition. *Breastfeeding, Biocultural Perspectives.* Ed. P. Stuart-Macadam and K. A. Dettwyler. New York: Aldine de Gruyter, 1995; 317-31.

6   Feldblum, P. J. et al. Lactation history and bone mineral density among perimenopausal women. *Epidemiology* 1992; 3(6):527-31.

7   Fildes, V. A. *Breasts, Bottles and Babies: A History of Infant Feeding.* Edinburgh, Edinburgh University Press, 1986; 48.

8   Gross, B. A. Is the lactational amenorrhea method a part of natural family planning? Biology and policy. *American Journal of Obstetrics and Gynecology* December 1991; 165(6):2015.

9   Hamosh, M. Nutrition during Lactation. *Nutrition in Pregnancy and Growth* Ed. M. Porrini and P. Walter. Basel: Karger, 1996; 31-32.

10 Hills-Bonczyk, S. G. et al. Women's experiences with breastfeeding longer than 12 months. *Birth* December 21, 1994; 21(4):212.

11 Hreshchyshyn, M. M. et al. Associations of parity, breast-feeding, and birth control pills with lumbar spine and femoral neck bone densities. *American Journal of Obstetrics and Gynecology* August 1988; 159(2):318-22.

12 Huggins, K. and Ziedrich, L. *The Nursing Mother's Guide to Weaning.* Boston: The Harvard Common Press, 1994; 105-06.

13 Kalkwarf, H. et al. Intestinal calcium absorption of women during lactation and after weaning. *American Journal of Clinical Nutrition* 1996; 63:530-31.

14 Kennedy, K. I. Effects of breastfeeding on women's health. *International Journal of Gynecology and Obstetrics* Suppl. 47: 1994; S18, S17. Rasmussen, K. M. Nutritional consequences of lactation for the mother: Definition of issues. Ed. M. F. Picciano, B. Lonnerdal. *Mechanisms Regulating Lactation and Infant Nutrient Utilization* New York: Wiley-Liss, 1992;105-06.

15 Layde, P. M. et al. The independent associations of parity, age at first full term pregnancy, and duration of breastfeeding with the risk of breast cancer. *Journal of Clinical Epidemiology* 1989; 42:966-72.

16 Mclean, H. *Women's Experiences of Breast Feeding.* Toronto: University of Toronto Press, 1990; 94.

17 Mohrbacher, N. and Stock, J. THE BREASTFEEDING ANSWER BOOK. Revised edition. Schaumburg, Illinois: La Leche League International, 1997; 373, 356-57,379. R. Newton, N. Psychologic differences between breast and bottle feeding. *American Journal of Clinical Nutrition* 1971; 24:994.

18 National Academy of Sciences Institute of Medicine, Food and Nutrition Board, Subcommittee on Nutrition During Lactation. *Nutrition During Lactation.* Washington, D.C.: National Academy Press, 1991; 229-33, 224, 218, 214.

19 Newcomb, P. A. et al. Lactation and a reduced risk of premenopausal breast cancer. *The New England Journal of Medicine* 1994; 330(2):81-87. S. Enger, S. M. et al. Breastfeeding history, pregnancy experience and risk of breast cancer. *The British Journal of Cancer* 1997; 76(1):120-22.

20 Newton, N. *Maternal Emotions: A Study of Women's Feelings Toward Menstruation, Pregnancy, Childbirth, Breast Feeding, Infant Care and Other Aspects of their Femininity.* NY: Paul B. Hoeber, Inc., 1955; 55.

21 Rosenblatt, K. A. and Thomas, D. B. Prolonged lactation and endometrial cancer. *International Journal of Epidemiology* 1995; 24(3):499-503.

22 Stern, J. M. et al. Nursing behaviour, prolactin and postpartum amenorrhoea during prolonged lactation in American and !Kung mothers. *Clinical Endocrinology* September 1986; 25(3):256.

23 Treckel, P. A. Breastfeeding and maternal sexuality in colonial America. *Journal of Interdisciplinary History* 1989; 20(1):38.

24 Weekly, S. J. Diets and eating disorders: Implications for the breastfeeding mother. *NAACOG's Clinical Issues* 1992; 3(4):697.

25 Weschler, T. *Taking Charge of Your Fertility: The Definitive Guide to Natural Birth Control and Pregnancy Achievement.* New York: HarperPerennial, 1995; 302-07, 359.

26 WHO/UNICEF. *On the Protection, Promotion and Support of Breast-Feeding.* August 1990.

27 Winkvist, A. and Habicht, J. P. A new definition of maternal depletion syndrome. *American Journal of Public Health* May 1992; 82(5):691-94.

28 Worthington-Roberts, B. and Williams, S. R. *Nutrition in Pregnancy and Lactation.* 5th edition. St. Louis: Mosby, 1993; 339.

29 Wray, J. D. Breastfeeding: An international and historical review. *Infant and child nutrition worldwide: issues and perspectives.* Ed. Frank Falkner. Boca Raton, Florida: CRC Press, 1991; 100-01.

chapter five
Glimpses into Other Times and Cultures

Nursing a toddler may seem unheard of these days in the USA, where 80 percent of babies are weaned by six months.[26] Mothers have written to me, describing similar circumstances in England, Germany, Sweden, and among mothers of European descent in southern Africa. Still, mothers who lived in East Africa in the 1960s or 70s have shared with me their pleasure in finding that it was still not rare to find children nursing for several years. Two North American women, one who had lived in New Guinea, the other in the Philippines, were pleased to see nursing extending past the first year. A mother in Sweden wrote of being blessed with support for her own extended nursing from an experienced mother of her husband's home country, India. "She said that in her country it is a minimum of two years if mother and child both want it, and usually breastfeeding continues for another couple of years. Her husband, she told me, had been nursed for seven years."

What follows is nowhere near a complete account of nursing and weaning around the world past and present. Rather it is my collection to date of observations and examples from published materials and from my correspondence.

History

Nursing a walking child has become so uncommon in the Western world that we tend to regard it as a novel innovation. Yet most of the children ever born in the world, the ones who survived at any rate, spent at least two years at the breast.

Nursing and weaning are, like most of our lives as human beings, guided by cultural considerations, so much so that it is all but impossible to say what is "natural" for us. Adaptable creatures that we are, we live in the space between what is ideal for our species and what our biological systems will allow. Adaptability is good; sometimes our lives depend on it. For example, our bodies tell us to sleep when we're tired; but, no matter what the internal clock says, it's not biologically advantageous to sleep through a tornado.

In such situations our reasoning brains often serve us well. At other times, however, we follow our thoughts until we forget where we started. To some degree we've thought up new ways to live until we've forgotten the basics of what human beings eat, or how and when we sleep. The great fluctuations in the "rules" for the care and feeding of infants over time indicate that we have definitely forgotten how humans care for babies. We can make better decisions about such matters, and thereby live better lives, if we can figure out what human minds and bodies expect and then deviate from those expectations only when we see a clear advantage in doing so—an advantage like knowing that we should stay awake until the tornado has passed.

Biological Clues to Weaning Age

Katherine Dettwyler's study of what she calls the "hominid blueprint" for nursing and weaning is an effort to work through the cultural confusion, back to the bedrock of human child care. Her work gives us the best information to date about the biological basis on which we build nursing and weaning decisions.[48]

In recent years, one indicator people have used to determine how long nursing should continue is achievement of a certain body size relative to birth weight. (Being "big enough" is a reason mothers all over the world give for weaning.) Mammals in general, Dettwyler writes, nurse until their young have tripled their birth weight, and many texts in use today base weaning advice on this "rule of thumb." For humans, tripling of birth weight occurs around the end of the first year. Large animals, however, do not usually wean until the offspring have come closer to quadrupling their birth weight. Humans quadruple birth weight sometime between two and three years, or somewhat later when undernourished.

Another weight-based marker for weaning, and one which works well in predicting weaning ages for other primates, is the age at which the young achieve one-third of adult weight. For humans, that would translate to a weaning age of somewhere between four and seven years, with boys nursing longer than girls. A belief that boys should nurse longer than girls pops up throughout time and all over the world, although it is probably expressed more often than it is practiced. The belief may reflect, not sexism as we generally assume, but a biological marker within us relating weaning to the anticipated adult size of the nursling.

Another "rule of thumb" is that nursing should last as long as gestation, which would equal the nine months that was often recommended through much of the twentieth century. Equating nursing duration with the length of gestation may be accurate as an average for all mammals, but does not work for primates, who nurse more than one-and-a-half times the period of gestation. And large primates nurse much longer, gorillas and chimpanzees nursing over six times the length of gestation. If humans follow a breastfeeding pattern similar to our closest primate relatives, nursing six times as long as we are pregnant, we would expect weaning to occur at around four-and-a-half years.

Another marker that works well for predicting the age of weaning in primates is the eruption of the first permanent molars. In humans, this occurs between five-and-a-half and six years, a time that also corresponds with the maturation of some aspects of the child's immune system.[13] Between five and six, children are as ready as they are going to be to deal with the world of foods and microorganisms in which they will live the rest of their lives.

Yet researchers do not report a great number of examples of children actually nursing through the fourth or fifth year. In 1970, in developing countries, average duration of nursing ranged from six to 27 months. By the late 1980s, breastfeeding duration had increased a bit, ranging from ten to 27 months.[20]

There are some examples of very long nursing in the literature, particularly in the islands of the Pacific, but not as many as we might expect. Observers probably miss a number of older nurslings, since nursing after four tends to be infrequent and private. But there is reason to believe that the numbers of these older nurslings are in fact relatively small. The nearly universal taboo against nursing while pregnant no doubt results in a majority of children being weaned because of a new pregnancy, usually well before the fifth year. (For discussion of the pros and cons of nursing during pregnancy, see Chapter 7.) The modest increase in duration of breastfeeding in some developing countries since 1970 is probably at least partially attributable to family planning and increasing birth intervals.

As a further explanation of the difference between her predicted weaning age and what is actually observed, Dettwyler suggests that humans started decreasing the weaning age a very long time ago, when we learned to grind foods and to cook them. Both these processes make it easier for children to eat adult foods, and we know from experience how most but not all children insist on sharing in family meals. The resulting changes in human diet no doubt led toward a somewhat earlier average weaning age, closer to the two to four years that researchers most often find.

People who moved to colder climates, such as northern Europe or the high Andes, may have also been able to survive a shorter nursing period because lower infection rates in cold climates made weaning foods less deadly. In northern Europe, the development of dairying led to the use of weaning foods that were more digestible for children than the high-fiber diet of the hunter-gatherers. A reduced nursing period probably also increased birth rates. All these factors may have led to increasing populations among dairying peoples in cool climates.[48]

It has been my observation that when pregnancy or social pressure doesn't interfere, a good many mothers and/or children tend to lose interest in nursing when the child is between three and four. But a significant number feel a need to nurse longer. Dettwyler's research suggests that to continue nursing past the age of three or four is consistent with the long-term human pattern developed over five to seven million years before the development of agriculture. Nursing six or seven years is well within the range of normal human behavior. Just a few generations back, in some tropical climates where a weaned child would be disadvantaged by exposure to the warm climate's microorganisms, such extended nursing was the norm, at least as long as the mother did not become pregnant again.

Prehistory

There has not been a great deal of research into breastfeeding and weaning in prehistory, but there are techniques emerging that give us some clues. Sophisticated tests on tiny fragments of ancient bone or hair in North America, the eastern shores of the Mediterranean, and the Sudan point toward nursing and weaning patterns similar to those in traditional communities just a few generations ago. Babies were breastfed exclusively for six to twelve months. Other foods were introduced slowly, and weaning came about gradually, with breastfeeding ceasing on average somewhere around two or three years.[48]

In other studies, some researchers use the average age of onset of lactase "deficiency" (or lactose intolerance) in modern populations to estimate the age of weaning for the ancestors of certain major ethnic groups. The onset of this normal absence of lactase has been widely studied in order to better understand when it may or may not be appropriate to offer dairy products to people from lactose-intolerant populations, since people who are lactose-intolerant cannot digest milk. As a result, there is a good body of research available.

The reason breastfeeding researchers believe they can use this data is that lactase production tends to decline in mammals soon after weaning. In some animals, in fact, the decline in lactase seems to help bring about weaning. The data are not entirely consistent, but in people from many non-dairy cultures, lactase declines sharply after age two or three, suggesting that their ancestors nursed for two to three years.[48]

Further research in paleonutrition should increase our knowledge of how people nursed and weaned long before there was anybody like me around with the hubris to write down how they ought to go about it.

Ancient History

The prophets of ancient Israel, as well as the merchants and the shepherds, were not weaned before two years. Infant feeding bottles have not been found in the ruins of pre-Ptolemaic Egypt,[10] so if Moses' mother, posing as a wet nurse, was bound by ancient Egyptian customs as she reared her son to be part of the Egyptian royal family, she nursed him three years. Hannah nursed the prophet Samuel for three years. Abraham and Sarah held a weaning party for Isaac when he was two. Centuries later (536 BCE) the Talmud set the nursing period at 18 to 24 months, stating that to nurse for a shorter time was to risk the baby's death. In *Breasts, Bottles and Babies,* an extensive history of infant feeding, Valerie A. Fildes writes, "Rabbi Joshua held that breast nourishment should continue as many years as desired."[12]

Soranus and Galen, first and second century medical writers who influenced European child-care practices through the eighteenth century, believed children should be nursed two or three years, respectively, and then weaned gradually, starting in spring, not in autumn. A poignant relic from second century Rome is a contract for a slave named Sarapias to wet nurse a little girl named Helena for two years.

The care and feeding of children in Europe has a very mixed history, however, a history that contains the roots of many questions and problems we struggle with today.[10] There is evidence from nearly two millennia ago that Greek and Roman parents did not necessarily follow their good doctors' advice on nursing and weaning. Soranus complained about babies being started on cereal at around forty days, well before the end of the six months of exclusive breastfeeding he recommended. Large numbers of infant feeding vessels are found in the graves of children in both ancient Greece and Italy. Remains of children with symptoms of rickets also suggest early weaning from the breast.

Recommendations about weaning age in later Byzantine literature, largely based on Soranus and Galen, ranged from 20 months to two years, earlier than advised by Galen. Jewish writings from the twelfth century recommend that mother or wet nurse suckle for two years and abstain from intercourse during that time.

Affluent women in medieval Europe continued a well-established tendency among some segments of society to avoid breastfeeding. Writers in the twelfth and fourteenth century complained about modern women being "delicate," "too haughty," and disliking the inconvenience of nursing their own babies. During this time, some physicians recommended nursing (or wet nursing) boys six to twelve months longer than girls; at least in one area of France girls were weaned at one, and boys at two.

The Arabian or Islamic school of medicine was built on classical Greek and Roman texts, and much of what we know about Greek and Roman medicine was preserved through Europe's Dark Ages in Arabic writings and translations. The Koran recommends breastfeeding for two years. Studies on the remains of children from the Medieval (800-1300 AD) site of Dor on the eastern Mediterranean coast near modern Haifa showed indications of a gradual increase in the amount of food added to the breast milk diet in a manner consistent with the practices of traditional Palestinian Arab communities in the twentieth century, that is, weaning between the ages of two and three.[48]

One ancient medical text in India recommends introducing solids, primarily rice, at six months. Another recommends exclusive breast-feeding for the first year, although solid food could be allowed when the baby started teething. Weaning from the breast was advised after the second birthday.

Dangers of Weaning

Weaning has long been recognized as a dangerous time. Children in England and northern Europe became especially susceptible to rickets at weaning. Many also developed "weaning illness" or "weaning brash," which is the weaning diarrhea that we see in the developing world today.[12]

Teeth were a widely used indicator of readiness to begin weaning. In the North American colonies, the appearance of teeth marked the time to begin feeding cornmeal, chopped or pre-chewed fish, fowl, and red meat.[50] In Europe the recommended weaning age was long determined by the age at which children had all their milk teeth. The presence of teeth was important in a child's readiness to wean, not only because they equipped the child to chew food, but also because it meant the child had survived the period of teething, which was often deadly. Although the danger of teething had more to do with weaning practices than with the teeth themselves, many infants and toddlers did not survive this transition and had "teeth" listed in public records as the cause of death.

During weaning, parents in pre-industrial Britain had to cope with the life-threatening problem of contaminated water. So they gave their toddlers what they drank themselves—tea, ale, or weak beer.

Toddlers might also receive broth or barley water. Parents who could afford it gave their toddlers wine and, believe it or not, hard liquors, although most, but not all, physicians disapproved. Gin was cheap, and midwives and low-income families sometimes gave it even to very small babies to keep them quiet. Upper class families did the same, but they used brandy.

In England before 1800, the ideal seasons for weaning were spring and fall, although practice seemed to vary widely from the ideal. It was also supposed to be better to wean while the moon was waxing.[12]

Protective Effects of Breastfeeding

In spite of general agreement about the protective effects of human milk, many in royal families were weaned early. Mary and Elizabeth Tudor, both English queens, nursed only twelve months, and thus were weaned sooner than many others of lesser status in sixteenth century England. On the other hand, there are accounts of English mothers who had lost previous children and subsequently nursed well into toddlerhood to protect their treasured nurslings.

Medical practitioners understood the restorative properties of human milk. In ancient Egypt mother's milk had been an ingredient in many oral and topical remedies for people of all ages. In the seventeenth century some recommended that the seriously ill of any age be allowed to suckle at the breast of a healthy nursing mother.[50] (This prescription brings to mind the closing scene in John Steinbeck's *The Grapes of Wrath.*)

The Less Distant Past

Fourteenth and fifteenth century North American children of maize horticulturists in the Ohio Valley appear to have had breast milk as their major source of dietary protein for two years, with other foods introduced before they were two years old. They seem to have continued to receive breast milk for at least six months after other foods were introduced. Chemical studies of the remains of members of the Akara tribe in South Dakota indicate that these seventeenth and eighteenth century babies breastfed for one year before receiving much supplementation. Nursing continued at least two years, maybe as long as six. In neither study did available techniques allow researchers to determine the exact age at weaning, but nursing appears to have stopped gradually.[48]

In Europe, from the Renaissance through the 1800s, a baby or young toddler was often better off if it was born into a poor family, one that could not afford a wet nurse or any of a host of infant feeding bottles, cups, and horns that were available. Fashionable dress of the time also interfered with nursing among the prosperous. An Italian physician said in 1552 "that Nature intended milk to last into the second or third year" and complained of modern women starting solids (sopped bread) too early.[12]

Meanwhile, lower-class English mothers generally nursed exclusively and weaned their children when they could eat the same foods as the rest of the family. In 1725 writers commented on nursing four-year-olds with disapproval, an indication that some eighteenth century four-year-olds were still receiving love and comfort at their mother's breasts.[43]

Starting in the fifteenth century, babies were artificially fed from birth in many parts of Scandinavia, Southern Germany, Austria, and Northern Italy. Breastfeeding was regarded as a filthy habit and a mother who would want to do such a thing reviled. The tight bodices worn in the Tyrol served to explain the phenomenon in that region, but why it happened elsewhere is not clear. Those of us with roots in northern Europe have several generations of ancestors who probably saw no nursing toddlers at all, and our families are no doubt heirs to some of the beliefs and attitudes that led to this widespread and often deadly (30 to 40 percent mortality) experiment in infant feeding.[48]

In England, a substantial number of middle and upper class parents—aristocracy and gentry, wealthy farmers and merchants, scholars, professional men and some clergy—sent their babies to the homes of wet nurses. By the 1700s even people of relatively modest incomes were not nursing their own children. Over these centuries, also, recommended ages for weaning decreased. The expense of retaining the wet nurse's services probably played a part in people's decisions to shorten the nursing period. Parents may also have been eager for weaning so the child could come home. In the eighteenth century, middle and upper class English children were being weaned before their first birthday. In France, they still nursed a bit longer.[12]

By 1800 most of the popular English writings on child care recommended weaning as young as twelve months. After 1850 the emphasis in discussions about weaning shifted from concern about the health of the child to the well-being of the nurse or mother, or to the quality of the milk. Historians debate whether the accompanying decrease in recommended weaning age reflects actual practice, or whether some parents ignored the experts and paid attention to what their children told them.

In what would become the United States, English women probably nursed for twelve to eighteen months, and weaning probably varied from abrupt to gradual. Wet nurses were required to wean their charges when menstruation resumed. Physicians believed that to continue nursing then would risk the child's health, or even his life.

There is disagreement among researchers over whether this prohibition applied only to nurses, or if it also applied to mothers nursing their own infants or toddlers.[43]

By 1850 most "experts" were recommending weaning by eleven months. At this time it was the nursing two-year-olds seen by child care advisors who drew official frowns. During the same period, in 1839, the head of a US exploring expedition to Western Samoa reported children nursing after they were running around, and that children often nursed until they were six.[33]

The Twentieth Century

Theories came and went while some little ones managed to thrive on their mothers' milk and the advice of old wives, advice that we've lost for the most part because it was almost never deemed worth committing to paper. At the beginning of the twentieth century, British writers took high infant mortality into account when they started advising a return to breastfeeding. They believed, however, that overfeeding caused the diarrhea so common in children, not realizing the true cause was contaminated foods. Here began the advice to feed by the clock. Nursing was to be replaced at nine months with diluted milk, with cod liver oil and corn flour added, because the experts thought nursing longer was causing rickets. Toddlers could also have meat soup, stewed fruit, and egg yolk, but little more before age three. This regime held until just before World War II, when babies were put on mixed feeding very early and adult foods at one year. Many poor children were spared some of the ill effects of these changing feeding regimens because of their parents' ignorance of the latest advice.[2]

The pattern in the United States was similar. There is evidence, however, that folk wisdom was also alive and well, because in spite of expert pronouncements, in 1911, 58 percent of babies in the US were still nursing at one year of age, 13 percent of them exclusively breastfed.[38]

Pre-Industrial Societies

Dr. T. Berry Brazelton says of modern, but isolated, Zinacanteco Indians, descendants of the Mayas in the state of Chiapas, México:

> *[When a new baby is born, if the mother] has older children, she continues to nurse them with the right breast, saving the left one for the new baby. Often a two-year-old and the infant will nurse simultaneously. By the age of four or five, children will no longer come to breastfeed at the mother's command, but before that they are expected to respond three or four times a day.*[6]

In the 1980s, children of Aztec or mixed descent in central México received sweetened chamomile or oregano tea from birth, tastes of other foods when they began reaching for them, and continued nursing from 30 to 42 months.[35]

An old tradition in India, anthropologist Alan Berg writes, holds that the longer a child received breast milk, the longer he would live. There some, like the father mentioned earlier in this chapter, were known to nurse seven to nine years. At the beginning of the twentieth century, mothers in China and Japan still nursed their little ones five to six years.[4] Several other writers in the early to mid-twentieth century noted breastfeeding lasting well into childhood in so-called "primitive" societies around the world. Most of the researchers did not specifically study breastfeeding, but when we read their comments about nursing toddlers and children, we can be reasonably certain that children nursing at age three or five—and beyond—did exist, because in many cases researchers saw them or talked with their mothers. Ford's 1940s study of 64 societies estimated an average weaning age of three years.[16] In another study, published in 1953, out of 52 societies, the authors listed only two that traditionally weaned before one year.[26]

These studies weren't done in a way to allow us to determine how most people in a society may have nursed and weaned. There is, however, enough information available for Katherine Dettwyler to estimate that before widespread distribution of infant formula, nursing worldwide continued for about three to four years.[48]

Valerie A. Fildes has shown that the median weaning age in twelve rural African societies in the mid-twentieth century was 24.1 months and in ten urban societies in Africa, 15.6 months. The samples included rural toddlers nursing 36 to 48 months, and urban toddlers, up to 27 months.[12]

Figures for some populations, however, do not represent mothering decisions, but grim necessity. In Bosnia before the recent war, for example, only about 30 percent of mothers started out breastfeeding. The European Journal of Clinical Nutrition reports that during the war (1992-94), 61 of the 70 newborns cared for by one pediatrician at the Dobrinja pediatric clinic in Sarajevo nursed for a year, and 17 nursed longer. "The findings from this study are a tribute to the people of Dobrinja, a settlement on the front line, cut off from the world, who despite terrible suffering were able to protect the new generation."[36]

Worldwide we see the highest incidence and longest duration of breastfeeding among the rural poor, who are frequently the most ill-nourished. Breastfeeding for eighteen months to two years is often the norm among mothers who have little choice but to keep nursing if their children are to have any hope of survival. In some of these places, the New Guinea Highlands for instance, children may continue nursing for up to four years. One survey of breastfeeding in rural Bangladesh showed the median duration of breastfeeding to be 30 months. At the time of the survey, 75 percent of the women were breastfeeding.[38] A 1982 survey in north Bangladesh found a mean duration of 22.5 months and solids were not introduced until a mean age of 13.5 months.[27]

It is hard to distinguish between those who nurse toddlers by preference and those who do so out of necessity. Throughout the developing world a combination of economic need and the desire for consumer goods is drawing mothers into the cash economy. Even so, the majority of infants in the developing world start life at their mothers' breasts, and the duration of breastfeeding remains longer than in industrialized communities.[33] Studies of segments of modern middle and lower income urban populations, published in 1988, found 41 percent of the study group in Bangkok, Thailand, still nursing at 12 months; in Bogotá, Colombia, 28 percent were still nursing at 12 months; in Nairobi, Kenya, 69 percent (49 percent at 15 months); in Semarang, Indonesia, 61 percent at thirteen months (41 percent at 19 months).[51] Among some groups in developing countries, duration of breastfeeding actually increased slightly through the 1970s and 80s.[20]

The poor, overworked, and often undernourished mother for whom breastfeeding is not a choice but a necessity may not get to enjoy all the warm, fuzzy feelings about nursing, especially when time spent with the baby interferes with her ability to feed herself and the rest of her children, or when work she has to do leaves her baby hungry.

> *The breastfeeding component of good infant care can be achieved only when adequate attention is given to the care of the mother. Women wanting to practice exclusive breastfeeding and full breastfeeding with complementation thereafter should be provided with correct information and relieved of nutritional and work burdens that stand in their way. Both the men in their families and society at large have roles to play in providing this support.*[19]

Oh, for a world in which all mothers have the resources and the freedom to choose (or refuse) the kind of life I talk about in this book!

Oceania

In Australia, many middle and upper class mothers make use of readily available breastfeeding support. Working class women, however, often end up weaning early, perhaps unwilling to "admit defeat" and ask for help. Immigrant women may have additional problems in getting help because of limited English.[32]

There are reports from the Solomon Islands of breastfeeding for three years.[33] In rural parts of Fiji, mothers believe it ideal to nurse until the little ones can walk, preferably run. Women of an earlier generation said breastfeeding used to go on longer, until the children could talk. The cities of Fiji, however, have a large tourist economy and have undergone westernization and urbanization. Here breastfeeding is on the decline, although in the mid-80s over half the babies were still nursing at six weeks. In Western Samoa, the weaning age has declined from about two years in the nineteenth century to closer to 15 months.[33]

In the mid-twentieth century there were many reports from Papua New Guinea of children nursing four years or more. Extended nursing was still common enough among the Enga people in the highlands that Thelma Becroft was able to conduct her classic study of the quantity of milk mothers produce at different times during a long course of nursing. Children in the study were nursing freely, mostly at two and three, but some at four years old. At that time, ten percent of Enga toddlers still nursed at five.[3]

In Papua New Guinea's next generation, urban mothers were more likely than rural mothers to use bottles, often weaning before one year to bottles of fruit juice or powdered milk. These mothers are wealthier than rural (island) women, with plenty of food to offer their children, and so are less likely to use the breast as a pacifier in the way island women do.

Unlike women in urban areas, mothers in the islands have to cope with serious malnutrition problems in themselves and their children. Most of these women breastfeed until they conceive again, usually between 15 and 30 months.[33]

Asia

In modern Singapore, breastfeeding declined among the poor from 90 percent in 1951 to 36 percent in 1981.[9] Today, the affluent breastfeed more than the poor and the educated breastfeed more than those with less schooling. The Chinese in Singapore are the ethnic group least likely to breastfeed, at least partially because of the inconvenience and discomfort of the diet and rituals tradition requires for proper nursing[14] and because of a belief that breastfeeding weakens the mother. Formula company advertising also furthers the belief that breastfeeding is only beneficial for six months and that nursing mothers must take special supplements.[15]

One study in India in the 1980s found more mothers in upper than in middle income groups nursing past six months.[40] Another study, in Agra, found different breastfeeding rates, depending on the surroundings, indicating that 52 percent of urban and 74 percent of rural mothers breastfed for at least 12 months. Rural mothers tended to nurse more than two years, but urban mothers did not. And in Agra women of lower socioeconomic status and lower education nursed longer. These mothers said that they continued to nurse because it was "still essential for child's health," "economical," or because "the child demands it." Of these mothers, 27.3 percent said it "enhances child's life span." A few said that continued breastfeeding was "convenient" or "offers contraception." A small number (2.3 percent) were advised to continue by health personnel.[29]

Findings were similar in Karnataka, India, where urban mothers weaned fairly early (13 months) while rural women nursed approximately 21 months. Only 53 percent of urban women nursed past one year, while 85 percent of rural women did so. In rural Jaipur in Rajasthan, the mean age at weaning was 27 months, with more than 92 percent of the toddlers nursing into their third year. Of these mothers, 24.1 percent did not introduce other foods at all during the first year, and this worried the researchers because of malnutrition plaguing both mothers and babies in this population.[46] Nursing patterns are similar in eastern Madhya Pradesh, where 96 percent of babies still nurse at 12 months, 35.4 percent of them exclusively. In spite of widespread malnutrition, these mothers fear introducing solids too soon, believing the foods will upset digestion and cause liver disease.[23]

Breastfeeding rates seem to be low in the cities of modern China. A late 1980s study in urban Shanghai found only ten percent of mothers planning to nurse more than ten months.[34] In a 1992-93 focus group study in Chengdu, Sichuan, out of 363 babies and toddlers, about a third of the four- to six-month-olds were still nursing, and only four percent of twelve-month-olds. Only one baby, seven months old, was exclusively breastfed.[21] Rates in rural Sichuan proved to be higher, with 67 percent still receiving at least some breast milk at 12 months.[22] A 1990 study of over 3,000 children in poor rural areas of Hubei Province reports 75 percent still nursing at one year, 26 percent of two-year-olds, and three percent at three years.[7]

In Vietnam in the early 1990s, the average diet was deficient both in calories and in essential nutrients, but true malnutrition was rare. Nearly all mothers started out breastfeeding and continued for a mean duration of 14.5 months. Government officials asserted that tradition and the high cost of formula protected breastfeeding in Vietnam, but researchers found less positive attitudes among overworked mothers convinced that breastfeeding drained their energy and that a bottle-fed baby would be less demanding. The duration of breastfeeding was longer among educated women, perhaps because they could afford to stay home.[37]

In a 1985-86 study in northern Thailand, most of the mothers started their babies on small supplements of glutinous rice by six weeks of age and slowly added fruit juices, bananas, and dishes containing meat. By one year, 60 percent of the babies studied were still nursing, and seven percent at two.[28]

Duration of breastfeeding in rural South Korea declined from 30 months in 1966 to 22.8 months in 1972. A study published in 1981 reported 35.6 percent of Korean toddlers still nursing at one year.[41]

Africa

A study published in 1985 says that the median duration of breastfeeding in Africa ranged from 14.5 months in Sudan in the north to 20.5 months in Lesotho. Women in cities, especially employed mothers, nursed for a shorter time than rural women.[25]

A more recent study reports that in rural Sudan, mothers nurse an average of two years. There is a lot of malnutrition among these mothers and children, and researchers worry when children in such circumstances don't receive adequate supplementary foods starting at six months, either because parents cannot afford them or don't know they are needed.[44]

Among the nomadic Turkana in Kenya, children stay close to their mothers for three to four years, nursing for two-and-a-half to three years.[18] In Kasongo, Zaire, all babies start out nursing and usually continue through the second year of life.[52]

A 1994 study in Ethiopia found 81.3 percent of rural and 69.1 percent of urban toddlers were nursing with a mean duration of 24.12 months in rural areas and 19.82 months in the cities. Here, as in many places where mothers are overworked and underfed, researchers express concern about malnutrition, both when babies are weaned too soon, that is before some time in the second year, and among those for whom supplementation is delayed too long after the first six months.[49]

In Mali, nursing toddlers are the norm. Upper class women nurse their own children, but relegate child care to nursemaids from among the Bella. Bella women, on the other hand, are rarely separated from their own young children. Babies may receive some food starting at six months, but breast milk is regarded as all that is needed for the first year. Complete weaning takes place at two, at least in town.[25] People in the community of Bamako told Katherine Dettwyler that in some rural villages children were allowed to nurse as long as they wanted to. In Bamako, however, mothers initiated weaning when the baby started asking for the breast or when the mother became pregnant again.[11]

A study of a representative rural population in Zimbabwe published in 1993 found most toddlers nursing 18 to 20 months, with a range of nine to 36 months. Mothers weaned either when they became pregnant or when they believed the child was "old enough."[8]

Traditionally, children in Botswana are breastfed two to three years, but both rates and duration are declining. A large 1984 survey found just over a third still nursing at 24 months. Factors that were related to shorter nursing duration were: more than two children under five in the family, a young mother, a mother who is salaried or self-employed. Duration is declining in urban areas, among better-off families, and among the wage employed. As would be expected, with nursing on the decline, birth intervals are also becoming shorter.[39]

Nearly 100 percent of babies in the Ivory Coast are still nursing at a year. Babies sleep close to their mothers during the whole breastfeeding period. Feeding frequency is higher than in similar West African communities, and breast milk production is higher. (Better nutrition may also be a factor in these mothers' good milk supply.) Children are weaned when they walk independently, about 18 to 24 months.[31]

Among the ¡Kung San of Botswana and Namibia, much studied because they are one of the few peoples on earth who continue to live as hunter-gatherers, frequent nursing continues for three or four years, with about ten percent of children still nursing at four.[48] Nursing is so frequent that without any other form of contraception, births are spaced more than three years apart.[47]

The Modern Near East

Researchers in Saudi Arabia and the United Arab Emirates write that mothers traditionally "breastfed for a long period as it is stated in holy Quran that 'a mother shall breastfeed her child for two years.'"[45] Avicenna (980-1037), an Islamic physician after the time of the Prophet, wrote about breastfeeding:

> *Breast milk and the suckling period is very important, because breast milk looks like the maternal blood which nourishes the fetus, so it is the most convenient food for the baby for his growth and development.*[30]

By the 1990s, however, supplementation often started very early, especially in the cities and among younger mothers, and these mothers tended to wean earlier as well.[1]

A study published in 1993 of a poor urban neighborhood in Cairo, Egypt, describes a community suffering a lot of malnutrition, illness, and death among children. Breastfeeding decisions in this community are influenced by Pharonic, Greek, Prophetic, and European biomedicine.

One example of non-European influences is how the mother's emotions are believed to affect breastfeeding. Grief may reduce milk supply and affect the milk. "Grief milk" or "sadness milk" is believed to cause diarrhea in the nursling. A mother experiencing grief must express some milk manually and discard it before she nurses.

These mothers nurse frequently and mostly wean when the child is old enough to eat adult food, when they run out of milk or the child loses interest because of mixed feeding, or when mothers become pregnant or want to become pregnant. There are also religious considerations about weaning, especially before age two. Mothers describe weaning as a stressful time, a time of conflict with the child, and discuss it with emotion.[24]

A published letter from two Turkish physicians states that the duration of breastfeeding in Turkey is longer and more satisfactory than in Western industrialized countries. But duration is declining among middle and upper middle class urban families. Also, small amounts of supplementary feeding are being started quite early, in the very first weeks of life.[30]

When researchers studied the breastfeeding patterns among the traditionally nomadic Bedouin in the Negev, Israel, these people were undergoing a time of transition to a more sedentary lifestyle, some moving into cities. Among a group of Bedouin children born in 1981, 37 percent of toddlers still nursed at 18 months.[17]

Using What We Learn from Other Cultures

Knowing that people in ancient or less technological cultures do something is not, of course, reason in itself to adopt that part of their lifestyle for ourselves. For example, it would be difficult, I would suggest, to sell many of today's couples on the practice of sexual abstinence during long periods of breastfeeding. Such sexual taboos were found in many cultures in the past and still exist in parts of Africa and the Pacific, including areas of Indonesia.[5]

It is a mistake, I think, to assume that people in pre-industrial societies are necessarily closer to their instincts than a mother watching the soaps or "Masterpiece Theater" on TV while she nurses her toddler. For one thing, parenting instincts seem to be a weak force among large primates. Gorilla mothers, like us, learn mothering by observation. Parenting is for the most part a social function, a learned behavior. That's why you're reading this book.

The second point is that we must, as Dana Raphael points out, understand that non-literate people are not necessarily unintelligent people.[42] The most human of all our instincts is that we must think.

A mother squatting on a dirt floor in front of her cooking fire loves her family and worries about what is best for her children in very much the same way as the mother popping a frozen dinner into the microwave. Both are influenced, for good and for ill, by ancestors and by others in the community. Both do what they conclude is best for themselves and their families. Their choices are often excellent, and practices that may seem bizarre to outsiders can prove to be ideal within the context of an individual family or community. On the other hand, their choices, like yours or mine, sometimes turn out to be wrong-headed and tragic.

For example, people may have parenting styles that are gentle and nurturing. They may get that part right, at least to my way of thinking. Yet these same people may, as people do in many cultures, deny colostrum to the newborn or wean a child who gets diarrhea. Research by non-judgmental anthropologists, who respect parents' rights and ability to make parenting choices for their own families, may find compelling reasons that lead to such practices. On the other hand, there is enough rigorous thinking (i.e., science) about the benefits of colostrum and about what produces the best outcome for a child with diarrhea that it would make no sense for anyone to emulate these particular customs, which are widespread among people who are supposedly living "closer to nature."

All of us are sometimes led astray by our logic. One theory about why so many societies deny colostrum to newborns is that people became alarmed at its cathartic effect. Because diarrhea is often a symptom of serious or even fatal illness, people may have assumed that the laxative effect of colostrum was endangering rather than protecting their babies. Such a conclusion, although incorrect, makes sense.

Ancient customs are sometimes abandoned for better ones, and some customs of "primitive" peoples, just like some "modern" practices, outlive whatever useful function they may once have had. They may end up working against people's best interests. The experience of other cultures widens our range of choices, but we must evaluate any practice we are considering on its own merits.

Still, knowing that in the past nursing almost always continued beyond infancy is proof that extended nursing is not debilitating in any significant way. In fact, records of illness and death among weanlings indicate just the opposite. Any serious harmful effects of long-term nursing would have crippled the entire ancient world. Knowing that children who are no longer babies still nurse in non-industrialized communities around the world today gives us a feeling of sisterhood and continuity in our mothering style. For, although we may have broken away from the child-rearing patterns of the immediate past, we join with mothers worldwide in preserving a tradition of tender nurturing from the beginning of mankind into yet another century.

References

1 Al-Mazrou, Y. Y., Aziz, K. M. S. and Khalil, M. Breastfeeding and weaning practices in Saudi Arabia. *Journal of Tropical Pediatrics* October 1994; 40:268-69.

2 Anderson, S. Changing practices in the weaning of babies in Britain. *Professional Care of Mother and Child* 1997; 7(3):59.

3 Becroft, T. Child-rearing practices in the highlands of New Guinea: a longitudinal study of breast feeding. *Medical Journal of Australia* September 23, 1967; 2:601.

4 Berg, A. *The Nutrition Factor.* Washington, D.C.: The Brookings Institute, 1973; 78.

5 Berg, A. and Brems, S. A case for promoting breastfeeding in projects to limit fertility. *World Bank Technical Paper Number 102.* The World Bank, Washington, D.C., 1989; 9

6 Brazelton, T. B. Parenting in another culture. *Redbook* May 1979; 153(1):94.

7 Chen, J. and Taren, D. Early feeding practices and the nutrition status of preschool children in rural Hubei Province, China. *Food and Nutrition Bulletin* 1995; 16(1):42.

8 Cosminsky, S., Mhloyi, M. and Ewbank, D. Child feeding practices in a rural area of Zimbabwe. *Social Science and Medicine* April 1993; 36(7):942.

9 Counsilman, J. J. et al. Breast feeding among poor Singaporeans. *Journal of Tropical Pediatrics* December 1986; 32:310.

10 Davidson, W. D. A brief history of infant feeding. *The Journal of Pediatrics* July-December 1953; 43:74-76, 30, 34-35, 39, 43, 47-48.

11 Dettwyler, K. A. Infant feeding in Mali, West Africa: Variations in belief and practice. *Social Science and Medicine* 1986; 23:657.

12 Fildes, V. A. *Breasts, Bottles and Babies: A History of Infant Feeding.* Edinburgh, Edinburgh: University Press, 1986; 12, 391-92, 366, 328-42, 99-100, 247, 370, 365.

13 Fitzsimmons, S. P. et al. Immunoglobulin A subclasses in infants' saliva and in saliva and milk from their mothers. *Journal of Pediatrics* April 1994; 124(4):571.

14 Fok, D. Cross cultural practice and its influence on breastfeeding—the Chinese culture. *Breastfeeding Review* May 1996; 4(1):13-15.

15 Fok, D. Breastfeeding in Singapore. *Breastfeeding Review* 1997; 5(2):28.

16 Ford, C. S. *A Comparative Study of Human Reproduction.* Yale University Publications in Anthropology 32. New Haven, CT: Human Relations Area Files Press, 1945; 78, 84.

17 Forman, M. R. et al. Undernutrition among Bedouin Arab infants: the Bedouin infant feeding study. *American Journal of Clinical Nutrition* March 1990; 51(3):347.

18 Gray, S. J. Infant care and feeding. *Nomadic Turkana: Biobehavior and Ecology of a Pastoralist Society.* Ed. M. A. Little and P. W. Leslie. Oxford: Oxford University Press, 1996; 247.

19 Greiner, T. Sustained breastfeeding, complementation, and care. *Food and Nutrition Bulletin* 1995; 16(4):318.

20 Grummer-Strawn, L. M. The effect of changes in population characteristics on breastfeeding trends in fifteen developing countries. *International Journal of Epidemiology* 1996; 25(1):99, 100.

21 Guldan, G. S. et al. Breastfeeding practices in Chengdu, Sichuan, China. *Journal of Human Lactation* 1995; 11(1):12.

22 Guldan, G. S. et al. Weaning practices and growth in rural Sichuan infants: A positive deviance study. *Journal of Tropical Pediatrics* June 1993; 39(3):170.

23 Gurudeva, R. K. et al. Infant feeding practices in Roe. *Indian Journal of Pediatrics* 1982; 49:817-18.

24 Harrison, G. G. et al. Breastfeeding and weaning in a poor urban neighborhood in Cairo, Egypt: maternal beliefs and perceptions. *Social Science and Medicine* 1993; 36(38):1066.

25 Hill, A. G., Ed. *Population, Health and Nutrition in the Sahel: Issues in the Welfare of selected West African Communities.* London: KPI, Ltd. 1985; 355, 193-94.

26 Huggins, K. and Ziedrich, L. *The Nursing Mother's Guide to Weaning.* Boston: The Harvard Common Press, 1994; 127, 6.

27 Isherwood, R. J., Dimond, C., and Longhurst, D. Breast feeding and weaning practices in relation to nutritional status of under-5 children in north Bangladesh. *Journal of Tropical Pediatrics* February 1988; 34:29-30.

28 Jackson, D. A. et al. Weaning practices and breast-feeding duration in Northern Thailand. *British Journal of Nutrition* 1992; 67:151-61.

29 Kalra, K., Kaira, A. and Dayal, R. S. Breast feeding practices in different residential economic and educational groups. *Indian Pediatrics* 1982; 19:422-24.

30 Koctörk, T., Zetterström, R. (reply) Yurdakök, M. (letter) Breastfeeding in Islam. *Acta Paediatrica Scandinavica* 1988; 77:907-08.

31 Lauber, E. and Reinhardt, M.C. Prolonged lactation performance in a rural community of the Ivory Coast. *Journal of Tropical Pediatrics* 1981; 27:76.

32 Manderson, L. To Nurse and to Nurture: Breastfeeding in Australian Society. *Breastfeeding, Child Health and Child Spacing Cross-cultural Perspectives.* Ed. V. Hull and M. Simpson. London: Croom Helm, 1985; 162-86.

33 Marshall, L. B., Ed. *Infant Care and Feeding in the South Pacific.* New York: Gordon and Breach, 1985; 298, 321, 241, 280, 255-68, 297-98, 196, 199.

34 Meehan, K. F. Breast feeding in an urban district in Shanghai, People's Republic of China. A descriptive study of feeding patterns and hospital practices as they relate to breast-feeding. *Journal of Tropical Pediatrics* April 1990; 36(2):76.

35 Millard, A. V. and Graham, M. A. Abrupt weaning reconsidered: Evidence from central Mexico. *Journal of Tropical Pediatrics* August 1985; 31:230-1.

36 Moro, D. Birthweight and breast feeding of babies born during the war in one municipal area of Sarajevo. *European Journal of Clinical Nutrition* 49, Supp. 2 (1995), S37-39.

37 Morrow, M. Breastfeeding in Vietnam: Poverty, tradition, and economic transition. *Journal of Human Lactation* 1996; 12(2):97.

38 Neville, M. C. and Neifert, M. R. *Lactation: Physiology, Nutrition and Breastfeeding.* New York: Plenum Press, 1983; 14. T. Woodbury, R. M. Causal Factors in Infant Mortality. *Children's Bureau Publication No. 142* Washington, D.C.: US Government Printing Office, 1925.

39 Omondi, L. O., Persson, L. A. and Staugard, F. Determinants for breast feeding and bottle feeding in Botswana. *Journal of Tropical Pediatrics* February 1990; 36(1):31-32.

40 Pant, I. and Chothia, K. Maternal knowledge regarding breastfeeding and weaning practices. *Indian Journal of Pediatrics* May 1990; 57(3):399.

41 Park, T. K. and Berlin, P. Prevalence of exclusive and extended breastfeeding among rural Korean women. *Yonsei Medical Journal* 1981; 22(2):110, 112.

42 Raphael, D. *Only Mothers Know.* Westport, CT: Greenwood Press, 1985; 17.

43 Ryerson, A. J. Medical advice on child-rearing, 1550-1900. *Harvard Educational Review* 1961; 13:302-23.

44 Sayed, Z. T. A., Latham, M. C. and Roe, D. A. Prolonged breastfeeding without the introduction of supplementary feeding. *Journal of Tropical Pediatrics* 1995; 41(1):29-33.

45 Shahraban A. et al. Patterns of breast feeding and weaning in the United Arab Emirate. *Journal of Tropical Pediatrics* February 1991; 37(1):15.

46 Singh, M. B., Haldiya, K. R. and Lakshminarayana, J. Infant feeding and weaning practices in some semi-arid rural areas of Rajasthan. *Indian Medical Association* November 1997; 95(11):578.

47 Stern, J. M. et al. Nursing behaviour, prolactin and postpartum amenorrhoea during prolonged lactation in American and !Kung mothers. *Clinical Endocrinology* September 1986; 25(3):abs.

48 Stuart-Macadam, P. and Dettwyler, K. A. Ed. *Breastfeeding: Biocultural Perspectives.* . NY: Aldine de Gruyter, 1995; 39-73, 100, 75-99, 88, 81, 43.

49 Tessema T. and Hailu, A. Childhood feeding practice in North Ethiopia. *East African Medical Journal* February 1997; 74(2):94-95.

50 Treckel, P. A. Breastfeeding and maternal sexuality in colonial America. *Journal of Interdisciplinary History* 1989; 20(1):36, 29.

51 Winikoff, B., Castle, M. A. and Laukaran, V. H. Ed. *Feeding Infants in Four Societies: Causes and Consequences of Mothers' Choices.* New York: Greenwood Press, 1988; 24.

52 Van Lerberghe, W. *Kasongo: Child Mortality and Growth in a Small African Town.* London, England: Smith Gordon, 1990; 62.

Nursing Your Toddler—How?

chapter six

When Nursing Presents Challenges

Nursing and Automobile Safety

How I miss the "good old days" when we just climbed into our cars with nursing babies in arms and took off, nursing as we rode. It was convenient, of course, but also quite dangerous. Today good sense—and the law, in most places—demands more caution and planning.

When we are accustomed to a parenting style that doesn't require our babies and toddlers to cry very much, it can be very difficult to teach them something as clearly "unnatural" as allowing themselves to be strapped into a plastic shell. But unless you want to stay home all the time, you have to teach them. From the beginning you have to insist that when the car moves, everybody, including the littlest passenger, be strapped in. He is strapped in. You are strapped in. Every time. This is not negotiable. If he has a hard time learning, you need to keep your trips short and/or break them with frequent stops. Few of us can safely maneuver through many miles of freeway traffic with a miserable child screaming from the back seat.

Today babies ride in rear-facing infant seats that make nursing all but impossible, even when mother is not the driver. Front-facing toddler seats aren't nursing friendly either. So on long trips, not being able to nurse on the road can be a dreadful problem. Driving with a crying baby or child is nerve-wracking and dangerous. Stopping along highways and in some neighborhoods is also dangerous. In the part of the

97

world where I live, there are often long distances between the relative
safety of highway rest areas or fast food restaurants.

We clearly need a good alternative to dangerous, and sometimes
illegal, practices that I hear about parents resorting to these days. I want
to challenge and encourage inventors and engineers to devise effective
restraints that allow mothers of infants and toddlers to nurse safely
while they are passengers in moving vehicles.

There may be no "natural" approach to this unnatural situation.
As much as I dislike the nuisance of pacifiers, I think that if I had a baby
today, I might try using one in the car, that is if the baby were willing.
The hardest times, of course, are when you must drive alone with your
child. Having you or someone else as a passenger in the back seat with
the little one can make the trip a lot easier. One thing in your favor is
that so many babies and toddlers find car travel soothing and will learn
to sleep on the road. If you're not driving, you can sometimes calm a
small baby by letting her suck your clean finger or knuckle.

With toddlers you have more options. Keep a bag of soft, not-too-
noisy toys in the car, and keep these special, as car-only toys, in order to
extend the period in which they are of interest. Before long trips I always
stocked up on a lot of very cheap new toys and games to stave off
boredom and fussiness. Some families have special tapes of children's
music or stories for car trips. Finger foods can be a useful diversion, but
beware of foods such as carrot sticks that could cause choking at a
sudden stop. Dry or salty treats can lead to thirst and then, with older
children, to bathroom emergencies.

Nurse right before you leave. Try negotiating with your toddler
about when and where you will nurse the next time (when you get to
Grandma's house, when you get to the visitors' center just across the
border, etc.). If it doesn't work this trip, you are at least moving toward
the time when it will.

If you stop to nurse a sleepy child, you may want to try nursing
him in his seat. The designs of the seats don't make this easy, but in a
safe parking area you can pretzel yourself into whatever position is
necessary to accomplish this feat. The advantage is that you can avoid
waking him by having to put him back into the seat and harness once he
has dropped off.

One mother wrote about driving along and hearing the
unwelcome click of buckles being opened by little hands. After that, the
parents explained to the children "that if they could get the straps
unbuckled, they could buckle them too; so they very proudly would climb
into their seats and buckle themselves in."

Teaching your child to use restraints pays off when you have one
or more toddlers and young children. Think what it used to be like trying
to drive with children bouncing around loose, parents constantly yelling

at them to sit down! Teaching automobile safety is not always easy, but the trouble you go through is definitely worth it. Your chances of keeping everyone alive and whole are much improved, and in the long run travel will be easier.

Breast Problems

Nipple Discomfort or Pain

One good thing about nursing a toddler is that sore nipples are usually behind you. Your body is used to nursing, and you and your child both know how to go about it. So it can be a surprise, and seem really unfair, if nipple pain decides to pay a return visit, or what may be for some a first visit.

Occasionally a mother will remark on a change in how her nipples feel when her toddler nurses, somehow different from the way they felt when he was an infant. The older child's nursing is uncomfortable sometimes, and tends to keep her awake at night. For many, nipple tenderness accompanies ovulation or the premenstrual period and subsides with the next stage in the cycle. If you are sure you are not pregnant, you may want to ask your doctor about a mild pain reliever and anti-inflammatory, such as ibuprofen, to use mid-cycle if needed.

Another explanation for the change some mothers notice is the decrease in milk supply coupled with the toddler's great efficiency in milking the breast. Nursing is comfortable as long as at least a bit of milk is flowing. As your little one grows older and nurses less frequently your production of milk decreases eventually to a point at which you no longer manufacture milk quickly enough to keep the sinuses behind your nipple from becoming completely empty when your child nurses for more than a few minutes. Without the lubrication of the flowing milk some mothers find nursing a little bit uncomfortable.

When nursing does not feel good because of no milk flowing, it helps to switch to the other breast if your child is willing (and when half-asleep he may not be). The other breast will have at least a little milk, so switching can relieve the discomfort temporarily—perhaps long enough for him to finish.

Such nipple discomfort, if you ever experience it at all, will probably not occur every time. You are most likely to feel minor pain when you are, for reasons of your own, impatient for this particular nursing session to be finished. Perhaps you tense yourself in eagerness to get away, or perhaps you focus your attention on the nursing and its sensations. At other times, when you are indifferent to the nursing or enjoying it, there may be no discomfort at all.

It is not uncommon to experience, on occasion, sore spots where the child's teeth rub. Soreness caused by your child's teeth should get better quickly if you consistently pat your nipples dry, apply a small amount of modified lanolin, e.g., Lansinoh for Breastfeeding Mothers®, and nurse in different positions so that his teeth do not rub the same part of your breast every time.

Occasionally after nursing for a year or more, a mother will develop true sore nipples like those which some mothers experience in their babies' first few weeks. If this happens to you, check all the possibilities a brand new mother checks—use of soap or alcohol on nipples, or detergent or fabric softener in your bra or other clothing, a deodorant, hair spray, or cologne causing irritation, inadequate air circulation around nipples because of plastic in bra liners or nursing pads.

Teething. For some, sore nipples in the toddler years are once again a matter of mechanics, much like the newborn period. A child's sucking may change as teeth emerge and make it necessary to reevaluate nursing positions. Make sure he is drawing the nipple well into his mouth and milking the sinuses behind the nipple, not the nipple itself. Check to be sure he is covering his bottom teeth with his tongue, not leaving them bare. Also be sure he is not sucking in his lower lip.

Sometimes toddlers try to combine gymnastics with nursing and just get too rough. Most of the gyrations are relatively painless, but they can result in nipple discomfort that is clearly related to nursing position.

The good thing about working on nursing position with a toddler rather than a newborn is that you can explain what you want her to do. The bad thing is that toddlers tend to have their minds made up about how they want to nurse. You'll want to be gentle with her, and patient. She doesn't mean to hurt you, so don't blame her. At the same time, however, you need to insist on your right to nurse without unnecessary discomfort. If you have to terminate a nursing because she won't do as you ask, offer to nurse again, and soon. Let her know you're glad to nurse her, but that she must do it in a way that doesn't hurt you.

Eczema. Another possible cause for sore nipples in a mom with an older nursling is eczema. Some mothers with this kind of allergic tendency may get a painful rash from contact with foods left in a child's mouth. If this seems to be a problem for you, check your child's mouth before nursing and make sure it is empty.

Pregnancy. Early pregnancy can produce nipple tenderness, too. See "Nipple Pain," in Chapter 7, for discussion of nipple pain in pregnancy.

Milk blisters. At any stage of nursing some mothers may experience painful white blisters at the tip of the nipple. These "milk blisters" are caused by a milk duct blocked with caked milk or a very thin layer of skin. Treatment involves softening the blockage so it will clear out on its own. Between nursings, soak the nipple in warm water and/or apply warm, moist compresses to soften the plug or covering skin. Nurse frequently, and try different positions. The combination of milk let-down and the child's strong sucking should open the duct.

If it doesn't open in a few days, have a medical practitioner open it under sterile conditions. As tempting as it may be to undertake this very simple procedure yourself, you shouldn't risk introducing an infection from your hands into a milk duct. As painful as a milk blister may be, the breast infection that could result would be worse.

Fungal infections (thrush/yeast). Thrush, that fungal scourge for some mothers of newborns, can reappear later. It can also be a vexing problem at the beginning of tandem nursing, when the newborn may infect your nipples, and then your nipples pass the fungus on to the toddler. The most familiar symptoms of this organism in the mother are the itchy or painful symptoms of a vaginal yeast infection (*monilial*

UDDER SIDE, MOMMY, UDDER SIDE!

vulvovaginitis). When it affects the nipples, it causes redness and soreness (possibly itching or burning) which is often severe, and sometimes a rash with tiny blisters. It usually affects both breasts.

If you develop nipple pain that lasts throughout the nursing, not just during the latch-on, seek the advice of a knowledgeable health care provider.

The nipple and vaginal symptoms are caused by the same organism. Such an infection is more common in a mother who lives in a warm, moist climate, is diabetic, has been treated with antibiotics or steroids (e.g., for asthma), or takes oral contraceptives. Other contributing factors in the mother include a sore or cracked nipple; warm, moist nipple environment (nursing pads, or bra that stays damp with milk); a diet with lots of dairy products, sweets, or artificial sweeteners; or a diet deficient in iron, folic acid, and vitamins A, B, C, and K.

Infection can follow antibiotic treatment of mother or child, or occasionally even of someone else in the family. Antibiotics disrupt the body's natural defenses against the ubiquitous fungus and allow it to take hold. Some infections seem to result from lengthy courses of antibiotics in the mother, even in the distant past.

If you have sore nipples caused by thrush, your child is almost certainly infected as well, although he may not be bothered by it. He may have a persistent perianal diaper rash, white patches inside his mouth, cheeks, or on his tongue, a whitish sheen inside his lips or in the saliva. His mouth could be sore, or he could be a little gassy. On the other hand, he may show no symptoms at all.

Anti-fungal treatment should involve both mother and nursling(s) and must last the full length of time recommended for the medication, although symptoms will probably disappear sooner. Let nipples dry between feedings by changing nursing pads at every feeding or leaving nipples exposed to air. Some stubborn cases may require systemic antifungal medication.

At least once a day, wash household items that go into your child's mouth, including rubber nipples or pacifiers, teething toys or other toys, cups, and eating utensils. Use hot, soapy water followed by scalding or boiling; a dishwasher is best if available because of its high water temperature and strong detergent. Also, be meticulous about washing your hands after using the bathroom, diaper changing, etc., to avoid spreading and reinfection.

Some much less common rashes or blisters. Two troublesome infectious conditions mothers occasionally have to deal with are impetigo and herpes simplex. Herpes can be fatal to newborns, but at any age you want to avoid spreading the virus. Uninfected people must not touch skin that is sore from either of these organisms. If either infection should break out on the nipple or areola, breastfeeding needs to be interrupted on the affected breast only for a few days to avoid infecting the child. Hand-express carefully so as not to open the lesion. When these infections are active close to the nipple, pumping or expressing from the affected breast may contaminate the milk, so the milk should be discarded. Consult a health care provider knowledgeable about breastfeeding for more specific advice on healing yourself and protecting your child.

Skin irritation caused by substances, such as poison ivy, on the breast or anywhere else on your body, is no danger to your child once you have bathed and washed the irritants out of all contaminated clothing. But if there are blisters or broken skin on the nipple or areola, you must take steps to avoid infection in the affected skin. You should get treatment immediately and not nurse on that breast until the blisters or broken skin heal. If you can express milk during the temporary weaning without opening the lesions, do so. In the case of poison ivy you need not worry about transmission of the condition, so you can safely give any milk you express to your child.[6]

Breast Infection (Mastitis)

Mastitis or breast infection is a painful inflammation of the breast, usually accompanied by fever, or so say the coldly clinical folk who write descriptions of such conditions. One necessary qualification of the coldly clinical is that they must never have suffered from the illness in question, or their description might be considerably more colorful. A less clinical definition of mastitis is a miserably sore breast, the aches and chills that go with fever, and an overall feeling of "Why did this have to happen to me?"

The best treatment for such an ailment is prevention, and most mothers have learned by the time they have been nursing a year or more pretty much what they individually must do and what they must avoid in order not to come down with a breast infection. What seems to bring this problem on varies from individual to individual. Some always have to be very careful about the fit of bras and other clothing. Many have to avoid overexertion or exhaustion. And most have to avoid allowing too long an interval to pass between nursings.

As your child gets older it continues to be important to remember the things you might do ("nursing indiscretions" Dr. E. Robbins Kimball named them) that could bring you down with mastitis. For instance, it is tempting to wear that pretty bikini you wore before you were pregnant now that you are all firm and back in shape. Yet you must treat that bikini top the way you would any new bra—with suspicion. If it does not fit you just right, you may not be able to wear it yet.

Avoiding exhaustion is a challenge for mothers of small children. For many women there is no more difficult time to keep from overdoing than during their children's second or third year. Frequently, women's expectations for themselves increase now that the baby is "older," and other people begin to expect more, too. Actually, you are likely to accomplish more beyond the business of caring for your child in her first year than in her second. Children between one and two, or even between one and three sometimes, require more physical exertion on the mother's part than at any other time in their lives. Many of them, besides being busy and needing lots of attention, nurse frequently so that milk production remains at a high level. A mother who undertakes too much— more for some, less for others—beyond nursing and caring for her child may find herself in bed with a throbbing breast and fever. Coming down with mastitis is not the end of the world, of course, but it is really uncomfortable and should serve as a warning to slow down and not ask so much of yourself right now.

As children grow older, their nursing patterns tend to become less regular, and there may be longer stretches between nursings. Sleeping through the night may produce a period of several hours without nursing. Whenever such an interval develops, you need to be aware of your body's reaction. Do your breasts become overfull? Do you begin to feel aches or any sign of breast tenderness?

If so, gently encourage your child to nurse immediately and often to keep the sore breast drained until you feel normal again. Cutting back on the amount of solids that you offer your child for a day or two can help, too. Then avoid the long time between certain nursings for a while by offering to nurse your child maybe a time or two during the night, or during the day—whichever is causing you problems.

Most mothers of children past about the middle of their second year adapt easily to uneven nursing patterns such as nursing only during the day, or only during the evening and night. A few do not. Keep in mind that a nursing relationship involves the needs of two people. It is quite right for you to let your child drop nursings, and yet also right that you should ask your child to nurse when you need him to help you avoid an illness. If he resists, however, don't try to force him. Pump or hand-express instead, just to the point of comfort.

For almost all mothers well-fitting clothes, adequate rest, and nursing patterns that are not too wildly irregular are all it takes to avoid mastitis. On rare occasion there is a mother, however, who is so subject to breast infection that her body cannot tolerate the normal reduction in nursing frequency that occurs in natural weaning.

If you are in the weaning process and find yourself ill every time your child drops a nursing, first of all you should upgrade your own self-care and diet and do what you can to get yourself in the best condition possible. Eat better—especially fresh fruits, juices, and vegetables. Suspend some project you have going right now so that you can have time for extra rest and enjoyable exercise. Taking extra care of yourself is a good investment, especially at such a time. Almost always, doing these things will be enough to help you through the weaning period. Only if you continue to have repeated breast infections would it become necessary to take the measures described in the next paragraph.

When you suspect a sore breast is beginning again, get off your feet, apply heat to the affected breast, and encourage your child to nurse frequently until all soreness is gone. Call your doctor if you need to. If he feels you need an antibiotic, take all the doses that are prescribed, and continue nursing often. If this is the third infection in the same place, have the doctor check your breast. In rare cases a breast tumor has been known to cause repeated blockage and infection.

Once you are well and assured that your breast is basically okay, think about the nursing pattern you had before you became ill. Prior to the time your child dropped a feeding (or more than one sometimes) and your breast became sore, how often was she nursing? From that you can figure out the maximum interval between nursings that your body can tolerate. When your child nurses, check the clock, add your maximum time interval to the present time, and make a note—mental or written—of the time you have just calculated. If your child has not asked to nurse by this time, then ask her to nurse. Be sure to do this every time you nurse. Of course you can nurse more frequently, but not less.

You should be able to avoid mastitis by taking life easy and not going too long between nursings. As the weeks go on you will gradually be able to let your child increase the maximum time interval that you can allow without nursing so that she will have the opportunity to move toward weaning in her own time, but still in a way that your body can tolerate.

Not nearly so rare as the mother whose system cannot handle the pace of natural weaning is the mother who takes off on an outing, maybe leaving her child at home, or sometimes even taking him along. In the excitement one or both may forget that they usually nurse one or more times, and much to mother's surprise, she has a sore breast the next day. You mustn't forget that you are a nursing mother on such occasions. Be sure to take time out to nurse or to express milk while you are out. You will be better off the next day if you do.

Breast Cancer

Breast cancer is quite rare in nursing mothers, but it is so important to catch this condition early that you must never ignore possible signs of the disease. I know, because my own family lost the mother of a nursing toddler to breast cancer.

You should always do monthly breat self-exams. Right after your toddler nurses is the best time. Your breasts will feel lumpy as long as you are lactating because of the filling and emptying milk ducts, but with regular checking you will get to know your own breasts. If you find a persistent lump, even a small one, do all the things you do to clear a plugged duct. Urge your child, if she will, to nurse more frequently on that breast. Apply a little heat and change nursing positions. (See THE WOMANLY ART OF BREASTFEEDING for more on treating plugged ducts.) If the lump stays the same or increases in size over about three days, have it checked.

It is not true that a baby's willingness to nurse from a breast proves it is cancer-free, so see your doctor about it. The lump is almost certainly something unimportant, like an inflammation, a fibrous mass, or a milk-filled cyst, but don't take any chances. If you need a biopsy to be sure, have it done. There is no need to quit nursing for this procedure. See THE WOMANLY ART OF BREASTFEEDING or consult La Leche League or your lactation consultant for more about nursing and biopsy or breast surgery.

Another very rare cancer, called inflammatory breast carcinoma, has on occasion been confused with a breast infection in a nursing mother. This happens because, although there is no fever, the breast reddens and swells as with an infection. To know for sure that you're not dealing with this most unlikely condition, if symptoms of mastitis don't clear after a ten-day course of antibiotics, have the breast examined by a doctor. If the skin of the breast starts to become pitted like the peel of an orange, see the doctor immediately. [8,14]

Mammograms of a lactating breast are hard to read, but there is probably some value in having them on the schedule recommended for your age group anyway. If it is time for your regular mammogram, or if one is recommended to help evaluate a lump, it may be necessary to shop around for a radiologist experienced with reading nursing mothers' mammograms. The x-rays do not affect your milk or interfere in any way with breastfeeding. Ultrasound can also be used to investigate a lump in the breast without interfering with nursing.

Right before a breast exam or other screening procedure, if your child will cooperate, nurse at the office or facility to minimize the amount of milk in the ducts. If you need an exam that requires the injection of a dye or chemical marker, consult your health care provider about the safety of this agent for your child.

I know it is unpleasant to read about such frightening possibilities, but I think all of you who never need any of this information will agree it's worth a little scare if including it here makes it possible for just one nursing toddler to grow up with mom because she knew what to watch for and got treatment in time.

Sensual/Sexual Aspects of Breastfeeding

We have so sterilized and idealized nursing in our minds that many of us have lost sight of the fact that breastfeeding is a sensual behavior for both mother and baby—beautifully and wholesomely sensuous. Yes, it is above all a nurturing relationship, not a prurient one, as evidenced by the great number of religious icons that depict a mother with bare breast and a child in arms. Despite what our puritan background may shout at us from inside our heads, it is not bad for something to feel good. It is not bad for nursing to feel good to mother, nor is it bad for it to feel good to the child.

Toddlers explore their bodies, sometimes while nursing, and this exploration will include genitals. In some cultures a mother may be startled at seeing her son's little penis stiffen, or at seeing her daughter fingering her private parts. These sensuous behaviors do not portend anything evil growing in our children, and in some cultures they seem to go unnoticed. John Bowlby describes these as "fragments" of reproductive behavior and observed them among the young of several species, not just humans. In the young, he writes, these behaviors are "non-functional and become so only when they become integrated with other systems."[2] They merely indicate that parts of what these immature beings will need for grown-up sexual behavior are present and in working order. Some research indicates that genital play is more likely to be present in well-mothered toddlers and absent "in cases of maternal unresponsiveness or neglect."[7]

We don't need to stop such activities in our children, just distract them gently and teach them over time that these are private behaviors. Dr. William Sears recommends treating touching of genitals like nose-picking, not as something depraved and dirty, just as something people don't do in the presence of others.[13] In the meantime, if the child's behavior is disturbing to you at a time when it is impractical to work on distraction (when you need to get him to sleep, for example) cover him up with a blanket, or clothing so you don't have to watch. Some parents of older toddlers require them to be wearing something, underwear at least, before they can nurse.

A few decades ago, several authors reported that mothers sometimes become sexually aroused while the baby is nursing, especially as their nurslings grow older and nurse less frequently. On rare occasion a mother was said to experience orgasm while nursing. As best I can tell, such reports are exaggerated. If there are more than a very few mothers having such strong responses to nursing, they are not telling me about it. The only experience of this sort I have heard about came to me secondhand, from a La Leche League Leader:

> Another mother I know well was dismayed to find herself having orgasms when she nursed her three-year-old son. Though she was pregnant again, she was committed to nursing her son until he no longer needed it, but she didn't enjoy the stimulation. In this situation, as in others where mother is feeling "uneasy" . . . about nursing, she can take her feelings as a cue to somehow modify the nursing relationship, i.e., shorter nursings, postponement, etc. This is the tack this mother took, and her son ended up weaning happily later in the pregnancy.

Sadly, some people turn reports of breastfeeding's sensuality against nursing mothers. One mother writes that her mother-in-law insinuated sexual pleasure was her reason for nursing. "Nothing could be further from the truth," the mother writes. "Nursing was hard work for me, a pleasure only because it made me feel good that I was doing the right thing for my child." Another mother with experience nursing through toddlerhood comments: "If you're looking for sexual gratification, there are certainly lots more efficient and effective ways to get it than from nursing a toddler!"

Ruth A. Lawrence in her medical text cites the various reports of sexual arousal while nursing, but then goes on to say that few women experience strong sexual arousal and that it is either "uncommon" or "under-reported."[6]

"Uncommon" seems more likely. La Leche League Leader Esther Schiedel writes of her research for a course in human sexuality:

> In my own totally unscientific survey of about ten people on whether they had ever experienced this (sexual arousal from breastfeeding) everyone said no. When I asked if they had heard about it from others, there were a few yeses. A couple told of mothers who stopped nursing toddlers because of this. One said she thought she might have experienced this once with her toddler, but that it might also have been part of a dream.

She goes on to say, "I wonder about the possible role of hormones and returning fertility; about changes in frequency of nursing and even style of nursing; I also wonder about the role of culture and of personal expectation. Are mothers who hear that nursing may be sexually arousing more likely to experience it themselves?"

Katherine Dettwyler's argument in "Beauty and the Breast" would suggest that the answer is yes. Dettwyler makes a case for erotic sensitivity in the breast being a learned, cultural response. In many societies, she writes, breasts are not considered erotic, do not seem particularly sensitive, and play no part in sexual interactions between men and women.³ Dana Raphael notes, for instance, that the Igorot language in the Philippines does not have any expression for cosmetic properties of the breast, having a single word for breast, which is also used to mean "nipple," "breast milk," and "breastfeeding."¹¹ Nor is breast eroticism a feature of culture in Samoa. "In rural villages breasts are often exposed, with no sexual connotation."⁹

But learned or "built-in," arousal does occur sometimes during nursing:

> *I experienced this recently. It's happened mildly more than once, but there is one time in particular that was a bit more "annoying." I got my period back when my little girl was twenty-three months old (she is twenty-six months old now). Perhaps some hormones or something to do with the return of fertility partly helps explain why I felt aroused. I think it may also have something to do with the way she breastfeeds. She seems to suck differently sometimes, more lightly, perhaps closer to the nipple. We aren't so careful with positioning these days as we used to be!*

A nursling not positioned well, nursing the nipple instead of the ducts behind it, can be a factor. The tip of the nipple is the only part of the breast with any really organized nerve ends. So you should be able to reduce the sensation by repositioning the child so the nipple is comfortably in the back of his mouth.

I know from nursing my own toddlers it can occasionally be mildly frustrating to find yourself aroused by nursing at a time when you really can't do anything about it. The feelings are harmless, of course. Scheidel writes that it is helpful for people to "understand that their sexuality is under their control. Physical signs of arousal have to be interpreted under the context they occur in. Both men and women exhibit physical signs of arousal at times when they are not mentally interested in sexual interaction—random arousal. Instead of worrying about those physical signs or interpreting them as sexual, we can choose to see them as sensual experiences or simply random occurrences."

What goes on in your head if you ever feel this way cannot possibly hurt or confuse your child. Thoughts without action are harmless. Nor do you need to fear embarrassment: No one has ever told me that they have experienced feelings of sexual excitement anywhere but in comfortable, private settings. In the best possible situation, after nursing a toddler to sleep, it may be possible to segue into real foreplay with your partner. In that case, the feelings wouldn't turn out to be annoying at all.

Most of the time, however, the pleasure of nursing is tranquil and peaceful—sensual, yes, but not at all erotic.

Nursing and Sexual Development

People sometimes come up with far-fetched "risks" of extended nursing. In some places people believe that nursing "too long" will make the child stupid. (In fact, increasing duration of breastfeeding up to the age of fifty weeks has been associated with a small but statistically significant *increase* in cognitive development,[12] and there is no reason to believe the trend necessarily stops at this age.)

Also without basis in fact, some parents in the USA have been told that nursing too long will make the child homosexual. No matter what you may hear, there is no evidence that breastfeeding (or not breastfeeding) has any effect at all on sexual orientation. It is clear in ancient writings from societies where extended breastfeeding was the norm that some people were homosexual. In industrialized society, after generations of widespread experience with early weaning (most babies weaned at birth), probably still about the same percentage of people are homosexual.

As one mother who nursed all her children well into toddlerhood wrote, "My son who is gay actually nursed for a shorter time than my other children." Another mother wrote about her former nursing toddler, "The long nursing relationship taught me a lot of lessons about respecting and loving my child for the person she is." Although not a factor in sexual orientation, a long and satisfying nursing relationship does help families form the bonds of love and trust that give them a solid footing for facing the challenges of the growing-up years, whatever those challenges may be.

Social Service Agencies and the Courts

Some parents today are afraid to admit to anyone that their toddlers are nursing for fear of interference by misinformed representatives of social service agencies. This fear, fortunately, has proved to be largely unfounded. Elizabeth Baldwin, Esq., Director of La Leche League International's Legal Associates Program, reports that no social service agency in the United States has found extended breastfeeding to be abuse or neglect, even up through age eight.

On the other hand, the pervasive ignorance about extended breastfeeding can cause problems in disputed child custody cases. Baldwin often suggests that mothers consider weaning a toddler if their custody and visitation rights are about to be decided by a judge who has never heard of extended nursing. In such cases, the custody decision may be based on the judge's perception that continued nursing could be an indication of an overall problem in the mother-child relationship. Baldwin points out that there is no "right to breastfeed" in family law cases or in social service agency cases. It is public policy in most states in the USA for a child to have frequent and continuous contact with both parents when the parents separate. Even though courts have recognized that breastfeeding is best for the child, they will not give it precedence over the father's bond with his child.[1]

Mothers must remember that in divorce or paternity cases they do not have the unilateral right to decide how to rear their children. Many states require shared decision-making between the mother and father and extended breastfeeding and other aspects of attachment parenting may become issues. The mother needs to consider how she will be perceived by people who may not share her parenting philosophy. Their impressions of her will determine the outcome of a custody dispute.

Biting

Rarely does a mother make it through an entire nursing career without being bitten at least once. Yet you can be sure that very few children bite very much, or no mother would be willing to nurse, much less enjoy it as most do. The vast majority of children learn quickly that they cannot bite if they want to continue nursing.

The most likely time for a child to bite is during the first year, usually in connection with teething. Such an incident can occur later, however, and sometimes even with a toddler teething is still involved. Your child is experimenting with using your nipple—inappropriately—to comfort painful gums. Your nipple will fare better if you manage to control the impulse to pull your little barracuda off the breast and instead use a finger to break suction and protect your nipple. It is best to temper your response to being bitten as much as humanly possible at the time so as not to frighten your child away from nursing.

Terminate the nursing for a few moments when you are bitten, and talk to your child. Tell him it hurts. Tell him he must nurse gently. Be sure to offer him things he can bite that will comfort his gums, for example, cold celery or carrots or a frozen bagel. Patting your nipple dry and applying modified lanolin the way you may have done when your baby was tiny will probably help if it becomes tender as the result of a bite.

When you talk to your child about biting, you will need to balance the severity of your tone with your child's sensitivity to verbal rebuke and, of course, do what you can manage under the circumstances. Sometimes children will refuse to nurse after a scolding for biting that is harsher than they can cope with. (For some children, it cannot be very harsh at all.) Some mothers, considering this possibility, especially with children under two or so, make an effort to curb biting without fussing at the child, but with only calm, determined, and consistent removal from the breast for awhile.

Karen Gromada writes that biting seems to be a greater problem for mothers nursing multiples, that is, twins or triplets. The problem can arise from holding a child to the breast when she's had enough and is ready to do something else.[4] This can bring on biting in any child, of course; but with multiples there is the tendency to hold on to both so that one doesn't get into trouble while you're still nursing the other. A bite tells you that you need to watch that child closely in the future for signs of being finished. It will also necessitate finding nursing positions that leave a hand free to break suction and thus protect yourself.

A few children, even if you have taught them not to bite at some previous time, may later experiment playfully with various "stunts," including nipping at your nipple. The child may pull your nipple out as far as she can, bite at it, blow it to tickle you, and on and on through all the tricks little ones invent for entertainment. When your child comes up with any game that hurts you, no matter how funny she may think it is, stop the nursing right then. Tell her why you are stopping and resume nursing when you are satisfied that she has agreed to your terms.

Allow me to reassure you again, your child in either of these instances is almost certain to learn very quickly to nurse without hurting you, although once in a while it is necessary to work for weeks with a child before she gets the message. Perhaps the reason that the vast majority of children learn not to bite so quickly is that we invariably react immediately and firmly to biting at the breast. There is probably no instance in which we apply behavior modification so immediately, decisively, and consistently. Besides, our children love us and respond to the urgency and sincerity with which we insist that they must not bite. Many a child who is old enough to talk will respond when you tell him he has hurt you with a sincere "Sorry, Mommy," and a kiss.

A few little people seem to grow bored after nursing a while and then bite. Occasionally a child bites because he is actually hungry. Terminating the nursing when your child first shows signs of restlessness indicating that he would really prefer something else can prevent such biting. You can make a point of shortening some nursing sessions a bit and follow these with interesting distractions or food.

Now and then biting can be a clue that your child wants to wean. "You don't have to nurse," one mother told her child who was nipping and playing at the breast. "Are you sure you don't mind, Mommy?" the little girl responded. Apparently this child thought for some reason that she was supposed to nurse at bedtime, even though she was no longer interested. It was certainly time to let the child know, as this mother did, that it is fine for her to wean if she wants to.

Your child may bite for the consistent and predictable reaction he gets from you. Not often, but once in a while the quickest way to stop the biting is to control your reactions—admittedly a difficult plan to carry out. Your child may become bored with the game and go on to something else that is fun for both of you.

It may be that your child is biting because he is upset with you and wants to hurt you. If biting begins at the same time as some change that may be upsetting to your child, you may want to consider the possibility that your child is signaling you for help, in an immature and inefficient way, certainly, but signaling nonetheless. One mother whose two-and-a-half year-old child persisted in biting, initiated the following interchange.

Mom: *Why are you biting?*
Tot: *Don't know.*
Mom: *Do you want to hurt me?*
Tot: *Yes.*
Mom: *Why?*
Tot: *Don't know.*
Mom: *Is it because you're angry with me?*
Tot: *Yes.*
Mom: *Why are you angry?*
Tot: *Because hm-hm-hm-hm. (Translated that means, I don't want to talk about it).*
Mom: *No, we're going to talk about it. Are you angry because the baby's here?*
Tot: *Yes. (Look of relief).*
Mom: *I understand how you feel. It's okay.*

It is tempting to say that after this conversation all biting disappeared like magic. It did not. From that time on, however, both mother and child understood better what was happening and were able to work on feeling better. The biting did diminish, and soon ceased altogether.

If your child is not verbal enough or refuses to enter into this sort of conversation, some sleuthing on your part may help you determine if the biting results from unhappy or angry feelings your child is not handling well. It may help to volunteer to your child that it is okay to be mad at you for having a new baby or for holding him down while he had stitches—or whatever you think might be troubling him. (You aren't admitting that you were wrong in these situations—just letting him know that his feelings about these things are worthy of attention, that you accept them and will help him deal with them.) Once in a while that will be all he needs.

Some biting can even be a simple attention-getter, and a very effective one. It is a way that your child can protest against being ignored while she is nursing. Many children at the breast, like many lovers, want to see your eyes. They may especially resent your talking to other people while nursing, but watching television or reading may annoy some children. It may eliminate any biting problem you have just to give your attention voluntarily to your child when she nurses. That will also make it possible to see when your child may be about to clamp down so you can slip a finger into the corner of her mouth and prevent the bite.

There are also occasions during which biting occurs by accident—for instance when a child is nursing in an awkward position and falls. I remember vividly the time when one of mine was nursing while standing on a narrow little bench. She fell, biting my nipple painfully and tipping the bench over onto my toenail, which later developed an ugly black bruise. I found the whole affair quite painful at the time and learned in the future to be more cautious about where and how I let my children nurse. It was almost worth it, though, to be able to watch people's faces when they asked what had happened to my toe. "It's a nursing injury," I told them.

Some children who fall asleep nursing will accidentally bite in their sleep. Not all children do this, and not usually during the first nine months or thereabouts, so there is no reason to worry about this happening unless or until it does. Mothers who are bitten once this way, however, quickly learn not to fall asleep anymore while their little ones are nursing, even though sleeping while nursing is such a precious luxury to relinquish. Still, it is not pleasant to be bitten, and it is possible to prevent such accidental biting if need be by staying awake until your little one is sound asleep and then getting your thumb or finger firmly between her teeth and removing your nipple.

Though biting does happen occasionally over the nursing years, we are invariably quick to develop the skills and tactics necessary to keep it from becoming more than an occasional problem.

Illness in the Nursing Mother

Reliable information on the effect of mother's medications on nursing babies and toddlers is slowly becoming more available. We know that most drugs, prescription or over-the-counter, do show up in breast milk. On the other hand, very few have been shown to cause problems for the nursling. The prudent course is always to avoid medications unless they're necessary. The older the child and the more other foods he is taking, of course, the less his exposure to drugs from breast milk. Also, older children are better able to metabolize the small amount of a drug they may receive through breast milk, and thus there is less concern about possible ill effects.

It is almost never necessary, nor even advisable, to stay miserable for want of medication that can help you feel better and it is almost never necessary to wean because you need to take medication. There is good research available on many of the more commonly used drugs, including analgesics, antibiotics, antihistamines, antihypertensives, hormones, etc. You can't use all these drugs while you are breast-feeding—even aspirin can be a problem for newborn babies—but with prudent medical advice you can probably find something that will help.

If you have questions about a specific drug, most La Leche League Leaders can refer to a condensed listing.[8] For a complete report and reference list on a specific drug, you, a pharmacist, or supportive health care provider should refer to a reputable source for the latest research, such as the newest edition of Briggs, Freeman, and Sumner, *Drugs in Pregnancy and Lactation* or Thomas Hale's current edition of *Medications and Mother's Milk*. If you cannot find a copy of these books locally, ask the reference librarian at your nearest library to order them for you through interlibrary loan. If you need the information quickly, you can almost certainly find these books in the library of the nearest medical school. (You don't have to have library privileges to read books in most libraries.) Or you can call the reference librarian at the medical school library and ask for information from these books. The librarian can probably read the entry to you or, for a fee, fax or mail you a copy of the pages you need. (Have the generic name of the drug you are inquiring about if you can. Otherwise, you will have to ask the librarian to look for the brand name in the book's index.) You can also ask your doctor or your baby's doctor to find out more information about a medication's effect on a nursing baby. He or she may be able to consult resources on the Internet or at a large, university-based hospital. Sources of drug information compiled by the pharmeceutical companies, such as the Physician's Desk Reference (PDR), take an overly cautious approach to the use of medications while breastfeeding.

There are a few drugs that definitely should not be taken by nursing mothers. When radioactive compounds are used for diagnostic tests, temporary weaning will be necessary until the mother's milk is clear of radioactivity. Larger doses of radioactive drugs given as treatment for certain diseases may require months of not breastfeeding. Some mothers have pumped for many months and then resumed breastfeeding, but this may not be a practical solution for the mother of a nursing toddler or preschooler. Weaning is also necessary during chemotherapy for cancer. Nursing mothers should not use illegal or so-called "recreational" drugs such as cocaine, heroin, or marijuana.

Dr. Ruth Lawrence, a great friend of breastfeeding, recommends that we have respect for the power, for good or ill, of herbal remedies as well. Herbs are the source of much of what is available in pharmacies and can be quite potent. Some, like rose hips, are mild and nutritious. Others have powerful effects and need to be monitored like any other drug. Effects of one herb, comfrey leaves (*Symphytum*), on the circulation and liver have so alarmed health officials that its use has been banned in Canada and Germany.

Properly formulated herbal remedies from a reputable source and taken in reasonable doses will probably not affect your child. But, like any medication, we need to exercise good judgment, avoid abuse, and keep a careful watch on our little ones for reactions. For listings of some commonly used herbs and their effects, see *Breastfeeding: A Guide for the Medical Profession*, Fifth Edition, pp. 346-348. (Your local La Leche League Leader can refer you to an LLL Professional Liaison Leader who has access to this and other references.)

Illnesses in Which Weaning Is Advisable

Breast cancer is extremely rare in nursing mothers, but it does occur, as it did in my own family. A mother newly diagnosed with breast cancer should wean her child and begin treatment. This can be true with other cancers as well. There is no evidence the cancer itself poses any threat to the baby. But treatment needs to begin immediately and will likely involve hormonal manipulation as well as drug therapies that would be harmful to the nursling.[6] The most loving gift a mother can give her child at a time like this is to save her own life.

A very few infectious diseases in the mother would require weaning for the child's safety. Although human milk kills the human immunodeficiency virus (HIV), there is still evidence of potential risk of transmission of the virus by breastfeeding. So at the time of this writing, mothers who have been proven HIV positive by a definitive test for the virus, not just a preliminary test for HIV antibodies, and who have access to safe, alternative ways of feeding the baby, are advised not to breastfeed, especially after the first three months. Also, at the time of this writing, advice to the mother of an older nursling who becomes HIV positive is that she should wean immediately upon learning of her newly positive HIV status.[10] However, because there is so much controversy and ongoing research about the transmission of HIV, no nursing mother who finds herself diagnosed as HIV-positive should rely solely upon these mid-1999 recommendations, but seek out the best and most recent information available.

Human T-cell leukemia (HTLV-I), so far uncommon in the United States, but a serious problem in some other countries, can be transmitted through human milk. Hepatitis viruses can be transmitted this way as well. But with appropriate medical diagnosis and treatment of the mother, and the nursling, and sometimes even other members of the family, breastfeeding can continue. In some forms of hepatitis, immunities the child receives through continued nursing may even be helpful to the child of an infected mother.[5]

In rare cases, certain skin infections may occur on a part of the breast with which the child will come in contact and possibly become infected, too. These may require a temporary weaning from the affected breast. (See the discussion of nipple soreness earlier in this chapter.)

Both breast cancer and infections contracted through intimate contact are subjects of intense study, so whatever I write today will be out of date tomorrow. If you find yourself or someone you know facing a decision about nursing or weaning because of a serious illness or infection, make sure you have the best information. You can look for the latest medical journals with the help of your library. Abstracts, and sometimes full texts, of articles from medical journals are available online. The US National Library of Medicine offers access to much of this material from home computers at http://igm.nlm.nih.gov/. However, the information needs to be interpreted for your situation by your own health care provider.

Multiples

The details of the joys and difficulties of nursing multiple toddlers are not much different from those that arise from nursing one. It's just that everything is compounded by the additional mouths, the additional bodies, the extra arms and legs, all interacting with each other as well as with you. In some ways nursing multiples may get a little easier when they grow into toddlers. At least when two need to nurse at once, you don't have the awkwardness of having to lift and hold two to the breast. Toddlers can climb into your lap and position themselves.

A mother of twin toddlers writes that hers is an uncommon experience:

> *I've been involved in two different "Mothers of Multiples" groups—and of the 200 plus moms of twins/triplets that I've come in contact with, I've only met one other mother who has continued breastfeeding into toddlerhood. It's sad to me that so many moms feel overwhelmed to the point that they quit. I genuinely can't imagine having done anything else.*

Another mother writes about some of the perils of nursing twins as they get old enough to express their own personalities and their own minds.

> *I'm a mother of four (ages nine, six, and eighteen-month-old twins). I've never nursed a toddler before (much less two) and am finding it a hoot! When my girl twin is finished nursing she'll let go, pat my breast, wave bye-bye, and then pull my t-shirt down to cover my breast. My boy twin will simply pop off (literally "pop") with a loud "aaaahhhhh" and run away. This concerns the girl, who is very meticulous and likes things in their place, so she'll come over, pat "his" breast, wave good-bye, and then cover it up. This concerns him, as he then decides he wasn't finished after all, so back he comes. This reminds her that perhaps another sip wouldn't hurt, so on she comes and we start again. Eventually I just have to stand up and shoo them away or distract them with books or toys. Otherwise it could go on forever.*

The reasons for nursing multiples into toddlerhood, of course, are the same as for continuing to nurse one—nutrition, protection from disease, comfort. By toddlerhood, the questions of milk supply and choices between alternate breasts or one for each have no doubt been resolved. Most of the nursing toddler issues faced by mothers of multiples are the same as the challenges of mothers nursing one child, only perhaps there are more of them.

The interactions between two at the breast can be tender and beautiful. They can also turn into brawls as the children work at asserting their own personal and territorial claims. Sometimes distraction with toys set aside for nursing time can help calm the conflict. Sometimes you have to be firm and terminate nursings until the fighting stops, usually by standing up. You can't, and probably shouldn't, prevent all their jealousy and competition; children have as much right to their bad feelings about one another as to their good ones. But you don't have to participate passively in their battles. If you are firm and consistent, it should be possible to establish nursing as a time of enforced cease-fire and a positive influence on their relationship. (For more on coping with multiple toddlers, see Chapter 29 in Karen Gromada's, MOTHERING MULTIPLES: BREASTFEEDING AND CARING FOR TWINS OR MORE!.)

Caring for more than one busy toddler is a lot of work, so take care of yourself. Don't ignore your thirst or your diet, because you will continue producing a lot of milk longer than if you were just nursing one. A greater strain on you than milk production, however, is the amount of chasing and lifting you have to do with your busy children. Encourage your children to take daytime naps for as long as possible, and lie down yourself during nap time. You need the rest more than you need any of the chores done. If there ever is a time when you need to take care of people before things, it is when you are caring for more than one baby or toddler.

Any mother nursing two is at increased risk of feeling "touched out" and may need to work on getting some minimum of personal space. With younger toddlers, if a helper can give you a break, even if it is no more than five or ten minutes of guaranteed privacy and time with your own thoughts, it may be enough to "reset your sensor controls" for the day. As your twins get older, you can negotiate nursing times so that you can be reasonably sure of a little time on your feet, on the phone, or in the bathtub. You need to keep your own emotional reserves built up most of the time so you have the best of yourself to give when you do sit down to nurse them.

It is important to learn to nurse twins lying down. To do this, lie flat on your back and support them, one on each arm and shoulder. Pillows under one or both may help, and toddlers can learn to arrange the pillows themselves.

Mothers of twins often hope to take advantage of nursing to get close to each child, one at a time. Twins tend to find themselves blended together in people's minds and get tired of being treated as one being. But these children interact as nurslings just as they do in everything else, so when one sees the other doing something, he'll probably want to do it, too. Most of the time, nursing one will soon mean nursing both. Their copycat behavior can be a lifesaver, however, because at least you don't have to worry about what one is getting into while you nurse the other. For toddlers who don't nurse at the same time, everyone will benefit if you create a closed-door, child-safe room where you can nurse one without having to worry about the child or children who choose to do something else.

It is good to try to find a little individual time with each child, especially when one is particularly needy. One-on-one time usually requires staggered naps or bedtimes or another person's help with the other child(ren). The others will have times of need, too; so you can pay attention to the needs of each as required rather than trying to dole out exactly equal portions of attention.

Each child will have his own style and motivation for nursing, and each may develop different routines. Nursing and weaning in her own time can give each child the opportunity to express her individual needs and have them met one-to-one.

Sometimes twins will wean at about the same time. Sometimes one will be through with nursing long before the other. They do not necessarily wean as a unit any more than they breathe as a unit. Like any situation in which you might be nursing siblings, you should regard each unique nursing relationship as a special beginning on that child's way to becoming her own adult self.

References

1 Baldwin, E. In the best interests of breastfed children? *Mothering* Fall 1997; 84.http://www.lalecheleague.org/LawMain.html

2 Bowlby, J. *Attachment.* New York: Basic Books, 1982; 157.

3 Dettwyler, K. A. Beauty and the breast. *Breastfeeding, Biocultural Perspectives.* Ed. P. Stuart-Macadam and K. A. Dettwyler. New York: Aldine de Gruyter, 1995; 167-215.

4 Gromada, K. MOTHERING MULTIPLES: BREASTFEEDING AND CARING FOR TWINS OR MORE! Schaumburg, Illinois: La Leche League International, 1999 revision; Chapter 27:269-287.

5 Lawrence, R. A. A review of the medical benefits and contraindications to breastfeeding in the United States. *Child Health Information Bulletin* Arlington, VA: National Center for Education in Maternal and Child Health, October, 1997; 31.

6 Lawrence, R. A. and Lawrence, R. M. *Breastfeeding: A Guide for the Medical Profession.* 5th edition. St. Louis: The C. V. Mosby Company, 1999; 548, 525-27.

7 Lieberman, A. F. Aggression and sexuality in relation to toddler attachment: Implications for the caregiving system. *Infant Mental Health Journal* 1996; 17(3):280.

8 Mohrbacher, N. and Stock, J. THE BREASTFEEDING ANSWER BOOK. Revised edition. Schaumburg, Illinois: La Leche League International, 1997; 404-06,426-27.

9 Nardi, B. A. Infant feeding and women's work in Western Samoa. *Infant Care and Feeding in the South Pacific.* Ed. L. B. Marshall. New York: Gordon and Breach, 1985; 299, footnote.

10 Newburg, David, Ph.D., Senior Scientist, Department of Biomedical Sciences, Eunice Kennedy Shriver Center, Waltham, MA, USA. Personal communication.

11 Raphael, D. *Only Mothers Know.* Westport, CT: Greenwood Press,1985; 35.

12 Rogan, W. J. and Gladen, B. C. Breast-feeding and cognitive development. *Early Human Development* 1993; 31:186-92.

13 Sears, W. and Sears, M. *The Baby Book.* Boston: Little, Brown and Company, 1993; 517.

14 Zeigerman, J., Honigman, F. and Crawford, R. Inflammatory mammary cancer during pregnancy and lactation. *Obstetrics and Gynecology* 1968; 32:373-75.

chapter seven

Pregnancy and Tandem Nursing

When nursing continues past the first year, a mother may become pregnant before the little child is ready to give up nursing. Becoming pregnant even in the first year of nursing is not unheard of (though frequent nursing and/or family-planning techniques can make such early conception unlikely), and it is quite common in the child's second and third years. If you do become pregnant while still nursing, you will be faced with at least some pressure to wean because of your pregnancy, whether it is for your sake, for the sake of your child, or for the sake of the tiny person inside you. There is no evidence that continued nursing would be harmful to any of you, but the pressure to wean has a history that is long and nearly universal.

Some Perspectives on Weaning during Pregnancy

In most of the world's cultures, weaning is mandatory. Aristotle wrote that pregnancy dried up the milk, or made it unfit to use. Soranus and Galen, authorities from the first and second century, both believed pregnancy would harm the milk and the nursling. Up through the eighteenth century, child-care experts in Europe and the Middle East based their writings on this advice. In medieval Europe, therefore, pregnancy was seen as a reason for abrupt weaning.[6] In Colonial America, it was thought that nursing while pregnant was dangerous for infants and would deprive the unborn child of nourishment.[21]

Many people all over the world today believe the milk of a pregnant mother will poison the child. In East Bhutan, where mothers regard the optimal duration of breastfeeding to be "as long as possible," people believe pregnancy causes breast milk to become "rotten." Pregnancy is the only circumstance in which a mother's neighbors would discourage breastfeeding.[2] Mothers in Rajasthan, India, who almost universally nurse more than 24 months, believe that when they become pregnant the breast milk spoils and will harm the child.[19] In Mali, too, if a mother becomes pregnant, the child is weaned immediately.[8]

In Pakistan a mother is expected to wean "as soon as she's sure she's pregnant." Both in East Bhutan and in Pakistan, however, researchers found a few exceptions:

Only one woman interviewed in Chitral said that she had taken the risk and actually nursed during late pregnancy; she added that she was pleasantly surprised to find that her child remained healthy and that her baby was born healthy as well.

Some Hindu mothers in Pakistan also did not hold the majority view:

For example, one woman told me proudly that she had breastfed through all nine months of pregnancy with no ill effects on the nursing child, who was a boy.[14]

In rural Zimbabwe, weaning because of pregnancy can be abrupt and includes treatment of the child with a purge that causes diarrhea and/or vomiting to "clean the dirty milk from the child." Once he recovers, he has a sudden transition from nursing on demand to scheduled meals of bulky starches that he must feed himself. The whole process is very stressful and increases his chances of suffering from malnutrition.[4]

In Bhutan and Bangladesh, on the other hand, although mothers regard nursing during pregnancy as harmful to the nursling, weaning is not abrupt, just less gradual than if the mother were not pregnant. In the Bhutan study, researchers noted a relatively large number who reported weaning in the ninth month and speculate that some of these mothers probably continued nursing the older child after the baby was born.[1]

Concern about the milk of a pregnant mother is unnecessary, however. A study of random samples of milk from pregnant mothers found changes, lower levels of lipids and lactose and higher levels of protein,[22] but nothing harmful. Another study tested the milk of three pregnant mothers over several months. About the second month of pregnancy the milk began to undergo changes similar to those observed during the course of weaning. Concentrations of sodium and protein gradually increased while milk volume, along with concentrations of glucose, lactose, and potassium, gradually fell. In weaning, these changes are brought on by decreased suckling, but they occurred in the pregnant women even when they continued nursing as much or even more than before the pregnancy.[17] No changes have been found in the milk of pregnant mothers that nursing children do not encounter during any gradual weaning process. Thus there is no reason to be concerned about ill effects in the nursing child.

Weaning during pregnancy: the "natural" choice? The widespread taboo against nursing while pregnant is probably natural in the strictly biological sense of the word. Pregnancy is a state in which your system focuses its resources on the needs of the new baby, no matter what you may think about it intellectually. As one mother put it, "I feel that my older son deserves to be nursed still, but my body is saying NO, NO, NO. It is very difficult."

The plan of nature seems to be that by the time a mother becomes pregnant again, the older child should be mature enough to have his needs met by more people than just his mother and by foods other than her milk. Most of the time when breastfeeding and mothering proceed without restriction, the maturity is there. Then the mother will gently urge her child to wean, and because he is ready, weaning will be easy. Still, most of us have seen continued nursing in nature—such as half-grown kittens nursing along with a subsequent litter. Similar behavior has also been observed in rats.[7]

In their 1970s study of 503 La Leche League members who became pregnant while still nursing, Niles Newton and Marilyn Theotokatos reported that 69 percent weaned at some time during pregnancy. "How many of these would have weaned if they were not pregnant is not known since no non-pregnant control groups are available. Since the child was getting older, it is likely that even without another pregnancy, there would be a high proportion of weaners."[15] Two decades later, in Moscone and Moore's study of 57 La Leche League mothers who were pregnant and breastfeeding, 57 percent weaned.[13] These mothers did not have to face the complex interplay of belief and harsh reality a pregnant mother may face in the developing world, where one mother said: "If I do not breastfeed the child it will die from starvation, and if I do breastfeed, the child will fall ill when the milk rots."[2] Yet over half of the highly motivated La Leche League mothers weaned during pregnancy.

Children mature at different rates, and any number of variables can affect how soon a mother becomes pregnant again. Many mothers who become pregnant when they have a child still nursing decide to continue the nursing relationship, or at least to give it a try. For many mothers this seems the obvious and, for them, the natural choice. They respond to the immaturity of the child in their arms. They feel strongly that ending the nursing relationship would deny the child advantages that they want for him.

> *I had the problem of deciding whether or not to wean. I had known one or two mothers who had nursed siblings, and I thought that was one thing I'd never do. But I did not anticipate an unplanned pregnancy or babies spaced so closely, either. I ended up deciding that if my son did not wean himself I would keep on nursing him quite willingly. I was very concerned about his being pushed out of the baby position so young. This seemed such a good way of reassuring him of my love.*

For many mothers, nursing through pregnancy is the easiest course to take. "When I was pregnant," a mother writes, "and needed to rest, nursing was the only way I could get the baby to lie down with me." Because of the changes weaning would require in the way these mothers cared for their children, weaning looked like a larger hurdle than any difficulties that might arise because of being pregnant and nursing.

There can be special joys, of course, as well as challenges, in nursing through pregnancy, for example, when your child is at the breast enjoying both you and the movements of her new sibling. Sometimes the only negative factor in nursing while pregnant is the surprise or disapproval of people, including medical advisors, who are under the impression that no one ever does such a thing.

Nipple Pain

For other mothers, nursing through pregnancy is not an easy, spontaneous behavior. According to Newton and Theotokatos, 74 percent of the mothers in their study experienced nipple discomfort or pain,[15] and Moscone and Moore name nipple and/or breast pain, followed by fatigue and irritability, as the reason mothers gave most frequently for weaning.[13] You may be among the fortunate minority who never have any nipple discomfort, or this pain may be the very first indication you have that you are pregnant. For many, nipple pain is part of the body's adjustment to pregnancy, a condition that does not respond to standard sore nipple treatments. The discomfort may be temporary—only a few days or weeks at some time during pregnancy—or it may last from the third or fourth week after conception until the new baby is born.

For some, the pain is mild. For others, it is strong enough that mothers use words like "extreme," "excruciating," or "incredible" to describe it. "Prepregnancy," one mother writes, "I was able to just let her lie next to me nursing in bed and we'd both fall back asleep. With my intense nipple pain, however, it was impossible for me to fall back asleep. So I weaned her from nighttime nursing." Another described the nipple pain as "so overwhelming that I had to stop my toddler nursing at night."

Your child does not want to hurt you and may be quite concerned, as was one three-year-old who told his mother, "I'm sorry if I hurt you when I nurse, Mommy; but my teeth don't make holes." This child needed the reassurance his mother gave him that he was not responsible for her discomfort. At the same time you do want to ask your child for help and cooperation.

Attention to positioning may help alleviate some of the pain. Try to pull your child in close to the breast, with a large portion of breast tissue in his mouth. That will at least eliminate pain from any unnecessary pulling on the nipple.

Work toward arrangements in frequency, duration, and positioning that are as agreeable as possible for both of you. Remember to give your child plenty of attention besides nursing and also easy

MY MOMMY'S NUMMIES ARE BROKEN!

access to snacks and good things to drink. The adjustments the two of you make may lead to total weaning, as in this case in which mom had to deal with a lot of nipple discomfort: "My son eventually decided nursing wasn't worth it anymore with all the limits. He just said 'no' one day when he woke up. I was so sad and had to call a friend to talk about how bad I felt."

Or your adjustments may result in very little change at all if your child still shows you a great need for nursing. Many mothers tell me that the breathing and relaxation techniques they learned in childbirth classes made it easier to cope with discomfort they felt while nursing. Others distract themselves from their restless, uneasy feelings by reading, checking their e-mail, watching television, eating or drinking something, or just deliberately thinking of other things while nursing.

Though there is no sure treatment for nipple tenderness during pregnancy, it may help, if you are still producing more than a few drops of milk, to get the milk flowing a bit by hand-expression before beginning to nurse. Even if your milk production is minimal, you may be able to make nursing less uncomfortable by pulling each nipple out gently before nursing to get it erect and reduce the friction when your child begins sucking. For many pregnant mothers, though, only the next change in your body, be that the passing of another week or the birth of the new baby, will serve as the "cure" for the tender nipples that many pregnancies bring.

Emotional Changes

In the Newton-Theotokatos study, a smaller number of mothers reported feeling very restless when nursing during pregnancy—30 percent frequently, 27 percent rarely or infrequently. This was described by some as an "antsy feeling."[15] This is probably a part of the natural weaning urge in a pregnant mother—a drive to wean by walking away from the nursling, as some of us have seen our pets do. In late pregnancy the child's wriggling and putting pressure on the abdomen is uncomfortable for some. Nursing also causes uterine contractions which bother some mothers, but not others.

If you find yourself pregnant and not happy with nursing, by all means tell your child about your discomfort, and not with an air of martyrdom that will make her feel guilty for needing to nurse. "By two," a mother writes about this experience, "one can usually communicate, 'Mom isn't comfortable with that,' and receive some understanding. We trimmed down the length of feeds during the pregnancy, because it was not something I enjoyed, and my child grew old enough to be sympathetic."

Milk Production during Pregnancy

Many mothers and toddlers notice a marked decrease in milk production during pregnancy.

> *I am 16 weeks pregnant and have continued nursing my now two-year-old. My milk production seemed to stop or slow significantly almost immediately after I discovered my pregnancy, however that never slowed my daughter's interest.*

A nursling who could talk kept her mother informed about changes in her milk:

> *My firstborn was three when she nursed through my pregnancy with her little brother. About the fifth month of the pregnancy I noticed that she seemed to be sucking really hard and getting frustrated. She let go of my breast, annoyed, and I asked what the matter was. She said my "numa" was empty. I offered to get her a cup of juice, but then she smiled and said "I don't mind. I'll drink numa anyway!"*
>
> *This went on for a couple of months and then one day while she was nursing she suddenly swallowed and then she pulled off with surprise and said "Mummy, your numa has apple juice in it!" That's when I knew that the colostrum production had started.*

When you think you may be pregnant, for your sake and your child's, be sure to make plenty of food available, especially nutritious snacks, so he can make up for a decrease in milk intake. If your nursling is young and taking little or no other food, you need to pay attention to his wet diapers and bowel movements, as well as the behaviors with which he signals hunger, in case you need to add more nutritious food to his diet.

Sometimes, especially if your nursing toddler is older, you may not be aware of any difference in your milk flow. With older nurslings, milk may be a less important part of nursing anyway.

Nursing and Nausea

Nausea during pregnancy dims some mothers' enjoyment of nursing. For some it may make continuing impossible.

*I personally could not stand nursing when I got pregnant.
My middle child (a boy) was/is fairly high need and loved
nursing, but I got pregnant with his sister when he was
sixteen months. I get horrible morning sickness when
I'm pregnant, and it was summer, and I was dehydrating.
I couldn't keep liquids down at all. I felt bad because
I couldn't meet my son's very reasonable desire to nurse,
but I really dreaded it. I felt sore and nauseous and tired,
so I weaned him halfway through my pregnancy. It was
hard on us both, but physically and mentally I couldn't
keep going.*

It is difficult indeed to manage a bouncing little person when you
are feeling that your stomach will turn at the slightest movement. For
many, nursing is not the problem; needing to hold your child is the
difficulty, and that is part of child-rearing whether you are nursing or
not. Improved diet, extra vitamins, especially vitamin B_6, rest, and small,
frequent snacks may all be helpful in overcoming the nausea of
pregnancy.

Nursing can be something of a lifesaver if you do feel nauseated,
because you can do it lying down. Caring for a child that way may be less
bothersome to your stomach than not nursing and, therefore, having to
sit up with him or carry him around.

If nursing itself seems to make nausea worse, as it does for some
mothers, let your child share in the first treatment that will be
recommended for you—frequent, small meals. If you can face nothing but
white crackers, as happens sometimes, pull a little wider selection than
that out of the refrigerator or pantry for the sake of your child's
nutrition. You might even end up tempting yourself to a few bites beyond
the blandness of saltines. By sharing these snacks with your child, you
may also succeed in reducing her need to nurse.

Nursing and Fatigue during Pregnancy

If you experience overpowering fatigue in early pregnancy as I did,
mothering a small child can take everything you've got and more. Your
toddler's nursing can be a great blessing if it enables you to get off your
feet. Or it can be an equally great problem if it keeps you awake. One
mother made the best of the situation by some nursing—and some
weaning:

*Nursing helped a great deal in the first trimester to get an
active toddler to settle down so I could get much needed
sleep. . . . I did cut out the night nursings so that I could
sleep better.*

Another pregnant mother tells how she talked her two-year-old out of nursing at night.

We did this by discussing how "ma-ma" had to go to sleep and she could do "ma-ma" when the sun came up. This worked amazingly well!

Nursing or not, you'll have to do the best you can to drag around after your child. Accept help when it's available. And don't despair; the middle trimester is usually much different, often filled with energy and good spirits.

One Day at a Time

Even through such difficulties as nausea or tender nipples, many mothers are motivated to persist with nursing by the obvious needs and uninhibited gratitude children show for having their mothers available to them in such a loving way.

But avoid making any fixed plans about how your nursing relationship will proceed over the next several months. As I have already pointed out, your own feelings and tolerances are unpredictable during pregnancy.

Children's reactions to pregnancy and the new baby vary a great deal, too. While some do not indicate that they notice any changes because of mother's pregnancy, others tend to wean very early on, presumably because of a change in the taste of the milk or the decreased flow. Others react to the changes in the milk that occur in later pregnancy, sometimes by weaning. Still others, like one eager little nurser I know, complain about the "yuck-o milk" but keep on. Sometimes, too, your abdomen in late pregnancy can become so large that your child may find getting to your nipple awkward, although a toddler with the will can probably find a way.

As if to add one more bit of confusion to life, there is no way of knowing whether a child who weans during pregnancy will stay weaned once the baby comes and you again have a good supply of milk—and milk that tastes good at that.

When the Pregnancy Has an Unexpected Outcome

I hate to bring this up, because I feel we do our best when we are motivated by positive rather than negative views of the future, but it is a fact that pregnancy is not always uneventful. Mothers have written about their disappointment over having weaned a child because of pregnancy when that pregnancy later ended in miscarriage. On the other hand, mothers who have lost their pregnancies at various stages have told me what a comfort their nursing child was to them while they were overcoming disappointment and grief.

When the new baby has been born prematurely or is too ill to nurse, the older child's nursing can be a great help in establishing and maintaining a good supply of milk—a boon for the tiny baby who needs that milk so desperately. You will, of course, want to hand-express or pump as much as possible of the colostrum and first milk for the little one before your toddler nurses. The toddler, then, will take some of the milk, but that is certainly a reasonable reward for making the milk let down and flow the way no pump would be able to do.

Nursing and Contractions

Some people wonder whether the uterine contractions stimulated by nursing could cause a mother to go into labor too soon. I am not aware of any controlled studies of this question. We have years of anecdotal experience with mothers who have been nursing through pregnancy, even those with a past history of miscarriage and premature delivery, and there is no readily apparent increase in either problem. Even at full-term, successful experiments with inducing labor by nipple stimulation required long periods, thirty to forty-five minutes out of every hour, using a breast pump or neuromuscular stimulator to induce labor. One article does caution against the use of nipple stimulation for the induction of uterine contractions except in a controlled clinical setting.[18] However, the duration and intensity of stimulation required to bring on labor even at full term appears to be more than a nursing toddler would be either willing or able to supply.

Still, we do not know for certain whether uterine contractions stimulated by nursing have some small effect on a high-risk pregnancy. So I don't have an answer for the mother who wrote:

> *I am currently seven weeks pregnant and still nursing my two-year-old son. I have suffered two miscarriages in the past six months. Though there seems to be no evidence of miscarriage associated with nursing, there also seems to be no evidence of a study specific to multiple miscarriages. Are there any studies that I may have missed and what are your thoughts?*

It is impossible at this time to know what advice to give to a pregnant nursing mother with a history of repeated miscarriage or premature delivery, or one who may be experiencing uterine pain or bleeding. The pregnant mother of an eighteen-month-old who was nowhere near being ready to wean found herself in this uncharted territory:

> *I had spotting at the beginning of my pregnancy and was concerned about miscarriage but continued to nurse. When I visited my obstetrician and told him I was nursing he said that was fine until I was five months. I told him that I did not plan on weaning and he said he did not want a baby born at thirty weeks. We continued to talk and he said that as long as I paid attention to my contractions later in pregnancy that would be okay.*
>
> *I read the information in* THE BREASTFEEDING ANSWER BOOK *and during my next prenatal visit asked my obstetrician if he'd read the research on nursing during a pregnancy. He said "no." I also asked how many patients of his had nursed during pregnancy and he said "none." So now I know that I am his test case.*

It may be that if sexual intercourse and orgasm, both of which cause uterine contractions, are not contraindicated, then nursing would not be a problem either. Until we know more, each mother in this tough situation will have to follow her own heart, guessing about the relative risks and benefits to her children from either course. Whatever you decide, there will be somebody to say you should have chosen otherwise; but until some careful research is done, nobody knows any more than you do. You deserve support in whatever decision you make.

Maintaining Adequate Weight Gain

Another concern is for adequate nutrition for both mother and unborn baby. If you had trouble maintaining an appropriate rate of weight gain during a previous pregnancy, you should evaluate the reasons. If your milk is a significant proportion of your toddler's diet, then you need to be sure you can take in enough calories and nutrients to maintain what will in any case be a decreasing amount of milk, to adequately nourish the unborn baby, and to build up sufficient fat stores in your body to support full lactation after the baby is born. For many mothers, such a need to eat may seem like a dream come true. But for a few, maintaining weight gain is an important problem. If you are having trouble eating enough to gain adequately after the end of the first trimester, you should work hard at getting your toddler to enjoy other foods and nurse less often, even if you prefer not to wean altogether.

Hormones in the Milk

There is also concern occasionally expressed that the hormones of pregnancy might be harmful to the nursing child. Small quantities of these hormones are present in the milk, as they are in the milk of mothers taking some oral contraceptives. There seems little reason to worry, though, about natural hormones present at natural levels, especially since some of the hormones we are talking about tend to reduce the amount of milk the child receives anyway. The developing fetus is exposed to the very same hormones at a much higher level. I doubt there is any more reason to worry about progesterone in the milk during pregnancy than there is to worry about the estrogen that was present in your milk once ovulation resumed.

So Should You or Shouldn't You?

In the judgment of most of the world, you should wean when you learn you are pregnant. But careful studies, even among mothers who insist that pregnancy makes weaning necessary, show that the nearly universal taboo is not universally observed, or at least not always as abruptly as the culture dictates.

Still, some physical cues and the accumulated wisdom of humankind tell you that you should wean when you are pregnant, and I am not about to argue with that kind of authority. On the other hand, your child may be telling you something altogether different. So far we haven't found evidence of any harm coming from continuing to nurse during pregnancy. I hope somebody with the expertise to do so will study any possible effects of nursing on high-risk pregnancies and look into possible nutritional strain on certain nutritionally vulnerable mothers. But, so far, everything we know indicates that whether to nurse or wean, or to nurse some and wean some, during pregnancy is a choice you can safely make based on your own evaluation of your child's needs and of your tolerance.

Nursing Two

If your child does continue to nurse all the way through your pregnancy, you may be entering into the unique experience of nursing two—something that happens occasionally, even in places like Mali where mothers have to violate taboos more serious than those in the modern West.[5]

A mother in East Bhutan told researchers:

I once gave birth to two boys, with only thirteen months between them. The first one was so small when I got pregnant again that he could not be weaned. I had to breastfeed him all through the next pregnancy. While I was pregnant he almost did not grow at all. Then his younger brother was born, and I breastfed both together for eight to ten months. At that time the eldest had recovered completely and was again big and strong.[2]

Tandem nursing is a challenging experience, but one that most mothers who have tried it find satisfying; only six percent of the mothers who had tandem nursed reported to Newton and Theotokatos that they would not nurse two again should the occasion arise.[15]

It Can Be a Joy

When I was pregnant and explaining to my son that the baby would nurse too and he would have to share, he told my parents and my friends, "I am having a baby. . . , and I'm not going to share!" Not long afterward, he decided it would be okay and then said, "This one is mine, and this one is hers!"

It gave me a laugh years ago, while all this was still new to me, when one mother wrote, "I guess we're going to try tandem nursing since my son nursed while I was in the early stages of labor." You cannot be sure, even at this point, though, because different children react differently to the return of your milk supply. Some children, just as mom gets adjusted to the idea of having two nurslings, dislike the gushing milk that appears shortly after the birth. When that happens, even if mother wants the child to nurse, he will not. Other kids are overjoyed at all the good milk, while still others don't let on that they notice any change.

What a kindness and comfort it can be to some children after the birth of that precious new baby—precious, but also a bit threatening to them—for their mothers to take them into their arms for that old familiar kind of loving! Your child may be especially grateful if you have been away in the hospital for a while.

We were a little anxious to see what our son's reaction to the new baby's nursing at bedtime, his special time, would be. Dad, Mom, and baby (nursing) crawled into bed. Our son stood beside the bed, shifting his weight from one foot to the other. I said, "Well, come on. Here's your place."

He heaved the biggest sigh, his face lit up, and in he scampered and began to nurse, too. That remains one of my most treasured moments.

Tandem nursing made the homecoming a great deal easier for another child, fifteen-and-a-half months old. When he saw mom nursing the new baby in "their" chair:

He threw himself down on the floor and sobbed. I made room for him on my lap and nursed them together for the first time. He curled his body around hers and reached across my lap to take her hand. As they nursed together they gazed into each other's eyes and I could see a special bond was being formed. That sweet memory has helped me through many a challenging afternoon.

Continuing to nurse your child is one way to show him that you still love the baby in him, too. And being a baby when he needs to be will help him grow into his big brother role with less conflict. He does not have to be big all the time, not before he is ready. Nor does he have to give you up entirely to the new baby. A little boy in Papua New Guinea was fortunate to have a mother who responded to his needs:

A boy of four or five was allowed to breastfeed while his newborn sibling slept. He had been weaned previously, according to tradition, but once "he saw his younger sister drink, he cried for milk again."[3]

Nursing can be a lifesaver for mother, too. Mothers with nursing toddlers often don't have to suffer with engorgement.

By the time my second daughter was born, my oldest was basically nursing only for naps and to fall asleep at night, maybe once or twice during the night. . . . So, when my second was born, she ended up nursing more, as I'd ask her to nurse when I was engorged, and she was happy to oblige.

When you're alone with a baby and a toddler and need to rest, you can often get a nursing toddler to lie down with the two of you. Even if he doesn't fall asleep, at least he is quiet for a while—and safe. You get a few minutes of relaxation.

*For nap time, I would nurse them both at the same time,
so they'd both fall asleep at the same time, and then
I could fall asleep. I am currently doing the same, but it's
harder when my six-year-old is home, because I can't keep
track of her while napping.*

We can (and most of us do) help our children make the transition
from being the baby of the family to being an older sibling without
tandem nursing. Dr. Herbert Ratner's philosophy of babying the baby in
the growing child is the essential concept; nursing is one good tool you
can use if it is available to you and if you want to.

THIS NONNY'S SO PERFECT, I WANNA PUT
IT ON MY SHELF AND KEEP IT FOREVER!

Changes in Mother's Feelings toward the Toddler

When a mother approaches nursing two with lofty motivation, it can be
quite a shock if she finds herself unexpectedly experiencing (as many
mothers do) waves of resentment at the nursing demands of this
suddenly *big* child.

*I had every intention of letting my older child wean
naturally. After the new baby was born, my feelings
changed and I began to resent my older child's nursing.
I would reread* MOTHERING YOUR NURSING TODDLER *and be
encouraged to keep going because I could see that my son*

*really needed to nurse. I struggled for eight or nine months
until I finally just couldn't go on, and I weaned my older
child. It's hard for me to describe how I felt. It was
something about the physical sensation of his mouth on
my nipple. Maybe it was that his suck was more vigorous
compared to the new baby. I just hated nursing him.
It made the hair on my arms stand up. It was awful.
I don't know what made me feel this way because before
my second child was born I thoroughly enjoyed nursing
my older one.*

Most mothers do not react this strongly, but negative feelings of
some sort are common. Actually, mothers often face the same kinds of
feelings toward the demands of their older children when there is a new
baby, even if their children are not nursing. When nursing is involved,
though, the negatives tend to focus there.

Such feelings are actually a part of rearranging and redefining
your mothering now that a new baby is part of your life. During
pregnancy, mothers fear that caring for the new baby will deprive the
young child whom they already love so much. A mother may also worry
that she can never love the coming baby as much as the child in her arms.

Once the baby comes, however, we find that nature has loaded
the dice very heavily in the tiny one's favor, especially if mothers are able
to have a good beginning with their newborns in their first hours and
days. In just a few hours, most are transformed from a guardian angel,
who was determined never to allow the newborn to intrude upon her
relationship with the older child, into a primitive mother, keyed to
defending the newborn's prerogatives at all costs.

Not all mothers experience such a dramatic shift in feelings, but
many do and suffer needless alarm and guilt. Once their feelings have
swung like a tire on a rope from one side of the yard to the other, they
will moderate and end up in a more functional middle place. Love for
each child will develop—different, rich, and exciting. We give love as one
candle gives its flame to another. Though we give all our love to one
child, as if by magic we still have all that love left to give to the next, and
to the next.[23]

One mother writes about the mental gymnastics that she uses to
help keep herself available to her children.

*There are times when the only way I can nurse is if I don't
pay any attention to what I'm doing. So I read or work on
the computer while nursing. When I'm not feeling so
cranky about nursing, I enjoy giving it my full attention
and gazing into my child's eyes; but there are times when*

*I have to either tune it out or I can't nurse at all. This
tends to happen more with the older one, and since it is
clearly important for her to continue nursing, it is a
compromise we have reached. In fact there are times when
I encourage her to nurse so that I can read something or
work on the computer! Disassociating oneself from one's
body is sometimes useful when breastfeeding is
uncomfortable.*

If you do find yourself resenting your older child's nursing
because of the baby, be reassured that what you are feeling is shared by
mothers here and there all over the world. Feeling this way does not
mean that you will never enjoy nursing your child again.

*I didn't know how I would feel about tandem nursing,
I just decided to see how it went, and go from there, one
day at a time. Some days I felt tandem nursing was awful,
other days I thought it was a godsend. I tandem nursed
my two children for eighteen months. What I will always
treasure in my memories of that brief but intense time was
watching my three-year-old reach across my lap to hold
his baby sister's hand. She looked up, still nursing, and
smiled. I knew then that all of the hard times of tandem
nursing were worth it—that this was a special love bond
that the two of them were able to share with each other.*

Most mothers find their doubts offset by positives:

*There were moments when tandem nursing had its
advantages, . . . [it] made up for the guilty feelings of not
enjoying the nursings. She certainly lit up when I would
ask her to relieve engorgement. And of course it helped
smooth the sibling rivalry. When she weaned one year
later she insisted I comfort my youngest at the breast
immediately.*

Considering that when you are troubled with negative feelings
your child may also be going through a mixed-up time, I would suggest
that with most children the weeks right after a baby joins the family may
not be a good time to discuss how you feel. You and your child will benefit
from a few weeks of nursing with as little conflict as possible while you
adjust to your new family setup.

How Do Mothers Manage?

Getting started. In my survey, a number of mothers wrote about nursing during labor, although doing so can bring on contractions. In a slow labor, a mother might even find this stimulation helpful. For most it would be uncomfortable but probably not harmful. "That was intense," one wrote, "but he needed that particular connection with me. So I nursed him."

Researchers using neuromuscular stimulation of the breasts to induce labor in full-term mothers found that in cases in which they applied too much stimulation resulting in too frequent contractions (more than five in ten minutes), stopping the stimulation was all it took for the uterine hyperactivity to resolve.[20] There is no experimental evidence, but logic suggests that nursing is less likely to cause such a problem and can be stopped as easily as artificial stimulation. Besides, few if any mothers having frequent contractions, are likely to be willing to nurse, no matter how the child may feel about it.

A mother wrote about her delivery room experience:

> *I had one, out of a whole group of attendants, comment something to the effect of "You're going to give her all your colostrum?!" as I was tandem nursing. I knew what I was doing was safe and remained positive. After all, my daughter had already nursed through my pregnancy and labor. I did call in a lactation consultant to confirm that all was well with my colostrum!*

Back in the 1970s we thought a good way to prepare our nipples was to express colostrum during late pregnancy. The practice didn't seem to do our nipples any good, but it did show us that the amount of colostrum isn't something fixed, that our bodies kept producing more up to the time the breasts switch over to making milk. The new baby does need colostrum, so your toddler shouldn't have a nursing binge the first day or two after delivery. But nursing a few times should be no problem, especially if you make sure the baby nurses first or more often. (If the toddler has to wait, ask a helper to provide distraction; right after the baby is born is not a good time to ask your child for patience. This is a time when you should try to avoid situations that may trigger sibling rivalry.)

A new kind of relationship. Some families begin tandem nursing in the hospital or birthing center, while for others it begins at home.

After his brother's birth, my toddler came into our bedroom and protested me giving the baby his "some." "My some," he said. Both my parents and in-laws were there, and they panicked. "What will you do?" And they gave me the "see what nursing so long does" looks and comments. I reassured everyone that we had discussed this with him and asked everyone to leave. I talked it over with my two-year-old. He wanted to nurse so we tried. He sucked a few times then let go and laughed. "There's milk in there! How you do that?" He never asked to nurse again but still needed mummy at night so I slept between the toddler and baby for months.

Families have to make adjustments to the special and complicated feelings that can come with nursing two. Many toddlers who have been nursing infrequently now backslide:

It's just very hard to understand my daughter's increased demands for nursing and to be patient with her when she nurses as much as he does! In some ways I feel like I've created a monster who is only satisfied by nursing. And I can only talk about it to other tandem nursing mothers, because I feel other people just wouldn't understand.

Another mother wrote:

Tandem feeding was difficult at times. Sessions could degenerate into tussles. I often complained that I felt like a sow, with scuffling piglets fighting over each nipple. I'm glad I had the right number of breasts to go around![16]

We need to remind ourselves that the arrival of a new baby is a time when toddlers, nursing or not, routinely return to behaviors parents thought they had outgrown, such as thumb-sucking, bed-wetting, waking at night, etc. Frequent nursing is a similar regression, but a healthy one that can help your child come out of this challenging time as a better person.

The mother of the "scuffling piglets" just quoted went on to say:

Overall, I would never question the wisdom of tandem feeding the girls. There are strong bonds all around. Because [the older girl] weaned so late, she may well retain memories of breastfeeding with [the younger one] into adulthood. And I'm sure that being forced to share the

*very thing that they were most attached to, i.e., my breasts,
must continue to make them feel close to each other, and
better able to share in general.*[16]

Together or separately. Many young toddlers seem to nurse
nearly as often as the baby does, especially in the early weeks. Nursing
infant twins separately can take approximately ten hours a day, fifteen
on frequency days. Nursing both together can reduce that time nearly by
half. Nursing siblings together is a great time-saver, and most mothers
do this at least part of the time. Some mothers, however, find the
physical sensations from nursing both infant and toddler at once
overwhelming and avoid doing so whenever possible.

Nursing both together isn't always agreeable to the children
either, and it's wise to pay attention to toddlers' jealousy as well as their
fascination with the usurper in the family. If the children don't cooperate
in sharing your arms, then other approaches are necessary, with some
renewed emphasis where possible on one-on-one parenting.

*My son, then eighteen months, wanted to nurse whenever
his newborn sister was put to the breast. After a few times
of nursing both together, during which he was trying to
push her away, I stopped and tried another tactic. My
daughter slept well from about 2 to 7AM every night. When
my son awoke at about 6:30, we would nurse while the
water boiled for his hot cereal, and then switch sides while
it cooled. That twenty to thirty minutes every morning was
enough to waylay the ugly green monster for the rest of the
day. We could cuddle while his sister nursed, and he was
able to accept her and her need to nurse. We tandem
nursed about fourteen months. My son and daughter are
very close, insisting on having their beds next to each
other, and having "hugging contests" as part of their play.
It is amusing now to see my twenty-six-month-old
daughter get jealous when her big brother wants some
cuddle time.*

When you don't want to nurse both at once, you may want to try
to divert your toddler's attention:

*I have a five-month-old baby and a two-year-old toddler.
My toddler will always want to nurse as soon as her baby
brother starts to fuss because he needs to nurse. I do not
like nursing both at the same time and cannot handle
hearing a baby cry. I get my daughter distracted with one
of her dolls and then nurse the baby.*

One way to reduce the toddler's urges is to nurse the infant in a baby sling so the toddler doesn't see what you're doing.

When you do nurse both together, experiment with positions to find what is most comfortable for everybody:

During the day, we used a nursing pillow and both in the football hold. The position we seemed to use most was the baby in the cradle hold and the toddler in football hold position. I tried this one the opposite way with the toddler in cradle position, but neither child was happy with that.

To avoid nipple soreness from improper latch-on by the newborn, many mothers start out by carefully positioning the baby and then letting the toddler figure out how to position himself, in both sitting and lying-down positions. In the lying-down position, the toddler often does best by getting behind you and draping himself over your back. As the baby gets older, they can sit on either side of you, or you can lie on your back with one arm under the head of each nursling.

Lactation consultant Beverly Morgan says that milk flow will be different when you nurse two children together than when you nurse one alone.

If one child has more difficulty handling the flow, try nursing the child that is having difficulty separately, at least when the breasts are firm and heavy. Once the breast is softened and the flow [slows down], he may be just fine if his sibling starts his meal.

It sometimes works the other way, too. If a newborn is having difficulty getting the hang of nursing, he may get [more] milk if he suckles while his sibling with a more organized suck is nursing.[12]

Plan your environment so you can be as comfortable as possible. A La Leche League Leader suggests:

Have a nursing station, ideally a couch, with lots of pillows, where you can comfortably nurse two simultaneously. Have water, tissues, and reading material for you and the toddler handy to make these sessions enjoyable. I get very thirsty nursing two, so I keep water bottles at several different spots all through the house.

Survival tips. Keeping everybody happy, including mother, can involve some ingenuity and willingness to rearrange schedules.

Sometimes we can get positioned cozily, and the boys pat each others' hands, and it is charming. But generally, nursing two at once makes my skin crawl. I feel put-upon, and not so motherly, like the piglet feeder in the movie Babe. *Over time, through distraction and letting daddy help with bedtime (I can go work out at seven and the older boys will be asleep when I return), the middle child's nursings have gradually reduced.*

Make sure nursing is not the only thing available for your child to do. A La Leche League Leader writes:

When the toddler asks to nurse, see if what she wants is actually food, water, a story, or someone to play with. Many times you can read, play, etc., with one hand and nurse the baby with the other, especially if you use a sling.

Frequent introduction of new toys can take a lot of pressure off mom. Toys don't actually have to be new, just new to the child. Swapping toys with other families with children the same age can accomplish the purpose at less expense. So can items from thrift shops and garage or jumble sales. Playgroups with other toddlers and young children can also provide your child with activities that are more interesting than nursing.

Cooking and housework will need to be kept to a minimum when you have two little ones. If there's nobody around to help and you find yourself going hungry because baby and toddler both insist on nursing when you sit down to eat, try eating on your feet with the baby in a sling. You may also have more luck getting your toddler to eat other foods when your position makes you less available for nursing. Soup in a mug and finger foods like fresh fruit or pre-cut veggies from the supermarket serve very well on such occasions. If you live where people eat yogurt with a spoon, learn to drink it the way others have been doing for centuries. Be creative, and do what works instead of what you're "supposed" to do.

For your own sake and your childrens' you must avoid letting your nutrition slide during these demanding weeks or months. If you go through a time in which your toddler nurses as much as the baby, you may temporarily need 1000 or more calories a day above your own body's needs just like a mother nursing twins, more if you are underweight.[10] When his nursing needs decline, so will your need for extra calories.

Making bizarre adaptations to taking care of yourself does not doom you to eating over the sink for the rest of your days. It's just another stage in the adventure. Doing a good job at parenting requires flexibility, but you can be sure that your adaptations to this stage will soon yield to a different set of adaptations for the next.

Remember too that this will pass and children do grow up. We only have one chance to make their childhood as sweet, innocent, loving, and as memorable as possible.

Cross-infection? Sometimes mothers worry that nursing two children may be sort of like letting them use the same toothbrush. Actually, siblings live so close together in the same environment that preventing cross-infection is nearly impossible. But the anti-bacterial properties of the milk itself probably work to reduce the likelihood of cross-infection.

One organism that defies everything I have just said, however, is the fungus that causes vaginitis and thrush (see p. 101). If you get sore nipples from thrush, it will be necessary to treat both children as well as your nipples. If you develop vaginitis, you will need to treat that as well, along with the diaper rash that one or both children may experience. Sometimes toddlers resist treatment; and since the infection in their mouths is not always a problem for them, some may even choose weaning over treatment. As painful as this infection can be for mother, I would think that most mothers would insist that anybody with thrush who wants to nurse has to undergo treatment. You would probably choose to insist on treatment for a young toddler, but an older one without symptoms should probably be able to decide between treatment and weaning.

In general, thrush aside, the only way to prevent cross-infection is to keep people from living together in anything so "unsanitary" as a family, doing such things as eating and breathing together. I cannot believe that whether they both nurse or not is going to cause much, if any, increase in their rate of infection.

Having enough milk. You may feel anxious about whether your new baby will get enough milk, and thus you may have a strong urge to restrict your toddler's nursing to certain times of day or to nursing only after the baby has finished. One mother said that she would fend off her toddler's requests for nursing by asking what she had eaten at her last meal. That seemed to work as a gentle reminder that the toddler could eat other foods while the baby could not.

If such restrictions work out easily for your children, it is fine to employ them with caution. Limiting the toddler's nursing is occasionally necessary if he consistently wants to nurse right before the baby awakens. After all, the baby has to have the milk to grow and the toddler doesn't. But such situations are not common. Most mothers nursing two find that they produce plenty of milk, enough to nurse the baby and the toddler, each whenever he likes. Researchers measured the milk volume of one tandem nursing mother and found a level of production similar to that of a mother nursing twins.[17] It is much easier to forget about the milk and pay attention to mothering these little people.

> *In the early weeks my toddler would ask to breastfeed every time she saw the baby nursing. This resulted in her having yellow bowel movements for a few days. I fed them both on demand. During the day, most feedings were simultaneous alternating sides at the next feeding. When baby fed alone then I would switch sides during feeding.*

One of the attractive reasons for nursing siblings is that this is one tool you can employ toward reduced sibling rivalry. If nursing becomes one more of the many pleasures in life over which your children have to contend with each other, taking turns and that sort of thing, then it may become part of their struggle with each other for their places in your affection. "Oh, wow, it'll be all gone then," griped one two-year-old asked to wait until the baby was through. The low level of conflict between the children has been most dramatic in the families who have felt free to allow both baby and toddler to nurse on demand. You can assure yourself that the baby is getting enough milk by watching her wet diapers and bowel movements just as you would if your toddler were not nursing.

One mother writes about her son who nursed along with two adopted brothers:

> *The "triplets" learned to care for each other at an early age. [The adopted babies], for example, were "high need" babies, probably due to prenatal drug exposure, and fussed quite a bit in their sleep. My husband and I learned to rub and pat their backs to calm them, without ever even opening our eyes. Early one Saturday morning, when my toddlers' ages ranged from ten months to twenty-five months, I partially awoke to the sound of [the baby's] restless groans. But someone was already patting his back gently and lulling him back to sleep so I closed the one eye I had opened and started to go back to sleep. Something told me to double-check the situation, however, so I pried open both eyes and the sight that met them is something that amazes me to this day. In the early morning light, there sat [the] eighteen-month-old, . . . sitting straight up in the middle of the bed with crossed legs and grinning proudly. He was alternately rubbing and patting [his brother's] back with precisely the same rhythm his Dad used! [The baby] was smiling in his sleep and calming beautifully.*

From the viewpoint of nutrition, too, it seems best not to employ a rigid pattern for nursing, always nursing one first and the other afterwards. Your milk is different at different times in a feeding. If your young toddler nurses frequently and always last, then the baby may not get his share of the relaxed flow of high-fat milk at the end of a feeding. Following a less rigid pattern (and allowing the baby to nurse without switching breasts until he indicates that he is finished by letting go or falling asleep) will allow him to get plenty of sucking time and the proper balance of nutrients over the course of the day.[11]

The baby, being the more frequent nurser, should have "first grabs" more often than not, but he needs to have some opportunities at "finishing up," too. In addition, the more frequently you nurse either child or both, the less variation there is in the fat content of your milk, and the higher the energy level.[9] The infant also needs to nurse on both sides in order for his eyes to develop properly.[11] So if you can relax and let your children nurse on demand, they will probably work out their own patterns without the problems caused by interference from mother.

Avoiding breast problems in the early weeks. For your own sake you may need to pay attention to how often your toddler nurses, especially in the early weeks. Do not let him vary the frequency so widely from day to day that your breasts become overfull some days, particularly if you are prone to breast infections. The great fluctuation in frequency of nursing that is common in nursing children is usually not much of a problem when your milk supply is waning. But when you are fully nursing a baby, you may need to encourage your nursing child not to get distracted and let your breasts get too full. Remember that if your toddler nurses frequently, you may be producing enough milk for twins. You may not be affected if your child nurses several times one day, and not at all the next. But if you are, do not hesitate to encourage him to nurse when he has forgotten to ask for too long a time.

Caring for two. Baby slings or carriers—the soft kind that hold the baby against your body—are great helpers when caring for one little one. When you have two needing your time and attention, a carrier is indispensable. You can cuddle the little one in the carrier while still meeting the needs of your bigger, but still little one. Your child may especially appreciate it if you can learn to carry your baby on your back part of the time, rather than in front, so you don't always have to work over and around the baby when you tend to your child. Having plenty of attention from you will help keep your toddler's need for attention through nursing at the minimum level for him.

If difficulties develop with either nursling—any of the difficulties you might encounter in nursing either one of them alone—you may be called upon for extra creativity in coping with both children's needs and with your own. Mothers sometimes make the mistake of thinking of the nursing relationships that they have with nursing siblings as one relationship, when in fact it is two separate nursing relationships. Yes, you are the same mother, and the little people do interact. But the nursing relationships are individual with each child.

Because tandem nursing is unfamiliar, even more so than toddler nursing, it is easy to say that such-and-such is happening because both are nursing. The truth is, however, that baby may have colic for whatever reasons there may be that babies have colic, and big sister may want to nurse all the time for the kinds of reasons that other people her age sometimes want to nurse all the time. You have to look at each child and do the best you can to help each one when needed.

The arrival of a new baby, like any one of many events in the life of your child, can cause her to need extra time at your breast. Though it may be quite a challenge for you for a while, especially with the new baby to care for, too, tending to her as completely as you can will be your easiest course in the long run.

Of course, extra loving from daddy will be a big help in meeting the needs of your children, especially the toddler. His loving can be administered directly to the children and also indirectly through his love and support for you at a demanding time like this.

Facing critics of tandem nursing. Nursing two in the presence of other people is not often necessary, because the older child is usually busy and distractible when you are away from home. There are situations that arise, however, when neither can wait and there is no privacy to be found, situations when you are best sustained by self-confidence and a sense of humor.

> *I do still struggle with a little bit of embarrassment. When he was a year, I was proud that I was still nursing him, and it was a little sad to me that I knew so few people who nursed their babies that long. Then he was two, and I was still very pleased with nursing him. Then I was pregnant and breastfeeding a two-year-old and started having to explain to people that it was okay to nurse during pregnancy, and no, I wasn't going to make him wean before the baby was born. Then it was tandem nursing: a newborn who (frustratingly) did not want to nurse often enough, and an almost three-year-old who wanted to nurse constantly . Now I'm tandem nursing two kids, not babies, who insist on sitting on either side of me (they each have a favorite side, and when one starts to nurse first, they usually invite the other to join, like it's social time).*

A mother of a three-month-old baby and a two-and-a-half-year-old child wrote of a "public" incident:

> *On the plane they both wanted to nurse at the same time,*
> *but the two-and-a-half-year-old had to nurse standing*
> *up—no other way would do—much to the astonishment of*
> *the two little old ladies beside us! It was all we could do to*
> *keep from laughing aloud, and my husband pretended he*
> *didn't know us. But both children were happy!*

Many a mother who has worried about how she would feel should she need to nurse both her little ones away from home has been relieved to be able to find a place to nurse alone, or has been gratified if her little ones cooperated and nursed discreetly.

You may wonder, with so many difficulties to overcome, why anyone would want to tandem nurse. First, of course, is that children seem to benefit from this kind of parenting. Besides, it is also a great joy.

> *I tandem nurse our girls (three-and-a-half and five-and-a-*
> *half) a lot and we all love it! . . . I just want to let you*
> *know I am here, because I am a mother who adores*
> *tandem nursing my two precious angels. I really can't put*
> *into words how special and beautiful it is for us.*

Will Tandem Nursers Ever Wean?

How either of these little guys is ever going to wean if he sees the other one nursing is a very common worry. We have been schooled to think of nursing as a bad habit that will go on forever if we do not somehow eliminate the opportunities for nursing and get the child to forget about it. But nursing is not a sneaky way little people have of dominating adults. Rather it is the manifestation of infantile needs in the growing child. When children wean spontaneously it is not because they forget about it, but because they outgrow the need.

As I have said, we must remember that even when mother is nursing two she is nursing two individual children. Rivalries between siblings over nursing and nursing only because the other is doing so can be kept at a minimum as long as both can come to you freely most of the time, whenever they feel the need to nurse.

When they will wean naturally is determined by their own individual development and in the long run will probably not be changed much by seeing the sibling nurse. There are likely to be changes and adjustments in nursing because of pregnancy and getting used to life with the new baby. But once these normal crises are past, each child should settle into the kind of nursing pattern he would have if he were the only one nursing. Usually the older one will gradually lose interest over the months or years until he just quits asking. Meanwhile the baby continues in his own individual pattern.

Responsive parenting, not a contest. It is not uncommon for mothers to find themselves nursing two toddlers at once (not as difficult as it sounds, because the older one is usually becoming less demanding all the time). It is not unheard of for both children to wean about the same time or for the younger one to wean first, but neither of these instances is the usual.

In a few families in which the older child has needed some nursing for several years, a second younger sibling has arrived while the older two were still nursing.

> *I just found out I am pregnant while tandem nursing a twenty-month-old and a three-and-a-half-year-old. . . . I felt very confident that I could nurse one through a pregnancy, but real unsure about two!*

I heard, in fact, from a mother, now a published author and a psychologist with a PhD, who found herself with a whole house full of nurslings for a few years after two babies joined her tandem nursing family through adoption. She writes that she had no trouble producing enough milk for all three boys and for their older brother, even though the babies didn't start solids until well past six months of age. All three boys self-weaned at different ages, the shyest one clinging the most and weaning himself long after the others, around age four years. This mother writes:

> *It was a wonderful time. In the mid-1980s, I was the stay-at-home mom of five children under age six, and four of them were nursing. For years, I didn't do much more than nurse, play, nap, change diapers, and load the washing machine, but it was one of the best times of my life.*

I feel some hesitation in describing situations like this, because I do not want to play a part in any pointless inter-mother rivalry over who can have the most children nursing at once. Such a contest would be nonsense. Besides, children are not likely to cooperate by nursing once they have outgrown the need.

What I hope to see is that nobody's counting. You can look at the needs of each child as an individual as well as a member of a family. It can be a kindness to a child to allow him to outgrow baby things at his own pace, even when little brothers and sisters join the family. Our children do not get bigger all at once when a new baby arrives; they just suddenly look bigger to us.

References

1   Bøhler, E. and Bergström, S. Child growth during weaning depends on whether mother is pregnant again. *Journal of Tropical Pediatrics* April 1996; 42:107.

2   Bøhler, E. and Ingstad, B. The struggle of weaning: Factors determining breastfeeding duration in East Bhutan. *Social Science and Medicine* 1996; 43(12):1809, 1811, 1813.

3   Conton, L. Social, economic and ecological parameters of infant feeding in Usino, Papua New Guinea. *Infant Care and feeding in the South Pacific.* Ed. L. B. Marshall. New York: Plenum Press, 1983; 112.

4   Cosminsky, S., Mhloyi, M. and Ewbank, D. Child feeding practices in a rural area of Zimbabwe. *Social Science and Medicine* April 1993; 36(7):943.

5   Dettwyler, K. A. Breastfeeding and weaning in Mali: Cultural context and hard data. *Social Science and Medicine* 1987; 24(8):642.

6   Fildes, V. A. *Breasts, Bottles and Babies: A History of Infant Feeding.* Edinburgh: Edinburgh University Press, 1986; 20, 29, 55.

7   Gilbert, A. N. et al. Mother-weanling interactions in Norway rats in the presence, of a successive litter produced by postpartum mating. *Physiology and Behavior* February 1983; 30(2): abs.

8   Hildebrand, K. et al. *Child mortality and care of children in rural Mali. Population, Health and Nutrition in the Sahel: Issues in the welfare of selected West African communities.* Ed. A.G. Hill. London: KPI, Ltd.,1985; 194.

9   Jackson, D. A. et. al. Circadian variation in fat concentration of breast-milk in a rural northern Thai population. *British Journal of Nutrition* May 1988; 59(3):abs.

10 Leonard, L. G. Breastfeeding twins: maternal-infant nutrition. *JOGN Nursing* 1982; 11(3):148.

11 Mohrbacher, N. and Stock, J. BREASTFEEDING ANSWER BOOK. Revised edition. Schaumburg, Illinois: La Leche League International, 1997; 93, 123, 281, 349.

12 Morgan, B. *Reading Your Baby's Body Language.* Audio tape. San Jose, CA: Milky Way Press, 1989.

13 Moscone, S. R. and Moore, M. J. Breastfeeding during pregnancy. *Journal of Human Lactation* June 1993; 9(2):85-87.

14 Mull, D. S. Mother's milk and pseudoscientific breastmilk testing in Pakistan. *Social Science and Medicine* 1992; 34 (11): 1280-82.

15 Newton, N. and Theotokatos, M. Breastfeeding during pregnancy in 503 women: Does a psychobiological weaning mechanism in humans exist? *Proceedings of the Serono Symposia,* 20B Ed. L. Zichella. London: Academic Press, 1980; 846-48.

16 Nursing Mothers of Australia. Tandem feeding. *Nursing Mothers' Newsletter* Summer 1998; 34(1):15.

17 Prosser, C. G., Saint, L. and Hartmann, P. E. Mammary gland function during gradual weaning and early gestation in women. *Australian Journal of Experimental Biology and Medical Science* 1984; 62(2):225 224-26. Garza, C. et al. Changes in the nutrient composition of human milk during gradual weaning. *American Journal of Clinical Nutrition* 1983; 37:61-65.

18 Segal, S. et al. Evaluation of breast stimulation for induction of labor in women with a prior cesarean section and in grandmulti-paras. *Acta Obstetricia et Gynecologica Scandinavica* 1995; 74:40-41.

19 Singh, M. B., Haldiya, K. R. and Lakshminarayana, J. Infant feeding and weaning practices in some semi-arid rural areas of Rajasthan. *Indian Medical Association* November 1997; 95(11):578.

20 Tal, Z. et al. Breast electrostimulation for the induction of labor. *Obstetrics and Gynecology* October 1988; 72(4):672-73.

21 Treckel, P. A. Breastfeeding and maternal sexuality in colonial America. *Journal of Interdisciplinary History* 1989; 20(1):37-38.

22 Vis, H. L. and Hennart, P. Decline in breast-feeding: about some of its causes. *Acta Paediatrica Scandinavica* October-December 1978; 31(4):197.

23 Zilberg, B. How my four-year-old haunted our midnight feedings. *Redbook* February 1972; 30-32.

chapter eight

Getting Enough Rest

One thing I remember about having small children is being tired. There were a few years when somebody was always up too early and somebody else up too late. I wish I had been smart enough to figure out this mother's nap-time technique:

> *For naps, drive the kids to sleep. This is the best way to ensure that both will fall asleep at the same time and stay asleep for me. You can then park in your driveway, and sleep too! Sometimes I fix something for lunch that I can eat while driving, like a pita bread sandwich, to save time.*

Night Duty

I originally wrote this chapter back in nineteen-mumble-mumble, sitting in bed with my youngest asleep beside me threatening to wake up any minute. So I know from long experience that this sleeping business is no joke. Parents' adult lifestyle and children's ever-changing sleep patterns keep interfering with each other. Just as you get everything worked out, your child changes again.

First of all, realize that nursing may not be the cause of your losing sleep. It's hard to be open to such a suggestion when the whole household is quietly asleep—that is, everyone but you. The little one nods

151

off, still clinging to your nipple, but like so many mothers who slept well while their small infants were nursing, you now find it difficult to sleep while nursing a little child. So you, little one attached, lie grudgingly awake in the peaceful night. Every time you remove your nipple from his mouth, no matter how carefully, he starts kicking and crying. Under these circumstances you are not likely to be very receptive to my suggestion that it might not be the nursing that is keeping you awake.

Well, technically, you are awake because of the nursing. Babies who nurse tend to wake more often than those who don't. But at least you're lying down, and bedsharing mothers are usually less disturbed by nursing at night than those whose children sleep elsewhere.[4] And you're in good company. Keeping a nursing child next to mother at night is the usual practice over much of the world. For instance, among Quechua Indians in the Peruvian Andes interviewed in 1985:

> *All mothers who had ever breastfed their youngest child had also co-slept with that child from birth. . . . It appears that breastfeeding at night may continue into a child's third year, long after the cessation of day nursing. Even without her mother's full participation, an older toddler could nurse at night unless her mother refused.[5]*

I would suggest that you and other mothers of older nurslings everywhere are awake mostly because of being the mother of your child at this time in her life. Instead of lying in bed, you could be stumbling around fixing a bottle or an apple slice, or rocking and patting, or fumbling among the toys under the bed looking for a lost pacifier. It was my experience that, even though I too at times felt really resentful of night nursings, they never disrupted my sleep as badly as did tending to the nighttime needs of my toddler who did not nurse and who was confined to his crib.

The best nursing-at-night times for me were when I discovered the warm, quiet of the night and the security of lying close between people who loved me. The worst times were when I wrestled with my own private nighttime demons and felt suffocated between the same bodies that made me feel secure the night before. The nursing situations were of course the same both times; the difference was what was going on in my head.

The status of your own health is a factor in how well you cope with interrupted sleep. You need to pay attention to your nutritional state, especially B vitamins, which you get from whole grains or supplements. (Brewer's yeast is a good source of B vitamins.) If your diet is deficient in these nutrients, the B vitamins will pass into your milk and leave you more susceptible to fatigue than you should be.[3]

When Needs Clash

Caring for children at night presents a situation in which mother's needs seem to be in direct conflict with her child's. Most of us become quite childlike ourselves when we go to sleep, so it often feels as if we are being asked to care for a little person at a time when we are not so big ourselves. Then all too often we carry an irrational resentment of the night's interrupted sleep into the day. Sometimes mother has big plans for the next day and is, of course, disappointed to be dragging because of lost sleep. Most days, however, mothers merely need to slow down their pace to cope with being sleepy. Sleepiness is one of life's many normal conditions that we can cope with very well if we don't fight it or push ourselves beyond what sleepy people can do.

Our initial, immature—100 percent understandable—reaction to interrupted sleep is to lash out at the child, to try to make him pay attention to our needs, too. Of course, when we do this (and most all of us do some time in one way or another), we communicate little and generally end up losing even more sleep. Many parent-hours of hard experience show that it is much more productive to apply adult heads to modifying living patterns so that children get the care they need twenty-four hours a day while adults get enough rest most of the time.

Night is a scary time for people—not just little people either. The nights of the first few years are when children learn how to cope with the fears that come with darkness. The very best source of comfort at night is the presence of another person, or other people.

Surely I am not the only one who remembers how it felt to be a very young child under the old "rules" that banished toddlers to their own beds. I can remember lying awake or sitting silently in the dark, terrified, full of rage, full of self-loathing. In the twisted logic of the very young, I figured I must deserve to feel that way or it couldn't be happening to me. I remember those feelings as intensely today as I did then, and those memories won't let me even consider the possibility that night waking is a casual game of manipulation and control that parents somehow need to win. Whether or not your child feels safe at night makes a difference in how well he will live his whole life.

You can teach your child to sleep alone if that is important enough to you that you want to put out all the effort outlined in many standard books of child care. You will no doubt need a regular bedtime ritual and, perhaps, a cuddly object to help ward off the demons little minds create in the night. As a parent you may also have to get extra rest in the day to minimize the physical drain on you from this arrangement. You will need to get up and present yourself bodily at your child's bedside from time to time during her growing-up years in order to prove to her that this sleeping arrangement is indeed safe and that you are still available when needed. A frightened child must not be left alone at night.

Some mothers tell me that toddlers in cribs sleep better, and perhaps some do. But I cannot reconcile this with my experience with my children, or with my own memories from distant childhood. Maybe my toddler was unusual when he awoke in his crib, but I doubt it. My experiments with this arrangement had me up several times a night for months. Many parents today claim better success than I had, saying they are only up a few times a year with their children. But I eventually found tucking that toddler into bed with me ever so much more restful than sitting beside his crib until the alligators went away.

I don't know how many children actually learn to sleep through the night, and how many parents just learn not to hear the smaller cries, only the loud ones. I don't know how many children simply learn, as I did, to turn their feelings in on themselves and keep quiet.

You can choose instead to teach your child to seek security in the night by getting close to people. Looking at humankind as a whole, it is clear that sleeping near other people has survival value. It is easier to keep warm and to defend ourselves from real dangers in the night if we are near other people. Only in a society in which we can burn fuel freely to heat large homes, and only where the danger of predators—human or animal—is very low, would we dare put a baby or small child in a room separate from his parents.

I must be quick to add, though, that I needed no such lofty goals as a desire to help my children grow up well-adjusted about nighttime or to protect them from danger to motivate me to teach my kids to seek company when they were scared at night. Laziness and distaste for lost sleep were motivation enough.

Nursing at night and doing it in bed is one way to increase your rest. (Some prefer to doze in a comfortable chair.) Another is to be flexible about sleeping arrangements. Your family may sleep best with Junior between you, or at your side. Learning to offer both breasts from the same side so that you don't have to roll over may help reduce interruption in your sleep and can enable you to keep your child in the safest or most comfortable part of the bed.

You may need to put your bed against the wall or your mattress on the floor for a while so you don't have to worry about his falling off. Two mattresses side by side is even better so you'll have room to get away from each other when you want to. Some families fasten a crib, with the side dropped, securely to the side of the bed. That way you can roll the child in and out of it easily. A mat, sleeping bag, or mattress for your baby or child on the floor near your bed may be your best bet.

It may even be that it will be more comfortable for you to have your child in another room for one reason or another. We moved one of our children out of our room while he was still a baby because he snored so loudly. Another family found it best to put their child in her own room for at least part of the night "since every sound woke her, including deep breaths and dropped socks." You may want to try putting your older baby or toddler into bed with an older sibling. Consider a bed or mattress on the floor or a recliner in his room where you can nurse in complete comfort, or where daddy or big brother can cuddle with the little one when that works out.

Night waking may become less wakeful for you if you provide your walking child with a place of his own to sleep that he can get out of easily at night, like a low bed or mattress rather than a crib, so that he can come to you when he needs to. Most parents are glad not to have to get up at night while still caring for their children who do awaken and need them.

Parents can divide responsibilities at times:

> *I've realized that any nursing child will wake for nighttime feeds if they're sleeping with you. When I've needed my space, in later pregnancy or with the third newborn, my husband has gone onto night duty, and slept with the other child/ren. This has worked well for our family, although I admit that it makes us a little more distant at the time. Many other cultures do this, and it seems to me that when a baby is little, it does take priority over the marital relationship for a time.*

This mother goes on to write about how she and her husband went about the pleasingly important task of getting together when parenting kept them apart at night. Later this same family changed to a different arrangement:

> *When he was just over two, I put him into bed with his two sisters, and he'll sleep until four or five, come in for a nurse, and sleep to seven. We both enjoy waking up with him, but get a bit of space back in the evenings. I remember that the girls didn't reliably sleep through until three to four.*

Some children disturb your sleep without losing a wink themselves. I have mentioned my snorer. We also had a tooth grinder who was eventually helped by a splint made by an orthodontist. But I lost the most sleep by far to the little guy who would, several times a night and without warning, clobber me with a hand or foot while completely dead to the world. And I lost sleep with him for well over a year after he had quit nursing, because this child needed to be close at night even after the other baby needs had passed. We survived by having lots of bed space to get away from him, or alternatively pinning him on his side with his back to me. He did eventually accept a bed of his own, and I'm still here to tell the tale. It was almost worth it to be able tease this now grown man about how he used to beat up his mother—almost. His wife assures me that he is sweet and loving, and no longer dangerous.

The bottom line is that you shouldn't accept any rules about how you have to sleep. Just make sure you provide secure feelings for your children at night, and make sure you do it in the least sleep-disturbing way possible for your family. Also be prepared to abandon your current easy approach in favor of a different easy approach as you notice things becoming different. Your child is growing and changing fast, and no one else in the family can be expected to stay the same forever either. Be adaptable. And be prepared to help with nighttime fears as long as your children live with you. School-age children are grateful to know that after the occasional nightmare there is a place near you where they can come quietly to sleep in the warmth of your protection, or to know that you will come and sleep near them.

Frequent Night Waking

It helps your child sleep and therefore helps you to get more rest at night if you do a few obvious things to help your child sleep better. One is helping her to keep cool enough or warm enough. On hot nights it may be necessary to use air conditioning more than you might otherwise to help a restless little one sleep. Or you can try hanging an electric fan high out of reach to use on such nights—much less expensive than air conditioning.

On cold nights, pajamas on a baby or toddler are helpful for those who will wear them, even if no one else in the house bothers with night clothes. Children are usually near four before they can sleep without kicking their covers off. So one way to avoid being awakened by a shivering tot is to cover him all up with warm sleepers—the kind with feet. Solving nighttime diapering problems helps a lot, too, because wet bedding and pajamas can make him even colder. (Be aware, though, that babies who sleep with their mothers should not dressed as warmly as those who sleep alone in cribs.)

Keep yourself warm, too. You will find nursing in a cold room when your shoulders have to stick out of the covers a less chilling experience if you wear a long-sleeved pajama top or robe. A loose-fitting pullover works fine; a nightshirt or robe that opens in the front or a specially designed winter nursing gown can be even more convenient for easy, warm nighttime nursing. Don't wear anything that requires much fumbling in order to nurse. The simpler the better, especially if the toddler can help herself without waking you at all.

Once in a while it is hunger that causes a child to wake frequently at night. If you suspect that this may be so, offer your child food more often during the day. Provide a filling snack (like a banana, a peanut butter sandwich, something good left over from supper, an egg, etc.) in the evening, before she gets really sleepy and brushes her teeth. If you suspect hunger in the middle of the night, you might offer a snack, starting with foods that are the least likely to cause tooth decay, foods like raw celery or cabbage. Crunchy raw carrots or raw fruit may be the best choice for some children, although these do contain natural sugar and acid. If your child is really hungry, you may need to offer other foods like crackers or a sandwich. You will have to balance what you offer at night, and whether you brush after this snack, with what your child's teeth seem to be able to tolerate. Remember that breast milk alone does not cause tooth decay, but mixed with sugars from food, it does.[2] Plan your strategy during the day so during the night, with your eyes only half open, you can do what works best for your child.

Some children, quite the opposite, seem to be disturbed by rumblings in their tummies if they eat at bedtime. They sleep better if they do their eating earlier in the evening.

There are health problems that can cause night waking too. Some children are troubled by stuffy noses at night—when they have a cold, or because of allergies. Your child is much less likely to be allergic than is a bottle-fed one, but some breastfed babies do grow into children with allergic sniffles. These children will sleep better if they are kept away from whatever substance it is that bothers them. Wool blankets or feather pillows top the list of things that can cause nighttime problems. Be sure to consult your health care provider if a stuffy nose stays around for a long time and disrupts your child's sleep. She will be able to help you identify the cause of the congestion and advise you in making your child (and thereby your whole family) more comfortable at night.

The onset of a cold or teething may reveal themselves in restlessness at night even before other symptoms appear. How often I remember resisting my children's waking at night "for no reason" only to find later that they were coming down with something. Of course I felt terribly cold and hardhearted once I learned what the problem was.

Other possibilities to check for when your child seems unusually restless at night include pinworms, earache, and constipation.

Mosquito or chigger bites can awaken little people (and big people too). It is wise to keep on hand whatever medication you find most helpful for itchy bites. In addition, after an active day children often experience leg aches which can make it hard to go to sleep or can wake them. Gentle massage and an extra cover usually relieve this discomfort.

Many children wake up while they are urinating or immediately afterwards. This can happen to any child, but is quite common in toddlers who are being toilet trained too early and too vigorously. Relaxing any efforts toward toilet training can lead to a gradual reduction in waking for this reason.

It is possible for caffeine in your diet to affect your child's sleep, although studies suggest that the amount of caffeine in a nursing mother's milk is usually too small to be clinically significant, even for young babies. The rates at which mothers' bodies metabolize caffeine vary, however, resulting in different caffeine levels in the milk of different mothers. Heavy maternal caffeine use has been shown to result in irritability and sleep disturbances in some nursing babies.[1] So if you use a lot of caffeine-containing drinks, cutting your caffeine intake back to less than the equivalent of five cups of coffee per day may be worth a try. It won't hurt anyway—unless you cut back too quickly and give yourself a caffeine headache, which I can tell you from personal experience does hurt! Take it slow, and don't bank on caffeine elimination for a miracle. If it proves to be one for you, great.

With the whole list of physical causes of night waking out of the way, the majority of you with questions about this matter are reading on, because physical factors do not seem to be involved in night waking most of the time. The reason that most children wake up at night is their normal, immature sleep pattern that will be changed only by the passage of time. I like to discuss the physical factors first, though, because by the time you have checked them all out, your child may have outgrown this up-and-down-all-night phase by himself, and thus you may have had an opportunity to take a bow for effecting such a marvelous "cure."

One fruitful place to look for reasons why nights may be restless is in the tensions of the day. The things we need to look at are not so much things that make parents tense, though our tensions cannot be ignored completely, but the things that make our children tense. Each child tolerates experiences differently, each in his own way, and on his own timetable. An increase in mother's activities, especially activities that consume her attention or take her away from her child, can result in more uneasy feelings during the day and an increase in children's wakefulness at night.

An overtired mother can also make a child tense and unhappy so that he is up more frequently at night. This situation can become a vicious circle, so it is wise when you see this happening to employ some of the "survival techniques" discussed later in this chapter in order to get more rest and break the cycle.

I do not want any of you who are living with a child who is wakeful at night to feel guilty, as if you must be awful parents to allow "tensions" into your child's life. He needs to learn to deal with the small, everyday situations that leave him tense, and he does this very effectively when he seeks the comfort of being near you and nursing— during the day and at night. He is learning to seek comfort by being near his most loved person. He gets into the warm, familiar nursing situation and lets himself feel good again. You are doing your part for his well-being in turn when you make it easy for him to do this. But it may indeed make you tired.

Mothers who work away from home especially notice their children's need for nursing at night.[4] Many employed mothers, even though they are really tired, tell me that they appreciate the closeness and softening of anxieties that night nursings provide for both mother and child. Frequent nursing at night can be a boon for toddlers whose mothers are away during the day. One mother writes:

> *I also respond quite defensively when I admit to colleagues that my daughter does not sleep through the night, and I have never attempted to [make her do so]. I state that because I am away from her for so many hours during the day, I feel I need to be available whenever she needs me throughout the night. I also state that I just can't feel comfortable letting her cry for a long period of time, which I imagine would be the case if I did not go to her during the middle of the night. I often ask others if they have read the book NIGHTTIME PARENTING, that advocates an approach which is very different from [the "cry it out" approach to night waking].*

Children vary so much in what makes them anxious that it is impossible for one mother to analyze another mother's activities and say for certain that this or that is why her child is up several times at night. The mother whose little one sleeps all night is not thereby proved to be a "better mother"; she probably just has one of those children who are not wakeful.

Some children seem to adapt easily to new situations. Others are so disoriented in their early years that they must have almost every minute of love and attention a full-time mother can give and still are restless at night. Nothing you can do will make the very anxious child become a completely easygoing one. You can make some difference, though, in how much tension your child takes to bed at night by gentling her days.

I would urge any mother who is walking around bleary-eyed because of being awake nursing so much at night to simplify the daytime routine, avoiding situations that make the child clingy (or wildly overactive—a kind of behavior that can signal the same threatened feelings in a child as does shy clinging). New people, new places, new activities, projects that occupy parents' or even siblings' attention for longer blocks of time than usual, activities that increase the separation of mother and child or father and child—all these are possible sources of tension.

Different children enjoy different kinds of challenges in their daily lives, so it is impossible to draw up a checklist that says, "Do these things every day" and "Never do these things." You can judge best by watching your own child's behavior. Watch for unusual signals of stress (one of my children avoided threatening situations by going to sleep), and sometimes you will be able to spot a situation that is just too much for your child right now.

There is one kind of tension that you would not want to eliminate if you could, however, and that is the one that results from your child's own eagerness to tackle new things. When your child wants to learn to walk, to talk with people outside the immediate family, to go out to the sandbox without a parent along, to tie his own shoes, to toilet train, to go to school, and on and on through the ambitions any young child may have—when your child pushes himself to accomplish more, he is going to experience some increase in his level of anxiety and require some babying to help him handle it. Cecily Lehrfeld Harkins, who some years ago trained many of us in the Southwestern USA for work in La Leche League, described this pattern of self-imposed tension and comfort-seeking as the "Yo-Yo Theory." The farther they venture away on their quest for independence, the closer they need to come back into baby things to make sure everything is okay. Both the venturing out and the coming back are necessary for growing up and away. And, like a yo-yo, they do gradually come back less and less urgently.

Surviving When Night Nursings Are Necessary

The key to surviving the active, unpredictable preschool years is laziness—well, laziness coupled with the ability to accept tiredness as a part of life sometimes. I know that what you do just to keep your toddler from dumping the laundry soap into the aquarium or from burning your shoes in the fireplace is far from laziness. But most of us have visions of shiny floors, kitchens that smell as clean as they look, and a germ-free bathroom bowl. If we do not meet the standards set by our mothers (or mothers-in-law) and the TV commercials, we feel inadequate and lazy. Well, in my opinion, if you are enjoying your time with your child and are having a happy give-and-take between what he wants to do and what you want to do, you are far from inadequate. If the day does not leave you time or energy to make the beds, then you may feel that you have been lazy. You have not been lazy at all really; but if you are like me, it will be easier just to say that you have been than to try to explain.

The most helpful lazy thing to do when you have lost sleep at night is to lie down during the day. You can usually find some time when you can lie down and nurse your little one to sleep. That is an excellent opportunity for rest for both of you. When you are being awakened at night, do not use your child's naptime to catch up on undone work that you are feeling guilty about. I repeat myself perhaps, but only because it is important and because parents are hardheaded about learning to take care of ourselves: be lazy. Lie beside your child and enjoy the warm, quiet time. Or drift off to sleep. He will help you dump that fizzy stuff in the toilet bowl later, or tomorrow. You will get done what you have to get done. I have learned from experience, no matter what "they" say, that a refrigerator is no harder to clean after eight months than after one. So don't worry about it. These things can wait when they have to.

If you reach a time when you are frequently exhausted while your little one is going strong, or a time when you need a nap but he does not, set up a safe, fun, locked room in which you can lie down and doze without fear of your child's hurting himself or you. You need to install a lock your child cannot operate—perhaps high on the inside of the door. The room needs to contain interesting books and toys—things your child likes—things that will not hurt you if he drops them on your head while you doze. Electrical outlets need safety covers, and things plugged into outlets (like clocks) need to be plugged in behind heavy furniture. Any piece of heavy furniture taller than it is deep or wide needs to be anchored to the wall behind it. There should be no appliances in the room for a child to practice operating, no plastic bags, medicines, cleaning supplies—nothing dangerous. Nor should there be anything fragile or valuable enough for you to have to worry about it.

It may be best for the "child-proof" room to be a playroom or child's bedroom, or you may prefer to fix your own bedroom to be safe for you and your child. This room is a place to which you can go, where you can lie down, relax your vigil over your child's inquisitiveness a bit, even doze if your little one gets occupied with something in the room for a while. Just lying down while he nurses, pries your eyelids open, flicks your fingernails, or tries all the other ways a child can use your body for entertainment—just lying down is more refreshing than you might expect. When she is bored with nursing, roll over on your stomach, and she will probably give you what one mother described as a "poor man's massage" by climbing all over you.

Another source of relief for you when you are up a great deal at night is another person with whom your child is comfortable. Perhaps daddy will entertain the little one for a while so you can get a nap or a leisurely bath. Some mothers go to bed early with the child for a while; usually doing this includes an understanding with their mates that they can wake their wives sometime later in the evening for conversation and whatever else may develop. Another great help can be a responsible older child—your own or a neighbor's—who is willing to play with your little one in a safe place (perhaps your baby-proofed room) while you nap. Since you are right there in the house, even a smart seven-year-old can fill the bill. You shouldn't give the children run of the house if your helper is very young, but a child this age may not even demand the going rate for babysitters.

By all means, be ingenious and clever. There are ways to survive without making anyone have to go without what she—or he—needs.

Expendable Nighttime Nursings

Many children need a lot of attention at night well into childhood. Many others drop one and then another nighttime nursing over the months or years just by beginning to sleep longer stretches. Now and then it is possible to hurry the progress toward longer stretches of sleep a little bit—not much, though—by gently avoiding nursing when you sense that your child is very sleepy and not really intent upon it. You can roll on your stomach and see whether your child's halfhearted whimpering and pummeling fades back into the steady breathing of sleep, or if it becomes more urgent. Or you can have daddy or an older sibling pat or rock the little one back to sleep. If you have guessed wrong and your child is feeling a strong need to nurse, there is no harm done. He is quite able to make it clear to you what he needs and will not hesitate to do so.

What I have not suggested for eliminating nighttime waking and nursing is the "letting him cry it out" approach. You may pretend to be fast asleep on your stomach while you make sure the child beside you is really awake and needing to nurse. Or you may snooze while one of your "reinforcements" tries to get him back to sleep. In either case you are doing quite a different thing from deserting him in a room by himself to "cry it out." Instead, there is a person with him to help him relax back into sleep, or you are there to respond finally if he tells you that nothing can substitute for nursing this time.

Caring for anxious, wakeful children at night can be tiresome, and we all resent it sometimes. But a combination of flexibility and creative laziness helps mothers survive these nights and the days that follow them. Keeping children secure and comfortable at night contributes toward a lifetime of easy sleep for them, an objective worthy of the weariness you may feel now. Hang in there; these nighttime needs will not stay so urgent forever.

The "No Nursing until Daylight" Contract

Some verbal children are able to make an agreement with their mothers not to ask to nurse until it gets to be light outside. Then they pounce eagerly, ready for a long, early morning cuddle-and-nurse.

Most mothers who suggest such an agreement meet either protests or blank stares from their youngsters. But an occasional child finds the idea acceptable, and mother gets a little more sleep as a result. A small, added bonus is the comic glee with which he flies into mother's arms, usually at the first glimmer of daylight.

An interesting corollary of this arrangement is the "No Nursing until Dark" Contract. Once in a while a mother has been able to reduce pressure upon herself from people around her by persuading her child to nurse only in the evening and during the night.

As long as the child is comfortable and is not showing signs of distress in other ways, there should be no problem with an agreement of this type. Do keep in mind, though, that a preschool child is not mature enough yet to make long-range plans about something so compelling as nursing. The agreement may be fine for a while, but when she reaches another stage in her growing, or a rough spot, the contract may need to come up for renegotiation.

Long Bedtime Nursings

Often we take a cranky tot to bed and lie down to nurse him to sleep— and lie there, and lie there. Sometimes it makes us really angry to be "trapped" when we would so much prefer to be involved in adult activities during the evening.

Many families, I must be quick to say, are comfortable with a long nursing at the child's bedtime. This is certainly a very peaceful way for your child to drift off to sleep. Some mothers take a nap at this time and find themselves refreshed for the late evening grown-up world. On occasion the child even puts mom to sleep instead of the other way around. In a delightful little family comedy it can be the child who reappears in the living room and then helps dad tease mom about who was putting whom to bed. At any rate, with or without comedy, if you are happy with these nursings, by all means do not interfere with something that is working for you.

If you have not achieved positive feelings, especially about nursing so long at bedtime, there are a number of options you may want to consider. First of all, is your child sleepy? Is your child who is so hard to get to sleep waking up very early in the morning or waking often at night? Preschool children require less sleep than most people wishfully may think. Crabby behavior in the evening can result from many things besides sleepiness. The first thing that comes to mind is that we adults are tired and start our own activities (or inactivities) that do not include our little ones. We may be less mobile and less interesting than during the day. Your child may like it better when you are sorting laundry and talking to her than when you are watching TV or writing letters. Another thing—children, like adults, may get tired and a bit irritable quite a while before they are ready to fall asleep. Sometimes they nurse a while, doze a bit, and then are (horrors!) their perky selves for another hour or so—just the way we adults are sometimes in the evening.

One approach to problems in the evening is to forget about bedtimes with preschoolers. School-aged children are into a scheduled world and have to adhere to some sort of bedtime; besides, they seem to need more sleep than do the younger ones. The little ones, however, can drop off to sleep whenever they are ready—tiny ones prone on daddy's knees or bigger ones sitting beside daddy, or in mommy's arms after nursing off and on throughout the evening, or on the beanbag chair in front of the TV, or wherever they curl up and conk out. As hallowed as the children's bedtime is in our motherhood lore, it is in practice many times a source of friction that is just as well done away with, for the little children at any rate.

The possible drawback of forgetting bedtimes is the fact that, in many families, the adults will have little people for company most of the evening. It is possible, though few believe it any more, to have enjoyable evenings with children around. Sometimes in a family of several children, after the school kids are in bed is the only time daddy gets to enjoy the youngest without competition from the others. And sometimes it is possible for parents to trade evening cocktails alone for breakfast alone for a few months or years. Some couples, however, may find that their time in the evening is irreplaceable; of course in these households it is wise to help the children get to sleep—at least a little while before the adults' bedtime. This may mean learning to enjoy a long nursing.

It could give you a kind of closed-in feeling, too, if you find that you cannot go out in the evenings because your child gets cranky and needs to nurse to sleep and really needs to do it at home in bed. Yet there are several constructive courses you can take. First, you can just wait. Your child will outgrow the time of having to nurse to fall asleep. Most children at a fairly young age, as long as they are happy with their caretaker, especially daddy, learn to fall asleep with rocking or walking, or just sitting with him as he reads or watches TV. A leisurely bath and reading a story can help.

Many children do not want to go to bed without nursing, but most will fall asleep as long as they can stay close to daddy or a familiar sitter. If your child is not yet comfortable with falling asleep in anyone's arms but yours, be patient. It will probably not be long before she is.

Another way to deal with the need to nurse at bedtime (or with the toddler who stays up very late) is to rearrange your plans to fit her schedule. There are many places—visiting friends or eating out for instance—that you can take your wide-awake child. If your child, on the other hand, needs you to be there for an early bedtime nursing, you can arrange to go out or to entertain after he is asleep. Either way the adjustments you are making are not permanent changes in your social life. They are temporary adjustments to make life easier. Besides, changes give you an opportunity to toy with different lifestyles. What is a cocktail party like with a two-year-old among the guests? What about a leisurely dinner well after 8:00 at a gourmet restaurant—or at the taco place for that matter? The possibilities are endless if you have imagination, and without your child's bedtime needs you might never have thought of them. As for the things you cannot do now, you will be able to do them again. The time during which your little one will need you so much in the evening is far short of forever. In fact it is hardly a moment in the space of your lifetime.

The way many families—mine included—have dealt with the problem of having mom feeling trapped at the bedtime nursing is to have dad take over the bedtime routine with the youngest. And freeing mothers like me who are impatient with bedtime nursings is not the only reason that families use this sort of routine. Many fathers enjoy this special cuddly time and responsibility for care of their little children.

This sort of arrangement can begin in infancy when dad holds the baby in the evenings until she wants to nurse. Mom nurses and then returns her to daddy and so on back and forth until the baby is sound asleep. Gradually there gets to be less nursing and more cuddling with daddy until the day when falling asleep goes more smoothly if mom is conveniently "busy" in another part of the house.

This type of routine for helping a child fall asleep is not as popular as having mother nurse the child to sleep, but it is a happy option for some families. Having dad help the youngest fall asleep can be an especially good arrangement when you have other children with bedtime needs, too.

There is a wide range of choices for balancing parents' needs and children's needs in ways that are comfortable for all. There are no rules about when bedtime must be, or how it must be structured, or by whom, so be creative. Adapt when and how you get him to sleep, not to what "everybody" in the neighborhood does, but to what works for your family.

References

1 Briggs, G., Freeman, R. and Yaffe, S. *Drugs in Pregnancy and Lactation*. 4th edition. Baltimore: Williams & Wilkins, 1994; 116c-17c.

2 Erickson, P. R., Mazhari, E. Investigation of the role of human breast milk in caries development. *Pediatric Dentistry* March-April 1999; 21(2):86-90.

3 Huggins, K. and Ziedrich, L. *The Nursing Mother's Guide to Weaning*. Boston: The Harvard Common Press, 1994; 105.

4 Stein, M. T. et al. Cosleeping (bedsharing) among infants and toddlers. *Journal of Developmental and Behavioral Pediatrics* December 1997; 18(6):410.

5 Vitzthum, V. J. Variation in infant feeding practices in an Andean community. *Multidisciplinary Studies in Andean Anthropology, Discussions in Anthropology 8*. Ed. V.J. Vitzthum. Ann Arbor, MI: University of Michigan, 1988; 141-42.

chapter nine

Marriage and Life with a Nursing Toddler

Changes in Sexual Interest

It worries me a bit to think of everybody who turns to this chapter looking for some definitive statements about how the relationships within marriages, especially sexual relationships, are affected by nursing and how to deal with these effects. There are people who actively research marriage and how it works, especially concentrating on human sexuality, but I am not one of them. All I have to offer is common sense to tide us over until someone comes up with satisfactory answers to all our questions.

There is little need to discuss relationships other than those in which people have lowered sexual interest, because these days it is when we are less interested in sex that we begin to have that "What's wrong with me?" feeling. A generation or two ago, people worried when they thought they had too much interest in sex, but all this is part of our cultural pendulum ride. I do want to be sure to say to those couples whose sexual feelings are unchanged or enhanced when there is a nursling in the family that you are not at all unusual. You are among the fortunate many. The way you feel is great—enjoy this time in your life. Skip this chapter (and what a lot of other writers have to say, too). Like the old poem's centipede who was able to walk happily only until the time she was asked "which leg comes after which," it is possible to think so much about something which is normal and natural that you lose it.

According to Gregory White, MD, the number one enemy of sexuality—greater than anything else I will discuss in this chapter—is excess fatigue. The previous chapter may, therefore, do more to help your marriage than this one. On sex and nursing, there is no clear evidence that nursing itself affects sexuality. There are families in which at night the husband "takes up where the baby leaves off," and that is that. Some people say that the low levels of estrogen following childbirth up until the time menstruation returns may decrease a woman's interest in sex, but this may or may not be the case. The role of different hormones in sexual response is still being debated and researched.

It may seem logical that one way nature might help protect the new baby from being followed too closely by another baby could be to reduce the new mother's interest in sexual intercourse. But in fact there are women—and no small number either—who have an increase in sexual desire immediately following childbirth.[1]

Attitudes toward nursing—and here I am talking about both husbands and wives—may have at least as much influence over sexual feelings as do other factors such as hormone changes. Do husband and wife see themselves and each other differently because of nursing?

I found it unsettling once in a group of couples to hear the men describe their wives' breastfeeding. Husband after husband described his wife as a Madonna (not the performer, but the Christian religious icon). The Madonna and Child do make a beautiful tableau, and we women put ourselves into that picture, too. But I wondered at that time how many couples in that group were affected by the fact that, in Christianity, the Madonna is the Virgin. The Virgin represents many wonderful things; but sexually she is strictly off limits, and that is significant. There is nothing wrong in seeing ourselves or being seen by our mates as a Madonna. The problem is in our ability to switch from the virgin and her consort to Caesar and Cleopatra when we want to.

We may also carry with us cultural messages like these from seventeenth-century England and America, where "influential theologians argued from a scriptural rather than a medical basis that women's breasts were created to provide milk for infants, not as erogenous zones, defining the dichotomous nature of women's sexuality in the eyes of Puritan men. They stated that the principal duty of Puritan women was to serve their Creator as mothers."[5]

If some images of the nursing mother seem to rule out sexual activity, overcoming the effects of these images will take patience and time and conversation. It may be healthy to read accounts of lusty ladies who nurse their little ones. The nursing mothers in Pearl S. Buck's *The Good Earth* and *Sons* come to mind. Some of the old Dutch painters like Jan Steen portray beautiful, robust mothers who clearly do not fit the image of the Madonna. Notice the "faint, bemused expression of pleasure"[3] on many of these mothers' faces. There are also quite a number of sexy screen stars who nurse their babies. All this, of course, is just to help you broaden your picture of the nursing mother a bit. The object is not to get you to adopt a whole new self-image, but to loosen up your options so that you can see more about who you are as, among other things, a parent of a nursing baby or child.

History

We may be annoyed by the way babies and hormones can combine to interfere with our sex lives. But in some ways we have it easy. In many times and places couples have had to cope with a total ban on sex for as long as breastfeeding continued. Some still do. No doubt frustration from living under these taboos added to the cultural pressures against extended nursing that we still experience today. William Gouge, a Puritan pamphleteer in New England, wrote:

> *Because giving sucke is a mother's duty, and hindered by breeding and bearing another child, man ought to doe what hee can to containe for that time: yet dare I not make this an inviolable law for man and wife to deny due benevolence each other, all the time that the wife giveth sucke.*[5]

People believed that milk was made from the menstrual blood, a way to explain why nursing mothers did not menstruate in the early months. They thought intercourse hastened the return of menstruation, which in turn caused the milk to change back into menstrual blood. So sexual relations could end up depriving the child of nourishment. Even sexual thoughts could "infect the milk." Later writers relented and only required mothers to abstain from sexual relations for two hours prior to nursing. During this time North American fathers had the power to decide about breastfeeding. They had to choose between sexual abstinence and hiring a wet nurse.[5]

Throwing Out Stereotypes

One thing that gives us trouble is a fixed view of what healthy sexual behavior is supposed to be. Whenever our feelings and behavior do not fit the stereotype we become worried that we are not normal, especially these days if we deviate on the side of being less interested in sex. But sexual feelings are like other feelings. They change and grow, and rest; sometimes they get to be too much for us, while other times we think they are gone altogether. There are many ups and downs along with subtle changes and shadings in how we relate as a couple at the dinner table. Why should we expect any less fluctuation in our relationship in bed? Being parents of a nursing baby is just one of the many stages of life that will reflect themselves in our sexual feelings. Whatever our feelings are now, it is nearly certain that they will have changed in some significant way by a year from now.

Fathers and mothers need to be wary of pressure from popular culture's propaganda on sexuality. The message is that if a couple does not have intercourse, complete with one or more orgasms, at certain regular intervals, they are doomed to occupy separate bedrooms from now on (or at least to undergo many months of sex therapy). If parents are devoted to one another, and if they are creative, the needs of young children will not stand in the way of their sexual relationship. In fact, when both parents together become deeply involved and interested in child care, their sexual interests are likely to be more in synch with one another.

Feeling Used

One statement most nursing mothers make at some time or another while little ones are nursing is that they feel used. They wish there were a time again when they could call their bodies their own. One mother talks about "a lack of privacy—an invasion of self" which carried over for a while to her relationship with her husband. These feelings come when a child wants a lot of nursing and mother does not feel that she can say no. At the same time husbands want sexual attention, and women may not feel they can say no to them either. These feelings are so common at one time or another during nursing that I would call them nearly universal.

> *Having a child is very disruptive to a relationship. We have both found that there are definite rewards but also some drawbacks. One is trying to establish the relationship as it was before. I don't think you can ever do that. You have to make allowances for change and find a happy medium. That's work!* [2]

This is a situation in which you may find feelings about nursing and feelings about sex interacting. The needs of two different people get lumped together and mother gets overwhelmed. She forgets the third person in the situation who also has needs—herself. But if we give up on ourselves with a sigh, "Alas, such is the life of a wife and mother," we are apt to become emotionally walled in so that we cannot enjoy either husband or child.

When one partner has little interest in sex, it is a time to show love in other ways—talk, touch, and be patient. A pause in sexual activity is a physical imperative when the man's sexual urges are at an ebb; it is equally imperative when the woman is similarly distracted. Love allows for pauses, even shutdowns in the lovemaking while either partner or both make adjustments, while they talk and mature and work things through.

This is a time to dialogue. Discuss your feelings about nursing with your child as best you can, depending on her age. Cut back on nursing a little bit if it helps and if your child can be comfortable with your doing that. Or give your child a chance for a "nursing binge" for a few days to see whether you can sate him and thereby reduce his demands on you afterward.

Discuss your feelings with your husband, too. He is the person who can aid you most. Do not use your discussion time to complain about how demanding your child is, how much he nurses, and so on. The response you will most likely get to such complaining is pressure to wean or send the child out to preschool, or both. These are not unkind suggestions on his part; when you complain that way, it sounds to him as if weaning or separation is exactly the kind of relief you are asking for.

Talk about your child's needs and your husband's needs for access to your body. Let your husband know that you feel that loving both him and your child is very important. Tell him what you are doing to reduce your feelings of pressure from your child and fill him in on any progress. Make clear your understanding and sympathy for his frustration when he has to wait because of the needs of the child you are rearing together.

Get him more involved in caring for your child or children. This offers two possible benefits to your sexual relationship. First, it will take some of the pressure off you so you will be less tired and less "over-touched." Second, time with his children will help fill his emotional reservoirs and make him less needy. Some fathers put pressure on their wives for sex when what they would find more satisfying is more love from their families.

Enlist his support for your need to have the final say over the use of your body. Do not be afraid to ask for some cuddling from him for yourself when you have been babying the baby all day—cuddling without sex if that is the way you need it to be. Learn to say no to sex when you need to, but learn to say no without rejecting love or the lover. Your life of love with your whole family will be much better in the long run if after a hard day of demands from your children, especially the little ones, you know you can fall into the arms of a man who, if you ask, will cradle you and not insist on making more physical demands on you that day. And don't worry that you are asking too much; there should be plenty of chances for you to do the same thing for him. Besides, for many of us there is sometimes no stronger aphrodisiac than being given love by a man who is not expecting to make love.

Re-Staging the Lovemaking

There are, of course, practical considerations about sex when you are parents of a nursing toddler—such as what to do if your little one spends most of the night in your bed. The parents' bed (renamed nicely by Tine Thevenin in her book *The Family Bed*) is a good and healthy place for little children,[4] as attested to by the fact that so many of them express a need to sleep there. The question is how to make love in a double bed without waking a three-year-old. Most couples don't even try; they leave the child in bed and make love somewhere else. Or they expand the bed space by buying bigger beds, getting more beds, adding mats on the floor.

I find it hard to understand the reasoning of those who warn that it can somehow damage a child if he should awaken and see you making love. From mankind's beginnings most people have been reared in dwellings with a single sleeping area. Even in Europe, the use of separate rooms did not appear in cities until the end of the seventeenth century and even later in rural areas.[6] Simple reason says that it is a very small minority of the world's babies and children who have reached maturity without the opportunity to awaken while adults were engaged in intercourse.

The only reason that interrupting parents happily involved in such a wholesome activity as lovemaking could be harmful to a little child, it seems to me, stems from social rules. Most adults in Westernized society would be absolutely scandalized should a child decide to tell the neighbors about it, or try to demonstrate in his childish way with his cousin. We should, for this reason, protect children over two years of age or so from adult attitudes by making love when they are soundly asleep or in another room. By school age, children are initiated into our culture and are therefore aware of what they are and are not "supposed" to see. Children this age would find it terribly embarrassing to see you enjoying sex, and so it's best not to let it happen.

However, as long as neither husband nor wife, nor baby or young toddler, are having uneasy feelings because of being in the same room during lovemaking, you need only concern yourself about not disturbing one another. You need only have enough distance between the two of you and the child to keep you from disturbing his sleep and to keep his presence from disturbing you. For some, that is the other side of the mattress; for some, the other end of the house.

Changes in Breast Sensitivity

Quite a number of nursing mothers report a considerable reduction in receptiveness to breast stimulation in sex play during the months or years they are nursing. Such a change in feelings is normal, though not universal, and I know of no way to alter it. It is a change that challenges couples to discover other things that please them under these circumstances. You may say wistfully that breast stimulation used to be really exciting; well, it will be again. Meanwhile you can have the pleasure of finding other ways to enjoy each other.

It may be that the various ways women react to breast sensations during the nursing years—occasional sexual arousal from nursing or lessened interest in breast stimulation in sex play—may be the result of factors that are as much mental as physical. These different feelings probably grow from the kind of adaptations our individual psychological machinery makes to the business of being a nursing mother. We have no direct control over this adaptation, which occurs without thinking about it. There is no reason to believe that it is better to have either sensitive nipples or not-so-sensitive nipples. Each is a circumstance to accept and enjoy; there are advantages as well as drawbacks either way.

Nursing Pads and Old Lace

One final suggestion that I have for nursing mothers comes from patient and supportive "nursing fathers." Please be conscious of how little glamour there is in many nursing bras—not all of them by any means; some of the newer styles are beautiful. Still, at some time, probably quite a while before your little one weans, you can return to fashion bras, especially those stretchy ones that you can pull up for nursing, or no bra if that is your style. You must still be cautious that any bra you wear fits well, not too tightly. Be alert, too, when you first try a new bra or no bra. Go back to what you have been wearing at the first sign of any breast soreness, and try again in a few weeks. As long as you are comfortable and not afflicted with plugged ducts or breast infections caused by a poorly fitting bra (and as soon as you are able to go without nursing pads which are cumbersome in a fashion bra), your mate will probably be glad to see the nursing bras go.

References

1   Masters, W. and Johnson, V. *Human Sexual Response*. Boston: Little & Brown, 1966; 144, 162.

2   Mclean, H. *Women's Experience with Breast Feeding*. Toronto: University of Toronto Press, 1990; 177.

3   Riordan, J. M. and Rapp, E. T. Pleasure and purpose. *JOGN Nursing* March-April 1980; 9:109.

4   Stein, M. T. et al. Cosleeping (bedsharing) among infants and toddlers. *Journal of Developmental and Behavioral Pediatrics* December 1997; 18(6):409.

5   Treckel, P. A. Breastfeeding and maternal sexuality in colonial America. *Journal of Interdisciplinary History* 1989; 20(1):32, 33, 31-32, 34.

6   Vis, H. L. and Hennart, P. Decline in breast-feeding: about some of its causes. *Acta Paediatrica Scandinavica* October-December 1978; 31(4):202.

chapter ten

Unique Circumstances

Employment Away from Home

If you have a commitment of some sort (a job, classes, etc.) that takes you away from a baby in his first year, the mechanics of nursing can be a challenge. One mother whose friends did not see how she could possibly nurse a baby while she was working, responded, "Oh, I don't. I wait until I get home." But of course there is much more than that to nursing while employed, especially in the early months.

As an employed mother of a nursing toddler, you join quite an exclusive set of mothers and babies. Numbers are probably increasing, but as recently as 1991 in the USA, out of a study group of 499 employed mothers who started out breastfeeding, 288 continued nursing after returning from maternity leave, but only five percent were still nursing at 12 months.[10]

Perhaps you have waited until your baby is older to go out to work or school. Or, if you were very fortunate or very creative, you may have been able to choose from some age-old alternatives:

> *I was able to take my daughter with me to work, when*
> *I returned at four months. I worked in a nonprofit that*
> *had a whopping local staff of two, and my office was*
> *housed in an old house. I kept her with me all the time.*
> *Now I am nursing again—although in my own home and*
> *I now own my own business.*

In any case, by the time your child starts toddling you are past the special problems of maintaining your milk supply while separated from your baby, so combining nursing and employment should no longer present any more difficulty for you than for any mother of a child the age of yours. It is mothering your child that will challenge you.

Mothers Have Always Worked

From the beginning, women have struggled to balance child care with their share of the work required to keep the family supplied with food, clothing, and shelter. In earlier days, most mothers worked in an environment reasonably safe for a young child, at tasks that were repetitive and could be easily interrupted. We all know the image of a hunter-gatherer at work with her child in a sling on her back or hip. Not many generations back in the southern part of the United States, the rural poor would place their babies on the tail of the long sacks they used to pick cotton and would drag cotton and baby along behind them, up and down the rows.

Nor is day care a recent invention. Mothers have been leaving their children in the care of others for a long time, too. Among the nomadic Turkana, poor women had to spend more time away from their nurslings than wealthier ones.[6] Households usually included grandmothers and/or co-wives who could help watch the little ones and nurse them on occasion. In some traditional farming communities, mothers may have to be away from their nurslings several hours each day. Mothers in parts of Nepal complain of seasonal fieldwork causing them to wean too early.[13] The French writer de Vallambert complained about mothers being "absent and held down by their work"—in 1565![5]

Sometimes in the past, as now, arrangements for mother's absence worked out well, sometimes they did not. The 1925 Woodbury study of infant mortality in the USA showed better survival chances for breastfed babies and for babies whose mothers were not employed or who did piecework at home. On the other hand, in this same study extreme poverty proved to be the greatest threat of all to infant survival.[19]

Worldwide

Today, women are losing "power over the nature and location of their work as needs for earning cash increase."[7] One researcher writes, "In developing, urbanizing, and industrializing communities, women are entering the cash economy, either pushed by social and economic necessity or pulled by increasing desire for consumer goods."[8] For most, the non-domestic tasks are in addition to, not instead of, traditional household duties. Often the new work seems incompatible with child care and breastfeeding. Yet despite the changes in mothers' duties, the vast

majority of babies in the developing world still start out at the breast.
A 1989 to 1991 study of mothers nursing toddlers in the United States
found that 68 percent had returned to outside employment within the
baby's first year.[9]

All over the world increased opportunities for paid employment
call to mothers. For some, "economic necessity, fueled by rapid inflation
in basic commodities, has forced women into wage work to help support
their families."[4] Many find themselves with long working hours, made
longer by long commutes. For some, rotating shifts complicate child-care
arrangements and make breastfeeding harder.

Answers to questions about which mothers were seeking
employment in the modern cities of Bangkok, Bogotá, Nairobi, and
Semarang (Indonesia) are the opposite of what we might expect. They
showed that outside jobs were most common among upper-income and
better educated women. At first glance, this may seem to reflect a greater
demand for goods among affluent families. But it also reflects the more
prosperous mothers' access to child care and help with work that might
otherwise keep her home.[18]

In 1989 among poorly fed urban families in Nicaragua, a mother's
paid work often resulted in better growth for her toddler. Researchers
theorize that better growth results stemmed either from the mother's
income enabling her to buy more and better weaning foods, or from her
increased power to influence how the limited family income was spent.[11]

Results of research worldwide are mixed on how large a factor
employment outside the home is in mothers' decisions about
breastfeeding, including whether to start breastfeeding, how soon to
introduce other foods, and how long to continue nursing.[4]

A strong breastfeeding tradition can make mixing employment
and mothering less difficult. Differing traditions are the reason that
employed mothers in Semarang and Nairobi nurse longer than at-home
mothers in Bangkok and Bogotá.[18] Although breastfeeding was thought to
be protected by long tradition in Vietnam, less educated women are now
nursing for a shorter time than the educated, who can afford to stay
home.[16] In 1991 in Rostov-Veliky, Russia, if mothers wanted formula, the
government supplied it without charge; and all were returning to work.
On the other hand, these women also had the advantage of maternity
leaves averaging twenty-five months and child-care facilities where they
worked. All the Russian mothers planned to continue their traditions and
breastfeed as long as they had milk.[14]

Economic Realities

No matter where we live, women have to think responsibly about family
goals. Does a child's life turn out better if he has a room of his own, or
might he thrive in a more crowded space with mom or dad around? Is it

in the best interest of children for mother to seek employment while the children are young in order to save for their college educations? Or would it make more sense for parents and children to pay these expenses together instead, with all of them working during the college years?

Women do have to find ways to take responsibility for their own financial security, whether it is they or their mates who actually produce the necessary income. Couples need to keep communication on the subject open and not risk making plans and decisions based on assumptions that both may not share. A mother can no longer assume that the father will provide financial support; couples need to discuss the matter and reach an agreement. As long as motherhood is not valued any more than it is in the world's economies, many mothers will have to struggle economically to meet children's needs for their mother's presence.

A mother who worked 16 hours per week during her child's first year has given some thought to mothers and money:

> *I wish there was some way to tell young women—go, get that big education and a tough job, but save your money so that when you decide to become a parent, you will have a choice. Education will not bring about the liberation of women. High-paying jobs (when coupled with expensive lifestyles) will not bring about the liberation of women. But money in the bank—it just might do the trick!*

The rise in single parent, female-headed households means that many women are the sole support for themselves and their children, and often have to return to work as soon as possible after childbirth, especially in societies with poorly developed social welfare services. Widowed, unmarried, or divorced women rearing children alone almost always have to generate income in addition to fulfilling their mothering role. And divorce, as I myself have learned in the most painful way, can surprise us even later in life and leave us strapped if we are not prepared to support ourselves.

When There Is a Choice

I realize that it is taboo these days to talk about the fact that children are able to grow up with less anxiety and therefore have the very best opportunity for full physical and mental development if they are able to be with their mothers all day, especially during the first three years. Talking about the disadvantages of mother-baby or mother-toddler separation is supposed to inflict guilt feelings upon mothers who must be away from their little ones—just as mentioning the risks of formula-feeding was once considered cruelty to mothers who do not breastfeed.

It seems to me that the mother who faces the kind of extremely rare problem that makes it impossible for her to breastfeed is not the one who is going to feel guilty. Nor is the mother in the not-nearly-so-rare circumstance these days in which she must be away from her young child, going to experience true guilt—disappointment and regret perhaps, but not guilt. These mothers are facing what all of us have to deal with at some time or another, that is, rearing children as best we can under less-than-ideal circumstances. The mother who has to be away from her child regularly can, as can any mother who must live in an imperfect world, do the very best for her child that the realities of life will permit.

It is when we voluntarily create a way of life that is not as good for our children as it should be that true guilt feelings surface, and rightly so. It may well be that when a mother chooses to be away from a child too young to function well in her absence that the long-range ill effects of premature separation are most likely to occur. For one thing, children may be able to perceive very early through their mothers' behavior that a necessary deprivation is one thing and that being deliberately shortchanged is quite another. Also, even under circumstances that make separation necessary for too long and too soon in the child's life, a mother who is doing her best for her child and knows it should be able to feel good about herself and be in the best possible frame of mind to overcome the kinds of problems that she may see arising as a result of regular separation from her child. "Your working in itself will not ruin your children," says Alice Skelsey, "but it does add one more factor to the interactions in all your family relationships. You have to interpret accurately the effects of that factor."[17]

A mother on the other hand who does have reasonable alternatives by which she could avoid separation (such as taking a job at home or being content, within limits of health and safety, with a lower standard of living) is more subject to being handicapped in her mothering by feelings of guilt. Guilt feelings, in turn, tend to compound any difficulties resulting from separation by interfering with a mother's ability to care for her child in ways that are both sensitive and sensible.

It is on the subject of voluntary separation of mothers and very young children that much of what we read these days is so misleading. All over the world, researchers have found that "the rising desire for manufactured goods, particularly those that are associated with modern, urban lifestyles, has influenced women to work even when the additional income is not critical for household survival."[4]

In a laudable attempt to overcome stereotypes and free women from irrational restrictions on what we could do with our lives, many have gone too far. They have undermined much of the support system for those who prefer to take primary responsibility for their children. And worse still, people these days have become much too casual in suggesting that families can do just as well using temporary mother-substitutes as with the real mother—just as a few years ago people talked as if they were certain that formula was just as good as mother's milk for babies. The truth is that, just as mother's milk cannot be duplicated, neither can mother herself.

John Bowlby, the pioneering attachment researcher, suggested early in his career "that the young child's hunger for his mother's love and presence is as great as his hunger for food, and that in consequence her absence inevitably generates a powerful sense of loss and anger." His continuing research served to confirm the validity of this early assertion.[3]

Seventeenth and eighteenth-century European writers worried about the effects on family relationships when siblings were fed by different nurses. And families who employed wet nurses were troubled because children would then prefer the nurse over mother.[5] Sensitive caretakers who do their best to serve not just as babysitters but as mother substitutes for babies and preschoolers are sometimes disturbed to find themselves experiencing moments of love and intimacy which they feel belong only to the child's parents. "She wouldn't want me to share such a special smile or moment with her husband," one woman said. "I don't know how she can let me have these moments with her child. She is missing so much."

Making the Best of Separation

Separation in the early years can have profound significance for both child and mother and should not be undertaken or recommended as if it were a choice without consequences. When separation from a baby or toddler is unavoidable, however, there are ways to soften the feelings of loss and anger that Dr. Bowlby mentions.

Nursing a preschooler when you are working away from him is one of those ways. Most mothers do not find it difficult. In fact, it is a great pleasure, a warm and intense greeting between mother and child after separation.

My son is about to be one in two weeks. We are still happily breastfeeding and plan to until he decides to wean. I had no choice but to return to work and did so when he was eight weeks. I agree that mothers should be home with their babies, but unfortunately it is not always financially possible. I am so glad I continued to breastfeed after returning to work. Not only did it help save money during his first year, it more importantly helps us maintain a bond only I can give him. I look forward to

*cuddling him and spending that special time with him
before and after work and all weekend. Even though
I can't be there with him while at work, it helps to know
he is getting a little piece of mom in his milk.*

And for employed mothers, too, nursing can extend long past the
first year:

*It was our special time. (I think he's finally weaned at
three years, ten months.) . . . I think my son would have
kept on going, but since January I've either worked full
time or close to it, so his afternoon nap nursing went by
the wayside.*

The difficulties for a mother with another career have to do with
adapting herself both to the rigidity of the adult world and the flexibility
needed to care for a rapidly growing and changing little child. Many
mothers who are away from their children appreciate nursing greatly
and use it to help maintain the intimacy and close communication with
their little ones that are essential in building a warm and healthy family.

But even nursing cannot guarantee complete security against the
risks of separating a baby or very young child from his mother. So
nursing mothers, like all mothers, must give very careful thought to any
decision to undertake a regular, frequent commitment away from a very
young child. First of all you will want to minimize your separation. Delay
your outside commitment for as long as possible, and then be away for as
few hours as you can manage. Try to have your child as close as possible
to where you will be so that you can perhaps have lunch or a break
together. If you have a long drive morning and evening, and if your
toddler rides well in her safety seat, then you and your little one may
enjoy it more if you arrange for child care close to the workplace so you
can be together during the drive.

Many employed mothers avoid two of day care's greatest
problems by leaving their children in the care of family members. In that
way their children do not have to adjust to the frequent changes in
caretakers often experienced because of the high turnover of day-care
employees. Nor are the children exposed daily to infection from so many
other children. Pediatricians express concern about children in day-care
centers because of the risk of infection from exposure to large groups of
children from other families.

Care by some family members, however, may not reduce, and
may even exaggerate, the difficulties in making sure your child is cared
for according to your instructions. Your mother or aunt may be less

willing than a stranger to follow your "orders." But if you can get past this obstacle, family members can be a great help because they often provide not only capable care but love that flows "thicker than water."

Co-parenting by employed couples. Many couples choose to share child-care responsibilities themselves, staggering their work schedules so one or the other is always available to care for the child. This arrangement has great advantages for the child because of the continuity in caregiving and environment. On the other hand, it is quite challenging to the marriage because it gives the couple so little time together. Finding times for companionship and communication sometimes becomes all but impossible for couples splitting child care, but they have to be found.

It is often difficult for each of the parents to realize that this is not just an eight-hour commitment to child care. Each will frequently have to stay "on duty" while the other sleeps.

Sharing child care this way, however, can be empowering for parents, giving mothers economic credibility and fathers domestic credibility. If parents can get past the very real difficulties, families can thrive on such a domestic partnership.

Family-Friendly Workplace

"Employment and breastfeeding are not in themselves incompatible, but being in the workforce can make it more challenging for mothers to breastfeed. Contrary to many common perceptions, there is little empirical evidence that women's employment of itself need necessarily affect breastfeeding negatively. This is not to suggest, however, that maternal employment is not a factor in decisions regarding breastfeeding. In most situations, modification of the work environment would increase women's options regarding infant feeding, so that women who choose to breastfeed would not incur a high opportunity cost for that decision."[2]

Most environments for wage work are modeled after the male workforce, with hardly a thought to the special needs of women as workers and mothers. It is painful, trying to divide our lives into public (work) and private (home) spheres. But one of the problems, as one mother writes, is that so many employers believe otherwise:

> *I am one of those people, albeit working part time, who is nursing (well, he hasn't in a couple of days) a three-year, ten-month-old. It has not been the easiest thing in the world to do at times. I had to educate a former boss on the subject, after she called my son "poor baby" because I was still nursing him when he was about two.*

Hostile attitudes or conditions can cause some mothers to quit work altogether in spite of the financial hardships. An employed mother says:

> *Some people are "self-conscious" about discussing their new mother needs with their employer or may feel like they are putting the employer on the spot to make special arrangements. I felt when I came back to work that my priorities had so drastically changed, that if I had been denied my right to pump (feed my baby) that I would have quit the job. (This never was an issue, my employer already had set up a pumping room.) I guess I think, "Baby first, work second."*

Some mothers in Thailand told researchers about slipping away from work to nurse their babies. "If they fire me I will have to leave," one mother said, ". . . but what can be done? The baby is mine, the baby is more important than any other thing."

There is a great need worldwide for full implementation of the International Labour Organization conventions passed in 1919 regarding maternity leave, nursing breaks, and creches. Families would also benefit from flexible working hours, job-sharing, and more part-time work. All these changes would make the work environment more compatible with the needs of children.

Many jobs, particularly those requiring substantial skill and training, do not permit extended maternity leave, and mothers have to go back to work soon after childbirth or lose their positions, their seniority, or their benefits. A mother's ability to get started at breastfeeding, and to continue past the first year, is affected by the length of her maternity leave, distance between the job and home or day care, and work breaks for nursing or pumping milk. A study among urban mothers in Nairobi, Kenya, showed that among women with a long lunch break and short commute, breastfeeding rates are higher, and breastfeeding continues longer.[18] Requiring a nursing-friendly workplace by law, however, can work against women. Where special consideration is required, employers have sometimes refused to employ women, or kept their female workforce below the minimum numbers triggering the regulations.[2]

Pumping — How Long? In such an environment, it is not surprising that nursing mothers can find themselves in a strange place. As your nursling grows older, you may feel as if you're from a different planet. One mother describes handling the questions of coworkers after the baby was six months old as "very tricky." She writes, "I was away from my daughter thirteen hours on the days I worked, so I needed to keep pumping."

If conditions for pumping or hand-expressing milk are uncomfortable for you because of either poor facilities or lukewarm support, or even hostility from your employer or coworkers, you may hope to quit pumping at work as soon as possible. Even without outside pressure, you may simply find yourself wishing to leave this little chore behind you so you can go back to socializing with coworkers during breaks. A mother wrote:

> *My baby is currently nine months old. I have no idea how long I should continue pumping. I was initially assuming I would until he was a year old, but have read nothing that gives recommendations for pumping once a child is a toddler. Should I continue to pump past that, and for how long?*
>
> *I brought up the question at my last LLL meeting. The other women who pumped said that they noticed when their children started taking less breast milk at day care, and stopped pumping then. . . . I figure at this point that as long as he really wants a bottle, I'll keep pumping for him, but that may change after he's a year old.*

Occasional business trips raise similar questions from another mother:

> *I also traveled on business occasionally . . . and it was difficult for me to know at what point I only needed to pump for comfort as opposed to trying to maintain my supply. In other words, if we are apart for two days when he is eighteen months old or two years old, do I need to try and pump as often and as much as I think he would nurse, or just pump enough to relieve engorgement? It would be nice to be able to get some information about such things.*

Another mother writes about how she managed breastfeeding and pumping, well into toddlerhood:

> *My son never was supplemented with anything (formula, early solids, etc.). Somewhere when my son was into his seventh or eighth month, he was eating more than I was producing at work. I even went to pumping three times a day at work. At the same time, he was grabbing the food off our table at mealtimes. This is when we started*

*solids—banana first, etc. After a couple weeks, I went back
to twice a day pumping. This continued until he was
about thirteen months, then I went down to pumping once
a day. I pumped once a day at work until he was eighteen
months old.*

*I always let my son tell me how much or how frequently
I needed to pump simply by monitoring how much he was
consuming during the day while I was at work. He is
twenty-one months old now and is still receiving expressed
breast milk when I am at work, at least during his lunch
time and some days for snacks. It depends on his mood.
I do not pump anymore at work, but I still have a reserve
of frozen milk that I am expecting will last for another
three months. It really was an easy process.*

On-site day care allowed another mother to quit pumping.

*When he was six months old he got into on-site day care at
my place of employment, and I went to nurse him there
when they called me one to three times per day (usually
twice). By the time he was eleven-and-a-half months old he
was asking to nurse during the work day only once,
usually at about 4:30 or 4:45 (we left work at 5:00).*

I would suggest pumping as often as the baby would nurse for
about nine months. Many mothers continue pumping much longer. Then
treat the decision to quit pumping as a "spot weaning" decision, as
discussed later in this book. (See page 276.) Pay attention to your body
and continue to pump for comfort as long as you need to. For mothers
like my daughter-in-law, who works three long shifts a week and nurses
freely the other four days, pumping will likely be necessary well into
toddlerhood because of the length of the separations after her milk
supply is built up by days of regular stimulation.

The decision on when to stop pumping will be affected by how you
feel about weaning or extended nursing. Some children will respond to
decreased milk flow after you stop pumping by losing interest in nursing.
Some mothers, noticing this decreased interest, have been motivated to
use the pump to keep up a good supply, even up to two years.[15]

*Some moms, who are on the top end of milk production,
can cut back on pumping sooner than others. The ones
who wish to cut back in pumping at work should
encourage the baby to sleep nearby and to nurse at night if*

*they want to protect their milk production. If the baby does
not nurse at night (eight hours, let's say) and mom doesn't
pump at work (ten hours) that means eighteen hours of no
breast emptying. It is hard to get enough stimulation in
the six hours that remain in the day—even if mom and
baby are willing to nurse straight through those six
hours.*[15]

When traveling, if you are going to be away for a day or more,
you will need to pump about as often as you would pump or nurse at
home.

*Unless your little one is only nursing for a few minutes
once a day, you would do better to take your pump. If you
find you don't need it—don't pump. However, if you have a
little one who likes a fast milk-flow, you may want to
pump anyway to keep the milk flow at the rate he is
comfortable with.*[15]

To know how much milk you need to collect by pumping, watch
for the signs the mothers above mentioned, the child taking less breast
milk while you are away or losing interest in the bottle. If you want your
toddler to keep nursing as long as he would if you were together most of
the time, watch the child for changes in behavior when you pump less. If
he begins losing interest faster than you feel he should, go back to
pumping more.

When you determine for yourself that pumping is no longer
helping you or your child in any significant way, then it is time to stop.

Reasonable Expectations

The greatest risk in any family to the mothering of a preschool child is
that mothers try to do too much besides working alongside, playing with,
and listening to the child. This applies to all mothers, whether they
spend time away from their children or not. A child in the second and
third year needs a great deal of attention. These busy years of rapid
growth are times when we all have to minimize our other commitments
in order to help our children grow.

If you find that you must be away from your child regularly, then,
with most children most of the time, your outside job will need to be your
only commitment besides being mommy. You may on occasion find time to
do other things, but you are wise not to make promises or to count on
time for other projects, and that may include forgoing much of the
housework.

Even finding time for yourself alone may be out of the question some days. As tempting as it may be to try to get your young toddler to nap for a while when you come home or to go to bed early, it is more important to the future happiness and security of your child—and therefore to the happiness and security of yourself and your family—that you be available to him as much as you can. If, for example, you need to lie down, perhaps you and your child can lie down together. Or maybe he'd like to join you while you unwind in a hot bath. You can figure out ways to calm yourself down and shift gears from the workaday world to your mothering world without shutting him out.

One of the most troublesome errors that we women make when we take on responsibilities away from home is that we try to add this job to the one we already have at home. So many women try to work an eight-hour day and then come home to do all the cooking, cleaning, and laundry. Few of us have that much energy to give. If you add a two-year-old to the picture, the situation becomes impossible.

Many children whose mothers spend several hours away from them daily wake several times at night for contact with mother and perhaps for nursing. Mothers who undertake two careers, mothering and the other one they have, need to appreciate how essential these nighttime get-togethers are. A baby or toddler who is away from her mother daily usually needs to be able to spend the night in her parents' bed.

Being awake at night with your child, however, or even partially awake, is going to put a strain on you unless you can go to bed earlier for a while or get extra rest some other way. The possibility of night duty as part of your mothering career is one of many reasons that you must take extra care of yourself and not require yourself to do much of what you have done in the past. (Actually no mother of a child in the second or third year should expect to accomplish great things beyond rearing a great kid.) You should expect to share household tasks with your partner, or just let go of as many as possible.

There is only so much time and energy available to you, and you need to set your priorities and work from the top of the list down. On those days when your mate has collected a whole load of laundry from under the furniture and supper is reheated leftovers, you must not allow yourself to feel bad about the housework. Your child needs your attention much more than he needs a clean house or gourmet meals. He cares nothing about whether his clothes are neatly folded or fished out of a basket from day-before-yesterday. But having you frenzied and worn out would bother him a lot. So keep first things first.

No doubt what you can get done will change from time to time. There are times for a mother who works away from her child, as for everyone, when the child enjoys helping around the house, when life is easy, when he sleeps well at night. Then mother and little one can spend their time together on whatever tasks seem important, be it cleaning, sewing, or visiting museums. At other times, the child cannot spare mother's attention for a moment, and then the family has to make whatever adjustments are necessary to function while mother is occupied exclusively with her two careers. Sometimes it becomes obvious that this child's need for mother is so great because of a crisis or illness, or just because of his temperament, that he cannot spare her for the other career. Then it is advisable to seek some way, if at all possible, to suspend not only the housework but the other job as well.

Organization is the watchword of most of the working world. The child's world at best is flexible and spontaneous and at its worst is unpredictable to the point of chaos. No wonder parents living with a foot in each of these worlds can feel as if they are being twisted apart by the pull of conflicting forces. But with persistence and ingenuity parents are finding ways to inject a little chaos into the workplace and a little structure into their family lives. With some luck and good humor, it can work out.

Your Adopted Child

If an unhurried weaning makes good sense for life with "homemade" children, it seems doubly reasonable for the mother who has made the extra effort involved in nursing her adopted baby. In fact mothers who have had to overcome challenges of any sort in getting started at nursing are, not surprisingly, often quite reluctant to give up nursing before they have to.

Dr. Rita Laws, mother of eight adopted children, three of whom nursed as toddlers, and co-author of *Adopting and Advocating for the Special Needs Child,*[1] encourages breastfeeding of adopted children.

> *I always tell people that adopted babies and toddlers need to be breastfed more than babies who stay with their biological parents for two reasons: One, they have suffered a terrible loss and shock. No matter how wonderful the adoptive family, it is strange at first, because it is not the family the baby knew in the womb. Two, internationally adopted babies and special needs babies are at risk of many kinds of physical, mental, and emotional problems due to risk factors like lack of prenatal care, unknown paternity, dangerous births, prenatal drug exposure, prenatal malnutrition, abuse, neglect, and incomplete medical histories. Breast milk and breastfeeding, the family bed, and kangaroo parenting all contribute to lessening the effects of these serious risk factors.*[12]

A mother who wants to should feel free to try nursing, even when the child is not placed until he is an older baby or toddler. Some adoptees who are more than just a few weeks old will take to nursing, and the possible physical and emotional benefits can make it well worth the effort. The first adopted nursling, and one of the first nursing toddlers I ever met, back in the 1960s, was over six months old when he first started nursing.

If you want to try nursing an adopted baby, however, no matter what the child's age, it might be advisable to determine his HIV status by medical testing, before offering the breast. There is some evidence that it could be possible for the HIV virus to be transmitted from baby to mother via the breast.[1]

Keep in mind that many older babies cannot be persuaded to try nursing, or cannot figure out how, and you will need to give them the loving and cuddling of nursing while feeding them in a way they can accept. Dr. Laws gave occasional cups of breast milk to some of her children who did not nurse.

She writes about how well her adopted children, now teens and young adults, have overcome (or learned how to compensate for) problems resulting from such things as inadequate prenatal care, oxygen deprivation during birth, and fetal alcohol exposure. The optimal emotional and physical benefits of nursing have helped her children, and the family, cope with very real problems—developmental delays, asthma, Attention Deficit Hyperactivity Disorder (ADHD), and speech disorders. These young people are doing far better, mentally and physically, than their doctors predicted, better than their biological siblings who grew up in other homes.

Nursing an adopted toddler may draw more attention from people who don't know this is possible, and the attention may be more pronounced if physical differences make it apparent you did not give birth to the child. I didn't notice this when I was nursing my adopted son, whose handsome features and coloring are clearly from a different background than those of his siblings. But I have always been sensitive to people's disapproval and so learned early not to look for it. Dr. Laws, on the other hand, was more inclined to look strangers in the eye:

> *When we went out in public with three beautiful same-size toddlers, we drew crowds. People always asked how two of the children could be black and one, white. We would smile and say "adoption." When I nursed any of the boys in public, but especially if I nursed [my adopted sons], the stares intensified. I made a conscious decision early on not to let this upset me by convincing myself that at least some*

*of the stares came from people who were considering
special needs adoption for their own families. I always
smiled back, even at the rude stares, which inevitably
resulted in one of two responses, both of them positive: the
person staring either stopped staring and turned away, or
the looker smiled back.*[12]

While many adoptive mothers do establish a full milk supply for
the baby's first six months or so, most do not. If you should be one of
those who does not have the experience of being able to nurse completely
without supplementation, the nursing time after nine months or one year
(or maybe even sooner) can be a special pleasure, because at last nursing
for you and your baby is no different than if you had given birth to your
child. Like other children this age, your child will eat whatever he needs
from the table and come to you for your comfort and your milk when that
is what he needs. Your special efforts have been rewarded; even if not at
first, now, for sure, you can meet nursing needs completely for that child
who, as the anonymous poem reads, grew not under your heart, but in it.

Your Last Child

We have all heard about a family's tendency to indulge the last child, to
enjoy his immaturity, and to allow him to stay a baby longer than
previous children in the family. Of course it is a mistake to indulge any
child to the point of denying him plenty of guidance, needed limits, and
opportunity for growth. But short of such an extreme, I see no reason to
worry about enjoying your youngest as much as you want to.

Perhaps, as some people suggest, we sometimes function
differently as parents in rearing the last child because of sadness that we
will have no one else to baby once this child is grown. It could be that in
many families, the desire to continue to have a baby in the family is one
reason that the last child nurses longer than her older siblings. As one
mother wrote:

*My twenty-two-month-old daughter is still nursing.
I expect she is my last child and right now I'd love for her
to nurse forever. I have not yet reached the point of
"burnout" with her. I remember hearing a mom say this at
an LLL meeting about her last children (twins!) and
I didn't really understand then.*

There are, however, simpler reasons, too obvious perhaps for us to see, that parents everywhere are more permissive with the youngest child, reasons that he may nurse longer than his older siblings. There are simply fewer factors that interfere with an easy, relaxed approach toward life with the youngest child and toward his nursing.

By the time the youngest is born, we have experience—not always a lot, but certainly more than we had the first time. We feel much less urge to hasten the youngest one's growing up. We are more confident and, therefore, much less easily shaken by the questions or criticisms of others. We know from experience that our children outgrow infantile behaviors, so these behaviors are not threatening to us any more. But the most significant factor of all is that we do not become pregnant again or have the needs of a still younger child to meet. He is likely to nurse longer, if he is so inclined, just because there is usually less to keep him from it.

References

1   Babb, L. A. and Laws, R. *Adopting and Advocating for the Special Needs Child.* Westport, CT: Bergin & Garvey, 1997; 54.

2   Berg, A. and Brems, S. A case for promoting breastfeeding in projects to limit fertility. *World Bank Technical Paper Number 102.* The World Bank, Washington, D.C., 1989; 13, 14.

3   Bowlby, J. *Attachment.* New York: Basic Books, 1982.

4   Carballo, M. and Pelto, G. H. Social and psychological factors in breast-feeding. *Infant and Child Nutrition Worldwide : Issues and Perspectives.* Ed. F. Falkner. Boca Raton, Florida: CRC Press, 1991; 178, 175-90, 178.

5   Fildes, V. A. *Breasts, Bottles and Babies: A History of Infant Feeding.* Edinburgh: Edinburgh University Press, 1986; 247, 113.

6   Gray, S. J. Infant care and feeding. *Nomadic Turkana: Biobehavior and Ecology of a Pastoralist Society.* Ed. M. A. Little and P.W. Leslie. Oxford: Oxford University Press, 1996; 275.

7   Greiner, T. Sustained breastfeeding, complementation, and care. *Food and Nutrition Bulletin* 1995; 16(4):315.

8   Gussler, J. D. Women's work and infant feeding in Oceania. *Infant Care and Feeding in the South Pacific.* Ed. L. B. Marshall. New York: Gordon and Breech Science Publishers, 1985; 321.

9   Hills-Bonczyk, S. G. et al. Women's experiences with breastfeeding longer than 12 months. *Birth* December 21, 1994; 21(4):211.

10 Hills-Bonczyk, S. G. et al. Women's experiences with combining breast-feeding and employment. *Journal of Nurse-Midwifery* September/October 1993; 38(5):261.

11 Lamontagne, J. F., Engle, P. L., and Zeitlin, M. F. Maternal employment, child care, and nutritional status of 12-18-month-old children in Managua, Nicaragua. *Social Science and Medicine* Feb1998; 46(3):411-13.

12 Laws, R. Personal communication.

13 Levine, N. E. Women's work and infant feeding: a case from rural Nepal. *Ethnology* 1988; 27:231-51.

14 Miner, J., Witte, D. J. and Nordstrom, D. L. Infant feeding practices in a Russian and a United States city: patterns and comparisons. *Journal of Human Lactation* 1994; 10(2):95.

15 Morgan. B. Private communication.

16 Morrow, M. Breastfeeding in Vietnam: Poverty, Tradition, and Economic Transition. *Journal of Human Lactation* 1996; 12 (2):97, 101.

17 Skelsey, A. F. *The Working Mother's Guide to her Home, her Family, and Herself.* New York: Random House 1970; 230.

18 Winikoff, B. and Castle, M. A. The influence of maternal employment on infant feeding. *Feeding Infants in Four Societies.* Ed. B. Winikoff, M.A. Castle, and V.H. Laukaran. New York: Greenwood Press, 1988; 124, 142, 133.

19 Woodbury, R. M. Causal Factors in Infant Mortality. Children's Bureau Publication No.142 Washington, D.C.: U.S. Government Printing Office, 1925. cited in Yankauer, A. A classic study of infant mortality—1911-1915. *Pediatrics* December 1994; 94(6): 876.

chapter eleven

Fathering and the Nursing Toddler

> *A father may or may not nurture his children differently than a mother because of his gender. But the fact that he does nurture, and the reflection of this nurturing in his children, is more important than the culture teaches any of us.*
>
> Richard Louv, *Father Love*[5]

A Father's Influence

Fathers' beliefs and attitudes don't necessarily determine how their children are mothered, but they can have a profound influence, one that has long been recognized. In 1622, William Gouge, a Puritan pamphleteer, wrote:

> *Husbands for the most part are the cause that their wives nurse not their owne children. If husbands were willing that their wives should performe this dutie, and would perswade and encourage them thereto, and afford them what helpes they could, where one mother now nurseth her child twenty would do so.*[4]

An eighteenth-century mother complained, "There are many husbands so devoid of sense and parental affection that during the first effervescence of voluptuous fondness, they refuse to let their wives suckle their children." A London apothecary wrote in 1753: "A man cannot be conversant with life and not see that many a sensible woman, many a tender mother, has her heart yearning to suckle her child, and is prevented by the misplac'd authority of a husband."[4]

But in spite of internal pressures for more of their wives' attention, and external pressures, at least in some cases, for very large families, there have always been men who understood how beneficial it is to families for mothers to nurse their own children. A minister wrote in 1695, "I have known some fathers at first averse to their wives nursing, who after some experience of those pleasing diversions that are to be found in the constant company of a little babe, would not on any terms lose the repetition of that pleasure, by turning the next abroad to a stranger to nurse."[4]

"Natural" Fathering?

What makes a father? Mothers have physical changes and hormonal shifts to trigger nurturing behavior, but fathers do not. Yet, whether or not we understand how the system works, history and our hearts both tell us that children ask more from their fathers than just the seed to begin life. Fathering counts.

In species with sexual pair-bonding, many birds for example, fathers are heavily involved in nurturing. In a few species, fathers are the only caregivers.

Experiments with rats, among whom the male ordinarily takes no part in caring for the young, found that males confined long enough with the pups will show nurturing behaviors ordinarily seen only in females with young.[1] This experiment reinforces what we observe in human families, in adoptions, for example: hormones may prod nurturing behavior, but nurturing relationships are built on proximity and contact. It is presence, not absence, that makes the heart grow fonder.

Among humans we find wide individual and cultural differences in fathers' participation in the care of babies and toddlers. At one extreme we see great numbers of children abandoned by their fathers at conception. At the other extreme—almost too far out to mention—is Dana Raphael's reference to "reports of lactation induced by sucking stimulation in adult men."[7] I have absolutely no desire to promote either of these extremes. Many a father who has found himself alone with a nursing baby when mother is away a little longer than intended has momentarily wished for breasts dripping milk. But at less trying times I am sure most fathers would agree that children are best cared for by two different parents, by what Dr. William Sears calls "the milk mother and the hairy mother."[8]

Western culture does not offer much encouragement to that "hairy mother." Margaret Mead and Niles Newton write that Western rituals of family-making, with our focus on weddings rather than births, emphasize the father's economic rather than nurturing role in the family.[6]

Devaluation of fatherhood has gone on long enough to create a backlash, a widespread longing to draw fathers back into the family. Some mothers don't even breastfeed because they want the father to share the parenting role by feeding the baby. This choice is sweet on the surface, mothers sharing one of parenthood's most gratifying aspects with their partners. But considering the biological and psychological needs for breast milk and nursing built into babies and toddlers, sharing the milk feedings with father seems a misplaced kindness, and one that can backfire for all concerned. There is plenty of parenting to share without sacrificing breastfeeding.

The Best for Your Family

As a father you are interested in growing the best children you can, children who are healthy and independent. You want children who love you and are glad they have you for their father. What a blessing it is to you and to your children to know that you can use the very approaches that make your children love you—gentleness and tenderness—to help them grow strong. From the solid base of your love your children can grow up prepared to face any challenge they need to.

We have neglected the art of fathering for too many generations, ever since men's work moved from the shops and fields around home to more distant centers of industry and commerce. The change in workplace enabled us to take advantage of the economic efficiency of centralized production. The new arrangement, however, has led to domestic inefficiency by decentralizing the family. Mothers have assumed traditional fathering roles for so long now that we've forgotten the life-affirming relationship fathers can have with their children. And men who are masters of negotiation, machinery, or spreadsheets end up feeling incompetent in their own homes.

A fifteenth-century French illuminated prayer book, called a *Book of Hours,* offers a rare image of fathering long ago. In the illustration, Mary pursues other interests, relaxing with her feet elevated and a book in her lap. Joseph sits on the floor cradling little Jesus in his arms and gazing into the baby's eyes.[9] The wordless picture teaches, within one religious tradition, about a precious relationship that is all but irreplaceable.

The Importance of Fathering

Fathers help their boys grow into men and their girls grow into women, but not in the ways put forward in popular culture. The measurable trait that results from good fathering is not competitive machismo but *empathy*, a quality essential for social order. This empathy does not come from rearing "good" or well-behaved children. Rather, it comes from the daily modeling of a man who is genuinely, and voluntarily, present. Interaction with a loving father tends to help girls grow up with more self-confidence and boys without what Richard Louv calls an "inflated, hyper-masculine view of manhood."[5] William Sears writes that increasing his time with family made him more sensitive, and that this filtered down so that "everyone became more sensitive to one another."[8]

A father can serve as a bridge between mother and the world, a function that is needed across the years. In the beginning, the father's influence begins on the near bank, reaching the child through the mother. As the child sits, walks, and runs, you, the father-bridge, can both lift and lure the child slowly and gradually away until the time, many years ahead, that you realize he has safely reached the other side, the shore of his own identity and his own life.

Mothers can, and do, accomplish this bridging, but not without cost to our children and ourselves. Taking on this task requires mothers to be less pliable, to close off some of the unconditional openness and acceptance that is a hallmark, and one of the pleasures, of motherhood. Boys without fathers have a harder time with developing morals and learning how to control their impulses. Girls need fathering to learn how to interact with men later in life.

Mushrooming Expectations

Today's fathers find themselves torn between taking on an overblown "provider and protector" role and heeding the emotional needs of their growing children. How can you do a good enough job at keeping the family fed, clothed, and sheltered and still have time and energy for the fathering business? It is difficult to come home exhausted from a full-time job only to have a cranky toddler thrust into your arms. It is difficult to respond to the morning's buzzing alarm clock when your sleep has been interrupted repeatedly all through the night. It is difficult to find the stores of energy and playfulness your child demands after a day of meeting the demands of other people. As much as you love your family, you begin to wonder if you'll ever again have a moment to yourself. And if you dare say anything about such feelings, you may get blamed for not caring enough.

As your family grows, you cannot just keep adding demands on your time and energy. Just as your wife must prioritize and set limits, so must you. Some things that were essential before you became a father may need to go on hold for a while. Some may need to be jettisoned forever. You and your partner need to determine what matters most in your lives and concentrate your energies there. Yes, there will be compromises between an ideal family life and a perfect work life; nobody ever has it all. But working out a plan will get you closer to your ideals, and the whole family will be better off for the effort.

Coping with a Mommy's Baby

If your child starts out as a mommy-oriented child, and most do, it can be hard on your ego. Of course you understand what a vital first step this first attachment is in a little person's ability to form relationships and friendships later—so important indeed that it is difficult or even impossible to compensate when the attachment process doesn't proceed normally in the first year. John Bowlby cites studies which indicate that babies who start out with an intense attachment to one person are significantly more likely to reach out to others.[2] Nonetheless, it is hard if your child seems to reject you, and especially if that seeming rejection lasts into toddlerhood. It's especially hard when you see other fathers playing with and tending to their babies and toddlers the way you are wanting to work and play with yours.

Such exclusive attachment, which can be as exhausting for mothers as it is frustrating for fathers, can be treated in several ways. First, of course is good old tincture of time; some babies seem to need a very long one-on-one attachment phase, occasionally remaining "mommyish" all through toddlerhood. With these little ones, you need to stay close and wait it out. Love the baby by loving his mother, and you'll be next.

The second treatment is included in the first—your presence. You have to be around enough for your child to learn to trust you. How much time together it will take before you can feel a difference varies from child to child, depending on how each little psyche is "wired." Periods of skin-to-skin contact in the early weeks, letting the baby lie on your bare chest, can be helpful. With some very sensitive babies, these periods have to be very brief at first. You just have to follow the baby's lead. Think about how immature your child is—how much she has to learn. She has to figure out how to love and trust one person before she can love and trust many people. If you are the person, next to her mother, who is around her the most and offers her comfort (although she may continue to reject your comfort for a while), you're in the right position to be the very next person she opens up to just as soon as she can. Pushing faster than she can go will only slow the process.

The best way to hasten the time when your child will be the companion you may have dreamed of is the opposite of what you might think at first. Do all you can to encourage and help your wife mother your child. Encourage her to nurse him and help her to baby the baby in him for as long as there is any baby left. Your wife will rejoice in your support.

If you want to hasten the time when your child will trust you and enjoy being with you, try making yourself available in unorthodox ways. For instance, psychiatrist-father Hugh Riordan suggests lying quietly on the floor. Once children become mobile, he says, like puppies, they usually cannot resist climbing all over you as long as you stay quiet enough not to make them shy away. As your child grows older, such play can evolve into as much roughhouse as the two of you want. It may need to start very calmly, though.

Another way to get your child's attention is to sit on the floor and play with his toys—not the ones he is playing with, of course. When you do this he may continue to play alongside you, or join you, or snatch the toys away from you; any of these games can be fun. Some fathers win over their babies even earlier by hanging around while the child is nursing, tempting her to reach out to you. When she does offer you a tiny hand or foot, you can kiss it or give it a tickle, thereby beginning the loving games you will be playing over the months and years ahead.

Preparing Children for the World "Out There"

Fathers of nursing toddlers sometimes find it hard to let go of control and to trust the slow, often inconsistent process through which children grow up. This can be especially difficult for men (and women, too) in careers that demand toughness and self-restraint.

We have grown up on the logic that we need to toughen up our children, to frustrate, abandon, or even hurt them "for their own good." But research into child development and the experience of countless parents leaves no doubt that strength grows out of nurture, adequate and timely support, and loving guidance. It is one thing (and often a good thing) to let a child experience frustration, staying aloof but available, watching, ready to step in if the situation seems about to overwhelm her. It is quite another thing to frustrate her deliberately or to abandon her when she's in trouble. A hurt child does not grow up strengthened, but wounded. The toughness some people develop from dealing with too much frustration too soon is not muscle but scars.

Fathering Your Nursing Toddler

Doubts

As babies grow and change, father's feelings about nursing may change. One mother says, "My husband was insistent on breastfeeding our children as newborns. It was when they could sit up and pull up my shirt that he wanted me to stop. He thinks . . . there should be a time limit. He felt embarrassed by my breastfeeding at that point." Another writes, "Although my husband was very supportive of the nursing relationship for the first twelve months of my son's life, he really struggles with it now."

It is hard to decide to go against the culture, especially in something as important as rearing your children. I hope the information in this book reassures you that, at the very least it, will not hurt your child to keep nursing. There is reason to believe it will be beneficial.

One father writes:

> *Some time ago a doctor said to my wife that maybe she should put our toddler in day care. . . . The doctor felt that our son was too dependent on his mom. However, this is not the case. Granted there are times when the little one wants to be with his mom all of the time, but usually I'm the one chasing him around the house . . . . He is very independent—I think even more so than the first one, who was bottle-fed. The health benefits and savings aside, I respect my wife for having the courage and commitment to continue to breastfeed our toddler. . . . He's developing just fine and whatever doubts I had about my wife nursing past 24 months are out the window every time I see the smile on my little one's face when he comes running for me, not for his mom's breast.*

Building a Parenting Team

You can make it easier for your wife to provide the mothering your child needs, or you can make it nearly impossible. Mothers and babies thrive with a supportive father, like the dad who seemed to get "offended" by negative remarks about nursing. "I remember the pride my husband showed when I nursed," another mother said.

A mother in India wrote about her husband's encouragement:

> *My wonderful husband . . . hated the idea of a separate bed for the baby and thought he looked so lonely—now we are all happy. I'm so proud of how much he has supported*

and defended all my "bizarre" ideas of how to care for our child! In fact many of those ideas originated with him. Nursing [our son] is probably the only area which is exclusively mine, everything else has been shared, and there have been many times when [our son] has preferred his father to me as a source of non-nursing comfort. Murmurs of "Poor man! His wife makes him look after the baby!" are beginning to fade, as people see what a wonderfully close bond they have.

Families blossom when fathers become involved with their children, and mothers take pleasure in watching the father-child relationship develop. Stay-at-home parents appreciate partners who serve as a link for them with the outside world. Families in which both parents are employed need a cooperative effort to keep the family time focused on family.

Families wilt in the face of insensitivity, such as that of the father of a frequent nurser who comments on undone housework. It is destructive when a husband whose wife does chores when he is home complains about her inattentiveness instead of pitching in to get the annoying tasks out of the way. Families can be hurt by unresolved fights over division of responsibilities.

You and your wife need to discuss your parenting goals, not just once, but periodically. Your discussions need not be aimed at reaching 100 percent agreement on everything to do with your children (or anything else for that matter), but life will be easier if you are essentially working toward the same objectives and supporting each other. Among the benefits children gain from a home with two parents is learning to live with differing viewpoints and inconsistencies. Your discussions should help you keep your focus on shared goals. When you do not see eye to eye, at least you can each be aware of the other's viewpoint so as not to undermine each other.

Just as your wife will help you, so you need to help her keep on the track you have chosen, particularly when you are not following the same course as the people around you. You can be a crucial factor in helping your child grow up well by being ready to show support for the parenting choices you have made about toilet training and bedtimes (or lack thereof). Especially when nursing is involved, you can be her best source of support, of encouragement, and of the mature judgment sometimes necessary to enable her to nurse your child as long as he needs it.

Pediatrician William Sears writes about the dilemma so many mothers face when there is conflict between their husbands' wants and their babies' needs. He advises against giving mixed messages, paying lip service to continued nursing on one hand, and daydreaming about weaning and "getting away" on the other.[8] Your family deserves better from you.

Protector Role Redefined

Mothers say that the most difficult problems they face in nursing past infancy result from criticism from other people—family, friends, medical practitioners. Sometimes this pressure, almost always from people who are as well-intentioned as they are misinformed, can be great enough to break a mother's resolve to give your child the best possible beginning. You can protect your wife, and thereby protect your child's birthright, by reminding her of your support for what she is doing.

You can also put a stop to conversations that work to undermine her resolve. There is little need to try to bring most other people around to your way of child-rearing; it is often more efficient just to change the subject of conversation firmly and unrelentingly. Some parents who find that certain associates persist in the rudeness of criticizing their parenting decisions choose to find new friends who are either more compatible in their opinions or at least have better manners.

Your wife may need your help most if criticism comes from members of your family. She probably has ways of coping when it comes from her own relatives (and with them, you may need her to stand up for you). But she may be unsure of how to communicate with your family. Besides, she does not want to embarrass or offend you. She will certainly benefit from any help you can give in establishing her as a competent mother in the eyes of your family. One mother writes, "My husband has been a wonderful advocate for me with his family. For him, the proof was in observing our children as they grew and developed, and in comparing doctor-visit stories with other parents."

There are times, too, when you may be called upon for mature judgment in helping your wife and child make the best of their relationship. Mothers sometimes feel obliged to pursue traditions (like holiday dinners) or family business (like putting up friends and relatives who come through town) or progress (like moving or remodeling). All this involvement can be enjoyable or satisfying when we have the means and are not feeling torn apart by the pull of other needs. A word from you will sometimes be all that is needed to head off disaster, small or large.

Advocating for the Child

Another way you can provide the best for your child is to help his mother through times when mothering him well is difficult for her. No doubt she will do the same for you when you tire and become exasperated with some of your tasks as a father. Many mothers, myself included, have gotten weary of a child's insistence upon nursing. When we mothers are not at our best, how grateful we are for husbands who calm us and gently stick up for our children. More than once I was set back on track by my husband's mild chiding, "She *needs* to nurse!"

When your wife complains about nursing, as doubtless she sometimes will, she needs you to slow her down and help her to take some other pressure off herself. (Has she suddenly decided all the closets need cleaning this week? Or started writing a book? Making holiday plans?) Remind her of what you both want life in your family to be like, and why you want to meet your child's needs as fully as possible. Help her to get her priorities straight again.

There is an impulse when she complains about nursing to write the nursing off as "her thing" and urge her to abandon it and get back to life the way it used to be. If you evaluate the impulse, though, you will see that it is an understandable, immature kind of thought that we all have when facing something difficult. It is a regressive and impractical impulse. Now that a child has become part of your lives, there is no returning to things as they were, nor would you want to.

Nor would weaning be an easy solution to difficulties in life with a young child. In fact it is neither easy nor a solution. Nursing or not, a young child needs much of her mother's time and attention, and mothers tire of pushing swings and finger-painting just as easily as they tire of nursing. Weaning a child who is not ready can also be quite an undertaking. It can be exhausting for both parents and cannot always be accomplished without emotional damage to the child, or even to the parents.

Nursing is not merely "her thing," but part of your whole family scene. Considering that nursing is something she does for a good reason, not for her own gratification, you shouldn't be surprised at what a resentful response you get if you answer her complaints by suggesting that she wean. Her complaints are likely a plea for help from you in caring for your child, or for help in figuring out how to make her life with him easier. They are almost always a plea for your reassurance and support for her continued nursing.

Finding Support

If you can't ask your colleagues at work about life with a nursing toddler, or bring up a question like, "What do you do when your kid picks her nose all the time?" then Richard Louv suggests you look for friendships with men who do share such concerns.[5] If your wife is in a breastfeeding or mothering support group like La Leche League, fathers of the babies in that group would be a good place to start. Most people, male and female, find it easier to swim against the social tide that treats children, in novelist Barbara Kingsolver's words, as "toxic waste"[3] if we don't have to do it alone.

Don't keep your good fathering hidden. Go places, and take your children with you. In time they'll probably bring you into contact with other like-minded men. They're out there, even if you haven't met them yet.

Husbanding Your Nursing Wife

Missing Intimacy

Some fortunate couples never face any problems in continuing their intimate relationship after children join the family. The loving feelings some mothers enjoy with their babies radiate over all their relationships, including passion for their husbands.[2] When it comes to sexual intimacy, however, life is often unfair to fathers, especially if your wife on occasion finds herself feeling "touched out" and low on desire. Add to this a toddler

I'VE JUST TALKED TO GOD AND HE
SAYS I CAN HAVE MORE NEE-NEE.

who may not sleep very much, and it can seem that your life as a couple is gone forever.

You have the same desires as before, but your mate has become unresponsive. It is hard not to feel hurt by this change. You may find yourself needing to re-start your romance. Dr. William Sears recommends a new and patient courtship that includes creative (and flexible) trysts at times and places that fit your family's new rhythms. Give it a try, especially the "patient" part; the rewards may be slow in coming, but ever so worthwhile.

There is a well-published notion that your marriage cannot flourish unless you have a periodic weekend, if not a whole week, away from your child. Since you and your wife loved each other enough to produce your child, I would bet that you are probably quite capable of figuring out ways to sustain that love without leaving a child who is too immature to do without your presence and protection.

There may be times when you need to take him along, times when you need to go out later, after he is asleep, or times when you find ways to entertain yourselves at home. You should not stop enjoying one another by any means; you just need to be inventive when the old ways prove not to be in the best interests of your family.

Redefining Domestic Responsibilities

Dana Raphael points out that human divisions of most nurturing roles into men's and women's domains seem cultural rather than biological. Among other species, the less colorful partner, regardless of sex, is the nurturer. Among species like ours in which the two sexes are similar, the nurturing of offspring is shared.[7]

Sadly, some fathers choose not to be much involved with babies and toddlers, even in families where wives are employed away from home. Some say they are waiting until the children get older, so they can talk to them like real people. Others find themselves so overwhelmed by work situations that they cannot manage any more commitment. As a result, children grow up not knowing their fathers, and the fathers feel like strangers in their own homes.

Life can be better. At the very least, you can make a point of expressing your appreciation to your wife for the massive investment of time and energy child care requires. Even better, you can get involved yourself, reducing your partner's workload and increasing your own satisfaction in family life. Better than just "helping out" is truly sharing in the responsibilities of rearing a child.

Some attitudes make it hard for fathers to care for their children. People persist in calling care by father "babysitting," as if you are substituting for the real parent. Some wives and mothers, too, may have difficulty accepting the idea of "real men" working in the home. But fathers who develop domestic competence and spend time at home would not trade the time with their children for anything.

If you feel inadequate for tasks around the house, apply the same mental and physical resources you used in learning your other jobs. The comedy sketches about men being klutzes with diapers and dishes are just that—comedy sketches. Domestic work is as important as any on earth and is worth doing well. A person competent to drive in freeway traffic is no doubt capable of refereeing quarrels among preschoolers or operating a vacuum cleaner. Besides, the more of life's essential business you know how to do, the more confidently you can live. If you make the effort to learn how to perform jobs like cooking or doing dishes well, then, when you're called upon, instead of being triggers for feelings of insecurity and stress, these will be tasks you can do on auto-pilot. But while you're learning a new task, ask for some slack—everybody is entitled to some "free" blunders at first.

If you've always been oblivious to household chores that madden your wife when they're neglected, try to learn what they are and take care of the ones you can. Be sure your partner knows, however, that you are pitching in out of love and not as a reproach for what she hasn't been able to get done. Under the right circumstances, tending to chores can so unburden a mother that it becomes the most passionate foreplay possible.

Feeling Left Out

Difficult as it seems, it is worth the effort to get past any sense of deprivation you may feel. You may find deprivation a greater challenge if you yourself didn't get enough loving as a child, or if you have painful memories of being displaced by a younger sibling. You may feel an urge to compete for your wife's attention, feeling as if the baby were a brother or sister rather than your child. Considering such possibilities may clarify some of your dissatisfactions and help you focus on the role you want in your present family. In this family you are not son or brother, but husband and father. We all have a right to enjoy being babied when it is possible and appropriate. But you can expect more enduring satisfaction from an adult partnership with your mate and shared status as a parent to your children.

It may seem strange at first, but the way to be closest to your wife is to help her stay close to your child. If you allow yourself to compete with him for her attention, you set up barriers between yourself and her that are hard to break down. You can, instead of seeking attention by coming between your wife and your child, embrace them together and nurture their love for each other. There is much to be gained from being the kind of father one woman wrote about, saying,

My husband learned about the baby's needs, my needs, giving up some attention from me for her security—but he also learned that his generosity gained him a close relationship with both of us. We are truly devoted to him.

As a result of fostering closeness among the members of your family, you are likely to be rewarded with increased love and affection from your wife and from an emotionally healthy child—a child who will love you as one of the most special people in his world for the rest of his life.

References

1   Ainsworth, M. D. S. Attachments and other affectional bonds across the life cycle. *Attachment Across the Life Cycle.* Ed. C.M. Parkes, J. Stevenson-Hinde, and P. Marris. London: Tavistock/Routledge, 1991; 41.

2   Bowlby, J. *Attachment.* New York: Basic Books, 1982; 308.

3   Epstein, R. The Progressive interview: Barbara Kingsolver. *The Progressive* February 1996; 60(2): 33-37.

4   Fildes, V. A. *Breasts, Bottles and Babies: A History of Infant Feeding.* Edinburgh: Edinburgh University Press, 1986; 104.

5   Louv, R. *Father Love: What We Need, What We Seek, What We Must Create.* New York: Pocket Books, 1993; 90-91, 137.

6   Mead, M. and Newton, N. Cultural patterning of perinatal behavior. *Childbearing: Its Social and Psychological Aspects.* Ed. S. A. Richardson and A. F. Guttmacher. Baltimore: Williams and Wilkins, 1967; 190-91.

7   Raphael, D. *The Tender Gift Breastfeeding.* New York: Shocken Books, 1976; 66.

8   Sears, W. Becoming A Father. Schaumburg, Illinois: La Leche League International, 1986; 139, 5, 61-62.

9   Walters Art Gallery, Baltimore, MD. Reproduced in: The Boston Women's Health Book Collective, *The New Our Bodies, Ourselves.* New York: Simon & Schuster, 1992; 489.

Nursing Your Toddler Year By Year

chapter twelve

Nursing in the Second Year

The Nursing Toddler—A Baby on Wheels

Somewhere along the way the idea emerged that babyhood ends with the beginning of walking and talking, and that with proper parental management, babyhood can end rather abruptly on the child's first birthday. Instead of standing in proper awe of the accomplishments that babies make around the beginning of their second year, we added demands for more. In addition to the big changes from crawling to walking and from body language and crying to talking, we also insisted that they be toilet-trained, sleep all night by themselves, and leave the bric-a-brac alone. It is little wonder that it is at this stressful age that our children are most likely to develop some attachment to inanimate objects. Such attachments are not harmful,[2] but sometimes inconvenient and often a sign of stress.

If we stop to examine a one-year-old child, the absurdity of some adult demands on them seems obvious. They are what someone has described as "babies on wheels," still infants, but mobile and therefore quite vulnerable. Their little foreheads remain babyishly high and broad; their legs are short and often still bowed, and they continue to have infants' round little bellies. The diapers or pants that stayed on pretty well while they were prone tend to fall victim to gravity now that they are vertical. They look like babies and act like babies. They will be three or four before their bodies and faces have stretched out into the shapes and proportions of childhood. The appearance of these mobile little people still makes us feel we are dealing with babies, and unless we are talked out of it by "experts," we will respond to them in a way appropriate to the care of babies for as long as their babyish appearance and mannerisms continue.

Nursing a child in his second year seems a reasonable way to help meet some of his continuing baby needs. How long he will nurse, how often, etc., is unpredictable. Some little ones this age are too busy with exploring to be bothered with much nursing. Some are happier to eat the family's food and nurse only to go to sleep or when they are hurt. Some even wean during the second year.

Frequent Nursing

By far the most usual behavior for a child in the second year, however, is to nurse a lot. According to a study done in an area of New Guinea where extended nursing was the norm, nursing continued at frequent enough intervals for mothers to continue producing 20 ounces of milk daily into the third year.[1] One researcher who recommends advising mothers to start solids gradually, starting at about six months, says to expect frequent nursing to continue. "The child should continue breastfeeding just as often during the second year, but offer solid foods a few times a day."[4]

A child who may have nursed less frequently near the end of her first year will often surprise her mother by going back to nursing almost like a newborn at times during the second year. Countless mothers have described this pattern to me, and it was observed among healthy children of nomadic Turkana pastoralists in Africa.[3] Mothers would be less distressed by their toddlers' seemingly constant needs to nurse if they were aware of how common frequent nursing is at this time of life. You need to be prepared for such needs and know they are normal and temporary. In fact, the first half of the second year may be one of the most intense nursing periods and the one in which children react most strongly to weaning.[5]

As children begin to walk and explore, they meet all kinds of new, unfamiliar situations. They become frightened by things that are new to them that we may never dream are frightening. They overextend themselves in their efforts to master new skills, even though we adults may not be aware that they are "working." All that babbling or patting or digging or running around is serious work in the business of mastering a new and expanding world.

Some children handle their work with ease, pace themselves, and cope well with their inevitable frustrations right from the beginning. Most are much more easily distressed and disoriented, especially when facing a new task like walking, and tend to venture too far and get hurt easily.

This busy time of life is wearing on mothers as well as on children. You may come to appreciate your child's time at the breast as did the mother who wrote, "Nursing gives me a break from having to be constantly monitoring his latest activity, which is usually more daring than he realizes." Rapidly learning toddlers have urgent and frequent needs for reassurance and encouragement that they are progressing well and that it is safe and worthwhile for them to try something again.

The child who needs a lot of nursing is just as likely to grow up emotionally stable and capable as is the child whose needs seem less overwhelming. Each child grows at his own rate emotionally just as he does physically and intellectually. Nor do we as parents have much to say about what kind of child we will have at this age. We can minimize a child's anxiety level by meeting her needs as fully as possible from birth on. But how much intense parenting she needs, possibly including frequent nursing, in the second year depends for the most part on her inborn timetable. As parents we can slow down emotional growth by leaving needs unmet, but there is little we can do to speed it up.

Our objective must be to help him grow into a child with the poise and self-confidence that will enable him to cope well with the world of school children and learning he will be meeting at age five or six. Our children do not need this kind of confidence at age one—or even two or three. We have several years to help them grow. There is no hurry, and your investment in your toddler who seems to be "always attached" will pay off when the time for independence does come.

Picking a Code Word

The second year is usually the time to promote your nursing code word if you are going to use one. Whatever word you pick, you should use it regularly with your child during this year and the next as he begins to talk. That will allow you to choose what nursing will be called in your family, rather than leaving it up to your child's choice as time goes on, and it will help your child by giving a name to something that is important to him.

Toddler Nursing Strike

Toddlers sometimes quit nursing suddenly, just as some babies do. Some mothers take this as self-weaning, and sometimes it may be. When a child has been nursing frequently, however, especially if she is under three, there is probably a reason for stopping, such as a stuffy nose or sore mouth. You'll want to look closely for a physical problem. Broken teeth have kept some toddlers from nursing even though they wanted to.

There may be a cause you'll never find, however, like hurt feelings over a scolding or having to do something she didn't want to.

Age is a clue. The closer to three or beyond, the more likely your child is just through with nursing. In the second year, there's a greater chance that nursing has been interrupted by something temporary. But age is an unreliable predictor of children's needs and behavior. The best instrument is your knowledge of your child. If he's happily too busy to be bothered with nursing, that sounds like self-weaning. If he's fussy and clingy but won't nurse, there is probably something else going on that could use your attention. One good thing about dealing with an older nursling at a time like this is that he may be able to tell you what is going on. By all means ask.

Whether or not they ever learn the cause, when a child quits nursing suddenly, many mothers pump or express milk for a few days, or even weeks, both for their own comfort, and to give the child the opportunity to go back to nursing once the problem is resolved.

> *After ten days, my toddler decided to start nursing again. We are very thankful. Nothing like having a non-nursing toddler for ten days to remind me about all the benefits of nursing a toddler! . . . I'm still not sure why my son decided to start nursing again. I had pretty much resigned myself to him weaning early but I am very glad things turned out otherwise.*

In toddlers, as in babies, "nursing strikes" do occur and can go on for some time. You can try the responses to a nursing strike you can find in THE WOMANLY ART OF BREASTFEEDING, including quiet, private nursing opportunities and offering to nurse when he is falling asleep or just waking up. He may or may not resume nursing. If he doesn't after what seems a reasonable amount of time to you, it may be another indication that you're dealing with weaning and not a strike.

Nursing Leaves One Hand Free

If not in the first year, then certainly in the second, most children find a favorite pastime for their "top" hand as they are nursing. (Until they start doing "acrobatic nursing," they usually lie on the other hand.) They stroke mother's face, force their fingers into her mouth, fiddle with her hair, caress her neck, play with mother's belly-button, pummel her with a little fist, and on and on.

That free hand can become a problem. One family was content with the choice of the code name "deedees" for nursing because it was unobtrusive at any voice level, even at church. But "the issue we had was that she liked to stroke my breast while she was nursing and wanted her 'deedees big.' The best I could do was try to explain that she had to have her 'deedees little' in church." As this family learned, during your child's first and second year you need to be aware, not only of words, but of the activities your child pursues with that free hand, and you need to give some thought to how you feel about them. What he does with that free hand will likely become an integral part of his nursing as time goes on, and getting him to change this activity later can be quite difficult—not always impossible, but difficult. Frequently children continue to enjoy their individual "free-hand game" whenever they are in mother's lap, even long after they have weaned from the breast.

By far the most common pastime for that free hand is flicking or pinching the other nipple. Many mothers find this nipple stimulation very annoying, especially as the child gets older, and some babies pinch painfully. Lactation consultant Beverly Morgan says this may be more than idle twiddling. "Milk flow is influenced by breast stimulation. That's why babies stroke or knead their mothers' breasts. Some enterprising young ones also stimulate the other nipple when they want a faster flow. It's sort of like turning up the volume on a TV set."[6] The result may be much like using a double breast pump. One mother interprets her child's twiddling differently:

> *I take fiddling as a sign my twelve-month-old doesn't really want to feed that badly. If he won't desist we stop nursing and I distract him. When he is really serious about his feed, he doesn't fiddle much. But I realize other babies might not be so amenable.*

It is not difficult to distract a baby from any game that you dislike if you are aware early on that whatever she is experimenting with now can become a permanent part of nursing. Breaking the habit later can be difficult.

> *I thought I would lose my mind! So one night at 3 AM, after two hours of nipple twiddling, I told her she could nurse, but she could not play with mommy's nipple. She naturally pitched a fit, but I remained firm, acknowledged her anger, told her I loved her, and held her (when she'd let me—she has my temper). These battles continued in diminishing fury for about three days every time she*

would nurse (I might add that getting her to sleep for about two days was difficult because her anger would energize her). Now, a few weeks later, she not only accepts it with grace when occasionally I have to stop a little hand from attempting to pinch a nipple (I actually admire her determination!), but she politely pulls my shirt down over the finished breast when she switches sides!

The urge seems all but universal. "My first was a real nipple-twiddler," says one mother. "I was reassured to see a picture of an Indian goddess nursing her son/toddler, and he had his free hand on the other nipple. I guess they're just fun things to play with."

Having been annoyed by my first nursing toddler's play with the other nipple, and then with her scratching at my navel with little fingernails, with later babies, I was quick to redirect tiny hands (and feet!) from where I did not want them to be for the next few years. But with the child for whom I discovered the need for "redirection" too late, I had to resort to clothing that kept most of my body inaccessible to her little fingers and fingernails. This was not difficult during the day, but it took a while to find a solution for nighttime. At last I came up with a scoop-neck gown with elastic in the neckline that was just firm enough that she had to hold it with both hands in order to keep it out of the way while she nursed. What a relief that was!

Another mother wrote:

My daughter (now twenty-one months) is a "twiddler" and a very determined child. The following tactics have helped me keep comfortable without getting into fights:

Instead of restraining her hand (instant frustration, wrath, hurt feelings!), I press my own wrist or arm against the "free" nipple under the pretext of supporting the nursing breast with that hand; she gets to hold or stroke the rest of the free breast.

While side-lying, I nurse on the lower breast first (to prevent plugged ducts when I roll onto it), using the technique above to protect the upper nipple; then nurse on the upper breast, with lower nipple tucked against the bed out of reach.

On the couch, I put her head on a pillow in my lap, with the rest of her body off to the side; she can't reach to put her hand down my shirt. (This is also very good for reading a book to my older child at the same time.)

Some types of bras and shirts are probably better than others at covering the unengaged nipple; mine are designed for easy access!

One useful ploy can be providing an object to occupy the free hand. At a recent La Leche League conference I purchased sturdy nursing necklaces for the mothers of my grandchildren to wear while nursing. The necklaces consist of strong cords strung with bright glass beads designed to attract a toddler's interest. Some mothers and toddlers use a nursing toy. A toy not only keeps the hand occupied, but adds one more bit of cover-up for you. You should make sure any toy used for nursing times is soft enough not to hurt you until you manage to teach him not to hit you with it.

A mother in Singapore writes that this approach does have some drawbacks. "When my son was younger (maybe about six to eight months), I started letting him hold a bear in his free hand. Maybe it wasn't too good an idea, because unless he's really tired, he needs to hold his 'bear bear' while nursing." Your child will likely be very upset if such a toy gets misplaced, so by getting him used to it, you may be committing yourself to keeping up with this item for as long as he continues nursing.

Your child may play with your clothing, starting at an early age to open buttons, raise your shirt, etc. Before you know it, this may become a part of nursing in private that you aren't comfortable with in front of others. Kathleen Huggins suggests in her book *The Nursing Mother's Guide to Weaning* that you keep your shirt "modestly down, even at home. Make it clear that your clothes are not for her to strip off whenever she feels like it."[5]

With some children, the activity is not confined to one hand. They move their whole bodies without losing the nipple. "He was a little monkey," one mother said of her son. "He tried and probably invented twenty positions to nurse in." Another wrote about her fifteen-month-old who always wants to nurse when mom sits down in front of her computer.

The other day as I was doing some typing and nursing at the same time (I've had lots of practice), he was doing his usual contortions. Soon, he was squatting on the desk in front of me, between me and the monitor! That has to be one of the most unique nursing positions yet! Would that be the reverse cross-keyboard hold?

On occasion you may want to discourage some of the acrobatics, if they should seem dangerous or become uncomfortable for you. If it hurts, don't allow it.

Rather than being negative about his activities while nursing, though, you can be observant and encourage your child toward habits you both enjoy—patting the other breast or mother's cheek are pastimes many mothers like. You should also consider whether or not what your child chooses to do will be acceptable to you when there are other people around; it's often the play while nursing rather than the nursing itself that mothers find embarrassing.

Some children insist on putting their hands down mother's shirt or holding her breast, and some do so when they're not even nursing. In some, weaning doesn't change this behavior. The best emergency measure parents have found to cope with the little hands in potentially embarrassing situations is to give the child something large and interesting to hold, something big enough to take both hands. For a toddler with this possibly annoying habit, father or friends can be a big help, holding and entertaining the toddler in public places or in front of judgmental guests. A child with her hand down Daddy's shirt won't raise anybody's eyebrows.

Some mothers point out, of course, that they're perfectly comfortable with the baby doing such things as nursing and playing with the other nipple. If that is the case with you, by all means don't worry about it! The same is true for the regular dental exams many toddlers provide while nursing. Some mothers hate them while for others there is no problem. The whole point is that you should begin to teach your child what you yourself, not somebody else, are comfortable having him do with that free hand, and start teaching as soon as he begins exploring with it.

Getting through the Peak Time for Criticism

The second year is the period in which you are likely to encounter the most questions and criticism about your little one's continued nursing. He is, as I have said, still very much a baby and still likely to find himself needing to nurse anywhere and everywhere, without regard to how you feel about the people nearby. This is not true for all nurslings this age, but for most of them it is. Few one-year-olds have the verbal or social understanding to respond reliably to explanations and delays. With babies in the second year it is frequently easier and more peaceful, and certainly kinder to the child, just to nurse whenever and wherever he needs it, and deal as pleasantly as you can with any questions or criticism you may receive. A sling can be a great help for discreet nursing with toddlers as well as babies.

It is too bad that mothers must cope with something so unnatural as a widespread belief that they should not nurse their babies, and that one-year-olds are not babies anyway. Little people in their second year offer their parents so much pleasure with their wide-eyed trust and exuberance. If you can rise above whatever criticism you may meet, you can enjoy your babies as babies far longer than many people think possible or advisable. How satisfying it is for toddlers—and for parents—not to have to rush through babyhood, no matter who says they should.

References

1   Becroft, T. Child-rearing practices in the highlands of New Guinea: a longitudinal study of breast feeding. *Medical Journal of Australia* 1967; 2:599.

2   Bowlby, J. *Attachment.* New York: Basic Books, 1982; 310.

3   Gray, S. J. *Infant Care and Feeding Among Nomadic Turkana Pastoralists: Implications for Fertility and Child Survival.* PhD Diss. State University of New York at Binghamton, 1992; 199, 202, 217, 282, 403.

4   Greiner, T. Sustained breastfeeding, complementation, and care. *Food and Nutrition Bulletin.* 1995; 16(4):317.

5   Huggins, K. and Ziedrich, L. *The Nursing Mother's Guide to Weaning.* Boston: The Harvard Common Press, 1994; 124, 132.

6   Morgan, B. *Reading Your Baby's Body Language.* Audio tape. San Jose, CA: Milky Way Press, 1989.

chapter thirteen

Nursing Through the Terrible Twos

"Terrible Twos"—No Longer Terrible

A wonderful thing seems to be happening lately. The Terrible Twos are being renamed: some parents now call little people in their third year "tantalizing twos" or "terrific twos." And a high percentage of those two-year-olds who have caused their parents to rename this stage of growth are still nursing.

Two-year-olds have earned a reputation for independent thinking and exploration through almost every minute they are awake. Their ambitions far exceed their capabilities, and they have been known to kick and scream out their frustrations in tantrums. Even with the careful watching required to keep them safe, they still get hurt and bring mother fingers and knees that need kisses and ceremonial bandages. They have no patience with adult schedules and the adult pace of life. Their drive to explore is constant, and they protest against being rushed past anything that catches their eyes, be it the neighbor's dog or one of those maddening candy and gum displays at the supermarket check-out line.

All these behaviors in the third year are normal and reflect the exciting growth of their baby minds toward childhood. We do a two-year-old quite a disservice if we become upset by his behavior at this age and try to teach him to behave much differently. Some wise advice given by D.C. Briggs back in 1970 still works today: "Fit his environment to his needs, eliminating as many frustrations as possible. His inner pressures are enough for him to handle. The child-proofed home beats tranquilizers."[1]

A two-year-old is inquisitive and eager to try new things—new things of his choice, not ours, no matter what a mother might wish on some of his especially busy days. He should begin to assert himself and make his wishes and opinions known. As he matures he will begin to learn that if he does not get his way right now it does not mean that he will never get his way again. But for now his newly discovered power to make his own decisions is precious, and he will fight anybody, anywhere if he fears he is going to lose that power.

The wise parent learns to work with this new assertiveness, not against it. You are not facing a potential lifelong behavior that must be "nipped in the bud." Rather, you are his guardian through an essential step in the development of a strong and healthy mind. Your child will move on to more reasoned and reasoning behavior over the next few years. Briggs, who understood kids, if not breastfeeding, went on to say:

> *Because establishing independence is such a monumental task, outside pressures become formidable roadblocks to the two. Yet, around this age parents often decide to take away the bedtime bottle, get the thumb out of the mouth, or remove the security blanket and pacifier. These demands are like asking a confirmed smoker to quit the habit at the very time he takes on a stressful new job.*[1]

Briggs goes on to say that because a child's internal pressures are at a peak during the third year, it is safer to wait until he's three to make major changes. If you're unsuccessful at three wait until he is five, which is normally another time of inner equilibrium.

During the fascinating, frustrating, always volatile third year, mothers and children alike find nursing to be a much appreciated leveler. Children use nursing to help calm themselves when mounting tensions—traumas or triumphs, either one—become too much for them and make them uncomfortable. Mothers use nursing to calm themselves and their overextended children.

"It is not a measure of your child's maturity if she does or doesn't wean before age three," Diane Bengson writes in *How Weaning Happens*.[2] Many children this age are weaned and are happy about it. Others nurse only to fall asleep or wake up. Others use nursing to get over tough spots at other times during the day. Quite a number of children this age still need to nurse quite often. Mothers with two-year-olds still nursing sometimes talk of feeling overwhelmed with how much their children still need them. Others tell how much they enjoy the nursing times. "It's the only time I get to cuddle her or see her sitting still" is a typical comment.

Tantrums

Nursing is an especially helpful tool in lessening, or even avoiding a two-year-old's (or any age's) possible tantrums. You or your child can usually recognize that a situation is becoming too tense for the child to handle and initiate nursing. It would be fascinating to know how many tantrums have not occurred because of nursing mothers' timely interventions; but that, of course, is the kind of statistic that is hard to pin down, like the number of cavities prevented by avoiding sweets or the number of colds prevented by hand-washing. If, however, you do find yourself facing a full-fledged tantrum, nursing will probably help you and your child to shorten it and come out of it more peacefully than anything else you can do.

Whenever you find that your child is crying but not too far out of control, you may be able to bring him out of it by making funny faces and jokes, by tickling, or by picking him up to nurse. For a verbal child, William and Martha Sears suggest wrapping him in an immobilizing hug and urging him, "Use your words. Use your words."[3] When your child does get well into a tantrum, something some nursing mothers tell me they have never experienced, he will probably not let you touch him, much less nurse. In that case, stay as near to him as he will let you. Tell him you are there whenever he is ready to cuddle or nurse. You might see whether he will let you stroke his leg or rub his back; if he will, that is a good start toward calming him. If not, then find something to do that will keep you from being bored and tempted to walk away from your very frightened and unhappy child. (Yes, I know, the tantrum is probably over something silly—the cat won't stay on the couch, or he can't go to work with daddy—but these things can become huge and overwhelming in a young mind.) Pick up a book. Grab your knitting or that article you were writing—whatever. You can go about your business quietly, as long as you stay close.

If he's in a full-blown tantrum, he may be embarrassed along with all his other overwrought feelings and may not even be able to stand for you to look at him.

After a while he will probably come sheepishly to you. This is difficult for him to do, and he needs your open arms and ready comfort, not a discussion of the tantrum and the events that led up to it. If he is still nursing, just hold him and let him nurse. Soon a good giggling and tickling session may be in order. If, instead of coming to you for nursing and for loving, he falls asleep where he is lying, you can assume that sleepiness was a contributing element in the upset. Let him sleep and go about your business, cuddling him and nursing him when he awakens if that is what he seems to want.

Of course tantrums do tend to occur at busy, hectic, often hungry times of the day when it is difficult to stop what you are doing and stay near your unhappy child. In fact, that is probably how the situation got out of control in the first place. If supper is about to burn on the stove or you have to pick up the older kids at school, you are in one of those situations so common in motherhood in which your family's different needs are pulling you in separate directions. All you can do is prioritize and work through the situation with the best effort you have in you that day (go ahead and pull the pots off the stove before you settle down near your child, or carry your crying child to the car and do the best you can to comfort her in her safety seat). These conflicts of needs crop up for all of us from time to time, and everyone seems to survive.

If you find that tantrums are occurring rather consistently at one time of day or in certain circumstances, you should look hard at what is going on and apply some parental brilliance to making life easier for your child right then. Can that particular bit of business be eliminated or moved to another time or place? What about trying to read a story or nurse beforehand? How long since she has eaten? Perhaps food and/or extra attention will fortify your child enough for her to be able to cope better.

Talking about Nursing

One of the joys of nursing two-year-olds is hearing what they have to say on the subject. Some of them will tell you not only when they want to nurse, but exactly where and how—"Not in bed, on couch!" "Don't pull up shirt; open buttons." One little one preferred to open mom's bra herself and would shout "Self! Self!" if mom started to unhook. At a La Leche League meeting where mothers were nursing their babies, a toddler ran to mother and said brightly, "Oh, many babies num-num. Me too!" Occasionally a two-year-old comes to a profound conclusion such as "milk inside Mommy!" What charming first steps these little people reveal on their journey toward understanding cultural anthropology and basic physiology.

It is during the third year, too, that most children become verbal enough to understand some of what mother has to say about nursing and to begin to adjust their requests for nursing toward times and places that are the most comfortable for the whole family. This is not to say that there is no point in saying anything about nursing to your child before her second birthday or that you will definitely have everything perfectly worked out by the time she turns three. In that vague, general time frame we must use in discussing individuals who develop at such widely different rates, the third year is when we are able to see some results from our attempts at setting limits and helping the child understand them.

Diversions start to become possible as verbal ability increases, as with one family's "snackies" (nursing) joke.

> *We bike ride to see our neighbors' cows frequently, and the cows often are nursing the new babies. As we pulled away on our bikes recently, my son, age two-and-a-half, was bidding farewell to his cow friends, and he said, "Bye, Merry Moo Cow. Bye, Brown Baby. Bye, Mama cow with snackies." We didn't even realize he had noticed the baby cows nursing! Now, when I'm feeling a bit burned out, . . . I tell him to go see the mama cow with snackies if he wants to nurse, and he gets hysterical laughing at the thought.*

It was when her child was about this age that one mother said, "I did insist that reading a newspaper on the floor did not mean I wanted to nurse." Another mother whose child was past two decided she was no longer willing for him to nurse instead of eating supper. She communicated her desire for this change mostly by not sitting down until he had begun to eat. On those occasions on which he still wanted to interrupt his mother's meal, she usually gently insisted upon her right to finish.

You make changes in nursing "rules" the same way you make other changes. You explain to the two-year-old, for instance, about staying inside the front door rather than running outside into the street. But he will be three or four at least before you can expect him always to observe that rule. Meanwhile, you remind him and help him comply. He learns the rules, not from how loudly you teach them, but from how often. The twos are a time of beginnings, not the age at which everything is settled once and for all.

With your two-year-old you can begin to see at least some results when you explain that there are situations in which nursing makes you uncomfortable. It is best, however, not to try to get her to understand several different changes you want to make all at once or suddenly jump in with restrictions on nursing when you have imposed none before. It's better to talk about nursing all along, starting in infancy. Then keep your eyes open to opportunities for changing this or that item from discussion to reality.

The time will come, for instance, when you can say, "I don't like to nurse at Grandma's house—let's wait until we get into the car," and your child will agree to the plan with a conspiratorial grin, or at least permit you to distract him easily. You can suggest to a child nursing at night that she finish up because mommy is sleepy. When your child wants to nurse, say, right after supper when you would love to sit down for a few minutes with your coffee and needlework, you can tell him, "Daddy will play with you for a little while; then we'll nurse" (or whatever you call it). These suggestions are not likely to be effective at all for quite some time after you begin making them, but someday, if you're alert to the possibilities, they will be.

When your child does respond to a request you make about nursing, be sure to praise him and thank him. He is making a positive step in learning to fit his needs in around those of others. It will take him his whole life to learn the art of meeting his own needs without interfering with the needs of others. He is on his way, and what a praiseworthy event it is!

Occasionally you may find it necessary to impose limits on nursing without waiting for your child to agree to the change. For example, if you should have to be away from your child for a while, then he will not have the opportunity to nurse at certain times of the day no matter what his needs might be. Or you could find that for the sake of other family members you have to be busy sometimes when your child might choose to nurse. In such cases you should tend to what has to be done and explain to your child as best you can. You will probably be surprised how well even small children can adapt to waiting when you really have to do something else. They often understand necessity remarkably well if you are honest with them about it. You need to do everything in your power, of course, to see that your child's needs are met—perhaps at other times or even by other people—but met fully.

The way you can tell whether you are succeeding in taking care of his needs is to watch him and to give him opportunities to tell you or show you how he is feeling. As long as he continues to grow and learn and is happy most of the time, you can be comfortable with the limits you have set. If he becomes whiny or aggressive, or shows regressive behavior, you need to make special efforts to baby him or to return to the old routine for a while if at all possible.

Any time you introduce a new "law," either by persuasion or by decree, you need to realize that it may be premature. If you find your child unable to handle new limits you either suggest or impose, don't despair. You need not repeal the law altogether. Just postpone its effective date a few weeks and then try again. Your child is growing all the time and after a while will indeed attain enough maturity to live comfortably within your family's routine.

Frequent Nursing in a Two-Year-Old

The third year is usually a period in which children find many other things to do besides nursing, even the ones who seem to nurse like newborns in their second year. Some stop nursing altogether. Often they are just as intense about needing to nurse as they ever were, but the need strikes them less often. But some two-year-olds still seem to want to nurse all the time. When a child this age still expresses a need for a lot of nursing, it may be that we have set up a new timetable for growth that does not fit this child.

Boredom/Overstimulation

We must keep in mind, too, that two-year-olds are demanding people. They need a great deal of parents' attention, and nursing is one way to get that attention. Attempts to get your attention are not an "evil plot" that you have to get under control; your two-year-old simply needs attention, and lots of it. Children this age can also need lots of extra nursing because of boredom (defined in their terms, not ours—little children's interests vary as widely as do other people's). Or some children

WOW, MOMMY, SHE'S REALLY FULL!

can need to nurse a lot because of overstimulation or having to face situations that are still too much for them.

A very common pattern at this age is nursing when waking, at bedtime, once or twice during the night, nap time, and any time mother sits or lies down. If you have a two-year-old who asks to nurse more frequently than most, you might take a good look at what is going on at your house. What kind of attention is your child getting from you? Having mother there with lots of closeness and cuddling is still nice—just the way it was in younger days, but your budding genius has other needs, too.

He announces his new ambitions clearly: "Me do it!" His hungry little mind will devour the activities and materials available to him at a good preschool—except that few little ones this age can be comfortable enough away from parents to make the best use of even the most fantastic facilities and programs in the world.

For a while yet the family provides the best learning environment. Maybe you will utilize all the clever ways mothers have always entertained two-year-olds, mostly by doing only what has to be done around the house, but doing these things slowly and teaching the little one how to help. Some children need lots of paints and crayons; some are big on toy cars and playing ball. I remember doing a lot of dancing with my little ballerina when she was still in diapers. Working puzzles and learning to count intrigue some two-year-olds, while others are not yet interested in such things. Two-year-olds do not usually enjoy listening to mommy as she talks on the phone or staying off the ladder while daddy paints the house. They do not readily share parents with their computers.

A great help in mothering a two-year-old is visiting other homes with small children. Playing in parks and such sports as swimming and skating can be fun for parents and little children together. Parents who find it difficult to provide enough interesting activity in their own homes have joined together to form playgroups and play centers where adults can go with their little children for fun and companionship. Other parents take jobs—paid or volunteer—at preschools or day-care centers so that the child can enjoy the other children and the facilities with the security of having mom or dad nearby. Parents also benefit from the companionship of other adults while caring for their children.

Of course, becoming so involved away from home with your youngster is quite an undertaking, and I don't want to leave the impression that such elaborate steps are necessary for all, or even the majority of children. Most children most of the time are quite adequately challenged by following mother around and manipulating ordinary household equipment. In fact, you usually don't need to plan your child's activities, but rather his environment.

Willfulness

The third year is known for the emergence of the child's will. We all experience this change in our children, but for one family this stage was especially difficult:

> *My son is nearly two-and-a-half, and has always been a frequent nurser. From infancy to age two, his usual nursing interval was twenty minutes. In the last four months, that interval has expanded to once every hour, and occasionally once every two hours. He has lived a great deal of his life in the sling, as he needs to be held a lot. He is reserved around other people, and needs his personal boundaries respected in order to be comfortable in their presence. When he feels safe, he radiates with an inward happiness. He is very focused in play, and is very exuberant in expressing his love. I have not questioned his need to nurse so frequently, as his requests to nurse are so soulful, and sometimes very urgent. I attribute the frequent nursing to his "high need" personality. However, there are times when he really clings to me and nursing. It usually happens when we need to run errands, or when I just want to get out of the house for awhile. He even turns down his favorite activities (the park, going for a walk or bike ride) and urgently says, "Nurney!" (his word for nursing). So I nurse him, and when he's through, I try to initiate the outing again. The process repeats itself. Trying to help him disengage from the house or his activity is met with further resistance. I get very frustrated, especially when I really need to get to the grocery store, etc. My skin crawls as I nurse him. He probably senses my feelings, which probably makes things worse. Usually, I then collect our things, and put a very unhappy boy in the car seat, hug him as he sobs, and tell him we'll nurse when we get there. Then he can usually let go of me till we get to our destination.*

Sometimes with children this age the issue is not that they want to continue what they're doing, be that nursing or something else, so much as an overwhelming need to exert control over their own lives. At this immature stage the urge comes out in inappropriate ways, but the child isn't able quite yet to make the distinction. Parents have had success sometimes in situations like the above by offering the child honest choices—park or bike ride?—instead of telling him what they are going to do. Grocery store first, or the post office? To give him, and you, any relief, the choices have to be real, and you need to honor his decision. If you are clever, you can give him some real power over acceptable choices and thereby help him with the anxiety that is making him miserable while still letting you get on with life.

Shyness

Shyness, anywhere from moderate to extreme, is characteristic of some two-year-olds and can be a special challenge to parents. Many children this age are not yet ready to cope with all the people in a playgroup, or sometimes even with visiting another home. When they are shy, children will often seek relief from too much contact with people by asking to nurse more often. These children need the same physical and mental exercise as do children who are more mature socially, but they need to do their work in an intimate family setting. The only way you can doom your child to a lifetime of shyness is to force her into situations that are too demanding for her immature capacity to deal with people, forcing her to cope beyond her capabilities.

The swings and sandbox in the park down the street may be great fun for the little girl next door. But you may need to swing and play in the sand in your backyard for a while yet until your little guy is ready to come out into the big world. He may not be ready to use that neat jumping horse or the huge set of blocks that the playgroup or preschool has, but you can have the same fun jumping off the porch with him or piling up your ever-increasing collection of cartons.

Stress

There are times, of course, when you expect an increase in your child's need for nursing: during illness, when you move, when a parent or sibling is away more than usual, during busy times like holidays, and so on—any time that your child finds stressful.

Sometimes situations arise in which mother and child must be separated for some reason or when the little one must be around more people than he can handle comfortably. A little bit of stress from these situations or others will not all by itself damage your child's progress in growing up with a healthy psyche. It is being forced to live with stress over too long a time and without plenty of comfort and security that will cripple her.

If your child chooses to cope with stress by nursing frequently, wonderful! Nursing is certainly a convenient, wholesome way to help a little guy grow past a rough spot. If nursing is not available, then a bright and attentive parent will follow the child's cues and find other ways to provide comfort and security in times that the child finds difficult.

Nothing's Wrong—Except Nursing All the Time!

If you have checked into everything you can think of in your two-year-old's life and can see little shortage of stimulation or security, and she is in good health and well nourished, yet she still wants to nurse "all the time," I'd suggest that you stop worrying about it. Some children just take a long time to come to terms with this world and need to be babies longer than what some of us may label as the norm.

These nursing-all-the-time little people are, I know, very wearing on their mothers; they make me think of young robins, bigger than their mothers, but still fluttering and cheeping to be fed. The robin mothers, like us, get really frayed and worn out babying their big fledglings. But they seem to know better than to abandon their young before they are ready to make it on their own. You can be sure that, provided you keep the opportunities for growth and more interesting "big kid" activities open and attractive, your child will, like the young robin, move away from such frequent and urgent demands on you as soon as he can. Eating hamburgers and playing with other children is a lot more fun than nursing, so it shouldn't be long before your child will choose the companionship of other children and his own place at the family table instead of your lap. And like the mother robin, you, too, will then have a chance to get your feathers preened and into place again.

Good, Wholesome Neglect

Some of us worry that frequent nursing is a result of "absent-minded" mothering, mothering in which we tend to our own business as best we can and just automatically nurse when the child asks. In fact, provided a child's surroundings are rich in people (like neighbors and relatives) and objects like pans, oatmeal boxes, stacks of plastic cups, paint and paper, etc., absent-minded mothering may be the best there is. "Good, wholesome neglect," La Leche League Founder Mary White calls it. Children learn much by being on the fringes of interesting adult activity, and mothers are happiest when they maintain some of their own interests.

The key to good "absent-minded" mothering is to keep the environment changing (which really is not absent-minded at all, but rather sneaky and creative) and to keep your own activities very flexible. What you choose to do must be easy to put down and take up again. Without great fuss you should be able to stop what you are doing (the secret is not ever planning to finish) and either nurse, help with your child's project, or just walk around and talk for a while. As long as you keep many and varied opportunities available, you can depend on your child to let you know what kind of attention he may need.

What I really mean by "absent-minded" mothering is non-manipulative mothering, not running every minute of your child's life.

Non-manipulative mothers learn to listen to their children and to help them when they are bored and fussy, but they do not interfere when children are busy with their own play and projects.

Getting Sick of Nursing

Many mothers during the time that the little ones need so very much attention, including so very much nursing, find themselves feeling manipulated, feeling that their entire lives are dominated by the needs of their children. Young children seem so unreasonable sometimes, refusing to pay attention to our need to fix supper or wash our hair, even to go to the bathroom by ourselves! (Really, they're unable to recognize these needs, but that is not how we see it when we are feeling low or stressed.) One mother complained, "Every time I sat down, there she'd be. I felt like a mother dog with a litter of puppies just waiting for mamma's knees to buckle so they could latch on."

No doubt the mother dog, who sees no option to natural mothering in her own canine fashion, and who is certainly not considering resorting to bottles or pacifiers to relieve her burdens with future puppies, still occasionally feels overwhelmed by her young ones' needs. We human mothers can at least comfort ourselves by looking into the future toward a time when our lives again will be more our own.

Few in my generation had any chance to observe and learn how people go about what is now being called "attachment parenting," especially in the second and third years. Parents around us usually believed they had to avoid being personally and intimately available to young children for fear of being manipulated by them and, as a consequence, spoiling them. Even today, responsive, sensitive parents have few role models and so face the double task of, first, meeting the child's needs and your own, and also of figuring out how. Caring for a two-year-old is a demanding enough path to travel; having to plan and clear your own trail as you go can sometimes make the second and third years unusually difficult. Let's hope your children will find the way already cleared for them when they are rearing my great-grandchildren's generation.

If you look carefully at your feelings about nursing, you will usually notice that you are not always overwhelmed by your children's needs—just part of the time. The worst times are likely to be when priorities are out of order. But there can also be physical causes at times for impatience with nursing. Right before a menstrual period many mothers are bothered by children's nursing, and often, in fact, by any demands that are made on them. Nipple tenderness at the time of ovulation or premenstrually can add to a tendency to resent nursing. Most mothers get some relief from possible bad feelings just by recognizing the cause and knowing that they will feel better in a few days. Cutting down on salt, increasing fluids, and getting some exercise can also help relieve premenstrual irritability.

As we are learning to be mothers, especially the first time, things do not always go smoothly. We are still growing up ourselves (though the truth is that we never stop learning).

> *Some days around suppertime both of us are uptight at the same time, and I do not want to sit down and nurse him. Then there are the just plain ugly days, and I find myself screaming for nothing. I thank God on those days for being able to sit us down and nurse and love after mom gets it out—calms us both down.*

There is no way more reliable than nursing to help us and our children get back to feeling good about each other after we have let feelings get out of hand. An Australian physician writes:

> *I cope with burnout by limiting the length of feeds, or distraction. I do find that sometimes he'll go on to hurt himself and end up on the breast anyway, which tells me that he has a real need. I've also noticed that when I get on the computer or telephone, or any other activity that's more focused, he'll want to feed. (I have Mary White's quote stuck on our phone to remind me; "When you're on the phone, you're gone from the neck up.") Still, it is a big commitment, and I choose to breastfeed rather than to work, as I don't have the energy for both this time around. I notice also how right-brained, for want of a better expression, it keeps me, and I think that's a good way to be with all of the children, and I don't attempt to do too much, which keeps my focus in the home. These are such brief and precious years, and I relish them.*

Resentment about how much our little children need us is likely to be a part of the picture for most of us. It is nothing to be ashamed of, and mothers can best alleviate it by acknowledging the feelings and sharing them and their various solutions with one other. (For more on coping with burnout, see *Parenting the Fussy Baby and High-Need Child* by William and Martha Sears, and Diane Bengson's How WEANING HAPPENS .)

References

1   Briggs, D. C. *Your Child's Self-Esteem.* New York: Doubleday, 1970; 126, 128.

2   Bengson, D. HOW WEANING HAPPENS. Schaumburg, Illinois: La Leche League International, 1999; 37.

3   Sears, W. and Sears, M. *Parenting the Fussy Baby and High-Need Child.* Boston: Little, Brown and Company, 1996; 193.

chapter fourteen

Nursing a Three-Year-Old

Babyhood's Last Shadow

Most nursing children nowadays are weaned by their third birthdays. Many children wean more or less spontaneously by this age in every culture. At the same time I am certain that the opinion held by most of the world, even those who are comfortable with prolonged nursing, that children aged three should not be nursing, influences parents toward weaning by three if not sooner. Where nursing longer is the usual practice, as among some people of the New Guinea Highlands, children just as routinely nurse up to four years.[1]

For this reason it is hard to say for certain whether millennia of practice among cooking and food-grinding humans have changed children's biological expectations. Have we in fact lowered the natural age of weaning from six or seven to three or four, or is three years another long-standing cultural landmark for the end of babyhood, like the more recent age limit of one year? The answer no doubt is different from one family to the next. There is no exact and universal age at which babyhood and nursing must end. At the same time there are enough changes both in behavior and physical appearance in the fourth year for us to feel that babyhood fades out and childhood fades in sometime around three.

Every passing day in the life of your child does bring closer the day when weaning will be easy—maybe by age two-and-a-half, maybe by age five-and-a-half. Somewhere along the way comes a time when you can wean without tears. At the same time, though, that the possibility of weaning becomes less overwhelming for your child, nursing usually becomes increasingly easy for mother. A three-year-old with whom you have been talking about nursing from infancy will usually go along with your nursing preferences and rules most of the time. Your growing child will rarely ask to nurse in embarrassing situations, nor should there be much problem any more with feeling that you have to nurse at times or places in which you dislike nursing.

A three-year-old may not be ready to understand the complexities of your feelings about nursing (or about writing on the walls for that matter), but most are ready to live with a few reasonable limits based solely on your feelings. Your child has no built-in understanding of why you may prefer not to nurse, let us say at a concert in the park. Nor will she necessarily agree that your wallpaper looked better before she added her own finishing touches in crayon. But she is learning some give and take—to make some adjustments to living with you, just as you make adjustments to living with her.

As a result of the three-year-old's slowly increasing ability to cooperate, mothers usually find a nursing child this age to be a genuine pleasure most of the time. Nursing is almost always private, intimate, and enjoyable, often spiced with lively and profound conversation. Three-year-olds tend to be unusually pleasant people to have in the family

THAT'S FOR MY MILKIE.

anyway, so it is little wonder that, if nursing is still a part of a child's family interaction at this age, nursing is unusually pleasant too.

The influences that work against nursing children in their fourth year are usually from sources other than just mother and the nursling. The most apparent events to lead a mother to decide against continuing the nursing relationship are pregnancy or the arrival of a younger sibling. A child does not have to be weaned because of the younger child of course; but in many families mother cannot be comfortable, be it physically, emotionally, or both, with the child's continued nursing. So she initiates weaning.

Probably the most common reason for weaning a three-year-old is an overwhelming feeling on the part of one or both parents that more than three years is just too long for nursing to continue. Three-year-olds walk, talk, and are often pretty well out of diapers. They do not look like babies any more, nor do they act much like babies. And even those authors who are comfortable with extended nursing usually suggest that most three-year-olds should be pretty easy to wean.

Of course many of these kids still suck their thumbs, sleep with teddy bears, throw an occasional tantrum, or exhibit some other holdover of baby behavior. Fortunately for children and parents alike we are learning to worry less about eradicating these traces of infancy that remain in the intricacies of our children's seedling personalities. Like the leaves emerging from the seed of a young bean plant, your child will grow and spread himself until hardly a sign of his infantile form, with all its folds and shadows, remains. What we cannot predict, however, is exactly which babyish behavior will be the last to disappear.

It seems to me that if child-care experts advise patience, as they most certainly should, with somewhat disturbing infantile behaviors like thumb-sucking and bed-wetting in children over three, there is every reason that they should be even more understanding of such a healthy behavior as nursing. No one has demonstrated that any harm can come from continuing to nurse. Many families feel much good has come from it.

Talking about Nursing and about Weaning

As children grow older and understand more about themselves and the rest of the world, most mothers want them to know that nursing is something they will outgrow and that mothers do not expect them to be nursing forever. When you mention the fact that he will wean sometime, however, a three-year-old who loves to nurse may seem incredulous. It is probably just as hard for him to believe that he will someday be happy without this loving closeness as it is for you to believe that he will not be nursing on the way home from the third-grade play. The child who is not ready to grasp even the concept of weaning will usually ignore any attempts you make to start a conversation on the topic—or will pointedly change the subject. It is not usually so much that the topic is threatening; the topic is inconceivable and unreal to him, not worth talking about. If your child should feel threatened by the thought, he will probably respond by needing to nurse more for a day or two.

One three-year-old, his mother wrote,

> ...*would hear me tell people that I'm going to let him wean himself. One day he said, "Why do you want me to wean myself? I don't want to wean myself!" It took a little explaining to get him to understand what I meant.*

The idea of self-weaning did not make any more sense to this little guy than the idea of performing brain surgery on himself.

When your child will not discuss weaning with you, forget it. Let it go for several weeks before you bother to bring it up again. By then she may have weaned quietly with never a word shared on the subject, or she may be ready to talk about the idea of weaning, or she may still turn down your offer for discussion.

The reasons for discussing nursing and weaning with your child are both serious and frivolous. One mother says, "I think one of the very nice things about nursing an older child is that you can talk, and thus is added another dimension to the relationship."

Some of children's observations about nursing and weaning are jewels to ornament your life, and you should unabashedly seek out such treasures. One three-year-old, for instance, schedules his day like a busy executive. "Don't go away," he said, "because I want to nurse when I finish this castle." When a father told his almost-three-year-old, "Big boys don't need Mommy's milk,'" he replied, "They sometimes do at bedtime!" When a mother's let-down did not come quickly enough, one little fellow said impatiently, "Turn it on, Mommy!" And when a mother asked her little girl, "Want to nurse now?" her daughter exclaimed with delight, "You have the bestest ideas!" She may comment halfway through, "This one all gone—other side," and after finishing, conclude politely, "All through. Please close door."

On a more mundane level—back from the pearls to the brown tape and thumbtacks of living—mothers do not see nursing as quite the same sort of baby behavior as is needing a teddy bear or thumb-sucking. On one hand nursing is less disturbing, because it does not suggest that some need or other for mothering has somehow gone unmet. But on the other hand, the teddy bear is a private matter for your child. Thumb-sucking is also mostly his own business—unless you are looking ahead to orthodontists' bills should the thumb-sucking continue into the school years. Nursing, however, involves two people, and mothers may feel apprehensive if they fear that nursing might last as long as some children continue thumb-sucking or sleeping with cuddly toys, comforters that some kids find themselves still needing in their college dorms.

Once your child is able to think about the idea of weaning, for your own peace of mind you can let him know that weaning will occur, that you expect it to occur eventually, and that you will both still be loving and close even when he no longer needs to nurse. You can point out other children, especially older siblings who no longer nurse, not, let me make haste to say, as competitive examples. ("Look, Gwen doesn't nurse any more, and she's only two!") Rather, you should use children who no longer nurse only as examples to show that life without nursing can be secure and happy. ("Gwen used to like to nurse the way you do. She and her mother like reading stories better now. Someday, when you're ready, we'll be that way too.") You are giving your child information which he will put to use in his own time—in a few weeks, or a few years, depending on his needs and his individual pattern for maturation.

The fourth year is a time when the child's incredible early growth seems to reach fruition. And children this age, even if they are not quite ready yet to leave behind all baby things, are usually eager to look ahead into childhood.

References

1 Bailey, K. V. Quantity and composition of breast milk in some New Guinean populations. *Journal of Tropical Pediatrics* 1965; 11:35.

chapter fifteen

Nursing Past Four

The Specter of Nursing Forever

Some have suggested that I should not write about nursing past the age of four in this book, and especially about preschoolers and school-age children who still nurse. They worry that mothers of young toddlers will be horrified at the thought of children nursing so long, as was the mother who wrote, "I found myself feeling uncomfortable with it, although I consider myself a lactivist [a person strongly active in support of breastfeeding] and truly believe in breastfeeding. Perhaps another book is needed." She does have a point. Chances are you did not start out intending to nurse even a toddler, much less somebody carrying a book bag. I know I didn't.

I have chosen, nonetheless, not to move information on older nurslings into another volume, even with the lure of the title one mother offered, *Through the Chain Link Fence*. (No, I don't know even one person who has tried such a thing, but the image kept me laughing a whole afternoon.)

Unless you have nursed a child of four years or more, the idea no doubt seems preposterous—such a big child! Of course most of us in Western cultures felt that way about nursing two-year-olds when we first encountered them. If you are nursing a child in those particularly demanding second or third years, the idea of a nursing relationship that may continue past your child's fourth birthday may make you want to run away from home. You are right, of course, because the thought of mothering (not just nursing) a two-year-old for years on end seems exhausting. But just as all mothering changes between two and four, so does nursing.

One mother asked her four-year-old about nursing and "what it tasted like, to which he replied (with a giggle and the sweetest shy smile), 'They're good like brownies!' After that he has asked for 'nursing brownies' a few times. It always makes me happy to think of myself as a dessert."

If, on the other hand, you find yourself nursing at this age and feeling uncomfortable about it, you should, as always, work for an arrangement with your child that both of you can be happy with. Don't stay in the place where one mother found herself:

> *Being burned out on nursing the four-year-old makes it hard for me to be enthusiastic to others about the fact that he nurses, and I feel a little embarrassed because almost nobody I know understands nursing a four-year-old.*

As your child grows, you need to be ready to make changes in your relationship. By four, you and your child can talk and come to a nursing, or weaning, agreement, an agreement that will last up until it is time to change again—one day at a time, one week at a time.

There is no way to know how long it may be before your child completely outgrows nursing on his own. Still, if you have been uneasily living with the thought that this child will not be able to go away to college because the telephone company has yet to devise a long-distance nursing system, you will feel reassured when you can see your child thinking about other ways to relate to you and other ways to feel loved and secure.

Most, but not all, children this age could be weaned much more easily than they could have been at two or three, but at the same time most of the reasons to do so have faded away.

Some, on the other hand, can still be pretty demanding. One study among nutritionally stressed children in Bangladesh found some children this age continuing to nurse seven to nine times a day.[3] Four-year-olds, in fact, are often at a more unsettled time of life than they were at three. Still, by age four you have long passed the time when you need to nurse every time she asks. Your feelings count. Negotiating about when, where, and how long to nurse is good for you in that it gives you more control of your own body. It's good for your child in that it teaches her the healthy give-and-take of an intimate relationship.

Lean toward negotiation here, I would suggest, rather than rules. I'm not saying that rules are bad. They're absolutely necessary, both for safety and for an orderly society. But rules are also arbitrary, and as a child-rearing tool result in less valuable learning than does negotiation.

Just think of what he'll gain from working with you through what you want and what he wants until you find a solution that both of you can live with. You can learn how his mind works so that you improve your gauging of what he wants and what he needs. He can learn how to meet his needs without embarrassing you or making you feel tied to the rocking chair. The learning will doubtless be slow, punctuated by times when one or both of you lose patience. You will probably have to weather an occasional battle, if not over nursing, then over something else of importance to both of you.

Keep your eyes on the larger goal. The kindness and consideration you're teaching in today's negotiations should help your child grow into a young person who has had some practice at empathizing with another and feeling empathy in return, even when his own needs are pressing.

For many of us, an early reward for teaching such kindness and consideration is getting to live with a five-year-old, nursing or not. Five to six tends to be a wonderful year, and most things you do with a child this age are as agreeable as they are ever going to get.

It may become necessary to deal with the occasional suggestion from someone else that your child will still be nursing after he starts school. "Why do you think they have recess?" many parents reply. Author Tine Thevenin writes of her daughter who weaned at six:

> *The last couple of years the nursing time was never very long. About a minute or so. It was easy, relaxed, and matter-of-fact. A fall, a scrape, a disappointment, some tears. "Do you want to nurse?" Without a word she would climb on my lap, snuggle and nurse for a minute, and that's all it took. Recharged, she'd slide off my lap. . . .*
>
> *And then one day I realized that she had not nursed for a couple of months. It surprised me that it had happened so quietly. I had been told that that is how it would happen. Suddenly you realize that that last tie had slipped loose. That was nearly twenty years ago. I still miss it once in a while.*

If the truth were known, we would soon learn that a number of fine adults today enjoyed a bit of nursing when they were in the early grades and that all around this planet today there are well-adjusted school kids who are not completely weaned, like two children about five years old observed nursing in Papua New Guinea[2] and a seven-year-old in East Bhutan.[1] A 1989-91 study of La Leche League conference participants in the United States reported weaning ages from one month to seven years, four months (with an average weaning age of three years).[4] As pointed out in the discussion of nursing and pregnancy, outside Westernized cultures the actual weaning age for many children is lower than what their parents regard as ideal because of taboos against nursing while pregnant. Most of the fortunate children who are able to nurse as long as they feel the need have not been displaced by younger siblings and so have a chance to continue.

One North American kindergartner used to ask coyly at bedtime, "Can I please n-u-r-s-e?" Her mother writes, "I chuckled to think what some people would say if they knew a kid who could spell it was still nursing." Another mother wrote about her daughter's weaning:

> *My daughter doesn't often let me come out of the closet, but I will share with you the little secret that she nursed until two months before her seventh birthday. At that time, she hadn't nursed in a couple of days, asked if it was okay, and started to nurse. She looked up at me and said, "You know, Mom, I really feel kind of silly." We both laughed and knew it was over. I can't believe I'm getting teary-eyed over sharing this with you. My daughter is now a college freshman.*

Yet, except for the secrecy that our social customs make advisable for those who are nursing past four, few mothers find any reason to insist on quitting. Nursing past four may give rise to some of the same concerns as other ages because of outside factors such as pregnancy or fear that nursing so long is somehow bad. The nursing relationship itself is usually not a source of much difficulty, but rather a pleasant cuddle.

Becoming Part of a Memory

Children begin to have conscious memories of their lives sometime past three or four for girls and usually a little later for boys, and nursing is one of the many things they may remember. You may be a bit frightened to think that your child, when he is grown and, say, an official in the Chicago city government, may still remember nursing. Would sharing such intimate memories with your son or daughter in the years ahead embarrass you? Probably not.

The memories people have of nursing are tender, warm, and fuzzy, the kind that lead to institutions like Mother's Day. These were certainly the feelings expressed years ago by an actual Chicago city official to a La Leche League International Conference when he talked about his memories of nursing when he was a child. What he had to say would not have made his mother uncomfortable; had she been there, no doubt she would have felt very much loved to have heard what her grown son had to say. Nursing is a healthy relationship, and your child's memories of it will be healthy.

Peer Pressure

Long before your child reaches four you have no doubt worked out systems that protect you from receiving unwanted comments or pressure from other adults. Keeping older siblings from translating your "code word" for the uninitiated may be the only problem along this line that you yourself still encounter. As your child, however, gets older—maybe indeed before four, but certainly at this age—you will need to stay alert to what is happening among her siblings or her friends. There will very likely be conversations about nursing—and there should be. There may also be teasing about nursing which you will need to monitor.

I would not suggest that you try to stop all teasing on this subject or any other among children the same age. To do so would be impossible, and probably not the best for their relationship if you could do it. Teasing is a significant part of childhood interactions, and of human play even among adults. You do need to watch your nursing child, though, to see how he is coping with teasing about nursing.

Teasing of younger children by older ones can be somewhat different, because the opinions of the big kids carry more weight than those of kids the same size. When a child, especially one who is three or four years older, is teasing a little one, we need to make an effort to teach him to limit his teasing to topics that are fun, and to a gentle enough level for fun. Older children need guidance on rules for the "teasing games" with little children, not only to protect their relationship with the young sibling or friend, but also as part of their education toward becoming parents themselves.

If your nursing child begins to show signs of distress because of pressure or teasing from other children, you will need to do what you can to help him. He may show distress by more frequent nursing, aggression or withdrawal in his relationship with you or with the other children, increased problems with sleep, an increase in bed-wetting or thumb-sucking, or any of the host of ways children tell us that something is not going right for them.

You can give your child relief by educating the children who are teasing about nursing so that it will not be such a hot topic for their verbal games. Also you and your nursling may decide on ways to keep nursing more private. A preschool child is certainly old enough to do some planning of his nursing times, particularly in his own defense.

Your little one will probably feel better just from having you bring up the topic of teasing if it is bothering him. Knowing that you are aware of the problem and want to help will take a lot of the pressure off all by itself.

Teasing on any topic, however, as I have said, is not to be eliminated even if it could be. Provided it is on a playful level and does not degenerate into ridicule, teasing is a valuable form of entertainment; people need lots of practice to be good at it, either on the giving or receiving end. Through teasing, children learn some aspects of how to behave in a particular society. Many conventions of our life together are learned through teasing—learned not from adults who set up rules, but from other people who are coping with pretty much the same things, i.e., peer pressure, at about the same time in life.

The role of adults in this process is the difficult one of keeping the "games" fair and relatively painless for children do not know how far they can go on the topic of nursing or any other without hurting their companions. It is our job to teach them what is fair play and what is not. This part of our parenting job begins when our children begin interacting with other children and continues until they are grown. If the job sounds enormous, that is because it is. But it is worthwhile, because helping your children learn to tease fairly and enjoy being teased fairly is to set them up with inexpensive entertainment for the rest of their lives.

The child who nurses to age four and beyond has an opportunity to apply her intellect to the kind of relationship she has with her mother and how this affects her interactions with her teasing peers and siblings. She comes face to face with inconsistent and contradictory feelings in herself, in her mother, and in other people around her. Observant parents notice their children are working back and forth through the differing impulses of babyhood and childhood.

The nursing child is blessed with safe retreat when the road out of toddlerhood becomes too complex and uncertain. Some growing children use nursing as a way to gain relief from the emotional strain of setting their own paths through the confusion. Feeling relaxed and secure, they can learn to see and accept themselves both as individuals and as members of society. Their nursing does not handicap children who nurse past four as they keep growing. Rather they capitalize on nursing, as they come through their "first adolescence" more smoothly than they might have been able to in any other way.

References

1   Bøhler, E. and Ingstad, B. The struggle of weaning: Factors determining breastfeeding duration in East Bhutan. *Social Science and Medicine* 1996; 43(12):1806.

2   Conton, L. Social, economic and ecological parameters of infant feeding in Usino, Papua New Guinea. *Infant Care and Feeding in the South Pacific*. Ed. L. B. Marshall. New York: Gordon and Breach, 1985; 112.

3   Greiner, T. The concept of weaning: Definitions and their implications. *Journal of Human Lactation* 1996; 12(2):127.

4   Sugarman, M. and Kendall-Tackett, K. A. Weaning ages in a sample of American women who practice extended breastfeeding. *Clinical Pediatrics* 1995; 34(12):643-44.

p a r t   f o u r

Weaning

chapter sixteen

"Natural" Weaning

The Child under Three

Because of the good results, both for their children and for themselves, parents are becoming more comfortable with allowing nursing to take its course and waiting for weaning to occur on its own. Some people choose such an approach because it makes the most sense to them, as did the mother who writes, "She hasn't shown any signs of weaning, and I'm not going to push it. Why put a strain into a so-far carefree experience? I believe it should end as it started—naturally." Others, like one mother of six, have more practical reasons. "She'll have to wean herself," she says. "I don't have the time to worry about it, and it doesn't matter." For these reasons and others, more children these days have the good fortune to be born into families in which they do not have to give up nursing in anyone's time but their own.

A few children, of course, come to a spontaneous finish to their nursing before their second birthday. For the few who leave behind this part of their babyhood very early it will be in some other behavior that parents will likely see signs of their immaturity for some time yet. They will continue to need babying, but they will need it in other ways.

One mother, disappointed when her fourteen-month-old weaned, realizes now that weaning came from her approach to breastfeeding, not an active weaning campaign. She emphasized solids, offered other food before nursing once her child was eating solids, and did not nurse her child just for comfort. As this mother found out, children who start taking other foods and liquids before four to six months may come to depend upon these foods for most of their nourishment in the second half of their first year, a time when most nurslings still thrive for the most part on mother's milk. Often, though not always, children who take in a great deal of food and liquid other than mother's milk at six to twelve months tend to lose interest in nursing sooner than they might have otherwise. Often they will wean from the breast and cling to other comfort objects.

Some children seem less interested in nursing and become easily distracted sometime between nine and fourteen months of age. Many advisors suggest that you take advantage of your child's decreased interest, if in fact her interest does show a decrease, to initiate weaning. If you don't want to nurse a toddler, this may be the least traumatic weaning time there will be for at least two or three years. But if you expect to find it easier to care for your child if she continues nursing, do not hesitate to remind her to nurse a few times daily until she outgrows this phase. If you do not want to wean, the time around nine months, a little later sometimes, may be a sort of danger time in which you may want to make sure your nursing relationship is not interrupted or disturbed.

Most children nurse without a pause through the months before and after their first birthdays, and a very few will wean in spite of efforts to the contrary, but you can nearly eliminate the possibility that your child might wean prematurely just by offering the breast a few times a day during those weeks or months.

Most youngsters around their first birthday still enjoy receiving a nice tummy full of milk when they nurse, and if other forms of feeding and sucking take the place of feedings at the breast, there will be, as a direct result, less of the milk that so many of these children look for. This is an effective way to encourage weaning, whether that is what mother has in mind or not. For many children such a pattern constitutes a satisfactory parent-initiated weaning. Also, if bottles and pacifiers are handy to offer children, mothers are likely to make use of them to put off a feeding while finishing this or that project they are working on. This also will lead to an earlier weaning, whether intended or not.

The way to achieve a natural weaning, if that is your objective, is to feed and care for your infant without contrived interferences. Nurse on demand from birth. Forget about other foods until your child shows he is ready for them. Then feed your child sensibly. Eating foods other than your milk in the first year is usually more for fun than for nourishment. Except in very hot weather, a baby who nurses often but has begun to ask for other foods does not need any more liquids besides your milk than he mooches from your cup or glass. Quenching his thirst with water or juice in a sippy cup can result in less interest in nursing. An excellent way to avoid overfeeding or over-watering your baby is to make tasty foods available and attractive, but let her feed herself, in her own way, and in her own time.

Unless you are in a situation where you absolutely cannot nurse your baby, a pacifier is no help to you or to your baby. It is mostly a nuisance that, unlike your breast, is always getting dirty or lost. There is no need for bottles, either. Both pacifiers and bottles tend to become mother substitutes and are not satisfactory replacements for the full embrace of nursing.

Without the distraction and confusion brought on by pacifiers, bottles, and too much other food too soon, your child can nurse and wean in his own time and have a chance to outgrow his baby needs so completely that he can leave them behind, whether that be in his second year, or fourth, or whenever.

Not all children give up nursing gradually. Some children seem to reach a new plateau in maturity all at once and turn their backs on this or that baby behavior seemingly overnight. One mother writes of her two-year-old:

> *He had always nursed to sleep, but one afternoon he got two new trucks and was afraid his brother would take them while he was asleep. When I sat down to nurse him he pushed me away, took a truck in each hand, and plopped down on the bed. He never nursed to sleep after that, though he did not wean from other nursings for several months.*

It is very common for little people to toilet-train themselves all at once. A few children also wean this way, especially when they are not nursing very often anyway. Surprisingly, the events that can bring on weaning in a child who is ready may be the same ones that may cause an increase in nursing at an earlier stage. A new baby, a move to a new home, or lots of company, often threatening to very little people, may at other times be so exciting and pleasant to your older child that he will drop nursing to have more time to devote to the happy new circumstances. If your child is weaning quickly just because that is her way of doing things, and if your breasts do not become overfull, then let the matter rest and go on to other ways of being with your child.

After Three

Most of my experience is with children who weaned between three and four, but clinical observations[3] and research suggest that a completely child-led weaning is unlikely to take place before the child turns four.[4] Mothers in East Bhutan, where nursing well into childhood is socially acceptable, say that self-weaning usually occurs between three and five years.[1] In any case, weaning may come dramatically enough that your child will brag about it as one little girl did, telling her grandmother, "I'm going to be a big sister when I'm almost four—and now I'm weaned!" Or it may be so gradual that no one will know for sure when it happened.

For most children in this age range weaning is a slow, unpatterned change in behavior, so unpredictable that it is not always even headed in the same direction. At times, maybe even for long periods, your child will nurse frequently and intensely. When conditions change, either around your child or as a result of his own growth, he will begin to prefer other things over nursing—playing, eating, sleeping, or even cuddling with you sometimes. Then things may change again for him so that he needs to be at your breast almost as often as before.

As the weeks go on, though, there will be movement, whether you notice it or not, away from many periods of frequent nursing toward more periods of less nursing. In some children this movement is regular and swift. In others it is so erratic and unpredictable that it is easy to understand how people come to believe some children would never wean without urging. Some children even wean from one breast long before the other.

Such is the unpredictable course of an uncoerced weaning. At some age, very young or "shockingly old," your child will not find nursing so absolutely essential to her well-being. And you may even miss it, as did a mother in India, who found herself unable to answer her e-mail messages as soon as she had gotten used to:

> *You know how things get with a busy four-year-old around the place! Sadly he's stopped automatically latching on when he sees me sit down at the computer, and pulls me off to play instead!*

Your child may be distracted from nursing by anything and everything. You can see that, though he may have some months to go yet, he is on his way toward a time when he will no longer need you in this exact way.

Is child-led weaning completely child-led? Yes and no, depending on your definition. You will probably respond, and appropriately so, to your child's increasing distractibility as he matures. He may pull you to your favorite nursing spot, sit you down, latch on, and then instantly abandon you to chase his sister or watch a TV commercial. When this has happened several times, you will very naturally and with hardly a thought respond less quickly to his requests to nurse, at least when he seems to be asking rather superficially, and when the world around the two of you is busy and interesting. In this way, even without planning it, you play your part in his weaning. You are following his cues and your own common sense.

You will probably come to a time when you yourself are impatient with nursing. If you have been enjoying loving your child this way, you may be puzzled at the change in your feelings. No doubt your impatience will flare at times and subside at others, depending on what is going on in the rest of your life. Some of what you may be feeling, though, is part of natural weaning and an indication that you are gradually outgrowing the relationship. You too are growing toward being ready when the time for weaning comes.

In time—how much time no one can say—your child will abandon all but a very few favorite nursing times, usually the times when he is falling asleep or first waking up in the morning. When you are down to these few times, your milk production will dwindle. Then some children who have especially liked the milk will quit nursing in favor of a breakfast or bedtime snack. Others continue to enjoy one or more of these special nursing times for a long time yet, dropping them slowly until a few days, then a few weeks, go by with no request to nurse.

Every spontaneous weaning is unique, however, so it is impossible to guarantee anything about it except that it will happen

Resuming Nursing after Weaning

For most children before age three or so, weaning, spontaneous or mother-initiated, is all but final when two or three weeks have passed without your child's tugging your blouse. After this amount of time most of these little ones do not ask again, or if they do, they find they have forgotten how to suckle. "Is it broken?" one little guy asked when he could not remember after a year just how to go about nursing.

Once in a while someone suggests that your milk may become "poison" or "spoiled" if your child does not nurse for some certain amount of time. This is an old wives' tale, one that is heard in many parts of the world. In rural Zimbabwe, for instance, mothers are told that if milk remains in the breast for a whole day, it will hurt the child.[2] But you can be assured that milk doesn't spoil in the breasts any more than blood does in the veins. Your child can nurse safely after any interval.

Occasionally a child will ask to nurse again after you have regarded her as totally weaned, but most forget how. A mother who was sad because her body just would not cooperate with her son's need to nurse during her pregnancy wrote:

> *I still have regrets because I see many LLL moms nursing their two-and-a-half-year-old sons, and I know that if I hadn't gotten pregnant I'd be nursing my son too. I think it would help because he doesn't talk, and it would be a great way to stay connected to him. He has tried to nurse since the new baby was born two months ago, but he doesn't remember how. I let him try whenever he wants (it's not very often).*

The most likely circumstance for such requests is when you have a new baby, but also once in a while when a child discovers that mom is pregnant. Or your child may be upset about something, as in this situation recalled by the mother of a now grown daughter:

> *It was a disastrous time ending up with a breast abscess and an angry weaning at about two-and-a-half. She missed nursing so much though that we gradually started up again, nursed through a pregnancy and tandem nursed. She finally weaned by contract a couple months after her sixth birthday.*

There is no reason that you can't allow your child to try nursing again, even though you have probably told all the relatives he is weaned. Chances are that he is weaned. A request to nurse from a child who has not nursed for a while is usually a request for reassurance and acceptance. You may not be able to discover any explanation for your child's desire to return to nursing other than the mysterious workings of his growing little mind. It feels good to a little child to know that if he ever did need you again that way, you would be there for him with open arms. One mother says of her weaned twins that they both had to try nursing several times when the new baby came, but gave it up after a few tries. It is much easier for a little person to wean himself if he knows that his decision does not have to be final.

One mother had nothing but positive feelings when her child wanted to nurse again a few times after over a year without asking for the breast: "I never realized just how important and memorable those nursing days were to her and that she would actually remember at all. This was her 'thank you' for the loving patience and time I took when it was needed." A brief return to the mostly outgrown way of loving can be a chance for mother and little one together to enjoy a bit of reminiscing.

Another mother writes of a child who resumed nursing—sort of:

*When our daughter, was about eleven months [her two-
year-old brother] started to become very interested in what
nursing was. He shocked me one day by pretending to
nurse on one breast while his sister was at the other.
I didn't try to discourage him because by now I had read a
little about tandem nursing and I hoped if he was to start
nursing again after two years that it would help our
relationship. I had already noticed the difference between
my two children's behavior that I attribute to our nursing
relationship. My son is a very energetic boy who likes to
tell me "No!" as often as possible while my daughter is
helpful and calm most of the time.*

*Now that she is fifteen months and he is two-and-a-half
years old, he still continues to pretend but doesn't actually
latch on. He even tells Baby, as he calls his sister, that it is
time to nurse and he directs her to the breast he chooses.
I am kind of sad that I didn't nurse him as long as I have
nursed his sister but it is wonderful that he has joined our
breastfeeding relationship.*

For a child who is apparently weaned to actually resume nursing
for a while, sometimes for no reason that you can perceive, might make
you feel panicky, especially if you are very happy for your child to relate
to you in a different way. Yet it will be helpful to your child for you to go
along with him if you can. Just as we adults sometimes make a mistake
in deciding to wean our children too soon, occasionally very small
growing people make mistakes in deciding to wean themselves too soon.
There is a reason, no doubt, whether we can see it with our adult eyes or
not, that your child needs to nurse again for a while.

Although it may seem like it at first, you and your child are not
going back to the beginning of the weaning process. After a few days of
adjustment your child is not likely to nurse any more than do other
children his age. He is not returning to babyhood, but picking up a
behavior that is appropriate for his age. He will nurse and wean also in a
way appropriate to his age—maybe in the next few days, or maybe some
months hence.

Weaning need not be any more dramatic and final than toilet-
training. We are not surprised when a child who is supposedly toilet-
trained forgets and "backslides" for a while. It should be no more
disconcerting that a weaned child would remember and backslide when
he needs to. In a household with a new baby, being welcome at mother's
breast, if he feels the need, can be quite a help in overcoming a child's

feeling of displacement. There is no harm done by stepping back to baby things for a while—probably considerable good in the long run.

Spontaneous Weaning in Children over Four

We commonly hear that most younger children do not ask to nurse again after they are weaned because they forget about nursing. This may be true, though I am not sure. It is certain, however, that children over four (or even over three sometimes) do not forget. As I have said, many of them will remember nursing as long as they live. So it should not be surprising that children over four are notorious for going about weaning in an irregular way. Many seem to give a lot of consideration to weaning. One little girl, asked when she would wean, thought about it and then replied, "Oh, probably I will try when I'm five, 'cause you can't come to school—can you?!"

Children usually wean at a time that is easy for them, when their lives are otherwise stable. From their behavior it is often evident that they are making quite a rational choice for so young a person. Some children tell their parents that they are weaning because they themselves decided to do so, and it is easy to see from watching other children that this is the case with them as well. In some children the process that leads to weaning is not readily apparent; but this is probably not because it is so much different for them, but because they are children who keep their own counsel about it.

In the months that follow a decision to wean (or at least what appears to be such a decision) many children encounter rough spots that cause them to reconsider. These times can worry you if you have regarded the child as weaned. But you have not lost all the progress you have made toward weaning. A child this age who goes weeks or months without nursing is definitely working on growing up. When she asks to nurse again after such a long time you can be sure that she has just come to a time in her life which she can handle better if she can still nurse a bit. Once she works her way past it, she will get back to the business of weaning.

Many mothers are quite hesitant to say that their over-fours are weaned, even after months without nursing. So often it seems that the minute mother pronounces her child weaned, he needs to nurse again.

Needless to say, spontaneous weaning with older nurslings can be gradual indeed!

References

1 Bøhler, E. and Ingstad, B. The struggle of weaning: Factors determining breastfeeding duration in East Bhutan. *Social Science and Medicine* 1996; 43(12):1809.

2 Cosminsky, S., Mhloyi, M. and Ewbank, D. Child feeding practices in a rural area of Zimbabwe. *Social Science and Medicine* April 1993; 36(7):944.

3 Lawrence, R. A. and Lawrence, R. M. *Breastfeeding: A Guide for the Medical Profession.* 5th edition. St. Louis: The C. V. Mosby Company, 1994; 345.

4 Sugarman, M. and Kendall-Tackett, K. A. Weaning ages in a sample of American women who practice extended breastfeeding. *Clinical Pediatrics* 1995; 34(12):646.

chapter seventeen

Time-Honored (or Time-Worn?) Approaches to Weaning

Initiating Weaning

The primary message in this book is that weaning is something you can forget about, and that you can forget about it in your own best interests and your child's. There is no specific situation in which to recommend weaning, because no one knows of a 100 percent reliable substitute for nursing, either nutritionally or emotionally. Nor does anyone have an approach to weaning that can be guaranteed to bring about weaning painlessly or in a certain amount of time.

There are many reasons that mothers feel a need to initiate weaning, by far the most common being disapproval from other people or embarrassment when the child insists on nursing in public places. Next comes the discomfort of nursing while pregnant or the cultural prohibition against it. (In the developing world, pregnancy is the primary reason for weaning.) Other less common reasons include medications being administered to the mother, persistent biting, frequent breast infections, uneasiness with continued nursing, worry that the child is not eating other foods, or even illness in mother or child. The items I have listed seldom make weaning mandatory. Some of them, in fact, such as most kinds of illness in the child, are best met with continued nursing, at least until the illness is resolved.

Certain conditions in the mother require weaning: addiction to drugs of abuse, including cocaine and heroin, the urgent need to take a medication that is incompatible with breastfeeding, a new diagnosis of breast cancer or any cancer that requires treatment with chemotherapy or radiation, HIV infection, or human T-cell leukemia (HTLV-I). But most do not.

Every family is different, however; every nursing relationship is different. What motivates one mother to nurse may so overwhelm another that weaning is very important to her. Nor does the decision to continue to nurse or to wean mark one mother or the other as superior. Each mother is coping in her own way with the problems that her family faces and is acting as best she can in her family's best interest.

Still, weaning before a child is ready is a difficult undertaking and full of risks for the nursling and for the whole family. Some weaning methods that we still hear recommended from time to time are so harsh that they can traumatize the child and leave him handicapped in his ability to interact warmly with other people for the rest of his life. For this reason, you should eye any "quick and easy" weaning method with suspicion.

The "Mother's Week Out" Approach, or Weaning by Abandonment

Ask for advice on how to wean, and the most likely response you will receive is incredulity that you would be nursing a child old enough that you would need to do more than give a bottle and take dry-up medication (not desirable or effective on either count, but this is what some people believe to be true). The most likely recommendation you would receive if you kept asking, especially among your grandparents' generation, is that you take a week-long vacation, leaving your child behind. When you return he will have forgotten all about nursing—or so they say.

This method of weaning has an extensive history and is still widely practiced in traditional societies. In the American colonies, "mothers weaned their children by leaving them at home while they visited friends or relatives far from their infants' cries, or by placing their children in the care of family or friends until the process was complete."[8] Families plan separations—vacations and such—in hopes that when mother returns the child will no longer want to nurse. Mothers may be part of the planning for these separations, or other family members may make the plans and coerce the mother into going along.

This approach to weaning has serious drawbacks. It is certainly not to be recommended casually. Separation from the child, for one thing, is most unpredictable as a plan to produce weaning without a struggle and tears. Though it is true that some children left behind will not ask to nurse when mother returns, other children will. There is just no guarantee that this risky practice will result in weaning. Even if it does, the cost can be great.

We adults may refer to the time we are intentionally away from a child as "separation," but to the young child it is desertion. One study among nutritionally at-risk children in Tanzania, where separation of mother and toddler is a traditional approach to weaning, showed a "highly significant correlation between development of protein-energy malnutrition and separation from the mother at the time of weaning."

> *In most cases this physical separation means loss of love, loss of necessary body-contact, lack of supervision, lack of caring help, especially during meals. All these facts, together with the child's grief at having "lost" the mother, turn it into a lone, unhappy, weeping creature, i.e., the child is in a condition which eases the way all too quickly—in the circumstances of developing countries— into malnutrition.[7]*

There is nothing that can explain a mother's absence to a child under three or so (give or take a year depending on the child). Each child can comprehend mother's absence for a certain amount of time—maybe five minutes for some, maybe all day for others, and for some older ones maybe even a weekend.

Once you are gone past your child's limit, she may begin to mourn for you as if you were dead. She will be frightened for herself, wondering how she can survive without you. She may be furious with you for leaving her. She will begin to reorder her world so that she can get along without you, and her new arrangement may be bizarre since she is not mature enough nor in a good mental state, considering her fear and anger, to undertake such a project. She may settle on unfortunate and inappropriate behaviors to compensate for her loss of you. For heart-wrenching examples of how babies and young toddlers react to the absence of their mothers, read Chapter 1, "The Trauma of Loss" in John Bowlby's *Loss*.[2]

Loss of the person to whom he is most attached, usually mother, can be so painful for a child that I could not recommend planning a lengthy separation from a dependent child, for the sake of weaning or anything else. A mother of a nineteen-month-old was able to see risk in an upcoming separation even before she was gone. She writes:

> *I planned on taking a trip for one week without him. (He was to stay home with his father.) I tried substituting things when he wanted to nurse: toys, dancing, a bottle (Ha!), books, reading, or carrying him in the backpack.*

*His attention was sometimes diverted, but only
temporarily. I felt terrible, and he was frustrated.
I canceled the trip, and I'm glad I did.*

As this mother realized, choosing to leave a little one for very
long can be like taking a deliberate risk, hoping that your child is one of
those who will be unscarred by having you tear yourself away from him
suddenly. The greater his attachment to you, the greater the danger that
he will suffer from your unexplainable absence. Even though he may stop
crying and calling for mother, he will likely continue mourning in other
ways; when you return, he may treat you with a cold shoulder or rage.

So real is the danger of a lengthy separation from a small child
that even in emergency situations many parents go to great lengths to
stay with their children. Parents and professionals have formed groups
like Children in Hospitals (Children in Hospitals, 31 Wilshire Park,
Needham, MA 02192 USA) to help families seek the best possible care for
children who have to spend time in hospitals, including around-the-clock
care-by-parent arrangements. These organizations also encourage
hospitalized parents to seek visiting rights for their children.

Children are increasingly on the scene when families face crises
or conflicts—while relatives bicker over an inheritance, at sickbeds and
funerals, and so on. Children do not suffer as much from being present
on such occasions as they do from being shut out and left behind by their
parents. Indeed, children gain a better understanding and acceptance of
life and death if they are included as much as possible. Besides, little
children can be a great comfort and joy to adults when events are trying
or sad.

Separations do come up sometimes that we cannot figure out how
to avoid. Of course a few years later somebody will come along with an
idea that would have solved everything—that good old 20/20 hindsight—
but the only thing that counts is what we can figure out at the time.
When such separations occur, we must make the best of them and do
everything we can to make them easier for the child—like keeping
everything around her as familiar as possible. Occasionally a trip with a
beloved family member, especially with father, can be joyful as well as
stressful.

*Before I had my son I never thought I would nurse for
more than a year. When that time came we had just
completed a move from South Africa to the US, and the
only constant in his life was nursing and me. So I decided
to let him wean when he was ready. When I got pregnant
I thought he might wean, but he showed no interest in
stopping. Then when I was eight months pregnant, he*

went back to South Africa to stand up in his uncle's wedding. They were gone ten days. I expressed to keep up my supply if he wanted to nurse when he came back, but since he didn't seem to miss it, I thought he was done for sure. I picked them up at the airport, and he was happy to see me, but didn't mention nursing. However as soon as we got home, that was the first thing he asked for. I have been tandem nursing now for almost eleven months and am so glad that I didn't wean him. My children get along great, and it has made my life much easier.

If you and your child are going to be separated, it may be necessary to pump or express milk for your own comfort while you are apart, depending on how often he usually nurses. Unless weaning is necessary, I would recommend pumping often enough to keep up milk production, as this mother did, until you and your child are reunited. That way you have a choice about continuing to nurse when you see how your child deals with the separation. You may choose to proceed with weaning at this point, or use nursing to smooth over any possible fear and hurt feelings. You may find that for your child this is a time to encourage nursing, not a time to deny it.

The "Spicy Burrito" Method

A technique commonly used to stop a child from thumb-sucking has also been used to bring about weaning. There is a foul-tasting liquid on the market that makes thumb or breast quite unpleasant for the child. In various parts of the world mothers use substances readily available in their own kitchens—a hot sauce such as taco sauce in some places. In Java, where mothers traditionally wean gradually and late, mothers tell of certain instances in which they would put turmeric or a crushed quinine pill on the nipple.[3] Igorot mothers in the Philippines have used ginger or chili-pepper sauce.[6] Mothers in East Bhutan report painting the breasts with the juice of a certain species of chrysanthemum or a mixture of ashes and water.[1] In eighteenth-century England, and no doubt in the North American colonies as well, breast and nipple were painted with bitter mixtures containing alum, mustard, or wormwood.[8] Mothers among the Turkana occasionally tried donkey's dung or juice from bitter euphorbia, but these proved largely unsuccessful.[5]

Like all quick-and-easy methods of weaning, this one seems risky. For starters, some of these substances, like chilies, must be painful for mother as well as for the child.

The young child is busy learning how to trust dearly loved people. Though children must in time learn to be selective in their trust, they first must learn to have faith at all. Trust is a fragile characteristic that is rarely learned anywhere if not in mother's arms. It seems too great a gamble to me to create even the possibility of shattering a child's trust in order to secure a quick weaning. We can only guess what passes through a child's mind when the sweetest and warmest part of his day suddenly becomes bitter, or even painful.

Nearly 2,000 years ago, the Greek physician Soranus expressed disapproval of the practice, citing the injurious effect of sudden change, added to the possibility that the bitter or evil-smelling substance itself might injure the child's stomach and make him ill.[4]

Besides, it doesn't always work. In 1664 Anne Bradstreet wrote about weaning in her *Meditations*. "Some children are hardly weaned. Although the teat be rubbed with wormwood or mustard, they will either wipe it off or else suck down sweet and bitter together."[8]

Of course it can be said that nature uses this very technique to bring about weaning when the mother is pregnant—at least this is what some youngsters tell us about the milk of a pregnant mother. It tastes bad. One three-and-a-half-year-old giggled, said the milk had turned to apple juice, and never nursed again. Others have less kind things to say about this milk.

In pregnancy, however, the milk must not become really awful, because so many children do continue to nurse. A pregnant mother is not deliberately making the milk taste bad. It is a natural change and an aspect of a real and natural condition. It would be very hard to keep a child in the dark about the source of the foul-tasting stuff if we were rubbing it on. Children cope very well with real situations—it is the deceit behind a contrived situation that makes it so threatening.

Even so, some children who wean suddenly because of changes in the taste of the milk in pregnancy do react as if they have been weaned by the "spicy burrito" method and need extra tenderness and attention for a while.

The Return of Frankenstein's Monster

A variation on the bitter ointment approach used in some places might be to do as Gussie's mother did in *A Tree Grows in Brooklyn*. In the novel, the mother painted an awful face on her breast with stove blackening and lipstick. The apparition so terrified the child that he screamed and hid under the bed for twenty-four hours. After that, Gussie was weaned.

Considering some of our artistic skills, or lack thereof, I would think a child would be as likely to burst out laughing as to be scared of a face painted on the breast. But if the face should do its work and succeed in terrifying the child as in the story, then what would we have done? Everything I have said about trust before seems worth double consideration. For a mother herself to create such fright in her child (not just a "boo" around the doorpost, but enough of a fright to cause weaning) seems terribly dangerous. The well-being of a child's psyche and the validation of a child's faith in those who are supposed to provide love and protection are too precious to endanger through such tactics as a monster where he has come to expect love.

Crying It Out

Often parents are urged to ignore their children's cries when "the time" comes for weaning. Some people think there can perhaps be no more convincing example of crying that is solely for the purpose of manipulating adults than a child crying for the breast. If your child's crying is for the purpose of controlling you, though, you should be able to perceive that in his behavior and distract him to a more interesting purpose, like controlling the dog maybe. Rarely does an observant parent see manipulation.

Instead, when your child cries to nurse, you are more likely to hear the need she communicates in her cry. You will sense her pain if you deliberately deny her the breast. Of course we cannot always give our children just what they are crying for, but still we do not ignore their cries. You yourself will likely be miserable any time you force yourself not to respond. Crying is a language for expressing need, and we cannot hear it without being affected deeply.

By "crying it out" I do not mean to encourage you to fret every time your child cries because you will not buy him candy at the gas station or let him hurt the cat. Situations like that come up almost daily with all our children, whether we are trying to wean them or not. Children can't and shouldn't get through a day without confronting some of life's ordinary frustrations. A few tears are inevitable. "Crying it out" refers to the practice of leaving the child to cry without comfort or distraction.

To ignore a child's cry teaches him a lesson, of course. It teaches a child that even when he is so small and miserable that he can't figure out anything to do about the way he feels except to cry, still no one will help him. And as ugly as this lesson is during the day, it is much worse at night, the very time crying it out is most often recommended. The night's fears can combine themselves with the loss of comforting parents to turn into the kind of nightmare we see in horror films.

Crying it out is just too painful both for parents and for the child and too likely to leave a scar of mistrust on their relationship. Flatly denying a child's expressions of need seems far too risky for anyone to urge a conscientious parent to do so for the sake of weaning or anything else.

References

1   Bøhler, E. and Ingstad, B. The struggle of weaning: Factors determining breastfeeding duration in East Bhutan. *Social Science and Medicine* 1996; 43(12):1810.

2   Bowlby, J. *Loss.* New York: Basic Books, 1980; 10-22.

3   Castle, M. A. et al. Infant feeding in Semarang, Indonesia. *Feeding Infants in Four Societies: Causes and Consequences of Mothers' Choices.* Ed. B. Winikoff, M.A. Castle, and V.H. Laukaran. NY: Greenwood Press, 1988; 142.

4   Fildes, V. A. *Breasts, Bottles and Babies: A History of Infant Feeding.* Edinburgh: Edinburgh University Press, 1986; 35.

5   Gray, S. J. *Infant Care and Feeding among Nomadic Turkana Pastoralists: Implications for Fertility and Child Survival.* PhD Diss. State University of New York at Binghamton, 1992; 238.

6   Raphael, D. *Only Mothers Know.* Westport, CT: Greenwood Press,1985; 37.

7   Schmutzhard, E., Poewe, W. and Gerstenbrand, F. Separation from mother at time of weaning. A rarely discussed aspect of the aetiology of protein energy malnutrition. *Tropical Doctor* October 1986; 16(4):177.

8   Treckel, P. A. Breastfeeding and maternal sexuality in colonial America. *Journal of Interdisciplinary History,* 1989; 20(1):37.

chapter eighteen

Some Less Dramatic Weaning Techniques

> *How you wean, in and of itself, doesn't make or break your child for life. Your child's personality and your relationship are more complex than that. But taking weaning considerations to heart and carefully weighing your choices can teach you and your child a lot about the fascinating process of growing up.*
>
> Diane Bengson, HOW WEANING HAPPENS[1]

Serious Business

The methods for weaning that have been discussed so far are intended to bring about an immediate weaning, a sudden weaning that is potentially hazardous both to mother and to child. Moreover, behind the advice for such weanings there often seems to be a mild, perhaps, but still sadistic attitude toward the child or perhaps toward the intimate mother-child relationship. Such advice is often, if not always, based on lack of respect for the intelligence and potential of the growing child.

Weaning is a serious business in which mother and child can both be hurt by a bungled job. (I said hurt, by which I do not necessarily mean ruined for life.) Weaning is not some kind of joke to be played on a child or foisted upon a mother. If weaning is to be undertaken before either of the nursing couple is ready, then the people dearest to them need to be ready, not with stunts and derision, but with extra love and support.

Parents need to be on hand to help the child being weaned if the going gets rough. Family and friends need to be ready to support the mother if she is giving up the intimacy of nursing before she is ready. Just as we offer care to someone whose appendix is cut out, so we should be ready to help a person, big or little, whose nursing relationship is cut off prematurely.

Weaning is also hard work. Mothers who have actively weaned little ones who were nursing more than two or three times a day talk about a time of being very involved in the weaning process, with little energy left for other things. A common remark about the weaning time is, "I didn't sit or lie down in the presence of my child for the duration."

"Don't Offer, Don't Refuse"

After the publication of the 1963 edition of THE WOMANLY ART OF BREASTFEEDING , La Leche League International's manual on breastfeeding and mothering, the weaning of choice in many families became the one recommended there. At that time the manual encouraged mothers to nurse whenever the child asks, but not to offer to nurse when the child does not ask. As the child becomes increasingly occupied with other things, the number of nursings gradually decreases until nursing stops altogether.

"Don't offer, don't refuse" is a safe and effective weaning technique as families all over the world who have used it can tell you. It does not come with a guarantee, however, of how long weaning will take; it may take months or years. Once you have seriously undertaken the "don't offer, don't refuse" course, though, you can be honest in telling anyone who asks that you are weaning your child.

Because the intent of this approach to weaning as presented in the original edition of the book was sometimes misunderstood as meaning that a mother must never offer to nurse, the wording was changed in the 1981 revision. After all, it would be a shame for anyone who was happy to go on with nursing and to let weaning come in its own time to feel constrained against offering to nurse whenever she felt the need. There are times when the best thing to do is to offer to nurse— when you sense a tantrum coming on for instance.

But at some point in the nursing relationship, particularly if it is a long one, you will probably find yourself waiting for your child to ask for nursing most of the time. As the child grows older most mothers just seem to make the change to "don't offer, don't refuse" automatically, even if they have never read THE WOMANLY ART OF BREASTFEEDING . This is what La Leche League's Founders had in mind all along.

It may seem surprising to some people that children do indeed quit nursing even while mother continues to offer at times, but they do. In fact, mothers occasionally find themselves feeling a bit rejected. These mothers will tell you how flatly a toddler or young child can turn down an offer to nurse once he has decided to wean. As one mother puts it, "Remember, if a baby wants to nurse she will, but you can't force a baby to nurse. If you try to force, you are subject to getting bitten—not hard, but enough to get the point across!" There is no way I know of to get a baby or child to nurse when he does not want to.

It is fine, then, to offer to nurse, or not to offer, depending on what you want. You should use some judgment about when and why you offer, but at the same time, do not fret and try to analyze every instance. Your feelings about your child and your relationship should influence what you do more than what you read about or reason that you are "supposed" to do.

Distraction

All of us use distraction to help steer our children past soft drink machines, or to halt a squabble over a toy, or even to avoid an occasional nursing. With some children this approach can be used to encourage weaning.

To wean by distraction involves considerable change in your pattern of living from day to day. You avoid familiar nursing situations and create new surroundings that your child likes. For one child this may include a great increase in outings to places she finds interesting and lots of company and excitement. For another child this will mean quieting life down a lot to minimize situations that he finds threatening.

Parents have to be like magicians ready with their bag of tricks whenever mother does not want to nurse. You need to anticipate the request and offer the distraction before the child thinks of nursing. If mother should chance to appear in the nude before a child she is trying to wean, for instance, she can probably forget about distraction at this time. Once a child has asked to nurse, distraction becomes difficult— often impossible.

One universal tool in parents' magic kit for weaning is to walk, carrying the child, talking or singing. Parents who have weaned by distraction start to look exhausted all over again as they tell about their weary feet and aching backs from pacing the floor at night carrying their youngsters or standing with a child in arms, rocking from side to side.

They have, however, the satisfaction of knowing they were able to do something to ease their children's distress during the process of a hastened weaning.

A change in routine may be distracting, too, like sitting up instead of lying down while helping your child go to sleep, or staying away from the old nursing places. Other possible distractions include reading stories, singing, new toys (even special "distraction toys") or new ways of playing with old toys, outings, bike rides, cuddles and tickles, visits from other children, and other fun things. For most children fathers are by far the best distracters.

The most effective distraction for many little ones is lots of attention from parents, "doubling up on the time spent with the child in activities other than being at the breast," a mother of a one-year-old writes. Such attentions can even be rather elaborate, as one mother describes:

> I would get out a little table of his about thirty minutes
> before a time when he often asked to nurse. We would sit
> on the floor next to the table and share a snack (slivers of
> liver were a favorite) and a drink. I vowed to give total
> attention to him for that fifteen or twenty minutes.
> I wouldn't even allow myself to think of what I was going
> to do after that. It worked: He didn't ask to nurse for a
> couple of hours unless nap time intervened.

Distractions of any type, including the very best ones that include lots of extra love, are limited in their effectiveness to what the child is mature enough to accept. Sometimes the distractions replace nursing very effectively; sometimes they don't. Only your child can tell you.

Substitution

Most mothers who initiate weaning through distraction usually combine that method with the substitution of food for some nursings. Sometimes children do ask to nurse because they are hungry. Parents who want to wean can try to anticipate these times and offer an appropriate food. Substituting food cannot be used very effectively to dissuade your child from nursing when hunger is not what is motivating him.

Like distraction, substitution does not work very well once the child has asked to nurse. Mothers who have used this technique like it best when it successfully satisfies a child who is wanting to nurse at a time when mother wants to be at work putting a meal on the table. Mothers like it least when it means giving up that universally enjoyed early morning cuddle-and-nurse and instead getting up to cook an early breakfast.

Substituting food for nursing is a technique that should be used in moderation and with good judgment. It is not in your child's best interest to be continually coercing him to do what you want with bribes of food, especially a sweet food like raisins or juice. Nor is it in his best interest for you to bribe him with inappropriate edibles—like cookies or candy (except on rare occasions—we all do it now and then). When I talk about substituting food, I mean whole, natural foods that you are happy to have your child eating. Your purpose is to forestall his hunger so that he will not be asking to nurse for that reason. You do not want to warp his appetite toward the wrong kinds of foods in the process.

Though you may for reasons of your own be trying to hasten weaning, it is hard to know how long your child may continue to have the need to suck, and of course such needs should be satisfied one way or another. Many children who are being weaned before they have outgrown this need begin to suck their thumbs or fingers. On rare occasion a child will turn to a pacifier. These behaviors are certainly second best to nursing, but can provide some relief for your child if the weaning is frustrating her sucking needs. It is not wise to discourage such sucking directly. Instead it makes sense to redouble the tender loving care she

MOMMY'S MILK IS AS GOOD AS STEAK!

receives so that the use of the pacifier or thumb-sucking serves only to provide needed sucking, and does not have to substitute for the parenting that children must have.

Mothers who have nursed their babies are intensely aware of the richness of the mother-child interaction when nursing. Nursing satisfies so much more than the child's need for milk or need to suck. So if you see your weaned or weaning child needing to suck—thumb, pacifier, whatever—make an effort to hold the child then, while he is sucking, and cuddle or rock and sing. Or if you notice this behavior in your child, you may want to slow down the weaning for a while. After her good start at the breast, it would be a shame for her to transfer some of that wonderful trust she has developed to an inanimate pacifier or bottle or for her to withdraw into herself.

Postponement

One of the most effective ways to hasten weaning over the long term is to put off nursing for a while whenever your child can accept the delay. Such an approach can be more flexible than attempting to eliminate a certain "feeding." Many children nurse so irregularly that identifying a nursing time to be eliminated would be impossible anyway.

Whenever you ask your child to wait for a nursing, you are weaning a little bit. It's an entirely appropriate part of the process. But, unlike the little delays mothers ask for almost every day, active weaning involves consistently postponing nursing several times a day or night.

The tactics used for delaying nursing are usually other approaches discussed in this chapter—distraction or substitution. Some verbal children will accept an agreement to wait for a while. You and your child will be comfortable with postponement only if he is ready to accept a wait, and only if you are able to come up with a suggestion that will keep him from being unhappy about waiting. Holding him at arm's length and saying "wait," as every mother finds out at some time or another, just makes your child more determined to nurse than he probably was when he first asked.

Postponement, used creatively and with a close watch on the child's reactions, can lead to weaning. It is useful, of course, only for those nursings that can be delayed. Nursing for falling asleep and upon awakening cannot be altered much by this approach. Postponement, however, can be a gentle way to urge a child on to other things, especially during the day. And it is an approach to weaning that is very easy to adapt to different kinds of days—hard days for your child when he needs more nursing, and easy ones in which he needs less.

Though there is no way to know how long it will take to wean a child using postponement, it can hasten weaning considerably. Often when nursing has dwindled to once a day or less, mothers who are eager to wean tell the child there is no milk. At some point many children will accept this, but by no means all. For those who are not moved by such a suggestion, weaning will come, but not quite yet.

Shortening the Nursings

A number of mothers have found it to be effective and relatively painless to nurse the child as often as he likes, but not to nurse as long. You can nurse for a little while and then use distraction or substitution. On hectic occasions, some children will agree to nurse to a count of ten. Like all efforts to alter nursing patterns, this one is comfortable for some children and not for others.

Sometimes shortening the nursing time seems to speed weaning, perhaps because it eliminates nursing for some children as a way to fill blank and boring times. Instead mother and child become involved in interesting diversions until eventually nursing is not needed at all.

For some mothers, finding it possible to shorten nursings removes their need to wean. Frequently it is the very long times spent nursing that leave some mothers feeling restless and resentful. There are ways of course to entertain yourself during long nursings, but there is no harm in trying to persuade a child to nurse for a shorter period of time when he is able to make that change.

Older nurslings, in fact, will eventually agree to nurse "just a little bit" or to "get through soon" merely because you ask them—and because you remember to thank them warmly and politely when they comply with your wishes.

Weaning by Contract

Sometimes parents say to their children, "After Christmas comes, let's not nurse any more. You'll have lots of new toys then, and we'll play with them instead." Or "You're getting so big now. After your birthday comes I think you'll be ready for us to read a story at bedtime instead of nursing." Some children reduce the frequency of their nursing or quit altogether when mother tells them—usually not completely honestly— that they need to save the milk for the new baby. A few children will go along with a contract of one sort or another, although, in truth, most will ignore you.

One way to wean by contract is by bribery. Once in a while a child is willing to trade nursing for a new toy or pet—and lots of mother's attention to go along with the new interest. It takes considerable maturity before a child can actually give up nursing comfortably for the sake of something else she wants very much, as in the case of the three-year-old who agreed to wean so her family could have a new baby. (Her mom was one of the few women who remain infertile the whole time they are nursing.)

Some children agree to the contract, enjoying the fun of making plans, but back out when the agreed-upon time actually comes. Though children must in time learn to live up to agreements they make, it seems to me that lessons about not breaking contracts should be taught over such matters as picking up scattered blocks or sharing treats. Nursing is so important to the child who is not ready to wean that his feelings about that are likely to overshadow any possible understanding of the meaning of a promise.

Weaning by contract does work sometimes:

> *My second child, a daughter, nursed until she was about five-and-a-half. I became pregnant again, we continued to nurse but then she was gone for a week on a family visit. When she returned home and tried to nurse again it was so uncomfortable we negotiated a reward for her weaning. It was no problem at all. I think she was obviously ready. She claims she doesn't remember nursing as long as I remember her doing it—which I take as evidence it wasn't that important for her after about age five. My third child, a boy, also nursed until about five-and-a-half. I had figured I would let him wean on his own, but I started finding that nursing became annoying to me. I wasn't getting any of the typical prolactin relaxation response, I assume because he wasn't nursing very often. Also I think he was starting to forget how to suckle properly. So I told him we were just going to have to stop and we had a reward for him doing so. He wasn't upset about it that I remember. When I ask him about it now he says he doesn't remember weaning.*

Success is most likely, as in these cases, with children who are older and nearly ready to wean on their own anyway. With these children a celebration of the event might be in order, rites for a passage in which they have been cooperative agents.

Father and Weaning

All of the approaches to weaning that have come up so far are fine for the light of day when you are awake and at your best. They can all be exhausting if a mother undertakes them seriously, however, all by herself. They are often near to impossible at night. Any father who is urging his wife to wean their child, especially a young toddler, needs to understand what a difficult role he is likely to have to play in the process. Just understanding how hard weaning can be is usually enough to change the minds of most loving fathers.

     Almost every parent-initiated weaning that I know of has involved a great deal of help from dad. A child who is immature enough to be meeting dependency needs through nursing still has very great needs in this department. Through nursing, mother and child have a relatively easy system for taking care of most of these needs.

     When a mother is weaning, however, and withdrawing from the surest and easiest way of meeting the child's needs, finding adequate substitutes is frequently more than she can do alone. Sometimes father can fill in and provide some of the close cuddling and affection that the child needs so much. If the weaning is to progress without great difficulty, we can hope the child will be far enough along in his social maturation to be able to take from father some of the affection he had been getting at mother's breast.

     Weaning at night is especially hard for mother to manage without help. In her arms the little one expects to nurse and cannot comprehend her unwillingness. Of course, neither mother or child is likely to be particularly rational at night. Yawning mothers do not distract or substitute with much finesse, nor are sleepy little people very open to any ideas beyond their most basic needs. That is why when weaning is deemed necessary in some New Guinea households, the child is sent to sleep with the father.[2] Fathers in many families have been the people who have made a comfortable, humane night weaning possible. They have walked, rocked, fed, and otherwise tended to their children at night for the duration of the weaning. Usually mother needs to stay out of sight while dad is tending to the little one. This way he is more likely to succeed in his efforts to keep weaning at night from becoming a nightmare for everyone.

     Even during the day many little children continue to expect closeness with mother to include nursing. Although a mother who is working on weaning may be redirecting the child with considerable success, she will be grateful when dad is able to provide the distraction for a while. The most common way for youngsters to be weaned from bedtime nursings, for example, is for dad to take over the task of helping the child get to sleep.

If the child is not ready, too much responsibility for weaning, especially night duty, can work quite a hardship on dad, even more so considering that most fathers, and sometimes both parents, still have to get up the next morning and spend the day at work. With this in mind, I would suggest that no one, particularly a father, should urge a parent-initiated weaning, especially of a child under two or so, except in the most compelling circumstances.

An additional role that a father needs to play during weaning is support for the mother as a mother. In some families this has meant an educated change in his own attitudes. If mother and/or child are clearly unhappy with the weaning, he can then be the one to encourage them to forget it for now. Or he can be sensitive to the feeling of loss many a mother has as her intimate physical relationship with the child changes. He may also need to support her if she faces criticism for her decisions regarding nursing or weaning. Mothers appreciate any of these kinds of support when they are appropriate. Without such love, a mother may find her job all but impossible.

Spot Weaning

When nursing seems to be just too much, there is an alternative to total weaning. Usually it is not the whole nursing relationship that is difficult, but one or two specific nursing times. Or the problem may not be the nursing, but that nursing sessions last so long. In these circumstances mothers don't have to stop nursing altogether; they can try "spot weaning."

Spot weaning can mean an attempt to eliminate a certain nursing just as if you were beginning a total weaning. Or it may be better to substitute nursing at a different time. In the case of long nursings, you might try to persuade the child to do something else after a comfortable amount of time at the breast. Or you could try offering more frequent, shorter nursing times to see if that might be more satisfactory.

Readjusting nursing, or spot weaning as I have called it, is always experimental, and always subject to more change. Your child may be comfortable with the restrictions for a while, then need to go back to the old routine. Then comes a time when partial weaning is okay again, and so on. I have not invented anything here, but rather have put a label on something we all do as our children grow so that we can continue to nurse without stress.

Weaning by Capitulation

Some families have actually hastened weaning by letting the pressure off. Children who are otherwise ready to wean may be made so insecure by the efforts to get them to stop nursing that they can't. One mother writes that she had had it with her three-and-a-half-year-old's heavy nursing demands, though it was clear to her that he needed it. At last in desperation she tried stopping all her weaning efforts and told him he could nurse whenever he wanted, and she meant it. Right away he tested her by asking to nurse every time he thought of it. Then, she says, "Two months after I decided to let him be and not worry about his all-night binges and seemingly constant nursings during the day—he weaned! All by himself."

Capitulation, or letting the pressure off, does not usually result in such a dramatic weaning. But it is one of the most effective "cures" for frequent or almost constant nursing, especially in a child of two or older. Of all the possible approaches to weaning, although it assuredly will not produce weaning in a child who is not ready, capitulation is certainly the safest and happiest for your child.

References

1   Bengson, D. HOW WEANING HAPPENS. Schaumburg, Illinois: La Leche League International, 1999; 5.

2   Tietzen, A. M. Infant care and feeding practices and the beginnings of socialization among the Maisins of Papua New Guinea. *Infant Care and Feeding in the South Pacific.* Ed. L. B. Marshall. New York: Gordon & Breach Science Publishers, 1985; 132.

chapter nineteen

Making the Best of Nursing or Weaning

Deciding to Wean

So often parents will find themselves feeling the need to wean and yet being torn between the improvement they expect to see in their lives and the fear of any hurt their child may experience as a result of a hastened weaning. First of all, they need to evaluate the child's need for nursing as best they can and decide whether they can really provide adequate replacements for nursing. They need to look honestly at the work ahead of them if they do undertake weaning and evaluate what kind of support system is available for both mother and child during and after weaning.

If you are considering weaning, and thinking the whole process through has not led you to discard the idea, then proceed gently, but decisively. Eliminate nursings (by whatever techniques you find work best for you and your child) as slowly as possible—no faster than eliminating one nursing every week.

While you are doing this, keep the burden of the decision upon yourself. Do not try to shift part of the responsibility to your child by being indecisive or becoming flustered if your child is upset with what you are doing. Unless you have made the firm choice in your own mind to give weaning a try, the whole process is likely to be fruitless and confusing for both of you. If you as an adult are going to make a decision about weaning for your child, you must act as the adult while weaning is underway. Your child is not equipped to comfort you and reassure you that this decision is okay. It must be the other way around. You must do what you can to comfort your child.

The kind of relationship you have with your child, along with all the intangible factors in your temperament and his, and, of course, his own rate of emotional growth are the determining factors in how nursing or weaning will proceed. Whether you are giving yourself lovingly to your child and are feeling warm, friendly, and cheerful is important in how well either nursing or weaning will go. If you are feeling guilty about weaning or about pushing weaning too hard, you will be angry with yourself and as a result probably will not be as loving with your child. He in turn may become anxious and demand to nurse more.

Don't undertake weaning until you can present yourself as confident and comfortable about your decision. Continue to offer first-rate parenting, the best you've got, during the process. Otherwise, your child is likely to have difficulties with weaning.

If you find that you cannot keep your child happy most of the time while weaning, then you can, unless your reasons are urgent indeed, make another adult choice. Just as decisively you can forget the whole thing for a while, or at least reduce the rate at which you are proceeding. With weaning, like so many other decisions in life, there is no harm in trying. If it goes well, good. Just be watchful and ready to back off or give up an undertaking that is not going well.

To give yourself an escape route, it's probably a good idea not to let your milk dwindle too far until you are sure that weaning is going to work for your family. Maintain your milk supply by pumping or expressing for a while, until you are sure. Knowing that you can change your mind should help you make an honest effort at weaning.

Knowing When to Abandon Weaning

If you undertake weaning, it is usually very easy to know when the approach you are taking will not do for your child or when weaning is proceeding at too fast a pace. If your child becomes upset and cries and insists upon nursing beyond your ability to distract him or comfort him, it is not difficult to figure out what the problem is. You clearly need to slow down the rate of weaning, change your tactics to ones he finds more supportive, or wait a while to try weaning. There may even be pleasant indications that your child is not really ready for weaning, as with the little one who hugged mother's neck and said, "I give you sugar; now you give me ninny."

Other more subtle signals your child may give you, especially if you are very skilled at distraction and substitution, may show up as changes or regressions in behavior. Disfluency (stuttering), which is very common in young children, is not always a sign of stress, but it can be at times. You may notice an increase in night waking or an increase in clinginess during the day. He may develop an attachment to an object, like a bear or a blanket, when there has been none before. There may be a new or increased fear of separation from you. A very common response to weaning that is going too quickly is a marked increase in mouthing objects or fingers and in thumb-sucking. Occasionally children who are being weaned too quickly begin biting people when they have never done so before.

Weaning may not be responsible, however, for the changes in behavior you see in your child. Children are people—complex beings with a lot more going on than just nursing and weaning. And, whatever the cause, you may be able to provide your child with lots of extra attention, love, and encouragement when these behaviors occur and thereby see them disappear without ever knowing their cause. It is not difficult, however, to make sure that your child is not fussy or clingy or up so much at night because of weaning: just suspend the weaning for a while.

Go back to nursing as much as your child wants, and see what happens. You may not see results immediately, though; it may take a while for your child's anxieties to subside if he found weaning very disturbing.

Keeping the Effort within Limits

Another measure of whether weaning is going too fast is its effect on you. Sometimes when a mother undertakes weaning, she feels that she must be committed to getting it done at all costs. This is not so. You can and should frequently give thought to whether you are progressing toward your goal at a comfortable rate, or if weaning is just too big a project to undertake right now.

An obvious problem from weaning too quickly is that your breasts may become overfull, making you uncomfortable or even ill. You can treat swelling and discomfort of engorged breasts by chilling cabbage leaves in the refrigerator and then wearing them inside your bra, replacing them with fresh ones every two to four hours, until the engorgement has subsided. Breast engorgement can lead to a breast infection or abscess that would have to be treated with bed rest, antibiotics, even minor surgery. Any of these problems is an indication that you are weaning too fast for your body to make the necessary adjustments.

You may also find yourself spending large portions of your day, or even of your night, working hard to keep your child happy without nursing. You can become exhausted and really resentful that weaning is taking so much from you. Such a physical and emotional state can detract from your child's ability to cope with the changes.

When weaning is keeping you busy for more than an hour or two each day or night, it is time to reevaluate your decision to wean. What do you hope to gain by weaning? Is weaning going to be worth what you are going to have to expend of yourself to bring it about now? What is the atmosphere in your home while all this is going on?

No one can answer these questions for anyone else, of course. Parents alone have to decide what limits to put on how much effort they will expend for the sake of weaning. Weaning is indeed serious business. Just as it should not be allowed to take too much from a child, neither should it take too much from parents.

When Weaning Will Not Work

It can be discouraging to see how much your child needs to nurse when what you really want to do is wean. If you are weary of nursing, the intensity of your little one's needs may seem staggering. Most of us come into parenthood unprepared for the amount of parenting young children need and for how long.

> *I am a true sufferer of nursing burnout! My five- and two-and-a-half-year-olds are always demanding "me me mama" and I do get very tired of hearing it. However, if I were to deny them, I would have two hysterical children on my hands and absolutely no idea how to calm them down, for nursing has been a godsend! Sometimes I daydream, or fantasize about one day when I will not be nursing. The reality is, my children will need me just as much, only in different ways. I often take a step back and remind myself of just how fast the time is going, so I appreciate it all more. This seems to help a great deal.*

If your child is not ready, his behavior urges you to look again at why you feel the need to wean now. Usually with creativity, perhaps with encouragement and shared experiences with other nursing mothers, you can figure out how to be comfortable with nursing a bit longer. You can be sure that nursing as you know it now will not stay the same forever, anyway. One mother says of her son's weaning once she had given up on leading the way, "I'm not sure whether he finally weaned because I quit pushing, or if it was a coincidence. I sometimes feel that nothing we did or omitted could change his inner timetable and that he weaned when he did simply because his time had come. On the other hand, he wasn't really free to do his own thing until I let the pressure off him."

Your child, like this one, will quit nursing whether or not you ever do anything about weaning. And should you still feel the need to wean after a few weeks you can always try again. The day is not far ahead of you when your child's needs can be satisfied in more mature ways.

Of course I do not urge any mother just to keep on nursing and hating it, if that is what it seems to have come to in her life. Rather I would urge a mother whose child clearly tells her that he cannot give up nursing yet without being miserable, but who is unhappy herself, to work very hard toward making her own life happier. Nursing all by itself cannot make anyone unhappy. One mother writes:

> *I got burnout during pregnancy at seven or eight months.*
> *I get burnout waiting for my ever-late husband. I get*
> *burnout cleaning, cooking, talking to negative people, etc.*
> *It is what I do with the burnout that gets me through it.*
> *My solutions may not be yours.*

Unhappiness with nursing usually comes from frustration at being unable to meet certain expectations and goals—like being socially acceptable or contributing to the family income the way you always have, or whatever—because of the unexpected demands on mother's time from the nursing child.

It seems much wiser, when a child indicates a need for much attention and/or for much nursing, to take those ever-so-important needs as a given factor in our lives and to restructure our goals around what we must do to help our little ones grow up as well as they can. But when a mother is unhappy, she should not just let things continue as they are. If she cannot see any better way to improve her situation than weaning, then she needs to give weaning a try.

Nursing, however, will sometimes not be the factor that can change. Often changes will need to be in some other part of a mother's daily expectations. What is surprising is the improvement that comes once we set our minds to making a different change, one less upsetting to human lives—such as maybe leaving the beds unmade for a month or two to make time for a little reading or a phone call, or trading chores with dad so that he is the one who puts the little one to bed, or . . . . The lists of parents' brilliant adjustments are endless. The truth that families usually learn is that nursing is not the problem really, and weaning is not the solution. (For additional discussion of this topic, see "When weaning isn't going well," Chapter 10 in Diane Bengson's HOW WEANING HAPPENS.[1])

Keeping Arms Open

Mothers all experience negative feelings about nursing from time to time. And all on occasion turn away from their children when they ask to nurse, turn them down, tell them "no," or push them away. These are unpleasant moments that leave behind feelings of guilt and defensiveness all mixed up together. These are moments when we are not at our best.

Yet in the normal course of events our children are very well equipped to deal with these grumpy times that we all experience. Like the little monkeys in the introduction to this book they fuss and cling and struggle until they force us to do our job and take care of them. It works out.

Problems arise when a mother begins to focus on nursing, begins to concentrate all her possible weariness and frustration there, and to push the child away almost every time he asks. This leads to a nasty struggle, with the mother feeling increasingly angry and the child feeling more and more rejected.

A mother may be looking so intently at nursing as the cause of the problems between her and her child that she cannot imagine receiving relief in any way besides weaning, especially if she is somewhat offended anyway by the idea of nursing a child as "old" as her little one is. Or she may feel so trapped in her resentment of nursing that the only first step she seems to be able to see toward resolving her feelings and needs is to attempt weaning.

Although each mother must do what she can to improve a genuinely unhappy relationship between mother and child, eliminating friction between mother and child by abandoning nursing seems rather like eliminating friction between husband and wife by abandoning sexual intercourse. In either case, the problem cannot be in the healthy physical union between people, but in the feelings and attitudes they are bringing into their interaction.

Nursing all by itself cannot make you so unhappy that you set up a pattern of pushing your child away. Nursing is a behavior that nature very carefully reinforces with pleasurable interactions and sensations. And nursing children are made cute and delightful so that we want to greet them with open arms. We begin to struggle with our nursing children because of other influences on our lives. Some, like pregnancy, we cannot alter. But many of the pressures on our lives that make it hard for us to enjoy our children we can change, or delay, or avoid.

Your child needs you to receive him with joy and enthusiasm most of the times he comes to you. For his sake and your own you must not let anything interfere with that acceptance between you. If you feel that you have to get away from nursing into a style of parenting that is more like what you may have grown up with, then give it a try.

Go about weaning without rejecting your little one. It is essential that, as best you can, you and other people dear to your child do as did the mother who wrote of weaning, "Nursing time was spent enjoying other interests with her, until she became too absorbed to notice the lack of nursing." The point is to move away from nursing if need be, but never to move away from loving.

Usually dealing with hard times in the relationship between mother and child brings us back to the business of testing our values and doing the best job we can of keeping first things first. Creative parenting, creative family living, learning to work for each other rather than only for the career or the house or whatever—these values and priorities will go far toward guaranteeing open arms for every family member.

Weaning in an Emergency

In the very rare instance in which weaning is so urgent that parents cannot change their minds, they may have the unhappy task of helping a miserable child adjust to weaning before he is ready. It is best if a mother in this circumstance can stay with her child, comfort him, accept his anger, and be sure he knows that it is okay to be angry and that mother is angry at the situation, too. Clothing that makes your breasts inaccessible may help when mom cannot nurse. Parents can substitute, distract, walk, or do anything that helps the child feel better. Weaning should occur as slowly as the situation permits.

Such a weaning can be very difficult for everyone involved, and fortunately it is uncommon that an unrelenting approach to weaning is unavoidable. Fortunately, children who must be weaned will often sense or understand the urgency of a real emergency and will cooperate as much as they can, making the whole process easier for everyone. For that reason it is certainly wise to explain, even to a young toddler, that weaning is necessary and why.

Abrupt Weaning

It is best if weaning can occur gradually, dropping a nursing time no more often than every week or so. There are instances, however, in which abrupt weaning is unavoidable, including rare medical crises such as the diagnosis of some cancers in the mother. The most tragic kind of abrupt weaning is the death of the infant or young nursling. When this happens the mother is left full of grief, surrounded by people and by things that must be done, and with painfully full breasts.

The mother whose nursing comes to a traumatic end needs care and support as she adjusts to and comes to accept her loss. She also needs rest and instruction in how to care for herself so that she does not become ill. For a mother who must dry up her milk, Gregory White, MD, of La Leche League International's Health Advisory Council, recommends that she abstain from salt, not restrict fluids, support but not bind her breasts, and express only enough milk to relieve discomfort. Some mothers find it comforting to donate pumped milk to a local milk bank. Gradually, they decrease their supply by pumping less over time.

Sometimes an abrupt weaning is not so tragic. It seems that some youngsters have not read what all of us author types have to say about weaning, that it should be gradual and all that. Some kids are nursing quite a bit one day and then decide the next day that they are weaned. One mother wrote,

> *Three years ago I had the good fortune of becoming unexpectedly pregnant at forty-one, having started [my mothering career] at 19. I was a little excited, and upset! I had my son on my forty-second birthday. He just weaned last year at two-and-a-third, and like his sister, he just quit one day and didn't tell me it would be the last! It was rather hard to say good-bye to this unplanned beautiful experience I thought I was far past in my life.*

Frequently there is a cause—like a sore mouth or tooth because of an injury, a sore throat, or a new tooth coming in—for such a sudden change in behavior (See Toddler Nursing Strike, p. 211). For this reason I would think it best to give a child who weans suddenly a chance to go back to nursing, especially if he is two or younger. It is a shame to let nursing end on a sour note if you can help it.

A few nurslings do wean abruptly in the natural course of life. When a child has made this decision, there is not much anyone else can or should do about it beyond making sure that he has ample opportunity to change his mind.

Living Short of the Ideal

If you should come to the end of your nursing relationship with a weaning that you regard as less than ideal, relax. Join the crowd. I don't know any mother who has been 100 percent happy with the way she and her children arrived at weaning. We each must do our best with nursing and weaning—and everything else we do with our children. When we fall short of this or that ideal (I do not say *if* we fall short), we should resolve to come closer to our mark next time, and otherwise shake off the thought of it.

Parenting covers many years, and nursing and weaning are only part of the whole picture. If you don't fail to measure up to your standards on one of these, then you will fall short somewhere else. Parenting is a job in which we need to do our best day by day. That is what books like this are for—to help us do our best. But we must not get bogged down in concern over every moment in our lives with our children.

We are not putting our children's lives together by some immutable scientific formula. Rather we are weaving a tapestry along with our children, a tapestry made up of our triumphs and our "If-only-I-had . . ." moments. The odds are on our side that years from now when we are finished, the tapestry will be beautiful, and the memories we and our children have of their growing-up years will be joyful.

Effects of Weaning on Mother

Weaning marks a significant but, I hope, not drastic change in the way you and your child interact with each other. Like any other such change there is a whole collection of feelings that go along with it. The more gradual the weaning, the more diffuse and easy to handle your emotional responses are likely to be.

Mothers usually notice few physical effects after slow, late weaning. There may be some breast fullness or engorgement for about a week after the final nursing. The younger the child and the more rapid the weaning, of course, the more likely this is. Remedies for breast discomfort include wearing cold cabbage leaves (see page 281), towel-wrapped ice packs applied to the breasts, and cautious use of analgesics, especially cautious if you may be pregnant. If a breast gets a reddened area, apply heat instead of ice. Contact your physician and take antibiotics if you need them. The best treatment for an infected breast includes frequent nursing to keep it drained. Therefore, if it is possible, it would be best to suspend weaning until the breast is better, that is, if your child will cooperate. He may not be willing, or able, at this point. In that case, until the antibiotic takes effect you may need to do some pumping or hand expressing to relieve pressure in the affected part of the breast.

Depending on your eating style and how much you were nursing before weaning, there may be some change in your weight. You may notice a decrease in appetite and lose a little weight. Or if you continue to eat just as you did while nursing, you may gain weight. The menstrual period following weaning may be early and heavy. Or you may notice no change at all.

Emotionally, most of us at one time or another during weaning experience a sense of loss—loss of the nursing relationship, maybe the loss of an early morning cuddle in bed, a funny kind of tug on your blouse, and the like. If the weaning is rapid, the change in hormone levels may trigger a depression in some mothers. Some of us wonder for a while if we have lost our status as the irreplaceable caretaker for the child, though of course we have not. Many of us miss the larger breasts that go with nursing. (When you have been nursing your children one after the other for several years, the possible decrease in breast size when the last one weans can be a surprise.)

We seldom think of ourselves as having an emotional need for nursing our babies, or if we think about it, we tend to believe that feeling this way must be unhealthy or a little bit selfish. Nursing is a symbiotic relationship, though, not just in the first few months, but for as long as we are nursing our children. A long and happy beginning at the breast is priceless for the well-being of our children; it is also important to the growth and well-being of mothers. We, as well as our children, can be frustrated by a premature weaning.

In reading letters about nursing from hundreds of mothers, I became increasingly aware of mothers who were sad or had mixed feelings when weaning occurred—the ones who were "singing empty nest songs" as it were. So many mothers whose children were weaned before two or so seemed to feel some sense of loss, as did the mother who, after her eighteen-month-old weaned, said, "At the time I was semi-depressed. . . . But soon I realized that weaning was not the end of things, but the beginning of a new growth and another 'time of wonder' for us."

When nursing continues past two or three, mothers much less frequently describe weaning in the same mixed terms. It seems that a time comes in the growth of the mother-child relationship when it is easier for both to move on and leave baby things behind.

Of course relating mothers' feelings about weaning to the age of the child is a broad generalization. Mothers' feelings also vary a great deal according to how the weaning came about and according to the warmth and closeness of the mother-child relationship before, during, and after weaning. It may indeed be that some mothers who are sad following weaning feel this way because of something in the mother-child relationship that has not worked out well, something that may in fact have led to the weaning. This could be true at any age. But having said this, it still seems to me that most of the sadness upon weaning that mothers have shared with me resulted from the fact that weaning came about before these mothers' nursing urges were completely satisfied. The source of such frustration for mothers is not usually from a child who chooses to wean too quickly on his own, but can be found rather in customs and social restrictions that interfere with the normal course of nursing and mothering.

While acknowledging the sad feelings that may go with weaning, let me emphasize the good ones. It feels good to reclaim our bodies and enjoy again an increased sense of privacy. Also, children who wean spontaneously do so because they are older and are becoming less immature. So along with the possible loss of status as the only one who can care for and comfort the child, most of us enjoy the freedom of knowing he can now sometimes get along very nicely in the care of other loving people. (This is true because he is older, not because he is weaned, and is less likely to be true of a child who is weaned before he is ready.)

One mother shares her pleasure in nursing and weaning quite eloquently when she says,

> *The entire nursing experience was a blessing that I can't find words to express properly. Weaning came about so naturally and mutually there were no feelings of loss or inadequacy . . . or anxiety. . . . To me child-led weaning is like a beautiful conclusion to a novel. I came away from the experience with a sense of completion and total satisfaction. The wonderful thing is that it isn't the end, but only the beginning of the childhood years of growing together.*

There are joys as well as difficulties in every part of parenting. The nursing years are not the only, or even necessarily the best, of our lives with our children. Babies are delightful to have around. So are school kids and teenagers, grown children and grandchildren. Through all the times of our lives, we need to stay physically close and not let weaning be the end of cuddling and loving. (You're never too old to kiss your mother, they say—or your father either.) Above all we must not lose the special joys of the present by spending too much time regretting the loss of a way of living we have outgrown.

The best way I know of not to find yourself singing those "empty nest" songs as your children grow is to throw yourself into every phase of your growth as a mother. Follow your maternal feelings with your babies and young children. Exercise your mothering urges; wear them out; use them up. These urges will not go away, of course, but, like your child, you can be satisfied and fulfilled. You can grow with your children so that the move from your nursing rocker to the Blue Birds or to being a grandparent is as exciting and joyful as your children's.

Weaning is a time when we all look back wistfully at those precious baby years. It's one of those times when you're likely to have a lump in your throat. But there is just too much good in living to use up very much of life trying to stay where you are. It's better to let a tear or two fall if need be, put an arm around that dear child, and plunge ahead into the rest of your life.

References

1 Bengson, D. How Weaning Happens. Schaumburg, Illinois: La Leche League International, 1999; 121-32.

Ahn, C. H. and Maclean, W. C. Growth of the exclusively breast-fed infant. *American Journal of Clinical Nutrition* 1980; 33:183-92.

Al-Mazrou, Y. Y., Aziz, K. M. S., Khalil, M. Breastfeeding and weaning practices in Saudi Arabia. *Journal of Tropical Pediatrics* October 1994; 40:267-71.

Alpert, G. et al. Outbreak of cryptosporidiosis in a day-care center. *Pediatrics* February 1986; 77(2):152.

American Academy of Pediatrics Committee on Nutrition. Fluoride supplementation for children: interim policy recommendations. *Pediatrics* May 1995; 95(5):777.

American Academy of Pediatrics Committee on Nutrition. Vitamin and mineral supplement needs in normal children in the United States. *Pediatrics* December 1980; 66(6):1015-21.

American Academy of Pediatrics Working Group on Breastfeeding. Breastfeeding and the Use of Human Milk. *Pediatrics* December 1997; 100(6):1035-39.

Anderson, S. Changing practices in the weaning of babies in Britain. *Professional Care of Mother and. Child* 1997; 7(3):58-59.

Avery, J. L. Closet nursing: a symptom of intolerance and a fore-runner of social change? *Keeping Abreast Journal* 1977; 2:212-27.

Babb, L. A., Laws, R. *Adopting and Advocating for the Special Needs Child.* Westport, CT: Bergin & Garvey, 1997.

Bailey, K. V. Quantity and composition of breast milk in some New Guinean populations. *Journal of Tropical Pediatrics* 1965; 11:35-49.

Baldwin, E. In the best interests of breastfed children? *Mothering* Fall 1997; 84. http://www.lalecheleague.org/LawMain.html

Barnett, E., Sienkiewicz, M., Roholt, S. Beliefs about breastfeeding: a statewide survey of health professionals. *Birth* March 1995; 22:15-20.

Becroft, T. Child-rearing practices in the highlands of New Guinea: a longitudinal study of breast feeding. *Medical Journal of Australia* 1967; 2:598-601.

Bengson, D. HOW WEANING HAPPENS. Schaumburg, Illinois: La Leche League International, 1999.

Bentovim, A. Shame and other anxieties associated with breastfeeding: a systems theory and psychodynamic approach. *Ciba Foundation Symposium 45.* London: Ciba Foundation, 1976, 159-78.

Berg, A. *The Nutrition Factor.* Washington, D.C.: The Brookings Institute, 1973.

Berg, A. and Brems, S. A case for promoting breastfeeding in projects to limit fertility. *World Bank Technical Paper Number 102.* The World Bank, Washington, D.C., 1989.

Bittman, S. and Zalk, S. R. *Expectant Fathers.* New York: Ballantine Books, 1978.

Boediman, D. et al. Composition of breastmilk beyond one year. *Tropical Pediatrics and Environmental Child Health* 1979; 25:107-10.

Bøhler, E. and Bergström, S., Child growth during weaning depends on whether mother is pregnant again. *Journal of Tropical Pediatrics* April 1996; 42:104-09.

Bøhler, E. and Ingstad, B. The struggle of weaning: factors determining breastfeeding duration in East Bhutan. *Social Science and Medicine* 1996; 43(12):1805-15.

Bøorresen, H. C. Rethinking current recommendations to introduce solid food between four and six months to exclusively breastfeeding infants. *Journal of Human Lactation* 1995; 11(3):201-03.

Boston Women's Health Book Collective. *The New Our Bodies, Ourselves.* New York: Simon & Schuster, 1992.

Bowlby, John. *Attachment.* New York: Basic Books, 1982.

Bowlby, John. *Loss.* New York: Basic Books, 1980.

Brakohiapa, L. A., et al. Does prolonged breastfeeding adversely affect a child's nutritional status? *Lancet* Aug 20, 1988; 2(8608):416-18.

Brazelton, T. B. Parenting in another culture. *Redbook* May 1979; 153 (1):90-97.

Bretherton, I. and Waters, E., Ed. Growing points of attachment theory and research. *Monographs of the Society for Research in Child Development* 50(209).

Briend, A., Wojtyniak, B., Rowland, M. G. M. Breastfeeding, nutritional state and child survival in rural Bangladesh. *British Medical Journal* 1988; 296:879-82.

Briggs, D. C. *Your Child's Self-Esteem.* New York: Doubleday, 1970.

Briggs, G. G., Freeman, R., Yaffe, S. *Drugs in Pregnancy and Lactation.* Revised edition. Baltimore: Williams & Wilkins, 1998.

Brown, K. H., Bégin, F. Malnutrition among weanlings of developing countries: Still a problem begging for solutions. *Journal of Pediatric Gastroenterology and Nutrition* 1993; 17(2):132-38.

Brun, J. G., Nilssen, S., Kvåle, G. Breast feeding, other reproductive factors and rheumatoid arthritis: A prospective study. *British Journal of Rheumatology* 1995; 34:542-46.

Cardozo, A. R. *Woman at Home .* Garden City, New York: Doubleday & Co., Inc., 1976.

Castillo, C. et al. Breast-feeding and the nutritional status of nursing children in Chile. *Bulletin of PAHO* 1996; 30(2): 125-33.

Chen, J., Taren, D. Early feeding practices and the nutrition status of preschool children in rural Hubei Province, China. *Food and Nutrition Bulletin* 1995; 16(1):40-48.

Cosminsky, S., Mhloyi, M., Ewbank, D. Child feeding practices in a rural area of Zimbabwe. *Social Science and Medicine* April 1993; 36(7):937-47.

Counsilman, J. J. et al. Breast feeding among poor Singaporeans. *Journal of Tropical Pediatrics* December 1986; 32:310-12.

Cross, N. A. et al. Changes in bone mineral density and markers of bone remodeling during lactation and postweaning in women consuming high amounts of calcium. *Journal of Bone and Mineral Research* 1995; 10(9):1312-20.

Cummings, R. G. and Klineberg, R. J. Breastfeeding and other reproductive factors and the risk of hip fractures in elderly women. *International Journal of Epidemiology* 1993; 22(4):684-90.

Davidson, W. D. A brief history of infant feeding. *The Journal of Pediatrics* July-December 1953; 43:74-87.

Dettwyler, K. A. Evolutionary medicine and breastfeeding: implications for research and pediatric advice. The 1998-99 David Skomp Distinguished Lecture in Anthropology, Department of Anthropology, Indiana University, Bloomington, Indiana, 1999.

Dettwyler, K. A. Infant feeding in Mali, West Africa: variations in belief and practice. *Social Science and Medicine* 1986; 23:651-64.

Dettwyler, K. Breastfeeding and weaning in Mali: cultural context and hard data. *Social Science and Medicine* 1987; 24(8):633-44.

Dettwyler, K. A. *Breastfeeding, weaning, and other infant feeding practices in Mali and their effects on growth and development.* Ph.D. Diss., Indiana University, 1985.

Enger, S. M. et al. Breastfeeding history, pregnancy experience and risk of breast cancer. *The British Journal of Cancer* 1997; 76(1):118-23.

Falkner, F., Ed. *Infant and child nutrition worldwide: issues and perspectives.* Boca Raton, Florida: CRC Press, 1991.

Feldblum, P. J. et al. Lactation history and bone mineral density among perimenopausal women. *Epidemiology* 1992; 3(6):527-31.

Fildes, V. A. *Breasts, Bottles and Babies: A History of Infant Feeding.* Edinburgh: Edinburgh University Press, 1986.

Fitzsimmons, S. P. et al. Immunoglobulin A subclasses in infants' saliva and in saliva and milk from their mothers. *Journal of Pediatrics* April 1994; 124(4):566-73.

Fok, D. Breastfeeding in Singapore. *Breastfeeding Review* 1997; 5(2):25-28.

Fok, D. Cross cultural practice and its influence on breastfeeding—the Chinese culture. *Breastfeeding Review* May 1996; 4(1):13-17.

Ford, C. S. A Comparative Study of Human Reproduction. *Yale University Publications in Anthropology 32.* New Haven, CT: Human Relations Area Files Press, 1945.

Forman, M. R. et al. Undernutrition among Bedouin Arab infants: the Bedouin infant feeding study. *American Journal of Clinical Nutrition* March 1990; 51(3):343-49.

Freed, G. L., Jones, T. M., Fraley, J. K. Attitudes and education of pediatric house staff concerning breast-feeding. *Southern Medical Journal* May 1992; 85(5):483-85.

Fuchs, S. C., Victora, C. G., Martines, J. Case-control study of risk of dehydrating diarrhoea in infants in vulnerable period after full weaning. *British Medical Journal* 1996; 313:391-94.

Gamez, S. Tandem nursing. LEAVEN Sept.-Oct. 1993; 28(5):69.

Gamez, S. Tandem nursing—What is it? Is it for you? *Couple to Couple League, Family Foundations* . May-June 1997; 6-7.

Garza, C. et al. Changes in the nutrient composition of human milk during gradual weaning. *American Journal of Clinical Nutrition* 1983; 37:61-65.

Gilbert, A. N. et al. Mother-weanling interactions in Norway rats in the presence of a successive litter produced by postpartum mating. *Physiology and Behavior* February 1983; 30(2):267-71.

Goldman, A. S., Chheda, S., Garofalo, R. Evolution of immunologic functions of the mammary gland and the postnatal development of immunity. *Pediatric Research* February 1998; 43(2):155-62.

Goldman, A. S., Goldblum, R. M., Garza, C. Immunologic components in human milk during the second year of lactation. *Acta Paediatrica Scandinavica* 1983; 72:461-62.2

Goldstein, A. O., Freed, G. L. Breast-feeding counseling practices of family practice residents. *Family Medicine* September 1993; 25(8):524-29.

Graham, M. A. Food allocation in rural Peruvian households: concepts and behavior regarding children. *Social Science and Medicine* 1997; 44(11):1697-1709.

Gray, S. J. Infant Care and Feeding Among Nomadic Turkana Pastoralists: Implications for Fertility and Child Survival. Ph.D. Diss. State University of New York at Binghamton, 1992.

Greiner, T. Sustained breastfeeding, complementation, and care. *Food and Nutrition Bulletin* 1995; 16(4):313-19.

Greiner, T. The concept of weaning: definitions and their implications. *Journal of Human Lactation* 1996; 12(2):123-28.

Gromada, K. MOTHERING MULTIPLES: BREASTFEEDING AND CARING FOR TWINS OR MORE! Schaumburg, Illinois: La Leche League International, 1999.

Gross, B. A. Is the lactational amenorrhea method a part of natural family planning? Biology and policy. *American Journal of Obstetrics and Gynecology* December 1991; 165(6):2014-19.

Grummer-Strawn, L. M. The effect of changes in population characteristics on breastfeeding trends in fifteen developing countries. *International Journal of Epidemiology* 1996; 25(1):94-102.

Guldan, G. S. et al. Breastfeeding practices in Chengdu, Sichuan, China. *Journal of Human Lactation* 1995; 11(1): 11-15.

Guldan, G. S. et al. Weaning practices and growth in rural Sichuan infants: a positive deviance study. *Journal of Tropical Pediatrics* June1993; 39(3):168-75.

Gurudeva, R. K. et al. Infant feeding practices in Rewa. *Indian Journal of Pediatrics* 1982; 49:815-18.

Hackett, A. F., Rugg-Gunn, A. J., Murray, J. J., Roberts, G.J. Can Breast Feeding Cause Dental Caries? *Human Nutrition: Applied Nutrition* 1984; 38A:23-28.

Hahn-Zoric, M. et al. Antibody responses to parenteral and oral vaccines are impaired by conventional and low protein formulas as compared to breast-feeding. *Acta Paediatrica Scandinavica* 1990; 79:1137-42.

Haider, R. and Begum, S. Working women, maternity entitlements, and breastfeeding: a report from Bangladesh. *Journal of Human Lactation* 1995; 11(4): 273-77.

Hale, K. J., Coping with dental caries: a pediatric dentist's perspective. New Beginnings January-February 1997;14(1):10-11. http://www.lalecheleague.org/NB/NBJanFeb97.dent.html

Hallonsten A. L. et al. Dental caries and prolonged breast-feeding in 18-month-old Swedish children. *International Journal of Paediatric Dentistry* 1995; 5:149-55.

Harlow, H. F. The development of affectional patterns in infant monkeys. *Determinants of Infant Behaviour* Vol. 1 Ed. B.M. Foss. NY: Wiley, 1961.

Harrison, G. G. et al. Breastfeeding and weaning in a poor urban neighbourhood in Cairo, Egypt: maternal beliefs and perceptions. *Social Science and Medicine* 1993; 36(38): 1063-69.

Hill, A. G., Ed. *Population, Health and Nutrition in the Sahel: Issues in the Welfare of Selected West African Communities.* London: KPI, Ltd. 1985.

Hills-Bonczyk, S. G. et al. Women's experiences with combining breast-feeding and employment. *Journal of Nurse-Midwifery* September/October 1993; 38(5):257-66.

Hills-Bonczyk, S. G. et al. Women's experiences with breast-feeding longer than 12 months. *Birth* December 21, 1994; 21(4):206-12.

Holt, R. D. Weaning and dental health. *Proceedings of the Nutrition Society* 1997; 56:131-8.

Holt, R. D. and Moynihan, P. J. The weaning diet and dental health. *British Dental Journal* October 5, 1996; 181(7): 254-9.

Hreshchyshyn, M. M. et al. Associations of parity, breast-feeding, and birth control pills with lumbar spine and femoral neck bone densities. *American Journal of Obstetrics and Gynecology* August 1988; 159(2):318-22.

Huffman, S. L. et al. Breast-feeding patterns in rural Bangladesh. *American Journal of Clinical Nutrition* January 1980; 33(1):144-54.

Huggins, K. and Ziedrich, L. *The Nursing Mother's Guide to Weaning.* Boston: The Harvard Common Press, 1994.

Hull, V. and Simpson, M., Ed. *Breastfeeding, Child Health and Child Spacing Cross-cultural Perspectives.* London: Croom Helm, 1985.

Hymes, J. L., Jr. "Behavior and Discipline." Speech presented before the conference of La Leche League International, San Francisco, CA, 1976.

Isherwood, R. J., Dimond, C., Longhurst, D. Breast feeding and weaning practices in relation to nutritional status of under-5 children in north Bangladesh. *Journal of Tropical Pediatrics* February 1988; 34:28-34.

Jackson, D. A. et al. Circadian variation in fat concentration of breast-milk in a rural northern Thai population. *British Journal of Nutrition* May 1988; 59(3): 349-63.

Jackson, D. A. et al. Weaning practices and breast-feeding duration in Northern Thailand. *British Journal of Nutrition* 1992; 67:149-64.

Kalkwarf, H. et al. Intestinal calcium absorption of women during lactation and after weaning. *American Journal of Clinical Nutrition,* 1996; 63:526-31.

Kalra, K., Kaira, A., Dayal, R. S. Breast feeding practices in different residential economic and educational groups. *Indian Pediatrics* 1982; 19:419-26.

Kendall-Tackett, K. A. and Sugarman, M. The social consequences of long-term breastfeeding. *Journal of Human Lactation* 1995; 11(3):179-83.

Kennedy, K. I. Effects of breastfeeding on women's health. *International Journal of Gynecology and Obstetrics* 1994; 47 Suppl.: S11-S21.

Kippley, S. *Breastfeeding and Natural Child Spacing.* Cincinnati, Ohio: Couple to Couple League International, Inc., 1989.

La Leche League International The Womanly Art of Breastfeeding. Schaumburg, Illinois: La Leche League International, 1991.

Labbok, M. H. and Hendershot, G. E. Does breast-feeding protect against malocclusion? An analysis of the 1981 child health supplement to the national health interview survey. *American Journal of Preventive Medicine* 1987; 3(4):227-32.

Lamontagne, J. F., Engle, P. L., Zeitlin, M. F. Maternal employment, child care, and nutritional status of 12-18-month-old children in Managua, Nicaragua. *Social Science and Medicine* February 1998; 46(3): 403-14.

Lauber, E. and Reinhardt, M. C. Prolonged lactation performance in a rural community of the Ivory Coast. *Journal of Tropical Pediatrics* 1981; 27:74-77.

Lawrence, R. A. A review of the medical benefits and contraindications to breastfeeding in the United States. *Child Health Information Bulletin.* Arlington, Virginia: National Center for Education in Maternal and Child Health, October, 1997.

Lawrence, R. A. and Lawrence, R. M. *Breastfeeding: A Guide for the Medical Profession.* 5th edition. St. Louis: The C. V. Mosby Company, 1999.

Layde, P. M. et al. The independent associations of parity, age at first full term pregnancy, and duration of breastfeeding with the risk of breast cancer. *Journal of Clinical Epidemiology* 1989; 42:963-73.

Leonard, L. G. Breastfeeding twins: maternal-infant nutrition. *JOGN Nursing* 1982; 11(3):148-53.

Lieberman, A. F. Aggression and sexuality in relation to toddler attachment: implications for the caregiving system. Infant Mental Health Journal 1996; 17(3): 276-92.

Little, M.A. and Leslie, P. W., Ed. *Nomadic Turkana: Biobehavior and Ecology of a Pastoralist Society.* Oxford: Oxford University Press, 1996.

Lopez, R. F. and Schumann, L. Failure to thrive. *Journal of the American Academy of Nurse Practitioners* October 1997; 9(10):489-93.

Louhiala P. J. et al. Day-care centers and diarrhea: a public health perspective. *Journal of Pediatrics* September 1997; 131(3):476-79.

Louv, R. *Father Love: What We Need, What We Seek, What We Must Create.* New York: Pocket Books, 1993.

MacLean, H. *Women's Experience of Breastfeeding*. Toronto: University of Toronto Press, 1990.

Maher, V., Ed. *The Anthropology of Breastfeeding: Natural Law or Social Construct*. Providence, Rhode Island: Berg Publishers, Ltd., 1992.

Marini, A. et al. Effects of a dietary and environmental prevention programme on the incidence of allergic symptoms in high atopic risk infants: three years' follow-up. *Acta Paediatrica Supplement* May 1996; 414:1-21.

Mark, B. S. and Incorvaia, J. A., Ed. *The handbook of infant, child, and adolescent psychotherapy*. Vol. 2. Northvale, New Jersey: Jason Aronson, Inc, 1997.

Marshal, L. B., Ed. *Infant Care and Feeding in the South Pacific*. New York: Gordon and Breach, 1985.

Masters, W. H. and Johnson, V. E. *Human Sexual Response*. Boston: Little, Brown and Company, 1966.

Matee, M. et al. Nursing caries, linear hypoplasia, and nursing and weaning habits in Tanzanian infants. *Community Dentistry and Oral Epidemiology* 1994; 22:289-93.

Meehan, K. F. Breast Feeding in an Urban District in Shanghai, People's Republic of China. *Journal of Tropical Pediatrics* April, 1990; 36(2):75-79.

Michaelsen, K. F. Value of prolonged breastfeeding (letter). *Lancet* October 1988; 2(8614):788-89.

Michie, C. A. and Tantscher, E. The long term effects of breast-feeding: a role for the cells in breast milk? *Journal of Tropical Pediatrics* February 1998; 44:2-3.

Millard, A. V. and Graham, M. A. Abrupt weaning reconsidered: evidence from central México. *Journal of Tropical Pediatrics* August 1985; 31:229-34.

Milnes, A. R. Description and epidemiology of nursing caries. *Journal of Public Health Dentistry* 1996; 56(1):38-50.

Miner, J., Witte, D. J., Nordstrom, D. L. Infant feeding practices in a Russian and a United States city: patterns and comparisons. *Journal of Human Lactation* 1994; 10(2):95.

Mohrbacher, N. and Stock, J. THE BREASTFEEDING ANSWER BOOK. Revised edition. Schaumburg, Illinois: La Leche League International, 1997.

Mølbak, K., Jakobsen, M. S., Aaby, P. Is malnutrition associated with prolonged breastfeeding? *International Journal of Epidemiology* 1997; 26(2):458-59.

Montagna, W. and MacPherson, E. Some neglected aspects of the anatomy of human breasts. *The Journal of Investigative Dermatology* 1974; 63:10-16.

Morgan, B. *Reading Your Baby's Body Language*. Audio tape. San Jose, CA: Milky Way Press, 1989.

Moro, D. Birthweight and breast feeding of babies born during the war in one municipal area of Sarajevo. *European Journal of Clinical Nutrition* 1995; 49, Supp. 2:S37-9.

Morrow, M. Breastfeeding in Vietnam: poverty, tradition, and economic transition. *Journal of Human Lactation* 1996; 12(2):97-103.

Moscone, S. R.; Moore, M. J. Breastfeeding during pregnancy. *Journal of Human Lactation* June 1993; 9(2):83-88.

Mull, D. S. Mother's milk and pseudoscientific breastmilk testing in Pakistan. *Social Science and Medicine* 1992; 34(11):1277-90.

Naggan, L. et al. The Bedouin infant feeding study: study design and factors influencing the duration of breast feeding. *Paediatric and Perinatal Epidemiology* 1991; 5:428-43.

National Academy of Sciences Institute of Medicine, Food and Nutrition Board. Subcommittee on Nutrition During Lactation. *Nutrition During Lactation*. Washington, D.C.: National Academy Press, 1991.

Neville, M. C. and Neifert, M. R., Ed. *Lactation: Physiology, Nutrition, and Breast-Feeding*. New York: Plenum Press, 1983.

Newcomb, P. A. et al. Lactation and a reduced risk of pre-menopausal breast cancer. *The New England Journal of Medicine* 1994; 330(2):81-87.

Newman, J. How breastmilk protects newborns. *Scientific American* December 1995; 273(6):76-79.

Newton, N. *Maternal Emotions: A Study of Women's Feelings Toward Menstruation, Pregnancy, Childbirth, Breast Feeding, Infant Care and Other Aspects of their Femininity*. New York: Paul B. Hoeber, Inc., 1955.

Newton, N. Psychologic differences between breast and bottle feeding. *American Journal of Clinical Nutrition* 1971; 24:993-1004.

Newton, N. and Newton, M. Psychologic aspects of lactation. *New England Journal of Medicine* 1967; 277:1179-88.

Newton, N. and Theotokatos, M. Breastfeeding during pregnancy in 503 women: Does a psychobiological weaning mechanism in humans exist? *Proceedings of the Serono Symposia 20B* Ed. L. Zichella. London: Academic Press, 1980.

Newton, N. and Theotokatos, M. Breastfeeding during pregnancy in 503 women: Does a psychobiological weaning mechanism in humans exist? *Proceedings of the Serono Symposia 20B* Ed. L. Zichella. London: Academic Press, 1980.

Noonan, M. Toddler Tips. NEW BEGINNINGS March-April 1994; 11(2):56-59. http://www.lalecheleague.org/NB/NBMarApr94.tod.html

Nubé, M. and Asenso-Okyere, W. K. Large differences in nutritional status between fully weaned and partially breast fed children beyond the age of 12 months. *European Journal of Clinical Nutrition* 1996; 50:171-77.

Nursing Mothers of Australia. Tandem feeding. *Nursing Mothers' Newsletter* Summer 1998; 34(1):13-15.

Ogra, S. S. and Ogra, P. L. Immunologic aspects of human colostrum and milk. *Journal of Pediatrics* April 1978; 92(4):546-49.

Omondi, L. O., Persson, L. A., Staugard, F. Determinants for breast feeding and bottle feeding in Botswana. *Journal of Tropical Pediatrics* February 1990; 36(1):28-33.

Pabst, H. F., and Spady, D. W. Effect of breast-feeding on antibody response to conjugate vaccine. *Lancet* 1990; 336:269-70.

Pant, I. and Chothia, K. Maternal knowledge regarding breast-feeding and weaning practices. *Indian Journal of Pediatrics* May 1990; 57(3):395-400.

Park T. K. and Berlin P., Prevalence of exclusive and extended breastfeeding among rural Korean women. *Yonsei Medical Journal* 1981; 22(2):108-21.

Parkes, C. M., Stevenson-Hinde, J., Marris, P., Ed. *Attachment Across the Life Cycle.* London: Tavistock/Routledge, 1991.

Petok, E. S. Breast cancer and breastfeeding: five cases. *Journal of human lactation* 1995; 11(3):205.

Picciano, M. F. and Lonnerdal, B., Ed. *Mechanisms Regulating Lactation and Infant Nutrient Utilization.* New York: Wiley-Liss, 1992.

Porrini, M. and Walter, P., Ed. *Nutrition in Pregnancy and Growth.* Vol. 53. Basel: Karger, 1996.

Prosser, C. G., Saint, L., Hartmann, P. E. Mammary gland function during gradual weaning and early gestation in women. *Aust J Exp Biol Med Sci* 1984; 62(2):215-28.

Raphael, D. *Only Mothers Know.* Westport, CT: Greenwood Press, 1985.

Raphael, D. *The Tender Gift Breastfeeding.* New York: Shocken Books, 1976.

Rasmussen, K. M. Nutritional consequences of lactation for the mother: Definition of issues. *Mechanisms Regulating Lactation and Infant Nutrient Utilization.* Ed. M. F. Picciano and B. Lonnerdal. New York: Wiley-Liss, 1992; 97-108.

Reamer, S. B. and Sugarman, M. Breast-feeding beyond six months: Mothers' perceptions of the positive and negative consequences. *Journal of Tropical Pediatrics* 1987;33: 93-97.

Richardson, S. A. and Guttmacher, A. F., Ed. *Childbearing. Its Social and Psychological Aspects.* Baltimore: Williams and Wilkins, 1967.

Riordan, J. M. and Rapp, E. T. Pleasure and purpose. *JOGN Nursing* March-April 1980; 9:109-12.

Roberts, G. J. et al. Patterns of breast and bottle feeding and their association with dental caries in 1- to 4-year-old South African children. 1. Dental caries prevalence and experience. *Community Dental Health* March 1993; 10:405-13.

Rogan, W. J. and Gladen, B. C. Breast-feeding and cognitive development. *Early Human Development* 1993; 31:181-93.

Rosenblatt, K. A. and Thomas, D. B. Prolonged lactation and endometrial cancer. *International Journal of Epidemiology* 1995; 24(3):499-503.

Ryerson, A. J. Medical advice on child-rearing, 1550-1900. *Harvard Educational Review* 1961; 13:302-23.

Saarinen, U. M. Prolonged breast feeding as prophylaxis for recurrent otitis media. *Acta Paediatrica Scandinavica* July 1982; 71(4): 567-71.

Saarinen, U. M. and Kajosaari, M., Breastfeeding as prophylaxis against atopic disease: prospective follow-up study until 17 years old. *Lancet* Oct 21 1995; 346(8982):1065-69.

Salk, L. *What Every Child Would Like His Parents to Know.* New York: David McKay Company, Inc., 1972.

Sayed, Z. T. A., Latham, M. C., Roe, D. A. Prolonged breast-feeding without the introduction of supplementary feeding. *Journal of Tropical Pediatrics* 1995; 41(1):29-33.

Schmutzhard, E., Poewe, W., Gerstenbrand, F. Separation from mother at time of weaning. A rarely discussed aspect of the aetiology of protein energy malnutrition. *Tropical Doctor* October 1986; 16(4):176-77.

Schrocksnadel, H., Sachsenmaier, M., Reider, W., [Experiences with breast stimulation for labor induction]. Erfahrungen mit der Mamillenstimulation zur Weheninduktion. *Geburtshilfe Frauenheilkd* July 1990; 50(7):569-71.

Schwartz, R. Failure to thrive, an ambulatory approach. *Nurse Practitioner* May 1996; 21(5):19-35.

Sears, W. and Sears, M. *Parenting the Fussy Baby and High-Need Child.* Boston: Little, Brown and Company, 1996.

Sears, W. and Sears, M. *The Baby Book.* Boston: Little Brown and Company, 1993.

Segal, S. et al. Evaluation of breast stimulation for induction of labor in women with a prior cesarean section and in grand-multiparas. *Acta Obstetricia et Gynecologica Scandinavica* 1995; 74:40-41.

Shahraban, A. et al. Patterns of Breast Feeding and Weaning in the United Arab Emirate. *Journal of Tropical Pediatrics* February 1991; 37(1):13-16.

Singh, M. B., Haldiya, K. R., Lakshminarayana, J. Infant feeding and weaning practices in some semi-arid rural areas of Rajasthan. *J Indian Med Assoc* November 1997; 95(11):576-8, 590.

Skelsey, A. F. *The Working Mother's Guide to her Home, her Family, and Herself.* New York: Random House, 1970.

Smith, B. *A Tree Grows in Brooklyn.* New York: HarperPerennial, 1998.

Specker, B. L. et al. Sunshine exposure and serum 25 hydroxyvitamin D concentrations in exclusively breastfed infants. *Journal of Pediatrics* 1985; 107:372-76.

Spitz, R. A. *Grief: a peril in infancy.* Film, 1947 (16 mm), 1988 (1/2 in.).

Staat, M. A. et al. Diarrhea in children newly enrolled in day-care centers in Houston. *Pediatr Infect Dis J* April 1991; 10(4):282-86.

Stein, M. T. et al. Cosleeping (bedsharing) among infants and toddlers. *Journal of Developmental and Behavioral Pediatrics* December 1997; 18(6):408-12.

Stern, J. M. et al. Nursing behaviour, prolactin and postpartum amenorrhoea during prolonged lactation in American and !Kung mothers. *Clinical Endocrinology* September 1986; 25(3):247-58.

Stuart-Macadam, P. and Dettwyler, K. A., Eds. *Breastfeeding: Biocultural Perspectives.* New York: Aldine de Gruyter, 1995.

Sugarman, M. and Kendall-Tackett, K. A. Weaning ages in a sample of American women who practice extended breast-feeding. *Clinical Pediatrics* 1995; 34(12):642-47.

Tal, Z. et al. Breast electrostimulation for the induction of labor. *Obstetrics and Gynecology* October 1988; 72(4):671-74.

Taren, D. and Chen, J. A positive association between extended breast-feeding and nutritional status in rural Hubei Province, People's Republic of China. *American Journal of Clinical Nutrition* 1993; 58:862-67.

Tessema, T. and Hailu, A. Childhood feeding practice in North Ethiopia. *East African Medical Journal* February 1997; 74(2):92-95.

Treckel, P. A. Breastfeeding and maternal sexuality in colonial America. *Journal of Interdisciplinary History* 1989; 20(1): 25-51.

Van Lerberghe, W. *Kasongo: Child Mortality and Growth in a Small African Town.* London, England: Smith Gordon, 1990.

van Lawick-Goodall, J. *In the Shadow of Man.* New York: Houghton Mifflin Co., 1971.

Victora, C. Discussion of papers by Hanson et al. and by Victora. *Food and Nutrition Bulletin* The United Nations University, 1996; 17(4):397-400.

Victora, C. G. et al. Prolonged breastfeeding and malnutrition: confounding and effect modification in a Brazilian cohort study. *Epidemiology* May 1991; 2(3):175-81.

Vis, H. L. and Hennart, P. Decline in breast-feeding: about some of its causes. *Acta Paediatrica Scandinavica* October-December 1978; 31(4):195-206.

Vitzthum, V. J., Ed. Multidisciplinary Studies in Andean Anthropology. *Discussions in Anthropology 8.* Ann Arbor, MI: University of Michigan, 1988.

Walant, K. B. *Creating the Capacity for Attachment: Treating Addiction and the Alienated Self.* Northvale, New Jersey: Jason Aronson, Inc., 1995.

Weekly, S. J. Diets and eating disorders: implications for the breastfeeding mother. *NAACOG's Clinical Issues* 1992; 3(4):695-700.

Weeks, S. and Weeks, M. Toddler Tips. New Beginnings March-April 1994; 11(2):56-59. http://www.lalecheleague.org/NB/NBMarApr94.tod.html

Weerheijm, K. L. et al. Prolonged demand breast-feeding and nursing caries. *Caries Research* 1998; 32(1):46-50.

Wendt, L. K.; Hallonsten, A. L.; and Birkhed, D. Analysis of caries-related factors in infants and toddlers living in Sweden. *Acta Odontologica Scandinavica* 1996; 54(2): 131-37.

Wendt, L. K. et al. Oral hygiene in relation to caries development and immigrant status in infants and toddlers. *Scandinavian Journal of Dental Research* October 1994; 102(5):269-73.

Weschler, T. *Taking Charge of Your Fertility: The Definitive Guide to Natural Birth Control and Pregnancy Achievement.* New York: HarperPerennial, 1995.

Wharton, B. A. Weaning in Britain: practice, policy and problem. *Proceedings of the Nutrition Society* 1997; 56:105-19.

WHO/UNICEF *On the Protection, Promotion and Support of Breast-Feeding.* August 1990.

Wickes, I. G. A history of infant feeding. Part I. Primitive peoples: Ancient works: Renaissance writers. *Archives of Disease in Childhood* 1953; 28:151-158.

Winikoff, B., Castle, M. A., Laukaran, V. H. Ed. *Feeding Infants in Four Societies: Causes and Consequences of Mothers' Choices.* New York: Greenwood Press, 1988.

Winkvist, A. and Habicht, J. P. A new definition of maternal depletion syndrome. *American Journal of Public Health* May 1992; 82(5):691-94.

Winstein, M. *Your Fertility Signals: Using Them to Achieve or Avoid Pregnancy, Naturally.* St. Louis, Missouri: Smooth Stone Press, 1994.

Wisniewski, P. M. and Wilkinson, E. J. Postpartum vaginal atrophy. *American Journal of Obstetrics and Gynecology* October 1991; 165(4):1249-54.

Woodbury, R. M. Causal factors in infant mortality. *Children's Bureau Publication No.142.* Washington, D.C.: U.S. Government Printing Office, 1925.

Worthington-Roberts, B. and Williams, S. *Nutrition in Pregnancy and Lactation.* 5th edition. St. Louis: Mosby, 1993.

Wray, D. Breastfeeding: An international and historical review. Ed. Frank Falkner. *Infant and child nutrition worldwide: issues and perspectives.* Boca Raton, Fla.: CRC Press, 1991.

Wrigley, E. A. and Hutchinson, S. A. Long-term breast-feeding: the secret bond. *Journal of Nurse-Midwifery* January-February 1990; 35(1):35-41.

Yankauer A. A classic study of infant mortality—1911-1915. *Pediatrics* December 1994; 94(6):874-77.

Yurdakök, M. (letter), Koctörk, T. and Zetterström R. (reply). Breast-Feeding in Islam. *Acta Paediatrica Scandinavica* 1988; 77:907-08.

Zeigerman, J., Honigman, F., Crawford, R. Inflammatory mammary cancer during pregnancy and lactation. *Obstetrics and Gynecology* 1968; 32:373-75.

Zenel, J. A. Failure to thrive: a general pediatrician's perspective. *Pediatrics in Review* November 1997; 18(11):371-78.

Zilberg, B. How my four-year-old haunted our midnight feedings. *Redbook* February 1972; 30-32.

La Leche League International
1400 N. Meacham Rd.
Schaumburg, IL 60173-4048 USA
Telephone: (847) 519-7730
web site: www.lalecheleague.org

Nursing Mothers of Australia Association
PO Box 4000
Glen Iris, Victoria 3146
Australia
Telephone: 61 3 9885 0855
web site: www.nmaa.asn.au/index.html
An Australian organization which provides counseling and support services to nursing
mothers and health professionals.

International Lactation Consultant Association
4101 Lake Boone Trail, Suite 201
Raleigh NC 27607-6518
USA
Telephone: 919-787-5181
Can refer you to a lactiation consultant who has been board certified as a health care
provider.

World Alliance for Breastfeeding Action—WABA
26 N. Jalan Mesjid
Negeri, Penang, 11600
Malaysia
web site: www.waba.org.br
The World Alliance for Breastfeeding Action has contact centers in several nations around
the world. In addition to other projects that promote and support breastfeeding worldwide,
WABA sponsors World Breastfeeding Week (August 1-7).

Children in Hospitals, Inc.
31 Wilshire Park
Needham MA 02192
USA
Parents and health-care professionals concerned about the need for ample contact between
children and parents when either is hospitalized.

Infant Feeding Action Coalition (INFACT) Canada
6 Trinity Square
Toronto, M5G 1B1
Canada
Telephone: (416) 595 9819
web site: http://www.infactcanada.ca
A non-profit, non-government voluntary organization which seeks to promote and protect
breastfeeding by producing and distributing educational resources to health-care providers
and the public.

Breastfeeding: A Guide for the Medical Profession, 5th edition
by Ruth Lawrence, MD and Robert Lawrence, MD
One of the most comprehensive breastfeeding resources available, including information on mother-baby bonding, breastfeeding in adverse conditions, drugs in human milk and the latest information on biochemical, nutritional and immunologic aspects of breatfeeding.

Breastfeeding: Biocultural Perspectives
edited by Patricia Stuart-Macadam and Katherine A. Dettwyler
Breastfeeding experts explore the biological, cultural, medical, and anthropological aspects of breastfeeding in order to encourage a more holistic view of its significance.

Drugs in Pregnancy and Lactation, Revised edition
by Gerald G. Briggs, B Pharm, Roger K. Freeman, MD and Sumner J. Yaffe, MD
The fifth edition of this book reviews over 800 types of drugs and their effects on nursing infants.

How Weaning Happens
by Diane Bengson
Written by an LLL Leader, this book includes the personal experiences of mothers who have weaned in a variety of ways. The author answers weaning questions from the understanding that weaning is a natural process that does not have to be stressful for mother or child.

Mothering Multiples: Breastfeeding and Caring for Twins or More! Revised edition
by Karen Gromada
This book covers all aspects of caring for multiple babies from possible complications of pregnancy, preparing for a multiple birth, coping with newborns who might need to spend time in the NICU, establishing milk supply for multiple babies, to adjusting as a couple and caring for toddler multiples.

Parenting the Fussy Baby and High-Need Child
by William and Martha Sears
Coping and survival strategies, techniques and tips to guide the development of the fussy baby and high-need child are presented in an easy to read format. Practical ideas from parents who have been there, including the Sears', whose first-hand experiences provide unique insights into parenting the baby and child who have above average needs.

The Baby Book
by William Sears and Martha Sears
From bonding to temper tantrums, this book emphasizes a baby's basic needs and helps new parents to meet those needs through a loving, nurturing, attachment style of parenting.

The Breastfeeding Answer Book
by Nancy Mohrbacher and Julie Stock
The revised and expanded edition of this LLLI resource book includes up-to-date references, expanded information, and three new chapters. Complete information on pumps and other products, new milk storage guidelines, and a whole new approach to newborn jaundice make this revised edition an indispensable resource.

The Nursing Mother's Guide to Weaning
by Kathleen Huggins and Linda Ziedrich
This book explores all aspects of weaning starting with historical aspects and ending with weaning a child over three and life after weaning. This book offers practical and helpful

The Womanly Art of Breastfeeding
Now in its sixth revised edition, this La Leche League International classic title is expanded to include important references and additional resources for the breastfeeding mother. Its vast depth of factual information makes this book essential for breastfeeding mothers.

Your Fertility Signals: Using Them to Achieve or Avoid Pregnancy, Naturally
by Merryl Winstein
This book can help to achieve or prevent pregnancy , reduce or eliminate contraceptive use, even enhance the intimacy on your relationship. It also includes information on low fertility, stress, breastfeeding, post-pill, and pre-menopause.

Nighttime Parenting
by William Sears
Newly revised edition includes the latest research on how sharing sleep may reduce SIDS risk. It also offers tips on safe sleep-sharing and an update in the benefits of breastfeeding at night as well as advice on other nighttime dilemmas such as how to get your baby to sleep and stay asleep; whether or not you should let your baby "cry it out"; dealing with toddlers who wake at night; and getting children to bed without a struggle.

Nursing Mother, Working Mother
by Gale Pryor
Mothers who have decided to combine breastfeeding with working will find this an immensely helpful and reassuring book. The author includes practical information about planning for and returning to employment, clear and concise tips on breastfeeding, pumping, storing, and transporting milk, and possible alternatives to full time employment such as job sharing, working from home, and staying home full-time. The book suggests numerous ways mothers can build and maintain closeness with their babies in spite of separation.

Becoming a Father: How to Nurture and Enjoy Your Family
by William Sears
Addressing the joys and problems of parenthood from the male perspective, Dr. Sears writes from experience about the ways in which a child can help strengthen a marriage and bring about increased love and maturity.

Michelle, the Nursing Toddler
by Jane M. Pinczuk
illustrated by Barbara Murray
This book is about growing up in a family that loves to the fullest. From mother's milk to daddy's hugs and special visits from grandparents, Michelle blooms from infant to toddler, developing confidence and pride along the way.

Maggie's Weaning
by Mary Joan Deutschbein
This is a delightful, child's eye view of the nursing experience. As Maggie reflects in the time she spent at her mother's breast, she offers her thoughts on the joys and the challenges of slowly leaving breastfeeding behind.

La Leche League International offers many benefits to breastfeeding mothers and babies. Local La Leche League Groups meet monthly in communities all over the world, giving breastfeeding mothers the information they need and the opportunity to learn from one another. La Leche League Leaders, women who have nursed their own babies and who have met accreditation requirements, are only a phone call away. They provide accurate information on breastfeeding problems and can lend a sensitive ear to women with breastfeeding worries. You don't have to be a La Leche League member to contact a Leader or attend Group meetings. However, members receive added benefits. They receive LLLI's bimonthly magazine, NEW BEGINNINGS, which is filled with breastfeeding information, stories from nursing mothers, tips on discipline and common toddler problems, and news about breastfeeding from all over the world. Members also receive a 10% discount on purchases from LLLI's extensive Catalogue of carefully selected books, tapes, pamphlets, pumps, and other products for families. Members may also borrow books from local Group libraries. Membership is $30 a year in the USA and helps to support the work of local LLL Groups as well as LLL projects all over the world. You can pay your dues to the LLL Group in your area or directly to LLLI.

For more information on a Group and Leaders near you, call 1-800-LA LECHE. (In Canada, call 1-800-665-4324 or 613-448-1842.) You can also visit our award winning website at www.lalecheleague.org for more information about LLLI and resources for breastfeeding support. In addition to finding information on membership or a Group near you, you can also find links to Group pages in the USA and all around the world. You can learn about the history of La Leche League International, browse the LLLI Catalogue, or peruse a collection of articles and selected passages from LLLI publications. The website also offers information and schedules for online LLL meetings as well as information on upcoming educational opportunities offered by LLLI.